E

Learning to read non-alphabetic script

Etsuko Toyoda

Learning to read non-alphabetic script

Development of L2 script-specific recognition ability among English-speaking learners of Japanese

VDM Verlag Dr. Müller

Impressum/Imprint (nur für Deutschland/ only for Germany)

Bibliografische Information der Deutschen Nationalbibliothek: Die Deutsche Nationalbibliothek verzeichnet diese Publikation in der Deutschen Nationalbibliografie; detaillierte bibliografische Daten sind im Internet über http://dnb.d-nb.de abrufbar.
Alle in diesem Buch genannten Marken und Produktnamen unterliegen warenzeichen-, marken- oder patentrechtlichem Schutz bzw. sind Warenzeichen oder eingetragene Warenzeichen der jeweiligen Inhaber. Die Wiedergabe von Marken, Produktnamen, Gebrauchsnamen, Handelsnamen, Warenbezeichnungen u.s.w. in diesem Werk berechtigt auch ohne besondere Kennzeichnung nicht zu der Annahme, dass solche Namen im Sinne der Warenzeichen- und Markenschutzgesetzgebung als frei zu betrachten wären und daher von jedermann benutzt werden dürften.

Coverbild: www.purestockx.com

Verlag: VDM Verlag Dr. Müller Aktiengesellschaft & Co. KG
Dudweiler Landstr. 99, 66123 Saarbrücken, Deutschland
Telefon +49 681 9100-698, Telefax +49 681 9100-988, Email: info@vdm-verlag.de
Zugl.: Melbourne, The University of Melbourne, 2006

Herstellung in Deutschland:
Schaltungsdienst Lange o.H.G., Berlin
Books on Demand GmbH, Norderstedt
Reha GmbH, Saarbrücken
Amazon Distribution GmbH, Leipzig
ISBN: 978-3-639-12373-9

Imprint (only for USA, GB)

Bibliographic information published by the Deutsche Nationalbibliothek: The Deutsche Nationalbibliothek lists this publication in the Deutsche Nationalbibliografie; detailed bibliographic data are available in the Internet at http://dnb.d-nb.de.
Any brand names and product names mentioned in this book are subject to trademark, brand or patent protection and are trademarks or registered trademarks of their respective holders. The use of brand names, product names, common names, trade names, product descriptions etc. even without a particular marking in this works is in no way to be construed to mean that such names may be regarded as unrestricted in respect of trademark and brand protection legislation and could thus be used by anyone.

Cover image: www.purestockx.com

Publisher:
VDM Verlag Dr. Müller Aktiengesellschaft & Co. KG
Dudweiler Landstr. 99, 66123 Saarbrücken, Germany
Phone +49 681 9100-698, Fax +49 681 9100-988, Email: info@vdm-publishing.com
Melbourne, The University of Melbourne, 2006

Printed in the U.S.A.
Printed in the U.K. by (see last page)
ISBN: 978-3-639-12373-9

TABLE OF CONTENTS

1 Overview

1.1 Introduction

Reading non-alphabetic script can be a serious challenge to second language (L2) learners with alphabetic backgrounds. Anecdotal evidence suggests that many L2 learners of Japanese or Chinese who are fluent in speaking the language do not necessarily acquire an advanced-level reading ability. One of the most important abilities of learners that needs to be developed for reading comprehension is efficient word recognition (e.g., Grabe, 2004; Koda, 1992; Stanovich, 1991; Haynes and Carr, 1990).

Research in word recognition processes has a long history, and research investigating alphabetic languages, particularly English, has made a significant contribution towards the understanding of word recognition processes. Not only word recognition mechanisms of adult native speakers, but also the developing word recognition skills of children learning to read in their first language have been vigorously investigated. Findings on word recognition skills employed by native speakers (both adults and children) in reading non-alphabetic script such as Chinese characters (including *kanji* used in Japanese) are also available although theories to describe these data are still limited compared to what is available for the processes involved in readers of alphabetic languages.

Studies on second language use and processes are gradually becoming available. However, most of them are in European languages and are confined to the issues of lexical representation. The goal of my research is to contribute to an understanding of the development of word recognition ability in non-alphabetic script among second language learners with alphabetic backgrounds at different levels of proficiency.

The aims of the current study were to gather information in order to develop an outline of the development of word recognition skills among English-speaking learners of Japanese (beginner to advanced learners), and to examine the development of their awareness of the word recognition. This study is thus different from studies that focus on models of fluent bilingual processing.

Recognition skills were measured for accuracy and speed of responses to visual representations (*kanji* characters) in various tasks designed to tap different processing levels. Awareness was assessed in terms of the participants' ability to reflect on behaviours using a verbal protocol method. In other words, this study attempted to bridge the gap between methodologically rigorous psycholinguistic studies and those more descriptive applied linguistics studies interested in aspects of the learners themselves.

To achieve the first aim, I investigated learners' *kanji* recognition skills using behavioural tasks which took into consideration both the learner's vocabulary size and the type of task and stimulus. It has been suggested that there are strong correlations between vocabulary knowledge and word recognition skills among native speakers of a language (Haynes and Carr, 1990; Koda, 1989b). Vocabulary knowledge is usually measured according to breadth, i.e., the number of words a person knows. In the present study, I categorised participants into beginner, intermediate and advanced groups in terms of the size of their vocabulary knowledge.

I then conducted experiments with the participants using various speeded tests that I had developed, which included different types of tasks and stimuli (*kanji* characters). The tests were designed to measure orthographic, phonological and semantic processing. The stimuli (*kanji* characters) of the test were selected with great care so that *kanji* characters with a wide range of stimulus properties were included, as it has been claimed that different stimulus properties, such as frequency of occurrence, may affect recognition processes (Akamatsu, 2002; Hong, 1998; Tamaoka and Hatsuzuka, 1995; Share, 1995; Tan, Hoosain and Peng, 1995; Taft and Zhu, 1995; McClelland and Rumelhart, 1981). The tests were computerised in order to automatically record correct/incorrect responses. Response times were measured to the millisecond.

For the purpose of investigating the second aim, I also conducted individual interviews with the participants in order to obtain their retrospective thoughts on the

3

processes that they used in responding to the tasks. These interview records provided a potential insight into the learners' awareness.

This book will be structured in the following manner. The initial chapter provides an overview of this book, and introduces the characteristics of the Japanese writing system. Chapter two discusses the development of word recognition skills and awareness in various languages, and the development of L2-specific skills and awareness. This chapter then looks particularly at recognition processes in character-based languages. Chapter three deals in depth with the research design and the subsequent development of tasks, and includes the rationale for my research questions and approach. Chapters four and five report and discuss the results of the series of experiments and interviews which investigated orthographic and phonological processing relating to aspects of character recognition. Chapter six presents the analyses of the results of the series of experiments, and discusses semantic processing relating to aspects of character recognition. The final chapter, Chapter seven, integrates the whole study and draws conclusions.

1.2 Definitions

The present study investigates the development of L2 readers' character recognition ability. **L2** in this study refers to a language other than one's native-tongue (**L1**), and includes a language being studied as a 'foreign language'. The term **L2**

4

readers refers to individuals who read or are learning to read in a language other than their native tongue. In this context, it is assumed that L2 readers have acquired a native-level reading ability in their L1. Although the difference between very advanced L2 readers and L1 readers may be minimal, most L2 readers have a smaller vocabulary in their L2 compared to L1 readers of the language. However, vocabulary alone cannot explain the different reading processes between L1 and L2 readers.

Although many processes are involved in reading, lower-level processing such as word recognition is claimed to be critical (Koda, 1992; Stanovich, 1991). Generally speaking, L1 and L2 readers differ in their efficiency in word recognition, although some L2 readers may be better than some L1 readers. The term **word recognition** refers to the process of retrieving orthographic, phonological and semantic information of the word. Word recognition process subsumes the whole process by which a word is recognized, including lexical access (the process of matching an input to a stored representation), checking, and decision (Tamaoka, 1992; Harris and Coltheart, 1986). Flores d'Arcais (1992:39) describes the process as follows:

> I will assume that from the moment in time at which a visual object such as a written character is put in front of the visual system of a literate native speaker of a language, a number of processes take place. This stimulus information has to spark some knowledge in the reader, which normally includes the pronunciation of the word, its meaning, etc. When this contact has taken place, we can say that the word is recognised.

Here, **word recognition skills** are defined as multiple skills required for word recognition. In this book, I adopted this broad definition of word recognition, and thus examined different sets of processing skills. Although many psycholinguistic studies focus on the much narrower domain of investigating lexical access (the process of matching an input to a stored representation), this is not the focus of the present study.

Word recognition is claimed to be supported by an underlying ability, **awareness** (Edwards and Kirkpatrick, 1999; Shu and Anderson, 1998). Awareness is defined in this book as 'insights into the structures and functions of words (spoken or written) that may or may not be consciously reflected on'. As exposure to words increases, readers become aware of how words and their constituent elements are formed and how they function in a particular language (Miller, 2002; Caravolas and Bruck, 1993).

The word recognition process needs to become **automatic** for readers to become skilled. Readers who are able to process words automatically, are referred to as '**skilled readers**' while readers who are still in the developmental stages are usually referred to as '**less-skilled readers**'. The concept of 'skill' may be ambiguous, as it can be interpreted in two related ways: skill as 'domain of performance' and as 'enhanced performance' (Birdsong, 1989). The term 'skill' as in 'word recognition skills' is used in the former sense. In this regard, there may exist multiple word recognition skills or performance domains (Birdsong, 1989:50). On the other hand, skill in 'skilled readers' suggests that the readers have obtained a high level of function within a given performance domain (Birdsong, 1989:50).

6

The present study focused on the skills and awareness used in processing *kanji* **characters**, which are an essential aspect of reading in Japanese. One might wonder why 'characters' and not 'words' would be the units of investigation. In this book, character recognition processes will be discussed in a similar way to word recognition processes for the following reasons. Although, in a strict sense, 'a character' may not be exactly the same as 'a word', the majority of characters have status as a word in their own right (Hoosain, 1991). Moreover, characters consist of components, just as English words consist of letters. For these reasons, in this book, word recognition processes will sometimes be discussed in relation to understanding the nature of character recognition processes.

Japanese writing includes a number of characters called *kanji,* which are used for most content words (e.g., nouns, verb stems and adjective stems). The recognition of *kanji* is therefore critical in reading Japanese (Dobson, 1997; Okita, 1995; Tollini, 1992; Hatano, 1986). The term *kanji* only refers to *kanji* characters used in Japanese, and characters used in Chinese will be called *hanzi*, the recognised term used in China (Wang, 1981). Hereafter, when I refer to *kanji* **recognition**, the discussion will be on the recognition of individual *kanji* characters.

The main interest in this study is the development of L2 readers' multiple character recognition skills and awareness of various aspects of the structures and functions of characters. In the present study, readers' word recognition skills were examined through their performances on various word recognition tasks in terms of **correct response rate** (accuracy) and **response time** (speed). In the course of reading, print representations stimulate the network of internalised knowledge of the reader, and information necessary to understand the text is accessed. In the process of information access, **stimulus properties** of words such as frequency of occurrence may affect the readers' performances. To this end, patterns of stimulus properties were also examined. The access to the necessary information for recognising words is assisted by readers' awareness of the structures and functions of words. In the present study, awareness was investigated using a verbal protocol, in the form of **retrospective interview**, in which L2 readers were asked to describe their task performance by consciously reflecting on their behaviours. Although verbalised accounts do not reflect a whole view, they can be an indicator of awareness.

1.3 About Japanese *kanji* characters

Before moving to the main body of the book, I would like to devote this section to describing the Japanese writing system focusing particularly on *kanji* characters and their components in order to provide some background information for the following chapters.

1.3.1 The Japanese writing system

Japanese employs four types of script: *kanji*, *hiragana*, *katakana* and *romaji* (Roman-alphabet). Historically, *kanji* originated in Chinese characters, and therefore there are many similarities between them, although some differences also exist. Records suggest that the Chinese writing system was brought to Japan around the 5th century with the introduction of Buddhism, and that it became the writing system for recording Japanese by the 8th century (Taylor, 1998, 1997; Sayeg, 1996). Later, the cursive script, *hiragana,* evolved through simplifying the *kanji,* and the angular script, *katakana,* was derived from part of the *kanji* (Taylor, 1998; Sayeg, 1996; Tomita and Sanada, 1994). The Roman alphabet was introduced to Japan with Christianity around the 16th century, and became part of the Japanese writing system in the 18th century (Tomita and Sanada, 1994).

Kanji characters, most of which are Chinese in origin, are widely known as logographs due to the belief that characters usually represent the minimal meaningful units of the language (Lee, Stigler and Stevenson, 1986; Wang, 1981). In fact however, pure logographic systems seem not to exist (Perfetti, Van Dyke and Hart, 2001). As the word 'logograph' can give the misleading impression that a character represents a word, recent researchers call *kanji* 'morphographs' (Mori, 1998; Koda, 1995; 1990; 1989a), as each character represents a morpheme (Hong and Yelland, 1997; Paradis, Hagiwara and Hildebrandt, 1985).

Both *hiragana* and *katakana* are often grouped into a 'syllabic writing system' called '*kana*' (Taylor, 1998), and *romaji* is an alphabetic script. *Hiragana* plays a supplementary role in a sentence, and is used to show grammatical functions such as verb/adjective inflections, tense, aspect, voice, mood, conjunctions and case markers. *Katakana* is mainly used for loanwords including foreign names, and foreign words not originating in Chinese. *Katakana* is also occasionally used for non-loanwords in order to add a special effect, for example, to attract attention. The use of *romaji* is becoming

9

increasingly popular in Japanese although it is still relatively rarely seen. Instead of translating words of foreign origin into *katakana*, *romaji* are sometimes used, in particular, in magazines targeting young people.

The approximate proportions of *kanji*, *hiragana*, *katakana* and *romaji* in a text are 30%, 65%, 4% and 1% respectively (Taylor, 1981). The number of *kanji* characters is enormous compared to 71 *hiragana* letters, 73 *katakana* letters (including a long vowel sign and a special letter for transcribing foreign words) and 21 *romaji* letters. Among approximately 50,000 characters included in the largest *kanji* dictionary in Japan, 1,945 Japanese general-use *kanji* have been selected by the Ministry of Education (Taylor, 1997; Tomita and Sanada, 1994).

Among these four types of scripts, *kanji* has attracted researchers' attention most for the following reasons: 1) *kanji* has a pivotal role in Japanese sentences as most nouns, and stems of verbs and adjectives, are written in *kanji* (Sayeg, 1996), and 2) this script is peculiar in that it is not phonologically transparent.

1.3.3 kanji word, character and component

One might think that a *kanji* word (a word written in *kanji* characters) and a *kanji* character are units equivalent to a word and a letter in alphabetic script. However, how a word is formed is different in alphabetic and non-alphabetic scripts. It is a common assumption that a word is constituted of a cluster of graphemes. A grapheme is the smallest unit in a writing system capable of causing a contrast in meaning (Crystal, 1987). In the case of alphabetic script, graphemes mainly refer to letters which are all

10

single non-separable configurations (Crystal, 1987), and with few exceptions each grapheme can be converted to a phoneme. For non-alphabetic scripts such as *kanji* (and *hanzi*), the term grapheme has been conventionally used to refer to a character. Characters were viewed as single non-separable configurations with only arbitrary phonological information. However, a character can in fact be further broken down to smaller units, and the replacement of a certain type of component may bring about a change in meaning. Moreover, some components carry phonological information.

The explanations of *kanji* word/ character/ component in the following sections may seem over-elaborate. However, it is vital to show readers, who may be relatively unfamiliar with Japanese, the structures and functions of *kanji*, as this is the main focal point of the book.

In the sections to follow, where statistics for *kanji* were not available, data on *hanzi* (Chinese characters) were drawn.

1.3.4 kanji word composed of character(s)

Structure

Japanese *kanji*-written words can appear in either single character or compound words (Morton and Sasanuma, 1984). A **single-character word** is a word written in a single *kanji*. For example, 語 /go/ is a word by itself meaning 'word(s)'. Another type of single-character word is a word with a single *kanji* with *hiragana*. For example 語る

/kata-ru/ is a single-character word meaning 'to tell', which consists of a character and a *hiragana*.

Most *kanji*-written words are **compound words** with two *kanji* characters (Hatta, Kawakami and Tamaoka, 1998). This is because a number of two-*kanji* compound words were created in Japan in order to translate the flood of new foreign words into Japanese during the 17-19th centuries (Takashima, 2001). It is said that about 70% of Japanese dictionary entries are two-character compound words (Shimomura and Yokosawa, 1991). 言語 /geN-go/, for example, is a two-character compound word meaning 'language'. There are also many three-character compound words. In most cases, however, they can be divided into a prefix and a two-character compound word or two-character word and a suffix. For example, 多言語 /ta-geN-go/ consists of a prefix meaning 'multi-' and a compound word 'language'.

Semantic function

A character may represent an object or an idea, but in some cases it only shows a broad semantic field. The characters that can be single-character words tend to have clear meanings although the degree of clarity varies. For example, the first character 認 of the word 認識 /niNshiki/ 'recognition' can be a single-character word 認める /mito-meru/, which can be translated to 'to accept', 'to acknowledge' or 'to recognise' depending on the context. This character 認 is used in many words, such as 認可

/niNka/ 'approval', 認定 /niNtei/ 'acknowledgement', and 確認 /kakuniN/ 'confirmation'. The meanings of these words are more or less related through the character 認.

On the other hand, the characters that are used only as a constituent character of a compound word may not have a clear meaning. For example, the second character 識 of the same word 認識 /niNshiki/ 'recognition' cannot be a single-character word. Therefore, what this character represents needs to be figured out by examining the meanings of several words containing this character. It is used in words such as 知識 /chishiki/ 'knowledge', 識別 /shikibetsu/ 'distinction', and 見識 /keNshiki/ 'insight'. However, it may not be simple to determine that this character represents the concept 'knowing'.

It is widely claimed that each constituent character in a word usually has the role of a morpheme (Taft and Zhu, 1997a; Zhang and Peng, 1992) although a few words cannot be segmented into morphemes (Taft and Zhu, 1997b). As shown above, characters that can be free-standing words act as free morphemes, and those that are combined with another character to form a word are bound morphemes (Taft, 2004). Occasionally, characters may not have morphemic status if they only occur in a particular word and have no meaning of its own: these are binding characters (Taft 2004). Of the 1,945 Japanese general-use *kanji*, 700 are used to represent free morphemes, *i.e.*, words (Yamada, 1998b).

Therefore a character has a potential semantic function in a word. However, the degree of semantic relatedness between a word and its constituent character(s) and between words sharing a common character varies. The relationship is sometimes transparent, and sometimes less so, depending mainly on whether or not the constituent character has a status as a free morpheme. There may also be other factors including social changes that influence the semantic relationship.

Phonological function

A *kanji* word has a sound or a **reading**. The reading could be one of, or a mixture of, two types of readings: ***kun*-reading** and ***on*-reading**. *Kun*-readings represent morphemes of Japanese origin whereas *on*-readings represent morphemes of Chinese origin (Paradis, Hagiwara and Hildebrandt, 1985). When Chinese characters were introduced to Japan, there were sometimes no Japanese concepts for the in-coming new Chinese words. In such cases, characters and their readings were used to represent objects, ideas or events, although the original readings in Chinese were altered to suit the Japanese phonological system (Hirose, 1998; Martin, 1972). These readings are *on*-readings. In some cases however, characters were used to represent native words that already existed in Japan (Hirose, 1998; Martin, 1972). These readings are *kun*-readings. For example, 言う /i-u/ 'to say' is a word of Japanese origin, and the *kanji* 言, in this case, is read in the *kun*-reading. Most single-character words (with or without *hiragana* to follow) are read in the *kun*-reading, with a few exceptions (e.g., the word 本 'book' is read in the *on*-reading /hoN/). In two-character compound words, the constituent characters are usually read in *on*-reading. For example, in the word, 言語 /geN-go/ 'language', both /geN/ and /go/ are *on*-readings. However, the constituent characters of some words are read in *kun*-reading, for example, 物語 /mono-gatari/ 'story'. There are few words that are read in the combination of *kun*-and *on*-readings.

Each constituent character carries phonological information. However, knowing the reading of a character may not be very useful in reading a compound word. For example, the reading of the character 認 as a single-character word (認める) is /mito-meru/, but this reading does not give any phonological indication in the reading of the word 認識 /niNshiki/.

Kanji characters are notorious for having multiple readings. Although an extreme case, the characters 生 and 下 have ten *kun*-readings and two *on*-readings (data drawn from a character database created by Tamaoka, Kirsner, Yanase, Miyaoka, and Kawakami, 2002). Although 726 of the 1,945 characters (37.3%) do have one-to-one correspondence with reading (32 characters have only one *kun*-reading and 694 characters have only one *on*-reading), the rest have two or more readings (Kaiho and Nomura, 1983). About 60% of the 1,945 characters have both *on*- and *kun*-readings, 38% have multiple *on*-readings and no *kun*-reading, and 2% have multiple *kun*-readings and no *on*-reading (Tamaoka, 2003). Nearly every *kanji* among the 1,945 has at least one *on*-reading (Nomura, 1981). *On*-reading *kanji* appear in print 4.6 times more frequently than *kun*-reading *kanji* (Hayashi, 1982). One would think, therefore, that knowing the *on*-readings of characters may be of help in reading words. However, as mentioned above, some *kanji* have more than one *on*-reading. Due to these numerous readings, it is widely believed that phonological representations of *kanji* are not immediately apparent from their graphical features (Wydell, Patterson and Humphreys, 1993).

When discussing the phonology of *kanji* characters, the two types of readings should not be mixed. *Kun*- and *on*- readings have no relationship (Tamaoka, 2003; Taylor, 1998), as they are from two unrelated languages, Japanese and Chinese (Taylor, 1998). *Kun*-reading usually shows the concept of the individual *kanji*, and *on*-reading only shows one of the readings of the constituent *kanji* (Taylor, 1998). For this reason, *kun*-reading is sometimes called semantic reading, and *on*-reading, phonetic reading (Hatano, 1986).

There is growing evidence that native Japanese speakers have separate 'entries' in the mental lexicon for *on*-readings and *kun*-readings (Tamaoka, 2003). It is claimed that native Japanese speakers mainly distinguish *on*- and *kun*- readings of a word based on the degree of semantic concreteness of the word and the speed of accessing the phonology of the word (Kaiho and Nomura, 1983). This suggests that they are functionally quite distinct in that processing *kun*-readings involves the activation of semantic representations prior to phonological activation while *on*-readings have direct links to the activation of phonological representations (Kaiho and Nomura, 1983).

16

Precisely, the dichotomy between *kun*-reading and *on*-reading as categorised in dictionaries may be too simplistic. It appears that when the reading for a character that occurs independently has concrete meaning, L1 readers tend to believe that it is a *kun*-reading of the kanji (Hirose, 1998). For example, many L1 readers of Japanese think that the readings /eki/ and /niku/ for the kanji 駅 (station) and 肉 (meat) are *kun*-readings when they are in fact *on*-readings (Tomita and Sanada, 1994). In this regard, it may be more reasonable to categorise readings into meaning-bearing readings (that are *kun*-readings in most cases) and non-meaning-bearing readings (that are *on*-readings in most cases).

1.3.5 kanji character composed of component(s)

Structure

Characters are composed of smaller graphic elements. The first character dictionary (around AD100) categorised approximately 10,000 characters using a system of 540 graphical elements. The 540 graphical elements were in later years reduced to 214, and the current radical system has developed based on the 214 graphical elements (Tomita and Sanada, 1994; Martin, 1972). Today, all character dictionaries (except a few innovative ones) follow this 214 radical system in classifying characters (Tomita and Sanada, 1994).

The term 'radical' is being used rather ambiguously in literature. According to Taft and Zhu (1997a:761), there are two different Chinese terms for 'radical': 部首 /bushou/

and 部件 /bujian/. In Japanese, those that are used as dictionary indices are conventionally called 部首 /bushu/, and the rest have no particular name. The majority of characters are made up of a combination of the 214 *bujians* although some characters may contain other graphical elements. In the case of the character 語 'word', it is composed of three *bujians*: 言, 五 and 口. In a character dictionary, this character 語 is classified under the *bushou* 言. In other words,, a character may have several *bujians*, but only one of them is the *bushou* in a character. In an attempt to avoid this confusion, some researchers use the term 'stroke patterns' to refer to all the recurring spatial designs, and 'lexical radicals' for dictionary indices (Chen, Allport and Marshall, 1996). However, these terms have not been widely accepted. In this book, in accordance with the meanings of the Chinese terms, *bujians* are referred to as **radicals**. When they have functional roles as dictionary indices (*bushou*), they are referred to as the **main radical**. The graphical elements, other than the 214 radicals that appear in characters, are referred to as secondary radicals.

Some radicals can become legitimate characters with slight changes in size and shape while others cannot (Shu and Anderson, 1998; Taft and Zhu, 1997a). According to the New Nelson Japanese-English Character Dictionary, 157 out of the 214 radicals may be legitimate characters. For example, each of the above-mentioned three radicals, 言, 五, and 口 can be a legitimate character with their own meaning and reading. However, the other 57 radicals cannot be legitimate characters on their own. For example, the radical at the top of the character 家 cannot be a legitimate character. A radical can be shared by a number of characters although some only appear in a limited number of characters.

Although combinations of radicals forming a character seem to be diverse, characters can be grouped, roughly speaking, into four patterns according to their graphical configuration (Nomura, 1984): non-separable (e.g., 日), left-right (e.g., 明), top-bottom (e.g., 星), and others (e.g., 間).

Characters with a non-separable pattern are called **single-component characters** in this book. For example, the character 火 has a non-separable pattern, although one may think that it has three separable parts, as this character as a whole depicts 'fire'. In passing some single-component characters originally had more than one radical. As a case in point, according to the Dictionary of *Kanji* Origin (*Kanji*gen) the character 言 was originally made from two radicals: 辛 (which has changed its form) and 口. However, under the current radical system, 言 is has a status as a radical. For this reason, the character 言 is considered to have a non-separable pattern, and is therefore a single-component character. As is in this example, a single-component character may be further decomposed into two or more radicals for etymological reasons. In this regard, a component and a radical are not identical although in most cases they are the same.

Characters with a pattern other than non-separable are called **compound characters**. Compound characters can be divided into two components: a main-radical component and a non-main-radical component (which may consist of radicals and secondary radicals). In a compound character, one of the radicals is designated as the main radical by which the character is indexed in a character dictionary. Therefore, every character has only one main radical, under which it is classified (Koda, 2002), even though it may also have a radical that has the exact same graphical shape as a main radical in other characters (Taft and Zhu, 1997a). For example, the main radical of the character 信 is 亻, and the other radical 言, which is the main radical of the character 語 does not in this case function as a main radical.

Some researchers use different terms such as 'simple character' and 'complex character' instead of 'single-component character' and 'compound character' (e.g., Li and Chen, 1997; Morton and Sasanuma, 1984). However, some simple characters may be graphically more complex than 'complex' characters. For example, when comparing the 'simple' character 魚 with the 'complex' character 化, the former looks graphically more complicated than the latter. In this regard, these terms are ambiguous. The two types of characters are also referred to as 'integrated characters' and 'compound characters' respectively (e.g., Leck, Weekes and Chen, 1995). Although the character 魚 may look like a compound character, this character consists of one component that cannot be decomposed etymologically, and is therefore an 'integrated' character.

However, this term 'integrated' also causes confusion. For example, the *kanji* 日 does not have separate parts to integrate. For these reasons, in this book I would like to use the terms 'single-component character' and 'compound character'

The numbers of single-component characters and compound characters have not been agreed upon among researchers due to varied interpretations of the term 'component' (some researchers use the term 'component' to refer to a 'radical'). Although the exact number of one-component characters in Japanese is not given in literature for this reason, the figure seems to be low, as it is reported that only about 10% of *hanzi* are single-component characters (Leck, Weekes and Chen, 1995). This suggests that the majority are compound characters.

Among the above-mentioned four graphical patterns, the left-right pattern is the most common. For Chinese, it has been claimed that about 90% of characters have the left-right pattern (Tan, Hoosain and Peng, 1995). The next common is the top-bottom pattern. For Japanese, the percentage of the left-right pattern is lower than that for Chinese, and it is reported as 56.3% (Nomura, 1984). According to Saito, Kawakami, Masuda, and Flores d'Arcais (1997), among the 1,668 *kanji* the left-right pattern *kanji* within the 2,965 *kanji* in the JIS, the total number of radical and secondary radicals used is 857. Among these, 97 (11%) are used only as main-radicals, 610 (71%) are used only as non-main-radicals, and 150 (18%) can be a main-radical or non-main-radical, sometimes with minor modifications. In left-right pattern characters, the main-radicals tend to appear on the left-hand side of the characters. In top-bottom pattern characters,

21

the main-radicals can sometimes be found at the top, but also sometimes at the bottom. According to the New Nelson Japanese-English Character Dictionary, 116 radicals can be left main-radicals, 106 can be bottom main-radicals, 91 can be top main-radicals, 57 can be right main-radicals and 31 appear in other locations.

Most main radicals have names which may indicate their locations. Left main-radicals are collectively called *hen*, and usually have *'hen'* or *'ben'* at the end of their names such as, *kihen, ninben,* and *tehen.* Likewise, top main-radicals are collectively called *kanmuri*, and usually have *'kanmuri'* at the end of their names such as *ukanmuri, kusakanmuri,* and *takekanmuri.* Right and bottom main-radicals are collectively called *tsukuri* and *ashi* respectively. These main-radicals also have names although they do not have *'tsukuri'* or *'ashi'* at the end.

Taft and Zhu (1997a), calculating from the Chinese Radical Position Frequency Dictionary, demonstrated that about 66% of all main radicals have fixed positions within characters: left, right, top, bottom or in the middle. There are a few main radicals that do not have fixed positions. For example, the main radical 日 can appear in various positions: left, 暗, right, 旧, top, 景, and bottom, 旨. However, in most cases main radicals have a preferred position over the other positions even if it is not fixed. For example, the main radical 言 usually appears in the left-hand side of the character with a few exceptional cases (e.g., 警). It is reported that about 80-90% of the left-right pattern compound characters have a main radical on the left-hand side and a phonetic (a radical or a combination of radicals that convey useful phonological information - this will be further discussed in the 'phonological function' section) on the right-hand side (Flores d'Arcaise, 1992; Huang and Hanley, 1995; Wang, 1981). For example, the compound character 認 has the main radical on its left showing a broad meaning category 'speech' and the phonetic (component that may give some indication of the pronunciation of the characters) on its right showing a broad sound category /niN/. Therefore, once the main radical has been identified, there is a good chance that the other component would be a phonetic. In this regard, knowing the positions of main radicals is essential, not only for accessing the semantic information of the main radicals, but also for finding phonetics and retrieving their phonological information.

Semantic function

The 214 radicals usually carry semantic information indicating a concept (or a broad meaning field). In the case of the character 語 'word', it is a compound character consisting of three radicals, 言, 五 and 口. According to the *Kanji*gen dictionary, this character was first formed by combining 五 and 口 meaning 'exchange' and 'mouth' respectively. The formed character 吾 meant 'discuss and exchange ideas'. Later the radical 言 was added to show that this character was related to the meaning category of 'speech'. This character is classified under the main radical 言 in a character dictionary.

Generally speaking, the radical that shows a broad meaning category of the character is designated as the main radical of the character.

If the main radical was the one that could not be a character, the concept shown by the main radical can only be arrived at by finding a common meaning among characters sharing it. For example, the main radical at the top of the character 家 'house' may be interpreted as 'a roof or a cover' after examining the broad meaning fields of the characters, 宿, 室, 宮, 安, 寝, which are 'inn', 'room', 'palace', 'safe', and 'sleep' respectively. However, finding a common meaning is not always an easy task.

As can be seen in the above examples, a main radical usually plays the role of a semantic indicator in a character. However, semantic relationships between a character and its main radical and between a main radical and the characters sharing it are sometimes not very clear unless the generic meanings of characters and main radicals are known. Available data for *hanzi* (Shu, Chen, Anderson, Wu and Xuan, 2003) show that 58% of compound characters are semantically transparent (i.e., the semantic relationship between a character and its main radical is clear), 30% are semi-transparent, and 9% are opaque. Without knowing the origin of their formation, some characters are difficult to associate to the category shown by a given main radical.

According to Tamaoka, Kirner, Yanase, Miyaoka and Kawakami (2002), among the main radicals, the 10 most frequently used main radicals appear in 34% of the 1,945 Japanese general-use *kanji*, and the 24 of them appear in 54%. The number of *kanji* characters sharing a particular main radical varies from very few to many (Flores d'Arcais, Saito and Kawakami, 1995). According to the *kanji* database created by Tamaoka, Kirsner, Yanase, Miyaoka and Kawakami (2002), there are 76 *kanji* that hardly have any other *kanji* sharing the same main radical, whereas there are 103 *kanji* that share the main radical representing 'water'.

Within the same semantic domain, the strength of the relationship between *kanji* characters varies widely (Flores d'Arcais, Saito and Kawasaki, 1995). Some are very closely related. For example, 語 'word' and 話 'story' share a common main radical, 言 'something related to speech', and are semantically closely related (semantically transparent). On the other hand, 語 'word' and 誰 'who', for example, are hard to relate to each other, despite their common main radical.

Phonological function

In a compound character, the non-main-radical component (a radical, or a combination of radicals) may have useful phonological information. The 214 radicals usually carry phonological information as well as semantic information. While the phonological information of most radicals is of no use for the recognition of the character, some radicals convey useful information. These particular radicals are often called 'phonetics' or 'phonetic elements' (Chen, Wu and Anderson, 2003; Shu and Anderson, 1998). Some researchers call them 'phonetic radicals' as a contrasting term to 'semantic radicals' (Flores d'Arcais, Saito and Kawakami, 1995, Taft and Zhu, 1995, Wang, 1981). In this book, I will call them **phonetics.** The terms such as 'radical' and

25

'element' were avoided, as a phonetic is not identical to 'a radical carrying phonological information' because it can consist of more than one radical. The character 認, for example, has a phonetic 忍 /niN/ that is composed of two radicals, 刃 and 心. A phonetic indicates a sound group (a group of similar sounds), which may suggest an *on*-reading of the character or a sound similar to it (this will be discussed later).

There is no consensus on the number of phonetics. However, it is estimated that 800-1,100 phonetics exist in Chinese *hanzi* (Shu, 2003; Hoosain, 1991) and approximately 700 exist in Japanese *kanji* (Koda, 2002). Some of them are single radical (e.g., 工 /koR/ in 功, 項, 巧, 紅, 貢), and some are composed of more than one radical (e.g., 利 /ri/ in 痢, 梨, 俐, 犁, 悧 - the last four characters are outside of the 1,945 general-use *kanji*).

A phonetic is useful only for a limited number of characters (Taft and Zhu, 1995, Hoosain, 1991; Lee, Stigler and Stevenson, 1986). They can only be found in a particular type of compound character called **phonetic compounds**, which are composed of a main radical and a phonetic. It has been reported that 66.1% of the 1,945 *kanji* are categorised as phonetic compounds (Tamaoka, 1991). In *kanji*, a phonetic can indicate only one kind of reading, namely the *on*-reading (Paradis, Hagiwara and Hildebrandt, 1985). Also, due to various reasons such as different readings at the time of introduction and the difference between the Chinese and Japanese phonetic systems

(Tamaoka, 1991), occasions where a phonetic represents the exact reading of the whole *kanji* are rare.

Similar to the case in a main radical, it should be noted that a phonetic shows only a broad sound category to which the character belongs, rather than the exact reading of the character. In *hanzi*, it has been claimed that of all the phonetics in Chinese, 36% give the reading of a character, 48% give partial information, and 16% give no useful information (Yin, 1991 cited in Shu and Anderson, 1998). In *kanji*, it is estimated that the phonological consistency between the sounds of the *kanji* and its phonetic range from 37 to 42% (Koda, 1999b).

The reliability of phonological information contained within a phonetic must be assessed both in terms of regularity and consistency. For regularity, the phonetic 包, for example, is a regular phonetic. This phonetic (包) and *kanji* containing this phonetic (e.g., 抱 and 泡) have the same sound /hoR/. On the other hand, the phonetic 占 is an example of an irregular phonetic. This phonetic (占) shows the sound /seN/. However, *kanji* containing it (e.g., 店 and 点) are read as /teN/, not /seN/. Some phonetics that are not legitimate *kanji* on their own, such as the phonetic shared by the *kanji* 脳 /noR/ and 悩 /noR/, are also considered to be irregular. For consistency, for example, the phonetic 交 /koR/ is one of the consistent phonetics. All *kanji* with the phonetic 校, 郊, 効, 絞 are read as /koR/. A less consistent phonetic is, for example, 毎 /mai/. The *kanji* with this phonetic, for example, 海 and 悔 are read as /kai/, 梅 is read as /bai/, and 侮 is read as /bu/; although as can be seen in the above example, the sound of the phonetic often rhymes with the reading of the *kanji* (Jackson, Lu and Ju, 1994).

Despite limited reliability, research emphasises that knowledge of main radicals and phonetics serve as a fundamental element of overall *kanji* knowledge (Tamaoka and Yamada, 2000; Leong and Tamaoka, 1995; Flores d'Arcais, Saito and Kawakami, 1995). According to the Path Model presented by Tamaoka and Yamada (2000), knowledge of the functional components (main radicals and phonetics) seems to be an important contributor to knowledge of *kanji* lexical orthography, phonology and semantics.

Although main radicals and phonetics do not show the precise meaning and reading of an unfamiliar *kanji*, they are potentially useful for the following reasons. Main radicals are useful for discrimination of a particular *kanji* from other graphically similar *kanji*, as a main radical often gives a good indication of the meaning category of the *kanji* (Koda, 2002). It is particularly useful for finding the correct *kanji* from a number of graphically similar homophones (Hatano, 1986). Phonetics are also useful for inferring (one of) the readings of the *kanji*, particularly when encountering an unknown *kanji*-written compound word in a text. Because the phonetic can assist the reader in reading out the *kanji*, there is a chance that the word containing the *kanji* is recognised via the phonological route.

Even if the semantic information of the main radical and the phonological information of the phonetic of the *kanji* are not readily available to the reader, the recognition of the *kanji* would be assisted with the general knowledge of the functional components (that *kanji* sharing a common main radical are in most cases semantically related, and that *kanji* sharing a common phonetic usually have similar *on*-readings). When encountering a new *kanji* at least the broad meaning category of the *kanji* can be known from the existing knowledge of other *kanji* sharing the main radical. Likewise, the new *kanji* can be read out (at least in a likely sound) using the existing knowledge of other *kanji* sharing the phonetic.

In summary, the understanding of the roles that the functional components play within individual *kanji* and across the *kanji* network seems to assist readers in recognising the *kanji* containing the functional components, which would consequently help them recognise the word containing the *kanji*. Becoming aware of functional components (main radicals and phonetics) therefore seems to be essential in developing word (character) recognition skills. Given the characteristics of *kanji* script, I hypothesise that readers who are developing *kanji* recognition skills need to become aware of 1) the positions of main radicals (which will then determine the positions of phonetics), 2) the potential of semantic and phonological information conveyed by the functional components, and 3) the limitations of such information.

2 Word recognition skills of skilled and less-skilled readers

2.1 Overview of word recognition skills

Chapter one provided an introduction to the book, followed by definitions of the terms used in the book, and a description of the Japanese writing system focusing on *kanji* characters. This chapter reviews literature pertaining to the word recognition skills of skilled and less-skilled readers. I would like to begin with a general overview of word recognition skills in relation to reading ability and vocabulary knowledge.

2.1.1 Role of word recognition in reading

Reading comprehension is 'a product of the integrated interaction between textual information and the reader's pre-existing knowledge' (Koda, 1996:450), a process which 'involves the operation of a wide and complex range of processes and strategies' (Davis and Castles, 1998:85). In other words, reading is a meaning construction process using information within, and outside of, the text. The internal information includes the outcomes of various levels of processing at letter, word, sentence and text levels. The external information includes the reader's already-formed conceptual schema and world knowledge.

For both internal and external information, several levels of processing are involved, and at each level, a variety of skills and strategies are required. While there is no doubt that higher order linguistic and conceptual knowledge are crucial for reading success, it also appears that lower level, perceptually based linguistic knowledge is crucial as well (Koda, 1994; Haynes and Carr, 1990). In this book, the focus will be on the recognition of words, an activity fundamental to reading comprehension (Harley, 1995; Vellutino, 1991; Perfetti 1986).

2.1.2 Word recognition, vocabulary knowledge, and reading ability

Research suggests that competence in word recognition is correlated highly with proficiency in reading comprehension in both L1 reading (Huang and Hanley, 1995; Stanovich, 1991, 1982; Vellutino, 1991; Cunningham, Stanovich, and Wilson, 1990; Perfetti, 1991, 1986; Barron, 1981), and in L2 reading (Koda, 1996, 1992, 1989b; Haynes and Carr, 1990; Adams, 1990; Segalowitz, 1986). Strong correlations between reading and both vocabulary knowledge and word recognition in L1 have also been reported (Cunningham, Stanovich and Wilson, 1990). Strong relationships between reading and vocabulary knowledge have also been found in L2 studies, with a very high correlation found between word recognition and vocabulary knowledge (Haynes and Carr, 1990; Koda, 1989b).

Although many processes are involved in reading, lower-level processing such as word recognition is said to be critical (Koda, 1992; Stanovich, 1991). It has been argued that higher-level processing (e.g., syntactic and discourse analyses) cannot be performed without proficient lower-level processing (Brisbois, 1995; Vellutino, 1991; Stanovich, 1991, 1982; Haynes and Carr, 1990; Brown and Haynes, 1985; Singer, 1982), as slower word recognition may result in fewer cognitive resources being available for higher order comprehension operations (Barron, 1981). Alderson (2000:80) advocates:

> It is clear that word recognition, and especially the automaticity with which this proceeds, is central to fluent reading, and the readers' ability to rapidly identify words and meanings at 'lower levels' is likely to be a key to any diagnosis of reading problems or abilities.

In short, word recognition is therefore an essential processing procedure in reading in L2 as well as in L1.

2.2 Development of word recognition skills

In this section, developmental processes of word recognition skills will be discussed. In order to investigate how less-skilled L2 readers develop their word recognition skills, after briefly discussing the differences in recognition skills between skills and less-skilled readers, I will examine how L1 children learn to read words in their first language. Although children learning to read in their L1 may be different from L2 adult readers in many cognitive aspects, it is worth investigating the developmental phases of L1 children in different orthographies. In the last part of this section, by examining some prominent word recognition models, I will investigate how skilled readers recognise words.

2.2.1 Skilled readers and less-skilled readers

As Castles and Davis (1998:93) stated, 'the acquisition of new word representations is not all-or-none, but may involve a process of shaping and modifying an internal discrimination mechanism'. With the development of the internal discrimination mechanism, readers gradually increase the accuracy of as well as the speed of word recognition (Takahashi, 1993; Perfetti, 1986; Segalowitz, 1986).

Many researchers emphasise that the speed of lexical access is particularly critical to efficient word recognition. Better readers demonstrate a response-time advantage over less-skilled readers when processing words (Kuhara-Kojima, Hatano, Saito and Haebara, 1996; Tamaoka, Leong and Hatta, 1991; Jackson and McClelland, 1981). Readers who have superior word processing skills are more likely to base their reading upon a bottom-up interpretation of the text. Indeed, evidence shows that fluent readers exhibit rapid context-free processes whereas less able readers show slower and more context-dependent processes (Perfetti, 1991; Cunningham, Stanovich and Wilson, 1990; Stanovich, 1980). This implies that readers who are slow in recognizing words may attempt to compensate by relying more heavily on context, which may result in inadequate comprehension. In fact, Horiba, van den Broek and Fletcher (1994) investigated how lower-level and higher-level processing interact, and found that L2 readers resort to context when the lower-level process breaks down. It has been claimed that slow word recognition hinders L2 readers from applying semantic and discourse restrictions efficiently or making use of background knowledge (Brown and Haynes, 1985).

When skilled readers recognise a word, it appears that they not only process it efficiently but also use information from the sentence and discourse to establish the precise meaning of it. When there is ambiguity between the information from the word and the context, skilled readers use their world knowledge. Research suggests that because their word recognition is efficient and does not require a large portion of their working memory (Osaka and Osaka, 1994; Kawakami, Hatta and Tamaoka, 1991), skilled readers are in a position to carry out higher-level processing (Brown and Haynes, 1985; Barron, 1981). This is not the case for less-skilled L2 readers however, as a greater portion of their working memory would be taken up in the lower-level processing, leaving less memory capacity for higher-level processing (Koda, 1989b; Stanovich, 1982).

In the following sections, in order to understand how less-skilled L2 readers develop into more skilled readers, I will first examine how less-skilled L1 readers (L1 children) learn to read words in their first language. Discussion will focus on English-speaking children learning to read English words, and then on Japanese and Chinese children learning to read *kanji* or *hanzi* characters.

2.2.2 Developmental phases in Alphabetic writing system

It has been claimed that children go through developmental phases before reaching the level of skilled reader. For example, Harris and Coltheart (1986) illustrate four phases of learning to read English. The first step is the 'direct procedure' phase, where children of 4-5 years old have a small set of words that they can read aloud. The second phase is the 'discrimination-net' phase where children read words using limited information such as word length, the initial letter or overall word shape. This phase is 'a choice from amongst the set of words that the child knows' (Harris and Coltheart, 1986:91). As the vocabulary size expands, it becomes increasingly difficult to distinguish a word from others by salient features of the word. The next phase of reading development is 'phonological-recoding'. Children at this stage can segment a word into letters and map the letters to their corresponding sounds. The final stage is the 'orthographic' phase where the readers pay more attention to how the words are spelt than how they are pronounced. Children read words by the orthography without necessarily going though grapheme to phoneme conversion. This process is thought to be the result of highly developed recognition skills. Harris and Coltheart advocate that phonological recoding is not the final stage of development, 'since skilled reading is only achieved if the reader can deal adequately with homophones and with exception words' (Harris and Coltheart, 1986:98).

The boundaries between the development stages may not be clear-cut. For example, Gough (1991) claims that there is a transitional stage between the selective association stage (which is equivalent to Harris and Coltheart's discrimination-net stage)

34

and the orthographic cipher stage (which is equivalent to Harris and Coltheart's phonological-recoding stage). In the selective association stage, children examine the word for anything that they can remember (e.g., length, overall shape or one letter of the word), and associate the word with that cue. Although this seems to work initially, recognising many words in this manner is not easy, because as the number of words increases, the more difficult this approach becomes. Children then gradually become able to recognise the printed forms of words by knowledge of the letter-sound correspondence of the language, or its 'orthographic cipher', via the transition stage (Gough 1991).

Furthermore, moving up the development stages may not happen all at once. Readers with higher skills may sometimes appear as if they read in a similar way to the readers with lower skills. For example, Ehri and Robbins (1992) claim that readers who have acquired phonological-recoding skills do not necessarily read words by converting letters to their corresponding sounds, but may read them by analogy. Phonological skills may assist beginner readers in reading words by analogy in two ways: it may enable readers to convert graphemes into phonemes and/or onset and rhyme, and to store the phonological information in the short-term memory (Ehri and Robbins, 1992).

Focusing on the fact that a reader can be more skilled and less skilled depending on the situation, Share (1995) discusses development of word recognition from a perspective of different word features. He proposed that development would be item-based rather than stage-based, arguing that 'the process of word recognition will depend primarily on the frequency to which a child has been exposed to a particular word' (Share. 1995:155). While lower frequency (and therefore less familiar) words are likely to be recognised by grapheme-phoneme conversion, higher frequency (and therefore more familiar) words may be recognised visually with minimal phonological processing.

It is probably not the question of either staged-based or item-based. It is more reasonable to think that children move through the stage-based developmental progression, but that the speed of the development is item-based.

2.2.3 Developmental phases in Logographic/Morphographic writing system

Unlike alphabetic script, in the logographic/morphographic script such as *kanji* and *hanzi*, breaking a character into smaller graphical elements (radicals) does not always lead to further phonological processing. Children need to be able to know the graphic features of 'functional' components (main radicals and phonetics) and their positions in a character, in order to identify them and to access phonological or semantic information though them (see Chapter 1 Section 3).

Nevertheless, studies pertaining to Chinese reading development suggest that the gradual development of character recognition of Chinese children is similar to how children learn to recognise the English alphabet (Shu, 2003; Ho, Ng and Ng, 2003; Ho and Bryant, 1997). It has been claimed that even children in early grades (i.e., Grade 1 or 2) have some rudimentary knowledge of the internal structure of characters (e.g.,

36

positional regularity of components), and that this knowledge grows with age (Shu, 2003; Ho, Ng and Ng, 2003).

Ho and Bryant (1997) claim that, just as children who learn to read the alphabet, Chinese children go through a phonological (analytical) phase after a logographic (holistic) phase. They investigated whether children who learnt Chinese characters (*hanzi*) without mediation of any phonetic system (i.e., neither Pin-Yin nor Zhu-Yin-Fu-Hao was used to teach pronunciation of *hanzi*), would utilise information of phonetics (components carrying phonological information that can be helpful in retrieving the phonology of the characters – see Chapter 1 Section 3 for details) for recognising *hanzi*. The participants were Grade 1 and Grade 2 children from Hong Kong. The results of the analysis of the children's performance in a naming task revealed that they named phonologically regular *hanzi* (the ones with a phonetic) more accurately than irregular ones (the ones without a phonetic). This indicated that the children utilised knowledge of the phonetics for naming the characters, which at the same time suggests that they were aware that the phonetics could be useful in reading the characters aloud. Evidence to support this was that the dominant type of error that the children made was phonologically related, showing overgeneralization of their knowledge about the roles of phonetics.

Ho, Ng and Ng (2003) investigated the impact of knowledge of main radicals and phonetics in Chinese reading development. Their participants were Chinese children in Grades 1, 3 and 5. Firstly, in order to examine the relationship between the knowledge of main radicals and reading ability, the researchers administered a battery of tasks (i.e., an IQ test, a Chinese word reading test, a Chinese sentence comprehension test, a character decision task, a radical position judgement task, a semantic relatedness judgement task, a semantic category judgement task, and a Chinese pseudo-character meaning judgement task). They found that even the Grade 1 children had some knowledge of the typical positions of main radicals, and that the Grade 3 children also knew the semantic categories of main radicals. The Grade 5 children were able to use the main radicals for meaning cues in processing a sentence. Secondly, for the investigation of the role of phonetics in reading, the researchers used a character decision task, a phonetic position judgement task, a phonological relatedness judgement task, a Chinese phonetic naming task and a Chinese pseudo-character naming task. Similar to the results for the main radicals, the Grade 1 children were found to have some knowledge of the position of phonetics. The Grade 3 and Grade 5 children were able to use the phonetics for reading words aloud. The findings suggest that Chinese children's reading skills seem to develop from visual and arbitrary recognition to analytic and rule–based recognition.

Apparently, however, the phonological (analytical) stage is not the final stage of reading development. As the number of phonetic families (characters with the same phonetic) increases in their vocabulary, Chinese children become aware that the phonetics are not a reliable cue for pronunciation (Shu, 2003), and they start to use this knowledge more selectively. Tzeng, Zhong, Hung and Lee (1995) asked third and sixth grade Taiwanese children to read three types of pseudo-*hanzi*: those with only regular neighbours (i.e., the pronunciations of the phonetic and the character with the phonetic

38

are the same), those with only irregular neighbours (i.e., different pronunciations), and those with both regular and irregular neighbours. The results showed that the children made regular responses to the regular-only condition, but not in the irregular-only condition, which suggest that skilled readers (older children, in this case) do not read characters solely based on the phonetics of the target characters, but use information in neighbouring characters. They utilise the information from the phonetics only when they are reliable. This stage, which follows the phonological stage, may be called the 'orthographic stage'.

Developmental phases for Japanese character recognition have not yet been firmly established in the literature. However, the above studies suggest that developmental phases for Chinese reading are similar to those for alphabetic languages: the recognition goes from holistic to analytical, and from analytical to orthographic. If this is the case, then Japanese children would also be expected to go from Stage 1 where the readers try to recognise a character relying on any familiar salient parts, into Stage 2 where they make use of the phonological and semantic information from the functional components of a character, and lastly stage 3 where they recognise a character using the functional components selectively. (The speed of this developmental progression is likely to be item-based.)

2.2.4 Word recognition by skilled readers

Optimum level of the orthographic phase - Automaticity

Children make gradual developmental progression, and eventually attain word recognition proficiency (lexicalisation), which is hardly distinguishable from whole-lexical processing (Share, 1995). When readers of a language become able to recognise words with optimum efficiency, they are considered to have attained automaticity (Driscall, 1994). Skilled readers appear to process words skilfully due to automatic or attention-free processing (Perfetti, 1991). This however does not necessarily mean that they can automatically process any existing word. It simply means that they have a certain number of words that can be decoded automatically (Perfetti, 1991). A reader can be fully skilled in recognising some words while the same reader can be less skilled in recognising others (Share, 1995). As Perfetti (1986) claims, although the concept of 'automaticity of word recognition' has been widely accepted, it may be more accurate to say that the resource demands reduce with practice. In this regard, it is expected that the more a reader sees a word, the more easily they recognise it (Share, 1995). Researchers indeed have revealed that developing readers become able to recognise high frequency words quickly and accurately from very early stages while they would need to rely on the slower process of grapheme-phoneme conversion for low frequency words (Tan, Hoosain and Peng, 1995; Taft and Zhu, 1995; McClelland and Rumelhart, 1981). As well, there may be other stimulus properties, such as the size of homophones and synonyms (Harley, 1995), affecting word recognition.

Models of word recognition by skilled readers

In this section the basic frameworks of some of the most prominent models describing how words are recognised will be outlined. For further review, see Davis, 1999; Harley, 1995; Foorman, 1994; Taft, 1991; Harris and Coltheart, 1986.

The Search Model (Taft and Forster, 1975) is a model that was developed based on the notion of library resources. This model proposes that a word in the mental lexicon (internal dictionary) is ordered in terms of a stored representation's frequency of occurrence: words that occur often as input are searched before rarer words. When the perceptual information input is matched with the entry in the lexicon, a stored entry in a modality free lexicon proper (called the 'master file') is contacted. The word is accessed when all necessary information contained in the master file becomes available.

Later, the notion of the serial search was replaced by the notion of activation. For example, The Logogen Model (Morton, 1980) proposes that each lexical entry acts as an evidence collector (logogen), which becomes activated when it detects a visual stimulus that contains features of the word it represents. Each feature of a word, such as the first or last letter, the number of letters, and letter positions can trigger the activation of logogens that have the feature. Each word has a different level of activation threshold according to its frequency of occurrence, and when this threshold is reached, the semantic and syntactic information related to the word becomes available in the cognitive system.

Overall, these models were proposed to explain the word frequency effect in which common words are recognised faster than less common ones. They also demonstrate why the recognition of a word is affected by sublexical features.

Among activation models, the most influential is the Interactive Activation Model (McClelland and Rumelhart, 1981). The concepts inherent in the Interactive Activation Model are important as these play a role in one of the few models of character recognition (which will be discussed later). This model demonstrates that the internalised system consisting of word, letter and feature levels is multi-layered, and that each level is hierarchically linked. When a word is presented visually, parallel activation occurs at the word, letter and feature levels, where knowledge and incoming information are processed interactively by passing the processed information up and down between neighbouring levels. There is excitatory activation between levels and inhibitory activation within a level.

The later version of the Interactive Activation Model includes the activation of phonology and semantics ('feedforward activation') and the activation of different words that share the same letters or features ('feedback activation'). In this model, high frequency words have a higher resting level of activation than low frequency words; therefore high frequency words reach their threshold of activation sooner than low frequency words, thus high frequency words may be recognised faster than low frequency words. The system is modified continuously over time by learning, which changes the strength of links between units.

This Interactive Activation model demonstrates links both within a word (feedforward activation) and between words (feedback activation), and offers explanations of regularity effect (regular words are recognised faster than exceptional words) and consistency effect (words that have neighbouring words with consistent features are recognised faster than words that have neighbours with inconsistent features). It also explains why word recognition is affected by neighbourhood size (the number of words that are graphically similar to the target word) and homophone size (the number of words that are homophonic to the target word).

The Dual Route Cascaded Model (Coltheart, Rastle, Perry, Langdon and Ziegler, 2001) may be viewed as an extension of the Interactive Activation Model, but offers a different perspective to the understanding of phonological processing in word recognition. As in the Interactive Activation Model, information processing occurs in a cascading fashion, instead of the thresholded processing that the Logogen Model has suggested. In the system of cascaded processing, as soon as there is any activation of an early module, it flows on to later modules. Just like the Interactive Activation Model there are multiple levels, visual feature units, letter units and orthographic lexicon, which correspond to the feature, letter and words levels in the previous model. This model is different from the Interactive Activation Model in terms of having a phonological system incorporated within it. As its name suggests, the model is based on the dual-route theory, which advocates that there is a direct pathway from the orthography to the lexical knowledge and that there is also an indirect phonology-mediated route. When a visual stimulus is presented, a series of activations occur between the levels in a cascading fashion, which leads to a build-up of activation in the phonological system via the lexical system and/ or via the phonologically mediated route (Grapheme-Phoneme Conversion).

Route models direct one's attention to the idea that word recognition (specifically reading aloud) might involve two different kinds of processing - that is, 1) simple associations by rules between print and sound and 2) the storing and access of whole word phonology.

Lastly, it is worth noting that there are models that do not presume the existence of a mental lexicon. The Parallel Distributed Processing Model (Seidenberg and McClelland, 1989) is one of them. This model proposes a processing mechanism that associates new information, which is accumulated via the interactions of a number of processing units, with previously stored information. There are excitatory and inhibitory signals, and the information is transmitted by synaptic-like links between nodes depending on which signal they receive. The strength of these links changes continuously through learning.

Recognition model for characters

An attempt to describe the recognition of Chinese characters has led to an alteration of the Interactive Activation Model. The Multi-level Interactive Activation Model (Taft and Zhu, 1995), which was constructed based on the Interactive Activation Model, explains simultaneous activation at the word, morpheme (character), sub-morpheme (component) and feature (stroke) levels. According to this model, when a word is visually presented, units in the multiple levels activate simultaneously, and the information generated at each level passes up and down interactively. This model focuses on the link strength (weight) between the units, which is thought to change through learning. If the weight between the neighbouring units is stronger, the speed at which the activation spreads from one level to another is also faster. The model also incorporated the concept of 'feedforward activation' and 'feedback activation'.

In a revised model of the Multi-level Interactive Activation Model reported in Taft and Zhu (1997a), position symbols were included in the component units. The researchers hypothesised that when the component units activate, in addition to the information of component features, component position information is spread, providing a mechanism to explain component position frequency effect on word recognition.

In later years, Taft (2004) introduced a unit called a 'lemma'. The term 'lemma' is usually defined as a sort of lexical hub that connects the three major aspects of a lexical item: form, pronunciation and meaning (Finkbeniner and Nicol, 2003). In Taft's model, the term 'lemma' is used as a synonym of 'concept' (Taft, 2004). Any orthographic unit that is consistently associated with a semantic feature has a lemma. All words are represented by a lemma, and most characters also have their own lemma. As mentioned in the previous section (Chapter 1 Section 3), a character can be a stand-alone free morpheme, a bound morpheme or a binding character, and as such, the strength of links between a character and its meaning varies depending on its morphemic status. A binding morpheme does not have its own lemma. While a bound morpheme does have its lemma representation, it is not as strong as that for a free morpheme. In short, the lemma is 'a layer of concept units that mediate between form and meaning' (Taft, 2004). Taft further argues that form and pronunciation may also be mediated by the lemma. Thus, the lemma is an integrated part of the hierarchy of form units (feature, component, character and word).

At the present time, the Multi-level Interactive Activation Model seems to be most suited to explaining the recognition of characters, as it incorporates the unique activation of units smaller, and larger, than the unit of 'character'. It emphasises particularly the role of components, and suggests that positions and frequency of components should be taken into consideration when designing, and interpreting the outcomes of, a study involving characters. The model illustrates not only the network within a character but also between characters, which is demonstrated by feedback activation. It further implies that links between a character and its meaning and pronunciation may depend on the morphemic status of the character. These are also important points to bear in mind when investigating character recognition.

In passing, given that recent findings of studies using neuroscientific methods have provided evidence of a complex network of connections broadly distributed across brain regions (Harm and Seidenberg 2004, Perfetti, Van Dyke and Hart, 2001), the interactive interaction of units at multiple levels may be performed at various locations.

To summarise, research findings suggest that children gradually develop recognition skills that are pertinent to the target language. Nevertheless, the overall developmental procedure appears to be universal, regardless of orthographies. L1 readers become fast and accurate, and ultimately attain automaticity (at least for high frequency words) in the recognition of their language via similar developmental phases. Although the processing mechanism has not yet entirely been revealed, as most word recognition models suggest, L1 skilled readers seem to process words using available lexical and sublexical information which is networked across multi-layered functional units. The models also suggest that the recognition of words may be influenced by variables such as word features, word frequency, component frequency, homophone size and neighbourhood size. The review of the literature pertaining to L1 word recognition suggests that when designing a L2 word recognition study, tasks with recognition units at different functional levels need to be prepared, and the aforementioned variables need to be taken into consideration.

2.3 Word recognition skills and awareness of structures and functions of words

This section will discuss the development of script-specific awareness in relation to the development of script-specific processing skills.

2.3.1 Script-specific word recognition skills and awareness of structures and functions of words

It is assumed that word processing ability develops as exposure to characters increases. Research suggests that word recognition skills are supported by underlying ability and insights into the structure and functions of words (spoken or written) (Edwards and Kirkpatrick, 1999; Shu and Anderson, 1998). In the process of attaining highly developed processing skills, the L1 readers are likely to develop such awareness. Perfetti (2003) states that learning to read is to be aware of how the writing system works with regard to both its basic principles and the details of its orthographic implementation. Research indeed suggests that skilled readers are aware of orthographic rules (Peng, Li and Yang, 1997; Perfetti, 1986: Barron, 1981; Fowler, 1981), that is, different types of information created by sequential and positional orthographic constraints (Singer, 1982:6), and that they are also aware of the structure and functions of phonological (Perfetti and Zhang, 1995, 1991; Koda, 1993; Mou and Anderson, 1981; Taft, 1991) and morphological elements (Koda, 2000; Tyler & Nagy, 1990).

Regardless of types of script, the written form of words represents spoken language and corresponds to sounds and meanings. In this regard, becoming aware of connections between orthography, phonology and morphology appears to be essential in any script. However, different types of scripts may require different types of awareness to be developed. Research suggests that the nature of the orthography shapes the early development of the awareness to some extent (Miller, 2002; Caravolas and Bruck, 1993). That is, L1 readers (children) become sensitised to the language features of their native language (Koda, 1997, 1994, 1993; Slobin and Bever, 1982).

2.3.2 Awareness of structures and functions of words in alphabetic writing system

Orthographic awareness

As discussed in the previous section, children start to read words using limited graphic information such as word length or overall word shape at an early stage of development, and they gradually learn to read words by making use of their orthographic information (Wagner and Barker, 1994). To this end, it is undoubtedly essential to become aware of orthographic features of words, such as letter probabilities, positional frequencies and sequential redundancy patterns (Perfetti, 1986: Barron, 1981; Fowler, 1981). However, studies focusing specifically on the development of orthographic awareness in relation to word recognition are scarce. While emphasising the necessity of knowledge of orthographic rules in orthographic processing of words, the vast majority of studies focused more on phonological awareness, as is shown below.

Phonological awareness

The most studied awareness in relation to word reading is phonological awareness. There is a vast amount of educational and psychological research to suggest that, although orthographic access to the meaning (orthographic route) is possible for familiar words, the meanings of unfamiliar words are accessed via the phonological route whereby readers parse strings of letters and convert them into sounds (e.g., Alegria and Morais, 1991; Adams, 1990). Numerous studies claim that phonological awareness plays a critical role in reading alphabetic scripts phonologically (for reviews see Rohl and Milton, 1993; Perfetti, 1991; Tunmer and Rohl, 1991; Adams, 1990; Wagner and Torgesen, 1987; Tunmer and Bowey, 1984).

Phonological awareness is commonly defined as 'the awareness that languages are composed of, and decomposable into, smaller units of sound, such as syllables, onsets and rhymes, and phonemes' (Reynolds, 1998:152). As the definition suggests, the unit of analysis may be a phoneme, syllable or rhyme. Among them, awareness of phonemes has been claimed to be particularly important for grapheme-phoneme conversion (see Perfetti, Van Dyke and Hart, 2001; Adams, 1990 for reviews).

Highly transparent orthographies promote the early development of phonemic awareness, while less transparent orthographies may delay the development of such awareness (Ellis and Hooper, 2001; Geva and Siegel, 2000). Goswami, Ziegler, Dalton and Schneider (2003), however, argue that not the speed but the gain size of units for reading differ with orthographic consistency.

According to Frost and Katz (1992), writing scripts can be classified on a continuum of orthographic depth, from shallow (phonologically transparent – such as Czech, Spanish, Indonesian) to deep (phonologically opaque – such as *kanji* and *hanzi*). Even within the alphabetic scripts, there are in fact phonologically shallow (i.e.,, the relationship between graphemes and phonemes are consistent) scripts such as Czech and Spanish, and phonologically deeper (i.e.,, the relationship between graphemes and phonemes are not consistent) scripts like English. Generally, in orthographically shallow scripts, the most important skill in the recognition of unfamiliar words is claimed to be to segment words into graphemes (letters) and convert them into phonemes (Wimmer and Goswami, 1994), in which the development of phonemic awareness is strongly associated. On the other hand, for a less transparent script such as English, awareness of a larger unit may also develop, as rhymes to sounds relationships are more consistent than letters to phonemes correspondences. Research indeed suggests that English L1 readers are aware of both phonemes and rhymes (Goswami, Ziegler, Dalton and Schneider, 2003).

Abundant research suggests that phonological awareness is important for the acquisition of alphabetic literacy (Shu and Anderson, 1998; Huang and Hanley, 1995; Rohl and Milton, 1993; Perfetti, 1991; Adams, 1990; Tunmer and Bowey, 1984). Findings also suggest that phonological awareness facilitates word reading development in alphabetic languages, and vice versa (Vellutino, 1991; Perfetti, 1991; Stanovich 1991; Tunmer and Rohl, 1991; Vellutino and Scanion 1991; Harris and Coltheart, 1986; Fowler, 1981).

However, Share (1995) claims that phonological awareness is not the sole predictor of good reading ability. He argues that readers need to have a good level of knowledge of letter-sound correspondence, as well as phonological awareness. Castles, Holmes, Neath and Kinoshita (2003) questioned the direct relationship between phonological awareness and word reading ability. They conducted a phoneme deletion task and a phoneme reversal task on both adults and Grade 5 children, and found that the participants performed better on items where there were direct correspondences between letters and sounds. Furthermore, it was found that the participants could not

51

suppress orthographic activation when it was disadvantageous to them. It appears that the orthographic information needs to be processed in order to have the phonological information processed (Foorman, 1994). Castles et al. (2003) concluded that there are substantial automatic orthographic influences on phonological awareness task performances, as the tasks used to estimate phonological awareness usually contain orthographic components that improve performance.

In fact, a meta-analysis of over 80 published papers that investigated the relationship between phonological awareness and word reading ability (Castles and Coltheart, 2004) revealed that the vast majority of the papers do not fulfil fundamental requirements such as measuring pre-existing word reading ability and knowledge of letter-sound correspondences of participants. A few papers that had observed the rigorous requirements showed little evidence that phonological awareness (which is purely spoken) has a direct influence on the development of word reading ability. Based on these findings, Castles and Coltheart (2004) argue that both phonological awareness and word reading ability develop through the development of orthographic skills.

What contributes more directly to word reading ability seems to be knowledge of letter-sound correspondences, which would be facilitated by awareness of links between orthography (letter or a cluster of letters) and phonology (phoneme, syllable or rhyme). Such awareness, which may be better referred to as 'orthography-phonology correspondence awareness', is an important subcategory of phonological awareness that supports the development of word reading ability.

A caveat is required here. Since Wagner and Torgesen (1987) claimed that phonological awareness is one of the three primary phonological processing skills, phonological awareness has been seen as a set of spoken *language skills* by some researchers (e.g., Carlisle, 2003) rather than *awareness*. However, phonological awareness is one type of awareness, and therefore should be separated from processing skills. This is similar to Shu and Anderson's view that 'learning to read requires becoming aware of the basic units of spoken language, the basic units of the writing system, and the mapping between the two' (Shu and Anderson.1998:1).

Morphological awareness

Compared to phonological awareness, morphological awareness is less clearly defined in the literature, but a morphologically aware person should be able to make use of the semantic information in meaningful units, and be able to map between morphological units and meaning (Shu and Anderson, 1998). A number of studies claim that in a phonologically less-transparent alphabetic script such as English, morphological awareness (such as the awareness of inflections, derivations and compounds) plays an important role in word recognition (Carlisle, 2003; Mahony, Singson and Mann, 2000; Tyler and Nagy, 1990; Nagy, Anderson, Schommer, Scott, and Stallman, 1989). In English, for example, the relationship between morphological awareness and word reading ability is hypothesized to be most important during the middle school years where there is a rapid increase in the number of words which children encounter that are derived from simple structures (Carlistle, 2003; 2000).

As in the case of phonological awareness, whether pure morphological awareness can be measured separately from orthographic processing skills is questionable. Tasks used to measure morphological awareness are often written tasks (e.g., judging whether a pair of words is semantically related), which require participants to *read* task items. Some researchers (e.g., Mahony, Singson and Mann, 2000) have prepared oral versions of such a task where task items were read out by the investigators. However, performing an oral version is not totally immune from the influence of orthographic processing skills, as morphological awareness tasks certainly contain orthographic components that improve performance. For example, the relationship between 'heal' and 'health' may not be easily noticed without referring to their spellings. In this regard, among various subcategories of morphological awareness, awareness of orthography–morphology correspondence may be most relevant to the development of word recognition skills.

2.3.3 Awareness of structures and functions of words in morphographic writing system

Orthographic awareness

The contribution of orthographic, phonological and morphological awareness to word recognition has also been discussed in the context of morphographic scripts such as *hanzi* and *kanji*. Although it is less well established compared to what has been known about the roles of awareness in alphabetic scripts, a number of studies suggest that readers of morphographic scripts are more sensitive to orthographical information than readers of alphabetic scripts (Geva and Wang, 2001; Tan, Hoosain and Peng, 1995;

Chen, 1992; Perfetti and Zhang, 1991; Wang, 1988). Research suggests that awareness of the internal structure of characters (e.g., positional regularity of components) develops at early stages (Shu, 2003; Ho, Ng and Ng, 2003; Shu and Anderson, 1998), as the phonological and morphological information of components are essential for the recognition of compound characters (see Chapter 1 Section 3 for details).

Phonological awareness

There is abundant research examining phonological processing of *kanji* or *hanzi* in relation to that of alphabetic scripts. Research suggests that phonological processing plays an important and universal role in reading regardless of differences in writing systems (Perfetti and Zhang, 1995, 1991; Koda, 1993; Taft, 1991; Mou and Anderson, 1981; Tzeng and Hung, 1980), and morphographic scripts are no exception.

For most Chinese words and Japanese *kanji*-written words, the orthography-phonology correspondence is character to syllable (McBride-Chang, Shu, Zhou, Wat and Wagner, 2003). McBride-Chang and Ho (2000) investigated Chinese children's awareness of syllables using a syllable deletion task. In the task, children were initially asked to delete the first or the second syllable from two-syllable words (that were presented to them orally). They were then asked to segment three-syllable words into syllables. McBride-Chang et al. (2000) found that phonological awareness measured in the syllable deletion task was a strong predictor of character recognition.

Huang and Hanley (1995) found that phoneme deletion was also related to Chinese character recognition in Chinese children. However, given that the phonological information in *kanji* or *hanzi* words cannot be obtained unambiguously with the grapheme-to-phoneme conversions as it can be in words in alphabetic scripts (Hoosain, 1991), the relationship between phoneme awareness and reading may be due to a general analytic attitude toward language.

Recent studies suggest that the phonological information of small units is accessed also for the purpose of recognising single character words, i.e., characters (Chen and Shu, 2001; Morita and Matsuda, 2000). It has been claimed that phonological representations emerge automatically during the process of lexical access (Tan, Hoosain and Siok, 1996; Leck, Weeks and Chen, 1995; Perfetti and Zhang, 1995, 1991; Taft, 1991). While smaller units in a word written in characters (compound words) are characters, in a single-character word (i.e., a character), would be components. Studies suggest that phonological information of phonetics of characters (i.e., components that may give some indication of the pronunciation of the characters) becomes available to skilled readers at a very early stage of character recognition, and that this information may even mediate a link between the character and pronunciation (Koda, 2002; Geva and Wang, 2001; Flores d'Arcais, Saito, and Kawakami, 1995; Flores d'Arcais, 1992; Shu and Anderson, 1998). For example, characters sharing the phonetic 工, such as 功, 項, 巧, 紅, 貢 are all read as /koR/. In this regard, skilled-readers of *hanzi* and *kanji* are likely to be aware of the function of phonetics.

Phonetic awareness, which is a subcategory of *phonological awareness*, is defined as 'insight into the structure and function of the phonetic component of compound characters' (Shu, Wu and Anderson, 2000: 57). The initial phonetic awareness may be crude and simple such as a vague feeling that the right-hand side of a character tells the pronunciation (Shu, Wu and Anderson, 2000). This rudimentary awareness, of course, needs to be more sophisticated as the phonetic is not always on the right and the phonetic does not always indicate the pronunciation of the character (Shu, Wu and Anderson, 2000). As phonetic components can only be identified visually, phonetic awareness is inextricably linked to orthographic units (cf., awareness of phonemes, syllables and rhymes is also influenced by orthography). In this sense, phonetic awareness is one aspect of *awareness of orthography–phonology correspondence,* which is a subcategory of phonological awareness.

Morphological awareness

Kanji and *hanzi* may enhance morphological awareness (Nagy, Kuo-Kealoha, Wu, Li, Anderson and Chen, 2002), as the morphemic function of a character is often clearly visible (Nagy et al., 2002; Taylor, 2002). For example, the character 時 (time) is a morpheme of the word 時代 (period / era). Focusing on this character-level morphological awareness, McBride-Chang, Shu, Zhou, Wat and Wagner (2003) conducted two morphological awareness tasks on Chinese children, along with other tasks including a Chinese word reading task, and found the children's performance on one of the morphological awareness tasks, the morphological construction task, was highly correlated with that of the Chinese word reading task. In the morphological construction task, the children were asked to make up a word using a given example as a model. For example, the children heard 'If we see the sun rising in the morning, we call that a sunrise (in Chinese). What should we call the phenomenon of the moon rising?', and were asked to construct new compound words for the objects in question (The correct answer in this case is 'moonrise' in Chinese). McBride-Chang et al. (2003) found that this task was a strong predictor of Chinese word recognition even when the effects of other reading related tasks were statistically controlled.

A study by Li, Anderson, Nagy and Zhang (2002) found the significant contribution of morphological awareness in Chinese word recognition both at the character and component levels. Component-level morphological awareness is often referred to as *radical awareness*. As described in Chapter 1 Section 3, the majority of characters are compound characters, which are composed of two components. One of the components is the main radical of the character, which sometimes offers a clue to the character's meaning. Radical awareness is usually defined as 'insight into the function of the semantic component (main radical) of compound characters' (e.g., Shu, Wu and Anderson, 2000; Shu and Anderson, 1997). For example, the compound character that can be a morpheme of a compound word 時 (time) contains a smaller morpheme (the main radical) 日, which shows the semantic category 'the sun / day'. The morphemic function of the main radical in a character is visually clear but it is not aurally conspicuous. Therefore, as in the case of phonological awareness, morphological awareness examined in studies dealing with *hanzi* and *kanji* is often closely tied to orthographic skills (*awareness of orthography–morphology correspondences*).

2.3.4 Comparison of awareness of structures and functions of words in alphabetic and morphographic scripts

The dichotomy between alphabetic scripts and non-alphabetic scripts and the controversy over the role of two aspects of processing, phonological or direct (non-phonological), have been the substance of much past debate. The emerging consensus is that readers process words orthographically, phonologically and morphologically regardless of orthographic types (Geva and Wang, 2001; Koda, 2002).

The review of literature has revealed that awareness is strongly associated with word recognition ability regardless of different scripts. Whether in alphabetic scripts or in morphographic scripts, orthographic awareness, phonological awareness and morphological awareness appear to develop along with the accumulation of knowledge through increased exposure to the script. The development of these aspects of awareness seems to be a universally influential factor in the development of word recognition ability.

This universal theory does not preclude script-specific awareness. Given that different orthographies require a variety of different script-specific processing skills (see Chapter 2 Section 2), the awareness emerging from word reading in different orthographies would be different. Adding to the examples shown above, there are many studies comparing the different nature of awareness in alphabetic and morphographic scripts. As a case in point, Ku and Anderson (2003) investigated the development of morphological awareness in Chinese- and English-speaking children. They used six tasks to assess different aspects of morphological awareness, vocabulary, and reading proficiency. The tasks were; recognising morphemes, discriminating between morphemes, judging pseudo-words, selecting interpretation (choosing an appropriate definition of a word), selecting vocabulary and reading comprehension (all in their respective L1). The results of the tasks indicated that both the Chinese- and English–speaking children's knowledge of morphology increased with grade level. The study suggests that the development of morphological awareness among Chinese- and English-speaking children is similar, despite the large differences in the two different scripts. However, the study also suggests that Chinese and English require different kinds of morphological awareness. The researchers found that the Chinese-speaking children displayed more awareness of the morphology of compounds than the English–speaking children. By contrast, the Chinese-speaking children displayed less awareness of derivational morphology than the English-speaking children did.

In a discussion of differences in the development of awareness between alphabetic scripts such as English and morphographic scripts such as *hanzi* and *kanji*, the orthographic differences of the two types of scripts need to be taken into consideration. There are clearly two functional grain units in *hanzi* and *kanji*: characters in a word and components in a character. One might argue that it is to some extent similar to rhyme and phoneme units in an English word. As noted earlier, Goswami, Ziegler, Dalton and Schneider (2003) found that English L1 readers are aware of both phonemes and rhymes. Similarly, gathering from the studies in morphographic scripts, readers of *hanzi* and *kanji* appear to be aware of small units both at the character-level and the component-level. However, the crucial difference between the two types of scripts is that main radicals and phonetics are not audible whereas rhymes and phonemes are. In this regard, the awareness associated with *hanzi* and *kanji* is much more closely tied to the development of orthographic processing skills compared to alphabetic scripts. Thus, different kinds of awareness develop as a higher order reflection of the features of the particular writing system. The development of those component-level awarenesses is one of the focuses of this book.

2.4 Development of L2-specific recognition skills and awareness of structures and functions of words

As demonstrated in the previous sections, abundant research suggests that regardless of different scripts children gradually develop word (character) recognition skills and awareness of structures and functions of words (characters) as they learn to read their L1. Normal adult L2 readers are assumed to have developed their word recognition skills and awareness in their L1s. When they learn to read in an L2, can they utilise the recognition skills and awareness developed in the L1? The answer is not always yes. As discussed in the previous section (Chapter 2 Section 3), required recognition skills and awareness vary according to the features of the target writing system. Adult L2 readers therefore may need to learn new skills and become aware of new orthographic features in order to efficiently read in the L2.

This section discusses L2 readers' recognition skills and awareness in terms of transfer and relearning. The influence of L1 recognition skills on an L2 and the development of L2-specific recognition skills will be discussed first, followed by a discussion on how L1 awareness influences the development of L2-specific recognition skills. I will first examine cross-language situations for L2 readers of English with different orthographic backgrounds as this is a more thoroughly investigated area than that for L2 readers of Japanese or Chinese. Although my study is about English-speaking learners of Japanese, an investigation of the reverse situation is insightful.

2.4.1. Development of L2-specific recognition skills (the case of English)
Use of L1 recognition skills in L2.

A number of studies suggest that L2 readers of English with different orthographic backgrounds have varied word recognition skills, which were developed from maturing processes in their L1 reading, and that they cannot avoid using those L1 processing skills in L2 word recognition.

For example, Brown and Haynes (1985) compared the differences in L2 (English) reading performance among readers from different non-English orthographic backgrounds: non-alphabetic (Japanese), non-Roman alphabetic (Arabic) and Roman-alphabetic (Spanish). Their test battery included an English word and pseudo-word naming test, a listening comprehension test, and a visual discrimination test (visual discrimination of abstract figures). The results showed that the non-alphabetic language (Japanese) group performed fast and accurately in naming familiar words, but this group was considerably slower than the other two groups on unfamiliar word strings, suggesting that the Japanese participants relied more on sight-word knowledge and less on rule-governed spelling-to-sound translation. The evidence of stronger orthographic processing skills and weaker phonological skills in the non-alphabetic language group (Japanese) was supported by the following findings: the Japanese group outperformed the other two groups in the visual discrimination task, and there was a strong positive correlation between the naming and listening performances of the Arabic and Spanish-speaking groups, but this was not the case with the Japanese group.

Similarly, Koda (1995; 1990; 1989a) examined the speed of silent reading of three alphabetic groups (Arabic, English and Spanish) and a non-alphabetic group (Japanese) using two types of English passages of similar difficulty on two different topics, one containing pronounceable English nonsense words and the other unpronounceable Sanskrit words (in Devanagari). The participants were asked to read the passages silently at a comfortable speed for comprehension (a short recall test was given for each passage). The (silent) reading speed decreased considerably when Sanskrit words were included in all the three alphabetic groups. However, the speed of the non-alphabetic (Japanese) participants remained relatively constant across the two types (Koda 1995; 1989a). These studies also indicated that non-alphabetic readers rely less on phonological information than alphabetic readers.

The above findings suggest that L2 readers continue using the recognition skills acquired in their L1. One might speculate that cognitive differences between readers from an alphabetic background and those from a non-alphabetic background would be due to the readers' insufficient experience with the L2 reading. Interestingly, as shown in the following two studies, it appears that L1 word recognition influence remains even after extensive exposure to an L2.

Akamatsu (2003; 1999) conducted an experiment using English passages printed in alternated case on three groups of *fluent* L2 readers with varied orthographic backgrounds. Two groups of non-alphabetic readers (Chinese and Japanese) and a group of alphabetic readers (Persian) were provided with English passages printed in either alternated case or in a normal manner (no case alteration), and were asked to read them as quickly as possible. The results showed that the fluent L2 readers were able to read the passage fast and accurately in the normal condition. However, when case was alternated, the reading speed of the non-alphabetic readers (Chinese and Japanese) dropped drastically, while the alphabetic readers were less affected, suggesting that the readers from a non-alphabetic L1 background were less efficient in phonological processing despite their fluency in the L2.

Haynes and Carr (1990) investigated the effects of L1 recognition skills in L2 reading at the word level. They examined the word recognition of L2 non-alphabetic readers (Chinese students learning English) in comparison with that of L1 readers of English. Two groups of Chinese students - freshmen (lower English proficiency) and seniors (high English proficiency) - and a group of L1 readers of English participated in

64

a visual same-different matching task using three types of orthographic units: illegal non-words (irregular letter strings), pseudo-words (not real words, but following orthographic rules), and real words. The results showed that while the three groups performed approximately equally well when the stimuli were real words, their performance on the pseudo-words was not uniform. The English readers showed no significant differences in their performances on the pseudo-words and on real-words. Conversely, the two groups of Chinese readers did not benefit as much as the English readers from orthographic regularity of the pseudo-words. There was no significant difference between the two Chinese groups on any conditions. The Chinese students, the senior students in particular, were not novice learners of English. On top of six years of experience in studying English during their high school years, they had taken a year of freshman English, which was conducted entirely in English, and had been using textbooks written in English. Nevertheless, their weak phonological skills continued to affect L2 word recognition.

The above studies suggest that even among advanced L2 readers, L1 orthographic features affect L2 reading procedure. However, it cannot be assumed that differences in L1 orthographic experience may generate differences in efficiency in reading in L2 (Akamatsu, 2003; 1999; Koda, 2002; Wade-Woolley, 1999).

The L2 readers of English with non-alphabetic backgrounds in the above studies did not differ in performance from those with alphabetic script backgrounds in *normal* English reading, although they experienced disadvantages in the reading of pseudo-words (or words with altered case). This suggests that L2 readers use strategies to deal with the new L2 script, while depending on the old recognition skills acquired through learning to read in the L1. In other words, they may be able to compensate for their deficiency in phonological skills with strong orthographic skills gained from practice (Akamatsu, 2003; 1999; Koda, 2002; Jackson Lu and Ju, 1994). When learning and storing English words, these readers may focus on orthographic information such as letter probabilities, positional frequencies and sequential redundancy patterns. When they read a word, they may use the stored information and read the word by analogy. They may also make use of morphological information in English words. Thus, L2 readers may attain a high level of L2 reading competence through qualitatively different paths (Wade-Woolley, 1999).

Development of L2 recognition skills

As argued, differences in L1 orthographic experience do not always generate differences in efficiency in reading in L2. In other words, efficiency differences in reading in L2 cannot be accounted for solely by different L1 orthographic experience (Koda, 1999). This is evident from the fact that L2 readers from the same orthographic background can be poor or good readers in the L2. It is plausible to think that efficiency difference may be at least partially attributed to the reader's L2 word recognition ability, which is likely to develop thorough orthographic experience in L2. Research indeed suggests that L2 processing experience is likely to be a major factor in developing L2 recognition skills regardless of L1 background (Koda, 2002; Ke, 1998).

As a case in point, Jackson, Chen, Goldsberry, Kim and Vanderwerff (1999) reported the importance of L2 processing experience for L2-specific recognition skills development. Jackson et al. investigated whether three groups of L2 readers with non-alphabetic home backgrounds (Korea, Taiwan and Hong Kong) showed any reliance on L1-specific processing procedures in reading English (L2) passages in different conditions including mixed case and pseudohomophone passages. The mixed case and pseudohomophone passages both had short high-frequency words in short and simple sentences, but letter cases were altered in the mixed case passage and some words were respelled (e.g., *phocks* for *fox*) for the pseudohomophone passage. Jackson et al. analysed whether simple text reading times and the effects of the experimental text manipulations differed between the participant groups. The results showed that while all the L2 groups with non-alphabetic backgrounds were impaired when orthographic cues were disrupted by mixed case words, the group from Hong Kong, who had the longest exposure to English, were less affected compared to the other two groups. The Hong Kong group showed a similar tendency in the pseudohomophone condition, but the difference between this group and the Korean and Taiwanese group was statistically not significant. This study suggests that exposure to a L2 writing system does facilitate the improvement in the L2-specific processing skills. Processing skills that work well in L2s thus would seem to develop through cumulative processing experience in the L2 (Koda, 1999).

Overall, the above studies all suggest that although L1 recognition ability continues to influence L2 reading even at highly fluent levels of L2 reading, L2 recognition ability develops through L2 processing experience.

2.4.2. Development of L2-specific recognition skills (the case of character-based languages)

Use of L1 recognition skills in L2.

Non-alphabetic readers may be able to read an alphabetic script using their strong orthographic processing skills. However, for alphabetic readers, reading a phonologically opaque non-alphabetic script using phonological processing skills may not be very practical. In order to discuss this issue, alphabetic readers' processing styles will first be examined. The following studies demonstrate that phonological processing is primary for alphabetic readers.

Chikamatsu (1996) asked American and Chinese university students who were studying Japanese (with only a semester's experience) to perform a lexical judgement task using Japanese *kana*. Test items were grouped into three types of stimuli: visually familiar words (*hiragana* or *katakana* words), visually unfamiliar words (*katakana* was used for *hiragana* words and vice versa), and non-words (created by changing one or two letters from real words). The results showed that the Chinese readers responded to the familiar words faster than they did to the unfamiliar words or non-words, whereas the English readers were relatively unaffected by the visual unfamiliarity. This implied that alphabetic readers rely more on phonological information than non-alphabetic readers.

Tamaoka (1997) examined differences in the putative reading processing mechanisms of learners of Japanese with a Chinese background or an English background by asking them to perform a lexical decision task on *katakana* loanwords (words originating in alphabetic languages such as English and French). The results showed that the English readers were more accurate in processing the loanwords than the Chinese readers, although their processing speeds for the loanwords did not differ.

The above studies indicated that the alphabetic readers processed the *kana* words more phonologically than the non-alphabetic readers, and that the non-alphabetic readers made more use of visual information than their counterparts. This tendency was observed even in a task requiring memory, as shown below.

Mori (1998) conducted an interesting experiment investigating the transfer of word recognition skills from L1 to L2, using non-*kanji* with and without artificial pronunciation markers (*katakana*) embedded within them. An alphabetic group (Americans) and two non-alphabetic groups (Chinese and Koreans with experience with characters) were tested on their ability to retain new non-*kanji* in their short-term memory. The participants were asked to identify the target non-*kanji* after studying a list of non-*kanji* with or without the artificial pronunciation markers (*katakana*). The alphabetic group found that phonologically accessible non-*kanji* (containing the artificial pronunciation markers) were easier to remember than the phonologically inaccessible non-*kanji* (without the artificial pronunciation markers). Conversely, the non-alphabetic group showed virtually no difference in recognising the two different types of non-*kanji*.

The above studies all suggest that the reliance on phonological information is stronger in alphabetic readers than in non-alphabetic readers. If *kanji* always have clear phonological information as in the case of the pronunciation-marker-embedded artificial characters in Mori's study, L2 readers of Japanese with an alphabetic background may be able to attain a high level of *kanji* word/character reading competence through their primary phonological processing.

However, the reality is that *kanji* are in most cases not phonologically transparent. For L2 readers of Japanese with an alphabetic background, the familiar phonological processing is not always readily applicable. This inaccessibility of phonological information may impair in the ability of an L2 reader to successfully recognize characters. As a consequence, alphabetic readers may be left with the unfamiliar non-alphabetic script without knowing how to deal with it. The following study provides an insight into how L2 readers with alphabetic script background might process non-alphabetic script in comparison with L1 readers' processing performance.

Hayes (1988) compared Chinese L1 readers (Taiwanese) and L2 readers of Chinese (American) in the processing of Chinese characters both with and without context. In the *hanzi* recognition task, the participants viewed a slide consisting of six random single characters without context. They were then required to circle the characters they had seen on an answer sheet. Orthographic, phonological, and semantic distracters (characters that had orthographic, phonological or semantic features similar

70

to or the same as the target characters) were randomly dispersed throughout the answer sheet. The results showed that the L1 Chinese readers made more phonological errors than did the L2 readers, and that they made significantly more phonological errors than orthographic or semantic errors. These results indicated that the L1 readers used phonological strategies in the task that required recall, whereas the L2 readers used mixed strategies in memorising the characters in random order. The L2 readers appeared to have been confused by a situation where their familiar phonological processing skills were not of any assistance.

In Hayes' sentence level task (Chinese characters in context), the participants had to decide whether Chinese statements were true or false. Each of the experimental sentences contained a phonological distracter (a homophonic to the target character), orthographic distracter (a character graphically similar to the target character) or semantic distracter (a character that had a similar meaning to the target character but was not appropriate in the target sentence). For control sentences, Hayes included some correct sentences and some conceptually incorrect sentences (e.g., 北的反方向是東 meaning 'the opposite of North is East'). In this sentence level task, the L2 readers made more orthographic errors than did the L1 readers, and they made significantly more orthographic errors than phonological or semantic errors. The L1 readers also made more orthographic errors than phonological errors, but not significantly more than semantic errors. As Hayes (1988:194) noted, it appears that 'L1 Chinese readers are

71

reading more for meaning at sentence level while L2 readers are still attending predominantly to orthographic features'.

The findings suggest that L2 readers with alphabetic backgrounds are confounded by phonologically inaccessible script. L2 readers, who are used to converting small units of words into sounds for reading unfamiliar words, may not know how to deal with Chinese characters without any phonological clues at hand. Furthermore, this study reminds us that L1 non-alphabetic readers do not always rely on orthographic processing. The view of primary phonological processing for alphabetic readers and primary orthographic processing for non-alphabetic readers is certainly too simplistic. As discussed in Section 3, the development of word recognition skills among alphabetic- and non-alphabetic readers is similar, despite the large differences in the two different scripts. They all learn to process orthographically, phonologically and morphologically. However, different orthographic features enhance the development of different kinds of recognition skills. L2 readers with an alphabetic background who learn to read in morphographic script are likely to develop recognition skills that are better suited to the orthographic features of the script.

Development of L2 recognition skills

As shown in the following study, it seems that alphabetic readers develop an effective L2 recognition ability with cumulative processing experience in the L2.

Chitiri, Sun, Willows, and Taylor (1992) reported a study by Sun (1991) that investigated the differences in word recognition processes among a group of L1 and two groups of L2 (high-proficiency and low-proficiency) readers of Chinese both with and without context. In the context-free word recognition task, two *hanzi* words were presented on a computer with a very brief interval between them, and participants were asked to decide whether the second item was the same as the first. Half of the words were presented with another word that resembled the target item orthographically, phonologically or semantically. In this task, which required speeded responses rather than recall, clear differences in visual processing skills between L1 and L2 readers, and between the high and low proficiency L2 groups, were observed, suggesting that the less-skilled L2 readers had not yet developed automatic visual processing skills. Sun's context-embedded task was a sentence validity judgement task. Again, a word was replaced with another word that was orthographically, phonologically or semantically similar to the target word in half of the sentences. In this task, accuracy in judging phonologically and semantically anomalous sentences improved with increasing skill (L1 > L2 high > L2 low).

Overall, the findings suggest that L2 readers with an alphabetic script background need to develop recognition skills for the particular processing and informational demands of character recognition.

2.4.3. Development of L2-specific awareness of structures and functions of words

Transfer of L1 awareness to L2.

Research suggests that L1 readers become aware of the language features of their native language (Koda, 1997, 1994, 1993; Slobin and Bever, 1982). L2 readers from different orthographic backgrounds indeed show superiority in the awareness that had developed from their L1 experience. For example, Wade-Woolley (1999) investigated the phonological and orthographic awareness of two groups of L2 readers of English on a number of tasks such as a phoneme deletion task and a spelling judgement task. One group of participants was from an alphabetic background (Russian) and the other was from a non-alphabetic background (Japanese), and they were matched on a measure of English word reading. The study found that Russians were superior in manipulating phonological segments compared to the Japanese, while the Japanese were better than the Russians at judging legitimate spelling patterns.

Numerous studies indicate that L2 readers utilise cognitive skills developed in their L1 when reading in their L2 (Comeau, Cormier, Grandmaison and Lacroix, 1999; McDonough, 1995; Carson, Carrell, Silberstein, Kroll and Kuehn, 1990; Sarig, 1987; Hatta, Hatae and Kirsner, 1984). Positive transfer of awareness developed in L1 to L2 may be possible if the two languages share orthographic features. For example, Comeau et al. (1999) found that English-speaking children in a French immersion program with good phonological awareness in English were also adept in phonologically processing

French, and vice versa. Their phonological awareness in English and French were both strongly related to achievement in word decoding in both English and French.

Gottardo, Yan, Siegel and Wade-Wooley (2001) investigated whether phonological awareness transfers between L1 and L2 even when L1 and L2 have different orthographic features. Their participants, Chinese children whose first language was Chinese and whose second language was English, were tested for their phonological awareness and reading abilities both in their L1 and L2. They found that the children's rhyme awareness in Chinese was significantly related to their English word reading ability. However, their phonemic awareness in English was not associated with their Chinese reading ability. This suggests that cross-linguistic transfer is not always bidirectional.

These findings from the above studies support those from the studies investigating the relationship between L1 recognition skills and L2 reading ability. Through exposure to alphabetic scripts, L1 readers of alphabetic languages become aware of orthography-phonology correspondence in their L1 and develop recognition skills that rely heavily on phonological processing. However, their phonological processing strategy that is governed by strong phonological awareness would not work in reading character words, as we have seen above (see Chapter 2 Section 4.2).

Awareness developed in the L1 may affect L2 reading even after a substantial exposure to the L2. As a case in point, Holm and Dodd (1996) found that adult L2 readers of English from Hong Kong (with non-alphabetic first language literacy) had limited phonological awareness (in English) compared to other Asian L2 readers with

75

alphabetic first language literacy even after 15 years of exposure to English literature. They also found that Hong Kong readers had difficulty processing English nonwords due to their poor phonological awareness. As evidenced here, awareness developed in an L1 does not cease to influence L2 processing skills, even after a long exposure to an L2. However, these Hong Kong L2 readers had a high level of English literacy, and performed very well in real word readings. The study suggests that phonological awareness is not a prerequisite for the achievement of high levels of literacy in English. Indeed L2 readers usually use a variety of strategies to compensate for weaknesses, and become advanced in L2 reading (as shown in Chapter Sections 4.1 and 4.2).

It should be noted however that Huang and Hanley (1994) reported that Hong Kong children performed very well (as well as L1 children) in an English phoneme deletion task. Huang and Henley found that Taiwanese children who had learnt Chinese in Zhu-Yin-Fu-Hao (symbols of phonetic pronunciation represented by unique characters) performed significantly better than Hong Kong children in the Chinese phoneme deletion test. However, the results of the English deletion task were the reverse: children from Taiwan found the task virtually impossible, and Hong Kong children performed the English phoneme deletion task much better than they did the Chinese deletion task. These results suggest that script–specific phonological awareness may develop with experience in the target script.

The inconsistent findings reported in Holm and Dodd (1996) and Huang and Hanley (1994) may be due to the difficulties of the tasks. Presumably, the phoneme deletion task that was used in Huang and Hanley's study was a very easy task, hence no significant difference was found between the results of Hong Kong children and English L1 children due to a ceiling effect. On the other hand, in the Holm and Dodd study, the English phonological tasks would have been much more difficult than the task used in Huang and Hanley. Therefore, although Hong Kong readers had developed some phonological awareness through experience with the L2, the results showed that their phonological awareness was not as developed as that of other Asian readers with alphabetic first language literacy.

2.5 Character recognition skills and awareness of structures and functions of characters

The previous section outlined support for the notion that as L2 reading experience increases L2 readers develop recognition skills and awareness that are suitable to the demands imposed by the L2 (although L1 recognition ability continues to influence L2 reading even for highly fluent levels of L2 reading). This section will examine particular aspects of *kanji* recognition skills and awareness that L1 readers possess, for it is these that L2 readers of Japanese are anticipated to develop.

2.5.1 Processing levels and influential factors

The Multilevel Interactive Activation Model (Taft and Zhu, 1995) proposes that L1 non-alphabetic readers receive information from the word, character and component levels concurrently, and that the information from these different levels is used to recognise a word. While earlier studies have viewed a compound word (consisting of

77

more than two characters) as an integrated unit, more recent research has identified the significance of elements smaller than a word. When a word written in characters is successfully recognised, it has been suggested that the reader also accesses the orthographic, phonological and semantic information corresponding to each of its constituent characters (Zhang and Peng, 1992; Liu and Peng, 1997). Furthermore, there is clear evidence that demonstrates that when recognising a word, L1 non-alphabetic readers access the *functional components* of the characters as well as the characters themselves (Shu, 2003; Taft and Zhu, 1997b; Peng, Li and Yang, 1997; Flores d'Arcais, Saito, and Kawakami 1995; Leck, Weekes and Chen, 1995; Flores d'Arcais and Saito, 1993). The present study deals with the character-level and component-level processing, as these are the demands imposed on readers in *kanji* word reading (see Chapter 1 Section 3).

In order to assess L2 readers' recognition skills focusing on the character-level and component level processing, how stimulus properties of *kanji* affect L1 readers will be examined first, as the general pattern of stimulus property effects as demonstrated by L1 readers is likely to be a good indicator of L2 readers' development in word recognition skills. The following section illustrates findings from previous studies on how certain stimulus properties of characters affect L1 readers' recognition of characters. Where studies of *kanji* are not available, studies dealing with Chinese *hanzi* will be used as guides, as both scripts are historically derived from the same source and still share many common features (Paradis, Hagiwara and Hildebrandt, 1985).

2.5.2 Stimulus property effects in character recognition

The word recognition mechanisms (in terms of variation of response times and error rates, etc.) of skilled readers of various scripts have long been investigated by psycholinguists, and it has been revealed that adult L1 readers show different patterns of responses to words that have different stimulus properties, such as frequency of occurrence and the number of words that share the same pronunciation, i.e., homophone size (see Chapter 2 Section 2). Processes involved in the recognition, or the duration of the processes, therefore appear to vary according to different types of words. In general, stimulus properties regarded as influential factors for word recognition include complexity (e.g., Nagy, Anderson, Schommer, Scott, and Stallman, 1989), frequency of occurrence (e.g., McClelland and Rumelhart, 1981) and homophone size (e.g., Ferrand and Grainger, 2003).

Therefore, the stimulus properties of interest in the present study in regard to developing a profile of processing characteristics are: complexity (the number of required strokes for writing), character frequency (frequency of occurrence in printing materials), and homophone size (the number of characters that share a common reading). As this study focuses on Japanese *kanji* characters, and since radical frequency is a highly influential factor in *kanji* recognition (e.g., Taft and Chung, 1999), radical frequency will also be included as a factor in the investigation. As will be discussed later, radical frequency can, in fact, refer to two separate concepts: type and token frequencies.

In the following sections, studies concerning effects of complexity, frequency occurrence, radical frequency and homophone size will be examined.

Complexity (the number of required strokes for writing)

Research suggests that the gap in word recognition ability between good readers and poor readers is more prominent for longer words in alphabetic script (Nagy, Anderson, Schommer, Scott, and Stallman, 1989). In *kanji* and *hanzi*, as characters are all written in a same-sized, square-shaped area, it is not the length but the density of strokes which determines their complexity (Li and Chen, 1997). Paradis, Hagiwara and Hildebrandt (1985) emphasise the importance of controlling the level of complexity when selecting experimental stimuli, as it may affect character recognition performance.

Hsu and Huang (2001) investigated minimal legible size characters in Chinese word recognition. Minimal legible size refers to the character size necessary to attain 95% correct recognition. L1 Chinese readers were shown characters with varied number of strokes ranging from 3 to 27, and were asked to read them aloud. The results showed that the minimal legible sizes were larger for characters with more strokes, indicating character complexity may affect readers' recognition performance.

Interestingly, Chen, Allport, and Marshall (1996) found that the number of strokes did not affect the recognition of characters for L1 readers. Using a same-different task (where participants were asked to judge whether stimulus pairs were same or different), Chen et al. investigated the effect of the number of strokes and of the number of radicals on L1 readers' character recognition. The results showed an effect of the number of radicals but no effect of the number of individual strokes.

In contrast, L2 reader who are not used to process detailed lines of characters may be affected by the number of strokes. Indeed Tamaoka (1997) found that in a lexical judgement task English readers were slower in processing *kanji* with many strokes, while Chinese readers processed two-*kanji* compound words equally well regardless of their complexity.

Character frequency (frequency of occurrence in printing materials)

Frequency occurrence is a fundamental variable in word recognition (Harley, 1995; Paradis, Hagiwara and Hildebrandt, 1985). It is a well-established finding that high frequency words are recognised more quickly than low frequency words, both in alphabetic languages (Harley, 1995; Taft and Zhu, 1995; Nagy et al., 1989; McClelland and Rumelhart, 1981; Morton, 1980; Taft and Forster, 1975) and in character-based languages (Hong, 1998; Tamaoka and Hatsuzuka, 1995; Taft and Zhu, 1995; Tan, Hoosain and Peng, 1995). The majority of word recognition models incorporate frequency of occurrence as an important factor in processing words (see Chapter 2 Section 2 for details).

Tan, Hoosain and Peng (1995) investigated the effect of print frequency at the character level using a backward masking paradigm in which they presented their L1 Chinese participants with a target *hanzi* followed by a pseudo-*hanzi* (orthographical, phonological or semantic mask) in rapid succession, and asked them to identify the

81

target *hanzi*. The results showed that the participants recognised high-frequency characters more accurately than low-frequency characters across the mask types. The effect of frequency of occurrence was confirmed by a study conducted by Hong (1998) which found a strong correlation between word frequency and participant response time.

However, the relationship between character frequency and the speed of recognition seems to vary according to the task and the position of the character in a word, although the fundamental trend of a processing advantage for the high frequency stimuli does not change. Tamaoka and Hatsuzuka (1995) investigated the effect of print-frequency for both left and right characters in two-*kanji* compound words. Frequency groups were determined according to the results of a survey conducted by the National Language Research Institute in Japan in 1976. Participants undertook naming and lexical decision tasks for four types of two-*kanji* compound words: H-H, H-L, L-H, and L-L (H = high frequency *kanji* – over 1,000 and L = low frequency *kanji* – less than 0.099. The range of frequency in each group were: H-H = 1.953-1.721, H-L = 4.461-0.053, L-H = 0.058-2.534, and L-L = 0.057-0.059). They found that the naming task was performed faster when the left character was high frequency (i.e., H-H and H-L faster than L-H and L-L), and the lexical decision was performed faster when the right character was H. (i.e., H-H and L-H faster than H-L and L-L). Tamaoka and Hatsuzuka explained this pattern of results in the following way: whereas the naming of a word can be initiated by the phonological activation of the left character, the lexical decision has to wait until the right character is also processed (Tamaoka and Htsuzuka, 1995:129).

Although some of the findings from the above studies may not apply to single-character recognition, they are consistent with word recognition models that build in an effect of print frequency.

A review of recent research pertaining to L1 alphabetic script recognition in children (Share, 1995) suggests that developing readers become able to recognise high frequency words quickly and accurately from a very early stage. Also, a recent study investigating word recognition skills in a L2 setting revealed that frequency effects were also evident among beginner L2 readers (Wang and Koda, 2005). Therefore, beginner readers in the present study may also show frequency effects. However, an effect of frequency of occurrence does not necessarily mean that beginner readers process characters in the same way as skilled readers. It is more plausible to think that novice readers (children and beginner L2 readers) are only able to recognise high frequency words, rather than think that they recognise high frequency words more quickly and accurately than low frequency words. In this regard, frequency data need to be dealt cautiously with when interpreting the data.

Radical frequency (the number of characters that share a common main radical)

When discussing radical frequency, researchers often fail to clarify two ambiguous issues. One of them concerns the use of the term 'radicals'. As mentioned in Chapter 1 Section 3, some researchers use this term to refer to all constituent graphical elements of characters while others use it to refer to only the ones under which characters are classified. In order to avoid confusion, in this study, the former is designated as 'radical' and the latter as 'main radical'. The chief interest of the present study is main radicals, which are functional components of *kanji* characters that may give some indication of meanings of the characters. The other ambiguous term is 'radical frequency'. There are in fact two types of radical frequencies: token frequency and type frequency. Token frequency refers to the number of times a main radical is seen in written materials regardless of the specific character in which it occurs, whereas type frequency refers to the number of different characters that contain the same main radical (Taft and Zhu, 1997a: 772; Li and Chen, 1997:148). In order to avoid confusion, some researchers call the former 'frequency' and latter 'neighbourhood size'. In what follows, the study of Taft and Zhu (1997a) is considered in order to illustrate the importance of a clear specification of the terms 'radical' and 'radical frequency'.

Taft and Zhu (1997a) investigated L1 readers' ability to discriminate real from artificial characters by using a task in which the frequency of the functional components within a character was manipulated. Both the real characters and artificial characters had a horizontal structure, i.e., they had left-side and right-side components. For the real characters, character frequency was held constant across the characters, but there were four combinations of component frequency: HH, HL, LH and LL (H = high frequency component and L = low frequency component). The frequencies were based on the Chinese Radical Position Frequency Dictionary (1984), and the average numbers of characters in which the components appear were: HH = 296-293, HL = 351-21, LH = 69-280, and LL = 51-34. The results showed that the frequency of the right component affected the responses; the responses were faster when the right-hand component was high frequency than when it was low frequency (i.e., HH and LH were faster than HL and LL). By contrast, the frequency of the left component did not affect responses. Taft and Zhu explained this null effect of frequency of the left component on the speed of character decision times by arguing that the processing of the right component began while the left component was still being processed, and thus neutralised any processing time difference between high and low frequency left components. In order to respond successfully, the processing of both components needs to be completed, and if left to right processing is assumed (as well as parallel processing) then it will be the processing of the right-hand component that will control the overall response time. Given that the majority of left-right pattern characters have the main radical on the left-hand side, this finding may be interpreted as an indication that frequency of the main radical may not affect the recognition of characters, but the frequency of the non-main-radical component (component that is not the main radical) does.

In the above study (Taft and Zhu, 1997a), both types of radical frequency effects may be involved. That is, research suggests that the token frequency (print frequency) triggers quick activation of higher frequency main radicals, and the type frequency (radical neighbourhood size) affects the activation of characters sharing the main radical (Masuda and Saito, 1999). The recognition process is fast if the main radical has high print frequency, but it slows down if the main radical has many radical neighbours, as these other competitors need to be inhibited in order to recognise the target one. Due to these potentially interwoven effects, the findings of the above study are difficult to interpret.

Masuda and Saito (1999) investigated the separate effects of token and type frequencies (of components in general). In their first experiment, dealing with token frequency (by controlling type frequency), the researchers presented pairs of *kanji* briefly to their participants, L1 Japanese readers, and asked them to write one of the characters down. The participants were instructed which character of each pair they should write and on which side (left or right) of the character they should start to write. There were two groups of character frequencies: a high character frequency group and a low character frequency group (these groups were determined based on their frequencies according to the norms published by the National Language Research Institute, 1976). In each group, there were four types of stimuli: HH, HL, LH and LL (H = high frequency component and L = low frequency component). (The mean frequencies of components in *the high character frequency group* were: HH = 3.34-6.03 with a character frequency of 2.58, HL = 5.40-1.37 with c.f. of 1.11, LH = 1.29-4.23 with c.f. of 1.09, and LL = 1.18-1.03 with c.f. of 0.75; the mean frequencies of components in *the low character frequency group* were: HH = 0.48-4.62 with a character frequency of 0.06, HL = 2.87-0.11 with c.f. of 0.02, LH = 0.03-3.82 with c.f. of 0.03, and LL = 0.01-0.27 with c.f. of 0.00). The researchers found that in general, the *kanji* recognition was more accurate when character frequency was high than when it was low. Within the high frequency group, the *kanji* that contained a high frequency component (HH, HL and LH) were recognised more accurately than the ones without a high frequency component (LL). The results of the low frequency characters showed that the *kanji* were recognised accurately only when both components were high frequency (HH). However, the correct response rate of this group was still lower than the LL group of the high character frequency group. Masuda and Saito explained this difference between the high and low character frequency groups in the following way: when the character was low frequency, it might have been necessary for both components to be high frequency in order to send sufficient information from the component level to the character level. The findings suggest that, when type frequency is controlled, high token frequency components including high token frequency main radicals are likely to facilitate L1 readers' character recognition.

In their second experiment, Masuda and Saito (1999) investigated the effects of type frequency (controlling token frequency) using a similar experimental design, although character frequency was not controlled in this experiment. The researchers found that *kanji* were recognised more accurately when the neighbourhood size of the left component (usually the main radical) of the characters was low (LH and LL) than when it was high (HH and HL). However, no such effect was observed for the right components (non-main-radical parts). The findings suggest that low type frequency of the main radicals facilitates L1 readers' character recognition at least compared to when the main radical has a high type frequency.

The above two experiments suggest that type frequency and token frequencies affect character recognition differently. However, radical frequency effects on character recognition may not be clear unless either of token and type frequencies is controlled.

Under natural conditions where the type of frequency is not controlled, the distinction between type and token frequencies may not be necessary, as these frequencies are usually highly correlated (Masuda and Saito, 2002; Li and Chen, 1997). The main radicals that are found in many characters naturally appear in print more frequently. Therefore, it is possible that radical frequency may not have a consistent effect on character recognition in the case of L1 readers, as token frequency and type frequency may be balanced out.

In the case of L2 readers, however, the two types of frequencies may affect the character recognition process differently. Type radical frequency may not affect their character recognition, as L2 readers are unlikely to know many characters that share a common main radical. However, given the well-known frequency effect, the token radical frequency effect may be observed, as frequently appearing main radicals should activate characters sooner than low frequency main radicals.

Homophone size (the number of characters that share a common reading)

A substantial number of homophones can be found in *kanji* (Paradis, Hagiwara and Hildebrandt, 1985). Owing to fewer syllables and the absence of tones in Japanese than in Chinese, *hanzi* that had similar readings and those that had the same reading but different tones resulted in many homophones in *kanji* (Taylor, 1998; Sakuma, Sasanuma, Tatsumi and Masaki, 1998; Tamaoka. 1991). The dual-readings of *on* and *kun* also contribute to the degree of homophony in Japanese (Leong and Tamaoka, 1995). In the present study, if a *kanji* has a large number of characters of the same reading, it is referred to as a 'high homophone size *kanji*'. Likewise, 'low homophone size *kanji*' refers to *kanji* that have few homophones.

Wydell, Patterson and Humphreys (1993) investigated whether access to the meaning would be mediated by the phonology of the *kanji*. L1 readers of Japanese performed a semantic categorisation task where they had to make a judgement whether or not the presented word was semantically related to the given category name. Wydell et al. used three sets of two-*kanji* compound words as their test words: visually similar homophone set, visually dissimilar homophone set, and visually similar control set. For example, for the visually similar homophone set, the category name was 'a kind of debt' and the word was 赤地 /akaji/ where 赤字 /akaji/ was the target word that would fit in this category. For the visually dissimilar homophone set, a category name was 'a kind of earth' and a word presented with it was 年度 /neNdo/ where 粘土 /neNdo/ was the target word. An example of the visually similar control set was 'a member of the government' and 大根 / daikoN/ for 大臣 /daijiN/. Wydell et al. found higher error rates and longer response times for the homophone sets, and that the effects were strongest when the homophone words were visually similar to the target words. Sakuma, Sasanuma, Tatsumi and Masaki (1998) replicated the above study using sets in which no pairs contained *kanji* that were identical to any *kanji* in the target words (as this could be a methodological problem in the study by Wydell et al.), and confirmed the above findings.

These findings can be explained in terms of the Two-way Street Model (Stone, Vanhoy and Van Orden, 1997) in which the orthographic representation of the stimulus activates other orthographic representations of homophones via phonological representation. In the above study, when the homophone of the target word was presented, all the homophones of that orthographical representation would have been activated, and one of them could have been the target word. The participants appeared to have made false positive errors due to this potential activation of the target word.

As can be seen in the above study, homophones affect the reader's performance in a semantic processing task in which phonological processing is not explicitly required. Tamaoka (2005) suggests that when a word is processed, all other orthographic representations of its homophones activate independently of the nature of the task. In this study, L1 readers performed a lexical decision task and a naming task on two-*kanji* compound words with varying degrees of homophony. The results showed that in both tasks the participants were slower in responding to the words with many homophones. Tamaoka explained that in order to perform the task, participants had to suppress the homophones of the target word, hence this inhibitory effect (although Andrews (1997) has shown using English materials that many neighbours actually facilitate word naming responses).

Homophones can be discussed at two different levels: word level and character level. Homophonic *words* may share a common character between them. For example, 清算 (liquidation), 精算 (adjustment) are homophones pronounced /seisaNi/.

Homophonic *characters* sometimes share the same phonetics (components that may give some indication of the pronunciation of the characters). For example, both 清 /sei/ and 精 /sei/ have a common phonetic 青 /sei/. In this regard, homophone size and orthographic neighbourhood size partially overlap, as homophones could also be orthographically similar due to common phonetics. Research suggests that phonological information of phonetics becomes available to skilled readers at a very early stage of character recognition (see Chapter 2 Section 3 for details). Bearing this in mind, I will re-examine the study of Taft and Zhu (1997a).

Taft and Zhu (1997a) found that participants responded faster to the characters with a high frequency right component than the ones with a low frequency right component. Given the fact that right components are sometimes phonetics (see Chapter 1 Section 3 for details), this study may suggest that phonetics that are located in the right side of characters may affect character recognition (the response times are faster for high frequency phonetics than for low frequency phonetics). Because a high frequency phonetic generally appears in many *kanji*, judging from the findings of the above-mentioned studies, one may expect longer character decision latencies and more errors for characters with a high frequency phonetic than ones with a low frequency phonetic due to the effect of competitors (activation of homophonic characters with the same phonetic as the target character would compete with the activation of the target character). In fact, the Taft and Zhu study showed that the characters with a low frequency phonetic induced slower responses and more errors than the ones with a high frequency phonetic. Apparently, as observed in the radical frequency, the interwoven effect of token and type frequency resides also in phonetics.

Although these studies did not directly take homophone *size* into consideration when selecting characters, the findings clearly showed that the phonological presentation of the word affected the semantic judgement. It is therefore plausible that homophone size may well affect the recognition of *kanji*. For L2 readers, however, as they would not know a large number of characters, homophone size is unlikely to affect their character recognition.

In order to assess the development of L2 readers' character recognition ability, their state of awareness also needs to be examined. A review of the literature suggests that orthographic awareness, phonological awareness and morphological awareness develop along with the accumulation of orthographic knowledge through abundant exposure to characters (see Chapter 2 Section 3.3 for details). The next section will examine how L1 readers process sub-word units (characters) and sub-character units (components), and will discuss what aspects of awareness would be expected to develop.

2.5.3 Awareness of structures and functions of characters

Research suggests that the nature of the orthography shapes the development of awareness (see Chapter 2 Section 3.3). As described in Chapter 1 Section 3, there are clearly two functional units in a compound word written in characters: 1) characters in a word, and 2) components in a character. While characters in a word are physically conspicuous, components in a character may not be so easily recognised. Less-skilled readers who have little experience with characters may look at a character as a whole or a cluster of stroke patterns (radicals). However, being able to segment a character into two functional components is an essential stage of development in character recognition (see Chapter 2 Section 3.3). The majority of characters are compound characters that are composed of a main radical (component) and a non-main-radical component. This non-main-radical side may be a phonetic component. The main radical may give a clue to the meaning of the character, and the phonetic may give some indication of the pronunciation of the character (see Chapter 1 Section 3 for details).

Research suggests that skilled-readers access the semantic and phonological information conveyed by these functional components as a process involved in the recognition of a character (see Chapter 2 Section 2.4). In this regard, becoming aware of positions and combinations of functional components would help readers to find the components, and being aware of the separate functions of main radicals and phonetics would assist readers to get useful information for character recognition. As the components are not always very useful (as described in Chapter 1 Section 3), being aware of the limitations of the components would also be helpful.

Methods of assessing awareness in morphographic scripts have not yet been firmly established. Most studies that discuss roles of awareness in character recognition use indirect tasks and therefore the results are ambiguous. In the following section I will examine some of these studies, and discuss how may support efficient character recognition.

Awareness of component positions and combinations

Peng, Li and Yang (1997) investigated whether L1 readers are sensitive to component position information in the recognition of *hanzi*. By relocating components of left-right pattern characters, they created four types of artificial characters: 1) artificial characters with both components in illegitimate positions (a main radical and a phonetic were swapped), 2) those with both components in legitimate positions (a main radical and a phonetic in a wrong combination), 3) those with two components, both of which are usually positioned on the left side of the character (two left components), and 4) those with two right components. L1 Chinese readers in three different age groups (Grade 3, Grade 6 and college students) were asked to undertake a character-ness judgement task. The results showed, for all the age groups, that the ones with both components in illegitimate positions (above #1) were most readily rejected, followed by those with one of the components in an illegitimate position (#3 and #4). The artificial characters with both components in legitimate positions (#2) were the least readily rejected.

Similarly, Shu and Anderson (1998) conducted an experiment investigating the effect of the component position on Chinese children. They asked Chinese L1 readers (who were in the first, second, fourth and sixth grades) to judge which of a series of items could be Chinese characters and which could not be. Half of the test items were real characters and the remaining half were artificial characters. The researchers created three types of artificial characters: 1) artificial characters with two real components in their legitimate positions but in an odd combination, 2) artificial characters with two real components, both of which were in illegitimate positions, and 3) artificial characters with two artificial components. The rate of 'false alarms' was very low across all the grades for the artificial characters with two artificial components (#3). This indicated that the Chinese children as early as the first grade had developed an insight into the basic structure of character components. On the other hand, the judgement on the artificial characters with the wrong combination of two real components in their correct positions (#1) was not easy for the children across all the age groups. However, for the artificial characters with two real components in illegitimate positions (#2), there was a decline in the false alarm rate for the older children (in Grades 4 and 6) while the younger children performed in this set as poorly as in #1. Shu and Anderson interpreted these results by suggesting that L1 readers gradually develop awareness of the detailed internal structure of characters.

These studies may not be direct indications of awareness of component positions, as one can respond correctly by rejecting any strange-looking artificial characters. However, the above studies have demonstrated that there were at least varied degrees of *strangeness* depending on the positions and combinations of components. Awareness of component positions and combinations would have definitely helped the readers in responding to the items accurately, as they could use the information conveyed by the components when judging character-ness. The awareness of component positions and combinations may also assist in locating main radicals (semantic components) and phonetics (phonetic components) in characters.

Awareness of information in components

Research suggests that *radical awareness* (awareness of the function of the semantic component of compound characters) and *phonetic awareness* (awareness of the structure and function of the phonetic component of compound characters) are essential elements of character recognition (see Chapter 2 Section 3.3). What follows is discussion on these aspects of awareness.

Main radicals

Leck, Weekes, and Chen (1995) investigated the role of main radicals in a compound *hanzi* using a semantic categorisation task. In this task, L1 Chinese adult readers were presented with a category name followed by a character, and were required to judge whether or not the character was semantically related to the given category name. Stimuli included two types of orthographically similar item sets: one set consisting of characters that shared a common left component (main radical) with the target character (for example, 恰 'as if' instead of 悦 'delightful' for the category 'emotion'), and the other set consisting of characters that shared a common right component (non-main-radical) with the target character (for example, 脱 'take off' instead of 悦 'delightful' for the category 'emotion'). None of these orthographically similar characters was neither phonologically identical to the target characters nor a member of the designated category. As can be seen in the above examples, the experiment was designed so that participants should have indicated that all of these characters were semantically unrelated to the category names. The results showed that the participants made more errors and took longer to reject the characters that shared a common main radical with the target character. On the other hand, no interference was observed in the characters in the other set that shared a common non-main-radical with the target characters. Leck et al. concluded that these results suggest that left components (main radicals) are very important for retrieving the meanings of compound characters.

These results suggest that L1 readers may be aware of the semantic function of main radicals. As described in Chapter 3 Section 1, not only a main radical, but each single radical has a meaning. In the study by Leck et al., if the participant had accessed the semantic information of all the constituent radicals, then there should have been no difference between the common main radical set and the common non-main-radical set. In fact, the participants experienced interference only with the main radicals. This could have been due to the participants' awareness that the main radical often determines the semantics of a character. On the other hand, the results obtained in the study by Leck et al. could be interpreted as merely that the participants took longer to reject the common main radical set because they had learnt that the characters sharing a common left-hand component would often have a synonymous relationship. By being exposed to a number of characters, readers might have learnt (as products of associative learning through exposure and practice) the association between the characters that share a common left-hand component. If this is the case, the awareness may not necessarily be of the semantic information of main radicals. However, Shu, Anderson and Wu (2000) argue that the initial awareness may be crude and simple. According to them, for example, a vague feeling of 'the left-hand side of a character sometimes tells the meaning' should also be considered as a rudimentary awareness. In this regard, the participants in Leck et al. at least had an implicit rudimentary awareness.

Shu and Anderson (1997) investigated the development of radical awareness in less-skilled readers (Chinese children learning to read Chinese). The testing items were all unfamiliar characters. There were three types of unfamiliar characters: 1) characters with a familiar main radical that was helpful for understanding the meaning of the whole character (transparent familiar), 2) characters with an unfamiliar main radical that was helpful for understanding the meaning of the whole character (transparent unfamiliar), and 3) characters with a main radical that was not helpful for understanding the meaning of the whole character (opaque). The participants were Grade 3 and Grade 5 Chinese children who were divided into three groups (high, average and low) according to their reading ability. The participants were presented with compound words that were made of one *hanzi,* and alphabetic letters to show the reading of the other *hanzi*. The task was to find an appropriate *hanzi* to replace the alphabetic letters from a list of four *hanzi*. The participants knew all the words from spoken language. The results showed that the participants performed significantly better on the items with transparent familiar main radicals than the items with transparent unfamiliar or opaque main radicals. The results showed that regardless of age groups the children with higher reading ability did better than those of lower ability only for the *hanzi* with transparent familiar main radicals.

In this study, the children had to choose one character out of four unfamiliar characters. In order to choose one, they were forced to use whatever information that was available in the characters. In this context, the result that the children performed significantly better on the items with transparent familiar main radicals than the items with transparent unfamiliar or opaque main radicals was not surprising. The children could have chosen the correct characters based on the familiar parts of the characters without necessarily being aware of the semantic information conveyed by the radicals. What was intriguing was the fact that the children with higher reading ability did better than those with lower ability for the characters with transparent familiar main radicals. If indeed the 'familiar main radicals' were familiar to all the children, why did the children with higher reading ability perform better than the children with lower reading ability? The children with higher reading ability may have been aware that the meaning of a character could be inferred by the meaning of its main radical whereas the children with lower reading ability may not have. Alternatively, the better readers could have used the semantic information from the main radical without knowing it was the main radical, and the poor readers may simply have been unable to identify the main radical as they looked at the character as a whole. The children in the above study therefore may or may not have been aware that the meanings of characters could be inferred using the semantic information of the main radicals. However, such awareness would have certainly helped them interpret unfamiliar characters on the basis of their main radicals. This study also suggests that knowledge of individual main radicals (knowing the meanings conveyed by individual main radicals) is also crucial.

Phonetics

Research suggests that phonological information of phonetics (components that may give some indication of the pronunciation of the characters) becomes available to skilled readers at a very early stage of character recognition (see Chapter 2 Section 3.3). Shu, Anderson and Wu (2000) investigated whether Chinese children use the phonological information of phonetics for pronunciation of characters. In their study, Chinese children who were in second, fourth and sixth grades were asked to name characters as quickly and as accurately as possible. The stimuli were all compound characters, half of which were familiar and the other half of which were unfamiliar to them. Three types of characters were included both in the familiar and unfamiliar sets: 1) regular *hanzi*, in which the reading of the whole was the same as the reading of its phonetic, 2) irregular *hanzi*, in which the reading of the character was different from the reading of its phonetic, and 3) *hanzi* with 'bound' phonetics. Whereas the phonetics in the regular and irregular *hanzi* were able to be characters in their own right, the phonetics of the third type were not able to be characters by themselves. The researchers explain that, in the characters with bound phonetics, the reading must be resolved by analogy with other characters containing the phonetics. Shu et al. found that both familiarity and regularity strongly affected the children's performance. An interesting aspect of the data was the accuracy of reading in unfamiliar *hanzi*. When the *hanzi* were unfamiliar, regularity made a significant difference in accuracy for the fourth and sixth graders, but not as much for the second graders. The older children made more errors in naming irregular *hanzi* than the younger children. These results were mainly because the older children had given irregular characters the same pronunciations as their phonetics. Another common error was caused by mispronouncing a character with a bound phonetic through an analogy with another character with a different pronunciation that contained the same phonetic. Shu et al. argue that phonetic awareness continues to develop over the elementary school years, as shown by the increasing influence of phonetic regularity on the performance of children in higher grades and the increasing percentage of phonetic-related errors among older children.

Chen, Wu and Anderson (2003) reviewed a few studies pertaining to phonetic awareness (including a thorough analysis of properties of school characters by Shu, Chen, Anderson, Wu and Xuan, 2003), and hypothesised developmental stages. At the initial stage, children become aware of the function of phonetics in characters and begin to *read* the characters by naming their phonetic. Naturally, according to Chen et al., children make many overgeneralisation errors at this stage. Chen et al. speculated that this stage evolves when children have acquired around 200 characters, and it is then followed by a more sophisticated stage where children become aware that the information conveyed by the phonetic might be unreliable.

In the study by Shu et al. (2000), the children could have read the characters by naming whatever part that could be read while not necessarily being aware of the phonetics. It could be the case that the older children were simply able to name phonetics without knowing their phonological function in the characters. Nevertheless, this sort of stage may be considered to be a rudimentary stage of phonetic awareness.

Awareness of limitations of component information

Chen et al. (2003) argue that, as vocabulary grows, children become aware that it is unreliable to pronounce characters based on the phonetics alone. At some point, children realise that phonetics do not always provide useful information, and become more selective when using the phonetics. As a case in point, the study by Ho and Bryant (1997) looked into the development of phonetic awareness. They investigated Chinese children's ability to utilise phonetic awareness in reading compound characters with different regularities. Participants were Grade 1 and Grade 2 children in Hong Kong. Their test battery included phonetic compound *hanzi* and pseudo-*hanzi* reading tests. The compound *hanzi* reading test consisted of *hanzi* with a phonetic of varied regularity (the distance between the pronunciations of the *hanzi* and its phonetic). The pseudo-*hanzi* reading test consisted of pseudo-*hanzi* that contained a phonologically regular phonetic. The results showed that the Grade 2 children outperformed the Grade 1 children in the pseudo-*hanzi* reading, suggesting that the older children may have had a greater ability to use the phonetic to infer the reading of the *hanzi* than the younger children. It was therefore expected that the Grade 2 children would show a stronger component regularity effect in the phonetic compound *hanzi* condition as well. Interestingly however, the size of the component regularity effect was bigger among the first graders than the second graders although the Grade 2 children were on average able to read more compound characters than were the Grade 1 children. Based on these findings, Ho and Bryant claimed that experienced readers have awareness of the limitations of component information. Less-skilled readers initially make many overgeneralizations (when they know about 200 characters), but, as they progress in reading and learn to read 500 or more characters, they begin to become aware of exceptions (Ho and Bryant, 1997: 288).

The results obtained in this study were inconsistent with the findings in the study by Shu et al. (2000), which found a larger influence of phonetic regularity of unfamiliar compound characters on the performance of children in higher grades. This was probably because the familiarity of characters was not controlled in the study by Ho and Bryant. As the same set of compound characters was used for both the first and second grade children, the older children could have known the pronunciations of some irregular compound characters, hence less regularity effect was observed. In this sense, the conclusion drawn in the study by Ho and Bryant that second graders have the awareness of the limitations of component information is somewhat questionable. Nevertheless, if indeed the phonological information of phonetics would be activated automatically as many researchers claim (see Chapter 2 Sections 2 and 3 for details), it is likely that children would face inconsistent information from the character and from its irregular phonetic, and therefore eventually become aware that phonetics are only occasionally useful for inferring the readings of characters.

Chen et al. further discuss the incomplete nature of phonetics from two aspects, regularity and consistency, which are related but separate concepts. According to Chen et al. (2003: 120), regularity (some researchers call it 'validity') represents the degree of congruence between the reading of a character and the reading of its phonetic, and consistency represents how much characters with the same phonetic agree in reading (i.e., intra- and inter-character reliability). Chen et al. proposes that, at a sophisticated stage, children become aware of both the regularity and consistency of characters.

The findings of the above research suggest that the underlying awareness that would be helpful for character recognition processes may be: awareness of component legal positions, awareness of information in components and awareness of the limitations of such component information. Given that awareness develops as reading ability develops, L2 readers' awareness in these areas in *kanji* recognition processes is thought to develop as their exposure to *kanji* increases, and as such might be able to be used as an indicator of this development. The review of relevant studies also indicated that awareness is difficult to assess in indirect tasks. In order to assess the development of awareness among L2 *kanji* readers, in the present study, a more direct method, a retrospective interview, will be employed (this will be described in Chapter 3).

2.6 Chapter two summary

The review of the literature pertaining to word recognition and reading development has revealed that recognition skills required to carry out necessary processes effectively vary according to the nature of orthography. Although orthographic, phonological and morphological processing is required regardless of scripts, the processes differ in alphabetic and non-alphabetic scripts. By going through several developmental stages, young readers develop appropriate recognition skills and awareness in order to efficiently process the L1 script. When reading in an L2, it has been shown that L1 recognition skills are applied to the L2, that is, readers tend to use word recognition skills developed in their L1, which in some cases may not facilitate the L2 word recognition. Research suggests that L2 readers gradually develop skills and awareness that are suitable for the L2 as their L2 processing experience increases. In character recognition, L2 readers are expected to show a pattern of character processing that is affected by character complexity, character frequency, radical frequency and homophone size. They are also expected to develop awareness of component positions and combinations, awareness of the information conveyed by components, and awareness of the limitations of such component information.

3 The present study

3.1 Rationale and design

3.1.1 Rationale

Background

The literature review has revealed that fundamental word processing procedures are universal regardless of orthographic differences, and that the prerequisites of efficient word recognition are: 1) readers have internalised vocabulary knowledge, 2) readers can access the orthographic, phonological and morphological information of words quickly and accurately and 3) readers are aware of the structures and features of words. It has been claimed that young L1 readers generally go through three or four stages to become skilled readers. Through cumulative exposure to words, readers gradually develop the orthographic, phonological and morphological processing skills suited to the features of their L1 script, and become aware of the structures and functions of the L1 script (see Chapter 2 Sections 1, 2 & 3). Even though Chinese *hanzi* and Japanese *kanji* have orthographic, phonological and morphological features that are distinct from those of alphabetic scripts, the gradual development of character recognition in children appears to be the same as how children learn to recognise the English alphabet (see Chapter 2 Section 2), although the nature of the word recognition skills and awareness varies according to the features of the script.

Research suggests that L2 word recognition procedures are shaped by cross-linguistic effects and L2 linguistic development. With respect to cross-linguistic effects, researchers have found that L2 readers utilise their L1 word recognition skills and awareness in processing L2 script. They have also found that not only beginner L2 readers but also advanced L2 readers are affected by their L1 word recognition skills and awareness (see Chapter 2 Section 4). This influence of L1 word recognition skills and awareness can be positive or negative depending on the orthographic distance between the L1 and L2. Given the distinct features of English alphabets and Japanese *kanji* characters, reading *kanji* can be seriously challenging to English-speaking learners of Japanese.

However, research also suggests that readers gradually develop L2-specific recognition skills and awareness through building knowledge of the L2 orthographic features (see Chapter 2 Section 4). In the case of English-speaking learners of Japanese, they develop recognition skills appropriate to *kanji* recognition, such as the use of component (main radical and phonetic) information, and become aware of the functions and limitations of functional components as the exposure to *kanji* accumulates (see Chapter 2 Section 5). These collective findings suggest that by identifying critical phases of development of character recognition skills and awareness of characters, some instructional implications for improving L2 readers' character recognition ability may be drawn.

Present study

The aim of the present study was to investigate how English-speaking learners of Japanese develop processing skills and awareness suitable to Japanese *kanji* recognition. Given that L1 children progress through three or four developmental phases as knowledge of the language increases, it seemed reasonable to assume that L2 readers of Japanese would also gradually refine their character recognition skills and sharpen their awareness (see Chapter 2 Sections 2 and 3 for details). One hypothesis was that L2 readers would also go through partial, analytical and orthographic phases, and with sufficient exposure and practice, eventually attain skilled L1 readers' level. However, it might not be correct to assume that adult L2 readers of Japanese take similar developmental steps to L1 children. Adult L2 readers have already developed word processing skills and awareness in their L1, and they tend to transfer those skills and awareness to an L2 reading setting (see Chapter 2 Section 3 for details). In this regard, L2 readers' developmental phases might be very different from those of Japanese L1 children.

Although studies investigating L1 and L2 word recognition abound, to my knowledge, none give an overview of the development of L2 readers' processing in Japanese *kanji* recognition. The present study characterised patterns of *kanji* recognition skills and states of awareness of L2 readers at different developmental stages as comprehensively as possible. The unit of investigation in this study was individual characters, hence *kanji* recognition and not *kanji* word recognition. *Kanji* words may consist of one or more characters, but the interest of this study was the characters themselves, which may or may not be words.

Approach

Although a longitudinal approach may seem to be appropriate for the investigation of development of word recognition skills, such an approach is prone to a number of unpredictable variables (e.g., attrition of participants). The present study took a cross-sectional approach, which seemed appropriate for investigating the development of broad characteristics of a sample. With respect to participant selection, it was necessary to ensure that participants with different levels of *kanji* knowledge were included. A group of L2 readers of Japanese were divided into beginner, intermediate and advanced groups according to their *kanji* knowledge level using a *kanji* vocabulary test as an assessment tool. A group of L1 readers of Japanese was also included as a very skilled readers' group, to provide a standard against which to contrast the measured aspects of L2 readers' development of *kanji* recognition processes.

In order to draw a broad outline of the processes of *kanji* recognition employed by L2 readers, several tasks were devised. The review of literature pertaining to word recognition and reading suggested that, although basic word recognition development may be similar regardless of orthographic differences of script (readers develop orthographic, phonological and morphological processing skills as their experience with

109

reading increases), some skills that are crucial for successful word recognition may be script-specific (see Chapter 2 Section 3 for details). For instance, converting graphemes to phonemes is vital for phonologically transparent languages whereas using component information is essential for character recognition. In order to examine the development of script-specific processing in L2 readers of Japanese, the tasks needed to be capable of assessing the ability to use orthographic, phonological and semantic information from both the characters and their constituent components.

A large body of research in word recognition suggests that the speed of word recognition varies according to different properties of the word (see Chapter 2 Section 2). Task items should therefore include *kanji* that vary in these types of properties. For example, the complexity of how a *kanji* is written might be an important variable affecting beginning L2 readers, as typically beginners recognise less complex *kanji* more accurately and quickly than more complex ones. However, this may not be the case for more skilled L2 readers who have become more familiar with complex *kanji*. In the present study, participants' orthographic and phonological skills were assessed by determining their accuracy and speed in performing different tasks for *kanji* stimuli that had different properties. For semantic processing, as will be discussed in detail later, the analysis of the effects of the stimulus properties was not conducted (this issue will be discussed in detail in Chapter 3 Section 3).

In order to examine the speed of processing, the tasks needed to take the form of a timed-test, in which stimulus exposure times were controlled and response times measured. Stimuli (task items) were therefore displayed using a computer that recorded both the accuracy and speed of responses for each item in each task.

Research also suggests that, in word recognition, awareness of the structures and functions of words plays an important role (Alderson, 2000). It is therefore essential to examine how such awareness relates to *kanji* recognition processing. L1 and L2 word recognition studies have proposed several possible aspects of awareness that may be critical for efficient *kanji* recognition (see Chapter 2 Section 5 for details). However, assessing awareness is problematic. In previous studies, awareness has been assessed by inference based on the results of the performance on the given tasks (see Chapter 2 Section 3). Results obtained from such tasks are, however, often ambiguous (see Chapter 2 Section 5), and whether awareness existed or not is not very clear from the results. This becomes even less reliable when readers' network of knowledge, which activates such features as the orthography, phonology and semantics of words, are not homogeneous. Some studies investigating less-skilled L1 readers (i.e., L1 children) have avoided this problem by limiting the stimuli (e.g., characters) to unfamiliar ones only. In the present study, however, as it is dealing with L2 readers with diverse *kanji* vocabulary knowledge, this was not possible. Even if it were possible, as mentioned above, inferring the state of awareness from task results is not always reliable.

In this study, a complementary interview was employed to elicit the participants' awareness using the *kanji* recognition tasks that they performed as a source of reflection. The *kanji* recognition tasks required the participants' instant responses, leaving almost no time for conscious, controlled processes. On the other hand, talking about their

111

performance required a conscious analysis of these automatic processes, which means that the interviewees were required to bring their awareness to the conscious level. Some researchers refer to this 'explicit conscious representation of the latent awareness' as 'metalinguistic awareness'. Metalinguistic awareness is claimed to be related to linguistic development, especially to the development of literacy (Alderson, 2000; Yelland, Pollard and Mercuri, 1993; Herriman, 1991; Birdsong, 1989; Yaden and Templeton, 1986; Tunmer and Herriman, 1984).

3.1.2 Design

Overall, the present study used a psycholinguistic, cognitive developmental methodology within an applied linguistic perspective, in order to develop a broad outline of *kanji* recognition in L2 readers of Japanese at various processing levels. A qualitative methodology was also used as a complementary measure.

The current study employed an experimental design, although, in a strict sense, it was not purely experimental, as it did not have the conditions of true experimental design (e.g., absolute random selection of participants and control of pre-existing differences), nor did it look for any causal relationship between treatment and result. The current study may be best described in the framework of the Ex Post Facto Design, which looks at the types of, or the strength of, connections between the variables without considering what went before. This is a common design used in reporting test results (Hatch and Lazaraton, 1991).

The dependent variables were response time and correct response rate. A between-subjects variable was the level of *kanji* knowledge (L1 readers, and L2 readers of Japanese - beginner, intermediate and advanced), and within-subjects variables were tasks, types of items and stimulus properties. A verbal protocol method was used to elicit knowledge of what a participant could declare about how they thought they performed each task, the purpose of which was to access their awareness of the structures and functions of characters and their constituent components.

3.2 Methods

3.2.1 Participants

L2 readers

Prior to the recruitment of participants, approval for conducting the research project was obtained from the Human Research Ethics Committee of the University of Melbourne. Participants were then recruited from universities[1] in Victoria, Australia, from students who were or had been enrolled in Japanese language subjects. A plain language statement that described the project was distributed to potential participants, and any queries were answered thoroughly. Those who expressed their interest in

---

[1]Participants were recruited from the University of Melbourne, Monash University, La Trobe University, RMIT and the Australian Catholic University. The Human Research Ethics Committee at the University of Melbourne, The Head of School at Monash University, the Head of School at La Trobe University, the Head of the School at RMIT, and the Dean of the Faculty at the Australian Catholic University all approved the recruitment of participants for the project.

participating were asked to sign a consent form. A small token of thanks (AUS $10) was given to them for their participation.

The L2 participants were asked if they had had experience of learning *kanji* or *hanzi* prior to learning Japanese. Anyone who answered 'yes' to this question was excluded from the final participant group. 109 graduate and undergraduate university students were selected from an initial pool of 224 volunteer participants for inclusion in the study. The criteria for inclusion were: 1) university students who are learning / have learnt Japanese, 2) have knowledge of at least 50 *kanji* characters, 3) English is the most comfortably spoken and read language, 4) are aged between 18 and 40, and 5) have normal or corrected to normal sight and hearing.

As the data were to be compared between different *kanji* knowledge levels, it was important that the participants were representatives of different levels of *kanji* recognition skill. To achieve this, three broad levels of skill were selected: beginner (less than 300 *kanji*), intermediate (more than 300 but less than 1,000 *kanji*), and advanced (more than 1,000 *kanji*) levels. Allocation to one of these categories was made according to the results of a *kanji* knowledge test (see the following section). The final participant group consisted of 39 beginner, 40 intermediate and 30 advanced L2 readers of *kanji*.

L1 readers

As a skilled readers' group, L1 Japanese readers who were resident in Melbourne were also recruited[2]. 16 native speakers of Japanese were selected to serve as participants in the skilled readers' group from an initial pool of 20 volunteer participants. The criteria for inclusion were: 1) have completed at least nine years of compulsory education in Japan, 2) Japanese is the most comfortable language to read, 3) are well-read in both Japanese and English, 4) are aged between 18 and 40, and 5) have normal or corrected to normal sight and hearing.

Another group of L1 readers was recruited for a semantic relatedness task, which will be described later. In this task, 45 native speakers of Japanese participated. The criteria for inclusion of the L1 readers of Japanese for this task were generally the same as above except that the required level of English proficiency was lowered slightly in order to increase the number of participants. Some of the participants resided in Japan at the time of the study.

3.2.2 Kanji knowledge test

Background

To assess the size of participants' sight *kanji* vocabulary, a *kanji* knowledge test was used (see Appendix A). Before describing the test, I would like to mention how assessments of sight vocabulary size are usually measured. In a vocabulary size test, a

---

[2]Volunteer participants were sought mostly from staff and students at the University of Melbourne but a few more came from the investigator's circle of friends.

large sample is a typical requirement in order to achieve reliable estimates (Nation, 1993). Also, it is desirable to have a test that can measure vocabulary size in a short period of time (Read, 1993). Well suited to these requirements is a checklist test, which presents test-takers with a series of words and simply asks them to indicate whether they know each one or not (Read, 2000). However, it is pointless to give test-takers materials that are outside of their vocabulary range or are at too basic a level.

An adaptive test is one solution. In an adaptive test, the participant only needs to respond to words that are neither too easy nor too hard. Adaptive tests are typically designed on the assumption that words that occur more frequently in print are more likely to be known than less frequent ones, and higher frequency words are likely to be known by a person who already knows less frequent ones (Read, 2000). One example of such a test is the EVST (Eurocentres Vocabulary Size Test) (see Meara and Jones, 1987 for details). While the EVST consists of both real words and non-words, the inclusion of non-words has been criticised, as non-words are not linguistically natural (Read, 2000), and typically, learners' scores do not differ on the test whether it contains non-words or not (Shillaw, 1996). This EVST was used as a model when devising a *kanji* knowledge test for the present study.

Manual adaptive *kanji* knowledge test

In order to estimate the number of *kanji* that the participant knew, a manual (not computerised) adaptive *kanji* knowledge test, which consisted of three lists of *kanji*, was designed. *Kanji* used in the test were all real *kanji* (i.e., non-*kanji* were not included), and participants were required to indicate which *kanji* they knew. It is acknowledged that knowing or not knowing words is not a dichotomous distinction: indeed as Vermeer (2001: 221) has stated, 'there is a continuum ranging from not knowing, to recognising, to knowing roughly, to describing very accurately'. However, as the purpose of the test was to simply group participants, and not to assess their *kanji* knowledge in detail, the current *kanji* knowledge test simply required a dichotomous yes or no response.

The *kanji* knowledge test was created using a *kanji* database that contained data from the standardised Japanese Proficiency Test. *The Database for the 1,945 Basic Japanese Kanji, 2nd edition* (Tamaoka, Kirsner, Yanase, Miyaoka, and Kawakami, 2002) consisted of 1,945 *kanji* with levels of the standardised proficiency test, the difficulty of which had been determined by two organisations, the Japan Foundation and the Association of International Education, in 1993.

The 1,945 general-use *kanji* are categorised into four levels[3], from the easiest (level four) to the most difficult (level one). Conventionally, learners of Japanese whose *kanji* knowledge is within the range of the levels three and four (less than 300 characters) are considered to be beginner *kanji* readers. If learners' *kanji* knowledge is

---

[3] According to the database, there were 80 *kanji* in level four, 165 in level three, 755 in level two and 926 in level one, which added up to 1926 in total. The other 19 characters fell outside of the four levels. In 2001, an article on the partial revision of the specifications (the Japan Foundation and Association of International Education, 2001) was published, with the result that a few *kanji* were moved up or down a level accordingly.

up to level two (300-1,000 characters), they are considered to be intermediate *kanji* readers. Learners who are above this level are considered to be advanced *kanji* readers.

For the selection of *kanji* to be included in the *kanji* knowledge test, firstly, all the *kanji* that were used in *kanji* recognition tasks (to be described in the following section) were marked as 1,2,3 or 4 according to their levels (1 is the most difficult level and 4 is the easiest). The ones marked as levels four and three were combined, as the number of *kanji* in these levels was relatively small. The total number of *kanji* selected was 315, with 27 characters in the combined group of levels four and three, 152 characters in level two, and 136 characters in level one. To make the number of items in each of the three levels more balanced, 108 characters from levels four and three were randomly drawn from the database, and formed a group of 135 *kanji* for the combined level. As a result, the test consisted of three lists of *kanji*: 1) a list of 135 *kanji* taken from the levels three and four of the standardised Japanese proficiency test (beginner list), 2) a list of 152 *kanji* taken from level two of the same test (intermediate list), and 3) a list of 136 *kanji* taken from level one of the same test (advanced list).

3.2.3 Kanji recognition tasks

Computerised *kanji* recognition tasks

In order to assess participants' character processing skills, several recognition tasks were devised. An experiment technique measuring response time and accuracy of response was employed in the *kanji* recognition tasks. There are several reasons for choosing such a method. Firstly, because skilled readers can recognise words more rapidly and accurately than less-skilled readers (Perfetti, 1986; Segalowitz, 1986), procedures should measure both response speed and accuracy. L2 readers at different levels were expected to exhibit different response times and varied rates of correct recognition. Secondly, although there are more direct methods to examine the recognition of words, such as brain scans and eye-movement, they are possible only with special equipment (Harley, 1995). Thirdly, setting a fixed time for a response did not seem to be appropriate in the current situation, where L2 readers had various levels of recognition skills. Further, these procedures have a long history in psycholinguistic research (Juffs, 2001).

The experiments in this study took the form of a series of computerised yes/no tests, which have been used extensively in cognitive research (Taft, 1991). Yes/no tests are simple to construct for a researcher and easy for participants to respond to (Read, 2000). In an attempt to eliminate guessing effects, an option for skipping items was provided in the experimental tasks in the present study.

Tasks

Six tasks were devised in order to investigate the *kanji* recognition processes of the different *kanji* level groups of participants, along with one warm-up task to familiarise them with the format of the timed yes/no tasks. All the tasks were more or less artificial (i.e., not the same as a normal reading setting), and focused on three essential aspects of *kanji* recognition, orthographic, phonological and semantic properties, respectively. The tasks used were two orthographic tasks (character-ness

119

judgement and radical identification), two phonological tasks (phonological judgement and phonological matching) and two semantic tasks (semantic judgement and semantic categorisation).

The character-ness judgement task was designed to assess participants' ability to discriminate real characters from non-characters. The radical identification task aimed to assess whether or not participants could find common functional components in characters (which were the main radicals of the characters used in this task). The phonological judgement task was designed to assess participants' ability to use phonetics (phonetic components of characters) to retrieve *on*-readings of characters. In the phonological matching task, the phonetics were highlighted[4] to draw the participants' attention to these functional components. In other words, the phonetics were explicitly, rather than implicitly, shown to the participants. The semantic judgement task aimed to assess participants' ability to use main radicals to infer the meanings of characters. In the semantic categorisation task, main radicals were highlighted in order to draw the readers' attention to them, and the words shown after the characters showed the categories of the main radicals.

---

[4] Compared to the character-ness judgement, phonological judgement, and semantic judgement tasks, the radical identification, phonological matching and semantic categorisation tasks provided more 'explicit' conditions in which participants were encouraged to pay attention to the components of the *kanji*. These three tasks were included for the purpose of inducing non-automatic processes, which are likely to induce explicit conscious representation of more subconscious-level awareness.

In order to familiarise participants with the format of the above tasks, a short and simple task was devised as a warm-up task. This task was to judge whether two characters were the same or different (i.e., same-or-different task).

Prior to the selection of the final seven tasks (one warm-up, two orthographic, two phonological and two semantic tasks), several tasks were trialled. Some earlier versions of tasks were devised and assessed by administering them in pencil and paper form to a group of L2 readers of Japanese. They were then revised according to the feedback received. A final selection of tasks was made, taking into account several parameters such as construct validity, feasibility, numbers of test items, and difficulties of the tasks.

Stimulus properties of *kanji*

The characters in the tasks were chosen carefully so that different levels of four stimulus properties would be included. The four stimulus properties that had been previously identified as relevant to *kanji* recognition were: complexity, character frequency, radical frequency and homophone size (see Chapter 2 Section 5 for details). The corpus of 1,945 characters was used to select a set of items that would represent each of the stimulus properties. Within each stimulus property, two groups of *kanji* were selected (e.g., for complexity, low complexity *kanji* and high complexity *kanji*). These contrasting groups of *kanji* were then used in each task, so that each task tested *kanji* with different stimulus properties.

Selection of *kanji* characters

Selection

In order to investigate the effects of the stimulus properties of the *kanji*, the *kanji* included in the tasks had to differ in only one dimension (complexity, character frequency, radical frequency or homophone size) keeping the others constant. The 1,945 characters were examined for their stimulus properties by referring to *the Database for the 1,945 Basic Japanese Kanji, 2nd edition* (Tamaoka, Kirsner, Yanase, Miyaoka and Kawakami, 2002). According to Tamaoka et al. (2002), the data for the four stimulus properties of interest were compiled in the following manner:

1) Complexity - based on the number of required strokes for writing. The data were taken from a particular Japanese *kanji* dictionary edited by Kamata in 1991, which followed the Ministry of Education guidelines.

2) Character frequency – The data were taken from a journal titled 'Japanese *kanji* in the newspaper media: *Kanji* frequency index from the Asahi newspaper on CD-ROM' written by Yokoyama, Sasahara, Nozaki and Long (1998). Character frequency was calculated based on all the *kanji* in the Tokyo edition of the Asahi newspaper printed in 1993.

3) Radical frequency - indicates how many of the 1,945 *kanji* share a common main radical (i.e., type frequency).

4) Homophone size - indicates how many of the 1,945 *kanji* share a common reading. Both *on-* and *kun*-readings were included in the calculation of character homophones although the majority of homophones were found in *on*-readings.

122

The 1,945 characters were categorised into low, medium and high groups for each of the four stimulus properties. Although, ideally speaking, each group should consist of approximately 648 characters, one third of the 1,945 characters, the number of *kanji* in each group varied due to various constraints. The final number of *kanji* in each group of each stimulus property is presented in Table 3.1.

Table 3.1 The number of *kanji* in the low, medium, and high groups of the four stimulus properties

	Low	Medium	High
Complexity	(1-7)	(8-11)	(12-23)
(# of strokes)	455	760	730
Character frequency	(1-1039)	(1050-5497)	(5522-257929)
(frequency of occurrence)	648	649	648
Radical frequency	(1-10)	(11-36)	(38-103)
(# of *kanji* sharing a main radical)	657	691	597
Homophone size	(0-7)	(8-21)	(22-60)
(# of *kanji* sharing a reading)	632	746	567

Note: Numbers in parentheses show the cut-offs; 'low homophone size' refers to a few homophones and 'high homophone size' refers to many homophones

Each of the total 1,945 *kanji* was then classified according to the above criteria. For example, the *kanji* 吸 was classified as LMMM type, as this *kanji* had low complexity, medium frequency of occurrence, medium radical frequency and medium homophone size. For the present study, only the *kanji* in the following eight types (four contrast pairs) were selected (see Table 3.2).

Table 3.2 Four contrast pairs selected

Type	Low	Type	High
LMMM	Low complexity and the rest are medium	HMMM	High complexity and the rest are medium
MLMM	Low character frequency and the rest are medium	MHMM	High character frequency and the rest are medium
MMLM	Low radical frequency and the rest are medium	MMHM	High radical frequency and the rest are medium
MMML	Low homophone size and the rest are medium	MMMH	High homophone size and the rest are medium

Note: L = low, H = high and M = medium

In order to maximise the number of items that could be assigned to each type, a number of adjustments for allocating *kanji* into the low, medium and high groups were carried out. Table 3.3 shows the final number of *kanji* in the eight types that served as a pool of characters for the tasks.

Table 3.3 The number of *kanji* assigned to each contrast pair in each critical property

Critical property	Low		High	
	Type	Number	Type	Number
Complexity	LMMM	16	HMMM	36
Character frequency	MLMM	52	MHMM	29
Radical frequency	MMLM	22	MMHM	36
Homophone size	MMML	28	MMMH	36

Note: L = low, H = high and M = medium

Four contrasting pairs - eight types of *kanji*

In order to investigate the effects of the four stimulus properties, first of all, a series of statistical analyses were performed to see if there was a significant difference between the two contrast types (e.g., LMMM vs HMMM) in the respective properties. For example, in the case of LMMM and HMMM, it was expected that these two types would differ in complexity, but would show no differences in the other dimensions.

Analysis

A series of independent t-tests were performed to compare the four pairs: LMMM vs HMMM, MLMM vs MHMM, MMLM vs MMHM, and MMML vs MMMH. The analysis showed each pair differed significantly in the respective critical property. The results of the analyses are presented in Tables 3.4, 3.5, 3.6 and 3.7.

Table 3.4   Differences in the four stimulus properties for the two types of characters that were intended to differ in complexity (LMMM vs HMMM)

	LMMM N = 70	HMMM N = 70	t	Sig
Complexity	7.9 (1.5)	13.8 (2.5)	17.12	0.001
Character Frequency	2620.6 (1984.3)	3465.3 (5303.0)	1.25	0.214
Radical Frequency	20.0 (10.9)	20.5 (9.1)	.28	0.782
Homophone Size	16.6 (8.8)	14.5 (8.2)	1.46	0.147

As intended, a significant difference was shown in the critical property, complexity, between the LMMM and HMMM types, t (113.2)=17.12, p<0.05 (equal variances not assumed). No differences were identified in the other properties.

Table 3.5 Differences in the four stimulus properties for the two types of characters that were intended to differ in character frequency (MLMM vs MHMM)

	MLMM N = 70	MHMM N = 70	t	Sig
Complexity	9.5 (1.4)	10.0 (1.7)	1.93	.055
Character Frequency	712.4 (1450.9)	21060.3 (30840.4)	5.51	.001
Radical Frequency	23.6 (14.8)	20.3 (12.6)	1.43	.154
Homophone Size	16.2 (6.7)	15.5 (6.0)	.64	.524

The contrast pair, MLMM and MHMM, differed significantly in the critical property, *kanji* frequency, t (69.3)=5.51, p<0.05 (equal variances not assumed). No differences were identified in the other properties.

Table 3.6 Differences in the four stimulus properties for the two types of characters that were intended to differ in radical frequency (MMLM vs MMHM)

	MMLM N = 70	MMHM N = 70	t	Sig
Complexity	9.4 (1.3)	9.2 (1.6)	.81	0.423
Character Frequency	3103.5 (2470.5)	2608.2 (1330.6)	1.45	0.142
Radical Frequency	7.5 (5.6)	66.1 (24.5)	19.50	0.001
Homophone Size	15.8 (6.5)	12.0 (5.2)	3.79	0.001

This pair, MMLM and MMHM, showed a significant difference in the critical property, radical frequency, t (76.3)=19.5 p<0.05 (equal variances not assumed). Surprisingly, however, it was found that the difference in the homophone size was also significant, t (132)=3.79, p<0.05 (equal variances not assumed).

Table 3.7   Differences in the four stimulus properties for the two types of characters that were intended to differ in homophone size (MMML vs MMML)

	MMML N = 70	MMMH N = 70	t	Sig
Complexity	10.0 (1.3)	9.2 (1.0)	3.75	0.001
Character Frequency	2955.8 (3335.4)	3451.0 (5140.4)	.68	0.500
Radical Frequency	20.7 (7.4)	19.2 (10.5)	.98	0.331
Homophone Size	3.9 (2.9)	35.2 (13.2)	19.42	0.001

Once again unexpectedly, significant differences were identified between the MMML and MMMH types not only in the critical property, homophone size, t (75.43)=19.42, p<0.05 (equal variances not assumed), but also in complexity, t (138)=3.75, p<0.05.

Discussion

Although the characters in each pair were selected to vary in only one critical property, it was found that there were unexpected differences in two cases. In pairs in which the radical frequency was the key property, the two types of *kanji* also differed significantly in their homophone sizes. In pairs in which the homophone size was the key property, their complexity was also significantly different, although the difference was by less than one stroke.

In reporting the results for the tasks (in Chapters 4 and 5), appropriate measures were taken in order to take these differences into account. For example, the L1 readers showed a radical frequency effect in the radical identification task. However, as mentioned above, the apparent radical frequency could have possibly been due to a homophone size effect. Therefore it was necessary to examine if the sets of low radical frequency *kanji* and high radical frequency *kanji*, which were used in the task, did not differ in their homophone size. To this end, an appropriate statistical analysis was performed to eliminate the possible effect of homophone size. The same measure was taken for all the cases where a radical frequency effect or a homophone size effect was found. In the subsequent sections, no further comments were made if it was found that the particular sets differed only in the key property. When further comments were necessary, they were footnoted accordingly.

Allocation of *kanji*

Allocating *kanji* characters to the tasks

In order to examine the effects of the stimulus properties of the *kanji*, each task needed to have a minimum of five (or five pairs) test items from each type. This number was a compromise solution after considering the maximum number of items that the beginner readers may be able to handle in a task and the minimum number of items needed for statistical power in the later analysis.

In the character-ness judgement task, 40 characters (5 LMMM, 5 HMMM, 5 MLMM, 5 MHMM, 5 MMLM, 5 MMHM, 5 MMML, and 5 MMMH) were used as stimuli for the real *kanji* group. 40 non-characters were created by shifting the locations of main radicals and non-main-radical components (5 LMMM, 5 HMMM, 5 MLMM, 5

130

MHMM, 5 MMLM, 5 MMHM, 5 MMML, and 5 MMMH). Together with 40 more characters that served as fillers, the task in total had 120 stimuli.

In the radical identification task, 80 (40 pairs) characters (10 LMMM, 10 HMMM, 10 MLMM, 10 MHMM, 10 MMLM, 10 MMHM, 10 MMML, and 10 MMMH) were used for the items that had a common main radical between the two characters. Other 80 characters (40 pairs) (10 LMMM, 10 HMMM, 10 MLMM, 10 MHMM, 10 MMLM, 10 MMHM, 10 MMML, and 10 MMMH) were combined carefully so that the pairs did not have a common main radical between the two characters. 80 more characters were added to form a filler group.

In the phonological judgement task, 80 (40 pairs) characters (10 LMMM, 10 HMMM, 10 MLMM, 10 MHMM, 10 MMLM, 10 MMHM, 10 MMML, and 10 MMMH) were used for the items that had a common reading between the two characters. For the items that had no common reading, the same 80 characters were used in a different combination. 80 filler characters were added.

In the phonological matching task, 40 characters (5 LMMM, 5 HMMM, 5 MLMM, 5 MHMM, 5 MMLM, 5 MMHM, 5 MMML, and 5 MMMH) formed a group of characters with a valid phonetic. Each of these *kanji* was paired with the pronunciation of its phonetic. Other 40 characters (5 LMMM, 5 HMMM, 5 MLMM, 5 MHMM, 5 MMLM, 5 MMHM, 5 MMML, and 5 MMMH) were paired with non-matching pronunciations. The pronunciation was in fact the reading of another *kanji* that shared the same non-main-radical component with the target *kanji*. In other words, these 40 characters were paired with an invalid phonetic. 40 fillers were added.

In the semantic judgement task, 80 (40 pairs) characters (10 LMMM, 10 HMMM, 10 MLMM, 10 MHMM, 10 MMLM, 10 MMHM, 10 MMML, and 10 MMMH) were used for the items that had a common main radical between the two characters. The same 80 characters were paired with non-matching main radicals for the group that did not have a common main radical. 80 filler characters were added.

In the semantic categorisation task, 40 characters (5 LMMM, 5 HMMM, 5 MLMM, 5 MHMM, 5 MMLM, 5 MMHM, 5 MMML, and 5 MMMH) were paired with the semantic category names of their respective main radicals. Other 40 characters (5 LMMM, 5 HMMM, 5 MLMM, 5 MHMM, 5 MMLM, 5 MMHM, 5 MMML, and 5 MMMH) were paired with non-matching semantic category names. 40 fillers were added.

The final number of *kanji* used in the six respective tasks is shown in Table 3.8 (see Appendix B for a full list of *kanji* used in the six tasks).

Table 3.8　The final number of *kanji* in the six tasks

Task	The number of characters in each group					
Characterness judgement	40	Real *kanji*	40	Non-real *kanji*	40	Fillers
Radical identification	40 x 2	Common main radical	40 x 2	No common main radical	40 x 2	Fillers
Phonological judgement	40 x 2	Common reading	40 x 2	No common reading	40 x 2	Fillers
Phonological matching	40	Valid phonetic	40	Invalid phonetic	40	Fillers
Semantic judgement	40 x 2	Common main radical	40 x 2	No common main radical	40 x 2	Fillers
Semantic categorisation	40	Main radical showing the category	40	Main radical not showing the category	40	Fillers

Task cards

Task card creation

In order to computerise the tasks, all necessary 'cards' were created using HyperCard for Macintosh. A 'card' refers to each image displayed on the computer monitor. The total number of cards was 1,426. These included all *kanji* cards used in the seven tasks (same-different, character-ness judgement, radical identification, phonological judgement, phonological matching, semantic judgement and semantic categorisation), *on*-reading cards used in the phonological matching task, and category name cards used in the semantic categorisation task.

All the writing (characters and letters) was in black with a white background. The characters were centred on each card, except for the ones in the phonological matching task where the characters were placed slightly off-centre. This off-centre placement was in order to show that the character was part of a compound word, for example, if the target *kanji* was the first *kanji* of a two-*kanji* compound word, it was placed slightly towards the left from the centre of the card, and a short line was added on the right of the character. This was to avoid possible instant rejection of the *on*-readings shown on the *on*-reading cards, as single-character words are usually read in the *kun*-readings.

The size of all the characters was 1.5cm x 1.5cm. For the paired *kanji*, two different fonts were used so that a short-term iconic-image matching strategy could not be used as the basis for a response. *Mincho* font was used for the first *kanji* (e.g., 長) and *Osaka* font for the second *kanji* (e.g., 長). In the character-ness judgement task, non-*kanji* were created by reversing the locations of components, right to left, left to right, top to bottom or bottom to top. Non-*kanji* used as fillers were created by adding extra strokes. In the phonological matching and semantic categorisation tasks, the *kanji* were shaded leaving the phonetics or main radicals intact in order to attract participants' attention to these functional components of the *kanji*.

Furthermore, cards for practice items were created for all the tasks. The practice items allowed participants to experience the task prior to the full display of task items. A confirmation card was inserted after the practice items in each task. The purpose of having this card was twofold. One was to show participants the results of the practice items, and another was to confirm if they understood what was expected in the task. If they pressed the 'no' button, the program would ask if they would like to go back to the instruction and practice items again. It also gave them an opportunity to ask questions.

I also created some other cards in order to provide 'signposts' to participants. For instance, an eye-fixation point (double circles) was inserted to show where the stimulus would appear. A mask with a black square that was of similar size to the characters was used in the radical identification task to erase any short-term iconic image of the first *kanji*. A blank card was used to provide a time gap between the cards. During the tasks, participants were allowed to take a break whenever needed. When the space-bar was pressed, the pause card appeared on the computer screen, and showed the time elapsed since the start of the pause. By pressing the space-bar once again, they were able to go back to the task.

Incorporation of sound

In the phonological matching and semantic categorisation tasks, an *on*-reading or a name of a semantic category appeared after each *kanji*. Simultaneously, the program played pre-recorded sounds (i.e., on-readings or the names of categories). All necessary sounds were recorded using the software, Sound Edit. In total, 132 sound files were created from the digital version of the sounds recorded, and the sound files were attached to the cards that required the sounds.

Exposure time

Exposure times for stimuli were decided after conducting pilot experiments that assessed their adequacy, as described below.

The first and second stimuli had to be displayed in rapid succession, as a longer exposure allows more attentive processing (Harley, 1995), which was not desired as it could encourage the use of conscious strategies. However, if the exposures were too short, this would possibly preclude accurate perception. The tasks had to be designed to accommodate learners of Japanese at all levels from beginners to advanced, and it was a prerequisite that they would be able to clearly see the characters. Therefore, the shortest possible exposure to the first stimulus that would suit learners of Japanese at all levels of *kanji* recognition ability needed to be identified.

Exposure time of the second stimulus was not set. Instead, individual participants' response times were measured. However, a time limit was required in order to encourage them to respond to the items as quickly as possible. The use of the limit was likely to curtail deliberative processing. On the other hand, the limit had to be sufficient to allow for adequate stimulus processing.

To find an appropriate exposure time for the first stimuli and a time limit within which L2 participants could appropriately respond to the second stimuli, the performance of people who had never formally learnt *kanji* before was examined. The exposure time that these novice Japanese readers felt 'barely manageable' was deemed likely to be the shortest comfortable exposure for the L2 participants.

The data of this pilot study, which compared the performance on a same-different task at three different exposure times, 250ms, 500ms and 750ms, suggest that the exposure duration of 250ms may be too short and it may preclude appropriate perception of the *kanji*, and that 750ms may be comfortable duration even for the participants who had never studied *kanji* characters. It appeared that 500ms was the 'barely manageable' exposure duration for these participants. The average response times of the three different exposure duration were well within five seconds (5000ms) although there were a few responses that exceeded the limit of five seconds.

It was thus concluded that the combination of 500ms exposure duration and a 5000ms limit would be appropriate for the L2 readers.

Programming

The *kanji* recognition tasks were programmed to automatically show the above-described 'cards' in a certain order (to be described in the following paragraph). The order of displaying *task items*, however, was randomised, and two versions with different orders of display were prepared in order to avoid any possible effect of a particular display order. After randomising, the order of the task items was adjusted in order to display 'considered-to-be-easy' items at the beginning of each task for the purpose of giving the participants initial success. The following is a brief description of how the program ran:

When a participant logged in, a new record was created by their ID number, and the date and time of the tasks taken were recorded. As the tasks progressed, new information was added to the record. Once the record was created, the program automatically moved on to the warm-up same-different task. After the warm-up task was completed, a question appeared and asked whether the participant would like to move on or to redo the task. If they chose to move on, the menu card showing a list of all the required tasks appeared on the monitor. In the present study, the order of doing the tasks was, however, set by the investigator. When one of the required tasks was selected by the investigator, the instructions for the task appeared and stayed on the screen until the 'yes' key was pressed. Prior to the task items, in each task, the program showed a few practice items followed by feedback (showing the key pressed, correct/incorrect and response time). Underneath the feedback table, questions appeared and asked if the participant had understood the task instructions. If they clicked on 'no', and chose to redo the practice items, the program displayed the instructions and the examples again. If they clicked on 'yes', it moved on and showed the first task item.

In each task, there were *kanji* or *kanji* pairs programmed to appear on the computer screen continuously unless the space-bar was pressed to request a pause. Underneath the *kanji* cards, two black lines showing the times were presented. The top line was created to show how much of time limit had expired, and the bottom line was to show how far they had to go to complete all the task items. When the top line came to the right end of the card, the program automatically changed to the next card. This only happened when the 'yes', 'no' or 'skip' key was not pressed before the time expired. When the bottom line came to the right end of the card, the program showed the 'end of the task' card.

The following information for each task item was automatically recorded: the card number displayed, the input, correct or incorrect, response time. Response times were recorded in milliseconds. However, because the computer clock was used for timing, and as one tick in the built-in clock is 16.6666....milliseconds (6 ticks = 100 milliseconds), response times, measured from the target onset until the participant's response, were only accurate to the nearest 16.7 milliseconds. The tasks were programmed not to respond to any keys other than yes, no, skip and pause.

3.2.4 Semantic relatedness rating task

The tasks were all programmed to record response times and correct response rates. However, what was correct or incorrect in the semantic tasks was not as well-defined as in the orthographic or phonological tasks. For the orthographic tasks and the phonological tasks, there was a clear-cut distinction between a correct and an incorrect response. For example, in the character-ness judgement task, if the stimulus was a real *kanji*, then the correct response would be 'yes', and if it was a non-*kanji*, then the response would be 'no'. Similarly, in the phonological judgement task, if the two characters had a common reading, then a 'yes' would be the correct response, and if there was no common reading, then the response would be 'no'. On the other hand, whether or not two characters belong to the same semantic category was not so straightforward. People could judge the same stimuli differently.

The semantic processing of readers is usually investigated using a task such as a semantic judgement task. However, it is not so simple to design a binary response semantic judgement task that compares known words (it would be problematic to design a word/nonword task, as one could never be sure at which level the person was responding). As the judgement of semantic properties of characters by individual readers may vary, for the same pair of *kanji* some may say that they belong to the same

139

semantic category while others may see them as unrelated. Unlike orthographic and phonological tasks, there are no absolutely correct or incorrect responses to the task, as the semantic network may not be homogeneous even among native speakers of Japanese.

The conventional procedure to overcome the difficulty of assessing semantic processing is to assess a group of L1 readers' rating of the semantic relatedness of word pairs, and then select only those pairs that were agreed to as being strongly related. Such a method is appropriate for a study investigating the effects of certain properties of words on word recognition in an L1 setting, as L1 readers are likely to have a more or less homogeneous semantic network. For my research, which investigates the *kanji* recognition patterns of L2 readers, this option seemed undesirable, as the semantic network of L2 readers might be very different from that of L1 readers.

Thus in order to assess the semantic knowledge of L2 readers, a novel approach was devised in which first a normative set of items with different strength of semantic relatedness was established using a non-timed semantic relatedness rating task (see Appendix C). This semantic relatedness rating task was devised in order to investigate how L1 readers perceive the semantic relatedness between characters. The stimuli were shared between the non-timed semantic relatedness rating task and the timed semantic processing tasks so that the response patterns of participants in the tasks in different conditions would be able to be compared. In the semantic relatedness rating task, two lists of items were prepared: a list of the 40 pairs of *kanji* (which were also used in the semantic judgement task) and a list of the 40 pairs of *kanji* and a semantic category name (which were also used in the semantic categorisation task). Each of the 40 pairs of

kanji shared a common main radical between the two characters. For the pairs of *kanji*

and semantic category names, the names of categories were English translations of the

meanings of the main radicals of the *kanji*. Next to each pair, a scale marked from 0 to 5

was provided to be used as an indicator of semantic relatedness. The scale was labelled

as 0, 1, 2, 3, 4, and 5; 0 meaning 'not related' and 5 meaning 'strongly related'. The

results of the non-timed task were then used to categorise the items into several

categories with different levels of semantic relatedness, which were used as a normative

set against which the results of the two processing tasks were compared (detailed

procedure and results will be presented in Chapter 6).

3.2.5 Retrospective interview

The interview took the form of a retrospective think-aloud report, which is also

referred to as retrospective protocol or episodic recollection (Pressley and Afflerback,

1995). The advantages of using this verbal protocol method are that it can provide data

about thought processes that otherwise could be inferred only from performance. It also

provides access to the overt reasoning processes that presumably underlie sophisticated

cognition, response, and decision making (Pressley and Afflerback, 1995:4).

The main reason for making it retrospective was because it would have been too

demanding to ask participants to describe their thought processes while performing the

timed tasks. The retrospective interview was given immediately after the task because,

in this way, the investigator would not need to guide the participants in order to be provided with information, as they would still have the necessary retrieval cues in their recent memory (Gass, 2001; Ericsson and Simon, 1984).

In the present study, therefore, the interview was conducted immediately after each task, instead of waiting until the end of all the tasks. As the purpose of the interview was to examine the participant's awareness, leading questions were avoided as much as possible. The questions prepared were 'How did you go about this task?' and 'Can you tell me what you were doing in this task?'. Some further questions were prepared for situations where participants' responses were irrelevant to the aspects of awareness that had been identified for *kanji* recognition. The questions included: 'Was there any particular part that you were focusing on?' and 'If you made a guess, based on what sort of information did you guess?'

3.2.6 General procedure

Kanji knowledge test

In order to assess the current *kanji* knowledge level of the L2 readers, each participant was asked to look at each list, starting from the advanced *kanji* list, and tick any *kanji* that were familiar to them. If the participant was able to tick more than five *kanji* on the advanced *kanji* list, s/he was considered to be an advanced reader, and was not further required to look at the intermediate and beginner lists. If the participant could not tick any *kanji* or ticked less than five *kanji* on the advanced *kanji* list, s/he was asked to look at the intermediate *kanji* list. Likewise, when the participant was not able to tick more than five *kanji* on the intermediate *kanji* list, s/he was required to try the beginner *kanji* list. The results of the test were used for dividing the participants into three groups of different *kanji* knowledge levels, beginner, intermediate and advanced.

Kanji recognition tasks

The devised tasks were administered to the L1 readers first, the results of which were to be used as a benchmark for comparative analyses. For the L2 readers, in order to avoid fatigue, only three or four tasks out of the six were assigned to each participant. The number of the participants in each task varied greatly (see Appendix D). This was due to the range of proficiency in Japanese of the participants. For example, the phonological and semantic tasks were beyond the abilities of the beginner L2 readers, as these tasks required a substantial amount of phonological and semantic knowledge. In order to give these participants positive reinforcement to continue with the difficult tasks, the beginner L2 readers were first asked to do relatively easy orthographic tasks (character-ness judgement and radical identification tasks). Nevertheless, a few beginner L2 readers refused to do the phonological and/or semantic tasks, and many others skipped most items in these tasks. In order to get adequate data across the task types, the intermediate and advanced groups were required to do more of the phonological and/or semantic tasks than the orthographic tasks.

The detailed procedures and results in each task will be described in the following chapters.

Interview

The retrospective interview was conducted on each participant after each task. Each interview was scheduled to be for 2-3 minutes per person per task although it varied in duration depending on how much the participant remarked. The interviews were audio-taped. The interview with the L1 readers was conducted in Japanese. In reporting the results of the interview, the data were translated into English by the investigator.

3.3 Analysis techniques

The previous section described the preparations and procedures for collecting data from the experiments and interviews. The current section will detail how the collected data were analysed. Needless to say, the experimental data and the interview data were analysed separately. However, even within the experimental data, several different analysis techniques were used due to the varied nature of the measures obtained.

3.3.1 Statistical analyses on the results of L1 and L2 readers in the orthographic and phonological tasks

The orthographic and phonological tasks were analysed using standard parametric analysis techniques (analyses of response times and error rates in correct responses). However, a few modifications to standard procedures were made in order to accommodate different requirements.

The first issue concerned the analysis of the different response categories. In the study, all tasks except the semantic ones had two response categories: 'yes' responses and 'no' responses. 'Yes' responses are based upon recognising that some property is present in the stimuli (e.g., the two characters presented share a common reading). On the other hand, 'no' responses are typically generated by the absence of some specified property (e.g., the two characters presented do not share a common reading). However, the situation seemed to be more complicated than that. In some cases, a participant can respond 'no' to the stimulus because it does not meet the 'yes' criterion, and at other times, a 'no' response may be made simply because of a deadline response strategy. In other words, the 'no' responses were given in lieu of 'skips'. Indeed in the interview, a number of the L2 readers, especially at the beginner and intermediate levels, remarked that they had sometimes pressed the 'no' key when they were not sure how to respond. Thus the nature of the process that might have generated this response type is not as clear as in the case of the 'yes' response type. For this reason, only correct 'yes' responses were analysed. Correct 'no' responses (for the task items where a 'no' was the correct response) were not analysed, except for the results of the L1 readers, which were thought to be fairly reliable, given their adequate *kanji* knowledge. Nevertheless, even the results of the analysis of the L1 readers on the 'no' items should be interpreted cautiously.

Response times were recorded in milliseconds. After analysing the results of the L1 readers' records, the minimum cut-off time was set to 266 milliseconds, which was the shortest response time for the L1 readers, as it is unrealistic that any L2 readers could process the *kanji* any quicker than the fastest of the L1 readers. In analysing the data, any values outside of the range between 266 ms and 5000 ms (see Section 3.2 for setting the maximum cut-off time) were excluded.

In psycholinguistic studies where native speakers are the participants, in most cases, not only response times in correct trials but also error rates become the subject of analysis (Harley, 1995), as error rates can provide additional information about the nature of what drove a response. That is, if response times were very quick and there were many errors, it would suggest that the participant was trading response speed for accuracy. However, in the present study, the participants were L2 readers (except for the L1 readers in the skilled readers' group) whose knowledge of Japanese may have been very limited, and therefore their error rates were likely to be high. Therefore, correct response rates instead of error rates were reported in this study, as correct response rates (i.e., scores) provide solid information about the *kanji* recognition skills of the L2 readers of Japanese.

The correct response rate (%) was calculated using the following formula:

# of correct responses / (# of correct + # of incorrect + # of skips) * 100

While most of the cases had 40 responses (# of right + # of wrong + # of skips = 40), a few cases had less than 40 due to pauses, too-quick responses and other unrecordable responses.

In the following sections, analysis procedures for the results of the orthographic and phonological tasks for the L1 readers and for the L2 readers will be discussed. Data for the L1 readers and L2 readers were analysed separately using different statistical

146

packages. There were two steps of analyses: analysis for the examination of general task performance, and analysis for the examination of effects of the stimulus properties (complexity, character frequency, radical frequency and homophone size), as shown below.

Analyses of response times and correct response rates for task performance and for effects of stimulus properties

L1 readers

For the results of the L1 readers, statistical analyses were performed using SPSS version 11 for Macintosh OS X. Firstly, each participant's individual mean response time and correct response rate were calculated. Then, the individual mean response times and mean correct response rates were averaged across the participants in the L1 group in order to obtain mean response times and correct response rates for the 'yes' and 'no' items respectively in each task. Subsequently, the groups' mean response times and correct response rates for the 'yes' and 'no' items were compared using the t-test for paired samples. Then, the results of the two orthographical tasks were compared using the t-test for paired samples. The alpha significance level was set at the 0.05 level. Similar comparisons were made for the phonological tasks.

In order to examine the effects of the stimulus properties on the L1 readers, each group's mean response times and mean correct response rates for the two contrasting categories (i.e., low and high) in each stimulus property (e.g., complexity) were calculated. Subsequently, for the property of 'complexity', differences in mean response times and mean correct response rates for low complexity *kanji* versus high complexity *kanji* were analysed using the t-test for paired samples. The same procedure was repeated for low versus high character frequency *kanji*, low versus high radical frequency *kanji*, and low versus high homophone size *kanji*.

L2 readers

The results of the L2 readers were analysed using the statistical package GenStat (Release 6.1 for Windows). The statistical procedure used was Restricted Maximum Likelihood (REML). REML is similar to Analysis of Variance (ANOVA), but is particularly helpful for analysing unbalanced data (i.e., where the number of observations is not equal across each combination of explanatory variables) within multi-level designs (e.g., subjects within groups, items within properties, and properties within categories of items – see Chapter 3 Section 2 for details). The REML analysis also weighted the observations for each student -task-property combination according to the number of items. Adjusted means (also called predicted means) were produced by the analysis to be used, instead of raw means, for presentation and comparison. An adjusted mean is an estimate of the mean that would be expected if the data had been balanced, i.e., if the number of observations for each combination of explanatory variables were equal. The use of raw arithmetic means would not have been as appropriate, as the unbalanced data could have resulted in a distorted estimate of the central tendency of the results. Due to the unbalanced nature of the data, standard deviations and standard errors across all the data were not very useful to report. The

148

variability in the data, in particular the comparison between means, was quantified and reported on using the least significant difference (LSD) statistic at the 5% level. The LSD equals the standard error of the difference between means (SED) multiplied by the 0.975 quantile of the t-distribution on v degrees of freedom, where v is the residual degrees of freedom from the analysis. However, in the current study, as all the relevant t-distribution values were very close to 2, SEDs were simply doubled to obtain LSDs.

If a pair of means being compared differ by more than the LSD, they are significantly different at the 5% level, and a 95% confidence interval for the difference does not include 0. If the difference between means is less than the LSD, the means are not significantly different, and the 95% confidence interval includes 0. It is then reasonable to believe that the observed difference may be due to random variation rather than being a real difference. In the result sections to follow, the statistics are reported as means, mean difference and LSD, such as 1251 - 923 = 328, LSD = 186, indicating that the difference is significant at the 5% level because the mean difference of 328 is bigger than the LSD value of 186.

For the results of the L2 readers, only the correct responses in the 'yes' items were analysed, as explained earlier. The following steps were used for each pair of orthographic tasks: Firstly, each participant's mean response time and mean correct response rate were calculated. Then, the individual mean response times and mean correct response rates were averaged across the participants within each group (beginner, intermediate and advanced) in order to obtain each group's mean response time and correct response rate for each task. Following this, using the approximate LSDs, the

149

mean response times and correct response rates were compared between the groups

(between the beginner and intermediate, and between intermediate and advanced)

within each orthographic task, and between the two tasks. The same procedure was

followed for the two phonological tasks.

Where an approximate P-value produced by the analysis suggested a significant

effect of either factor, differences in the mean response times and correct response rates

between low versus high in property (e.g., low complexity vs high complexity) and

between the participant groups were compared to the relevant LSDs.

3.3.2 Analyses of the results for L1 and L2 readers in the semantic tasks

For the results of the semantic judgement and semantic categorisation tasks, the

above-described procedure was attempted initially. However, it became clear that while

it was appropriate for the orthographic and phonological tasks, it was problematic for

the analyses of the results of the semantic processing simply because the concept of

correct and incorrect responses is not appropriate to the semantic task. Therefore, as the

semantic tasks did not have well-defined correct or incorrect expected responses,

statistical analyses were not performed. Instead, a descriptive approach to the data was

used such that the response patterns of the L2 readers were contrasted with those of the

L1 readers. Data from the semantic relatedness task (which was conducted on the L1

readers) were analysed initially using a normative approach, and then the data from the

semantic processing tasks were analysed for the L1 and L2 readers separately by comparing them with the results of the analysis of the semantic relatedness task, as described below.

Results for the semantic relatedness task

As described in Section 2 of this chapter, a non-timed semantic relatedness rating task was used as a guide to the degree of the semantic relatedness of stimuli used in the two semantic tasks. The stimuli in the semantic judgement task were pairs of characters that had a common main radical between the two characters (hereafter, common-radical items), and those in the semantic categorisation task were pairs consisting of a character and the semantic category name that was equivalent to the semantic information that the main radical of the *kanji* depicted (hereafter, radical-category items). These two sets of stimuli (40 common-radical items and 40 radical-category items) were rated for their semantic relatedness by a group of L1 readers using a scale marked from 0 to 5 (0 meaning 'not related' and 5 meaning 'strongly related').

A mode value of the rating was calculated for each of the 40 common-radical items, and for each of the 40 radical-category items respectively (the mode rather than mean was used because it preserved the rating structure of the scale, i.e., mean values would result in decimal scores which do not correspond to any actual rating score). Then, the 40 common-radical items were grouped into six different mode categories (as the rating scale was in discrete categories from 0 to 5) according to their mode values, which showed the strength of semantic relatedness (e.g., mode category 5 showed that

151

the items that fell in this category had a strong relationship). The procedure was repeated for the 40 radical-category items.

Comparing the results of the semantic relatedness rating task and the results of the semantic tasks

The results for the semantic relatedness rating task and the semantic processing tasks (semantic judgement and semantic categorisation) were compared in order to see how the participants responded to the items with different degrees of semantic relatedness (shown in mode values) in the timed environment.

L1 readers

Each participant's individual mean response time and mean percentage of 'yes' responses to the items in each mode category were calculated separately for the common-radical items and the radical-category items. Following this, the individual means were averaged across the participants for each mode category. The same procedure was conducted for the 'no' responses. As the purpose of the comparisons was to obtain the participants' response patterns rather than numerical differences between the mode categories, a statistical analysis was not performed. Trends observed in their response patterns will be discussed in Chapter 6 Section 1.

L2 readers

Each participant's individual mean response time and mean percentage of 'yes' responses to the items in each mode category were calculated separately for the common-radical items and the radical-category items. As with the LI procedure, individual means were averaged across the participants, in this case, for each participant group (beginner, intermediate and advanced) for each mode category. The 'no' responses were not analysed for the reason described at the start of this section. The L2 readers' response patterns were compared against the patterns shown by the L1 readers. Trends observed in their response patterns will be discussed in Chapter 6 Section 2.

3.3.3 Protocol analyses

The audio-taped interview was transcribed and then coded to examine particular aspects of processing skills and awareness.The number of participants who made a particular remark is given for reference. However, it should be noted that the remarks were made freely without guided questioning. Therefore the numbers do not reflect the significance of a particular view of the participants.

4 Orthographic processing skills and awareness

Chapters 4, 5 and 6 report and discuss the results of a series of experiments and interviews which investigated orthographic, phonological and semantic processing relating to aspects of character recognition. This chapter will first deal with the results of orthographic tasks for L1 readers followed by those for L2 readers.

4.1 L1 readers of Japanese: Objectives and Methods

4.1.1 Objectives

The process of visual word recognition can usefully be conceived of as involving a series of analyses that tend to become more abstract. Although some processing operations may proceed in parallel, it seems reasonable to assume that initially, some processing of orthographic features (such as shapes, locations, and combinations of orthographic units) is necessary. That is, orthographic information needs to be processed in order for phonological and morphological information processing to occur.

154

This idea of a flow of information processing seems to apply regardless of script type, and indeed, *kanji* recognition is no exception.

When presented with *kanji* characters, skilled readers of Japanese are most likely to process them, as a first step, using orthographic information from the character as a whole and in terms of the combination of components. Recent word recognition models (see Chapter 2 Section 2) propose that skilled readers process characters at multiple levels including the character level and the component level. Given that *kanji* are made of components and that some components carry useful phonological and semantic information, it is reasonable to think that readers need to have the skills to process the relevant orthographic information from the *kanji*. Performance on orthographic processing tasks focusing both on character level processing and on component level processing may indicate the reader's current level of processing skills.

In the process of attaining orthographic processing skills, skilled readers are likely to develop awareness of the structures and functions of orthographic units (see Chapter 2 Section 3). Although awareness may or may not be consciously reflected, verbalisation of metacognitive processing may indicate the extent to which such awareness to a certain extent (see Chapter 3 Section 2 for discussion).

Two orthographic tasks and a retrospective interview were used in order to investigate the development of orthographic processing in character recognition among readers of Japanese with different levels of character knowledge. The tasks used were the character-ness judgement and radical identification tasks (see Chapter 3 for a details). The tasks were designed to tap into the orthographic processes used in character recognition and to determine the associated response patterns of readers. The open-ended interview questions were designed to supplement this data in order to gain greater insight into the readers' orthographic awareness. These tasks and the interview were administered to a group of L1 readers first, and then to three groups of L2 readers. The results of the L1 readers provide a benchmark against which L2 readers' orthographic processing development can be compared.

In this section, L1 readers' performances on the two orthographic tasks and their reflective accounts are reported. Firstly, their response patterns to two types of stimuli, real *kanji* and non-*kanji*, were compared. The effects on their performances of four stimulus properties (complexity, character frequency, radical frequency and homophone size) were also examined. Secondly, the L1 readers' ability to identify a common main radical in two characters was determined. The effects on their performance of the four stimulus properties were also examined. Then, their performances under the two different conditions (character-ness judgement and radical identification) were compared. Finally, the L1 readers' spoken accounts were considered.

4.1.2 Methods

Participants

16 native speakers of Japanese participated in this study. All of these participants met the selection criteria (see Chapter 3 Section 2 for details).

Materials

The two orthographic tasks used were character-ness judgement and radical identification. The character-ness judgement task assessed how quickly and accurately the participants could judge whether or not presented stimuli were real *kanji*. The stimuli were either a real *kanji* or a non-*kanji*. The radical identification task was designed to assess how quickly and accurately the participants could decide whether or not two *kanji* had the same component, which was in fact a main radical. The *kanji* were pairs of characters that shared a common main radical and pairs of characters that did not have a common main radical between them. This task taps how top-down knowledge and familiarity affect a largely perceptual processing (i.e., one can perform this task without having to know any *kanji*).

In each task, eight types of *kanji* with the following stimulus properties were included: low and high complexity, low and high frequency of occurrence, low and high radical frequency, and low and high homophone size. Two versions of the tasks with differently-ordered items were prepared in order to avoid any effect of a particular order of presenting items. A same-different task (a warm-up task) and interview questions were also prepared (see Chapter 3 Section 2 for details).

Procedure

The participants were randomly assigned into two groups. One group of participants undertook the character-ness judgement task before the radical identification task, and the other group did the tasks in the reverse order. Prior to the tasks, as a warm-up, all the participants did the same-or-different judgement task, which consisted of five pairs of graphically identical *kanji* and five pairs of graphically different *kanji* (see Chapter 3 Section 2 for details). After the warm-up task, half of the participants took the character-ness judgement task and the other half took the radical identification task. They then did one phonological task (see Chapter 5) and one semantic task (see Chapter 6) before doing the other orthographic task. In each task, three practice items were provided. The participants were given the results of their performance on the practice items before the start of the full version of each task, and were asked if they would like to move on or redo the practice in order to make sure they understood the instructions for the task.

In the character-ness judgement task, 120 figures (40 real characters, 40 non-*kanji* and 40 fillers) were displayed in succession. An eye-fixation mark (double circles) was displayed for 600 ms before each stimulus, and there was a brief (200 ms) blank frame between the stimuli. Items were presented until a response was made, but the time for the response was limited to five seconds in order to encourage a quick decision.

In the radical identification task, each of the 120 pairs of *kanji* (40 pairs with a common component, 40 pairs without a common component and 40 fillers) was displayed on the computer monitor one *kanji* at a time, one after the other, with an exposure duration of 500 ms. Each test item was centred in the viewing screen. Prior to the first *kanji*, an eye-fixation mark (double circles) was displayed for 600 ms, and between the two *kanji*, a mask (black squire) was displayed for 200ms. The second stimulus was presented until a response was made, but, again, the time for the response was limited to five seconds in order to encourage a quick decision.

The participants were tested individually on one of the two order scrambled versions, which were selected randomly by the computer. They were asked to respond as quickly and as accurately as possible by pressing the 'yes' key for acceptance of the task questions (e.g., Is the figure a real *kanji* character?) or the 'no' key for rejection of the question. The 'skip' button was provided in case the participants could not make a decision. No feedback was given except for the first three practice items.

Immediately after each task, a short interview session was held in which the participants were asked to talk about how they thought they performed the tasks. The retrospective reports were audio-taped, and were later transcribed for qualitative description.

4.2 Results and discussion

In this study, the results of the items for which 'yes' was the correct response ('yes' items), and those for which 'no' was the correct response ('no' items) are both shown (see Chapter 3 Section 1 for detailed explanation of the items). However, as described in the analysis section (Chapter 3 Section 3), the results of the correct 'no' responses should be interpreted cautiously. Only the correct responses in the 'yes' items were analysed for further discussion.

4.2.1 Character-ness judgment task: Reaction times and correct response rates

In the character-ness judgement task, each participant was asked to judge whether or not the stimulus (e.g., 励) was a real character. A 'yes' response was expected for the real *kanji* items and a 'no' response was expected for the non-*kanji* items. Table 4.1 presents the mean response times and mean correct response rates of the L1 readers in the character-ness judgement task for the real-*kanji* items and non-*kanji* items.

Table 4.1 Mean response times and mean correct response rates of the L1 readers in the character-ness judgment task for the real-*kanji* and non-*kanji* items

Group (N)		Character-ness judgment Is the figure a real *kanji* character?					
		Correct Yes responses to the real-*kanji* items			Correct No responses to the non-*kanji* items		
	S1	RT (ms) SD	CR (%) SD	S1	RT (ms) SD	CR (ms) SD	
L1 (16)	較	681 168	97.2 3.8	主亻	661 134	98.4 3.3	

RT = response times in milliseconds; CR = correct response rate in %; N= the number of participants; SD = standard deviation

The L1 readers responded to the character-ness judgement task in less than 0.7 seconds on average. There was no significant difference in response time between the real-*kanji* and non-*kanji* items, t(15)=1.25, p>0.05. There was also no significant difference in correct response rate between the two types of items t(15)=1.52, p>0.05. As expected, the L1 readers obtained near-perfect scores for both real-*kanji* and non-*kanji* items in this task. Moreover, the SDs in this task were low. These results indicated that the performance of the L1 readers was homogeneous with regard to judging character-ness.

4.2.2 Character-ness judgment task: Stimulus properties

Next, statistical examination of the correct responses in the real-*kanji* items was conducted to see if there were any effects of the stimulus properties on the L1 readers' performance.

Complexity

Differences in the responses to the *kanji* that differed in complexity (i.e., low complexity *kanji* versus high complexity *kanji*) were analysed both in terms of mean response times and correct response rates using t-tests for paired samples. Table 4.2 shows mean response times and mean correct response rates for the low and high complexity *kanji*.

Table 4.2 Mean response times and mean correct response rates of the L1 readers in the character-ness judgment task for low and high complexity *kanji*

		Character-ness judgment				
		Is the figure a real *kanji* character? - Yes				
		Low complexity			High complexity	
Group (N)	S1	RT (ms)	CR (%)	S1	RT (ms)	CR (ms)
		SD	SD		SD	SD
L1 (16)	栄	659	95	願	692	95
		142	11.5		179	8.9

RT = response times in milliseconds; CR = correct response rate in %; N= the number of participants; SD = standard deviation

There was no significant difference in response time for the L1 readers' performances between the means for the low and high complexity *kanji*, t(15)=1.79, p>0.05 and none in correct response rate. Clearly, the complexity of the characters did not have an impact on the L1 readers' performance.

Character frequency

Table 4.3 shows mean response times and mean correct response rates for the low and high frequency *kanji*.

Table 4.3 Mean response times and mean correct response rates of the L1 readers in the character-ness judgment task for low and high frequency *kanji*

Group (N)	S1	RT (ms) SD	CR (%) SD	S1	RT (ms) SD	CR (ms) SD
		Character-ness judgment Is the figure a real *kanji* character? - Yes				
		Low character frequency			High character frequency	
L1 (16)	娯	790 199	96.3 8.1	移	667 191	100 0

RT = response times in milliseconds; CR = correct response rate in %; N= the number of participants; SD = standard deviation

The L1 readers responded to the high character frequency *kanji* significantly faster than to the low character frequency *kanji*, t(15)=3.89, p<0.05. On the other hand, there was no significant difference in correct response rate between the low and high frequency *kanji*, t(15)=1.86, p>0.05, although this comparison obviously suffers from a ceiling effect due to the no errors for the high character frequency items.

Radical frequency

Table 4.4 shows mean response times and mean correct response rates for the low and high radical frequency *kanji*.

Table 4.4 Mean response times and mean correct response rates of the L1 readers in the character-ness judgment task for the low and high radical frequency *kanji*

163

	Character-ness judgment Is the figure a real *kanji* character? - Yes					
	Low radical frequency			High radical frequency		
Group (N)	S1	RT (ms) SD	CR (%) SD	S1	RT (ms) SD	CR (ms) SD
L1 (16)	耐	628 151	100 0	板	647 217	100 0

RT = response times in milliseconds; CR = correct response rate in %; N= the number of participants; SD = standard deviation

Similar to the variable of character complexity, differences in radical frequency had no significant effect on the response times, $t(15)<1$, $p>0.05$, and none on the correct response rates, although this comparison also suffers from a ceiling effect due to the no errors both for the low and high character frequency items.

Homophone size

Table 4.5 presents mean response times and mean correct response rates for the low and high homophone size *kanji*.

Table 4.5 Mean response times and mean correct response rates of the L1 readers in the character-ness judgment task for low and high homophone size *kanji*

Character-ness judgment

	Is the figure a real *kanji* character? - Yes					
	Low homophone size			High homophone size		
Group (N)	S1	RT (ms) SD	CR (%) SD	S1	RT (ms) SD	CR (ms) SD
L1 (16)	敏	711 191	92.5 14.4	将	660 170	98.8 5.0

RT = response times in milliseconds; CR = correct response rate in %; N= the number of participants; SD = standard deviation

The L1 readers showed a tendency for processing the high homophone size *kanji* more quickly and accurately than the low homophone size *kanji*. However, the statistical analyses indicated that there were no significant differences either in response speed, t(15)=1.49, p>0.05, or accuracy, t(15)=1.58, p>0.05.

4.2.3 Radical identification task: Reaction times and correct response rates

In the radical identification task, each participant was required to judge whether or not the two stimuli (e.g., 礎 and 硬) shared a common component (e.g., 石). All shared components were the main radicals of the characters. It was envisaged that a 'yes' response would be given for the pairs of characters that shared a common component (hereafter, common-component items) and a 'no' response for the pairs of characters that did not have a common component between them (hereafter, no-common-component items). Table 4.6 presents the mean response times and mean correct response rates of the L1 readers in the radical identification task for the common-component items and no-common-component items.

Table 4.6 Mean response times and mean correct response rates of the L1 readers in the radical identification task for the common-component and no-common-component items

	Radical identification task Do the two figures share a common component?					
	Correct Yes responses to the common-component items			Correct No responses to the no-common-component items		
Group (N)	S1 - S2 Ex	RT (ms) SD	CR (%) SD	S1 - S2 Ex	RT (ms) SD	CR (ms) SD
L1 (16)	礎 - 硬	844 255	83.9 6.8	鎖 - 救	861 222	93.9 4.8

RT = response times in milliseconds; CR = correct response rate in %; N= the number of participants; SD = standard deviation

There was no significant difference in response time between the common-component and no-common-component items, t(15)<1, p>0.05. However, the L1 readers made more errors when judging that there was a common component between the pairs than when judging that there was no common component for the pairs that did not share one. The results of the paired samples t-test showed that the L1 readers responded to the no-common-component items significantly more accurately than to the common-component items, t(15)=4.54, p<0.05. The relatively low correct response rate (83.9%) for the common-component items in this simple task was an unexpected

166

outcome and it suggests a bias towards judging that pairs did not contain a common element.

4.2.4 Radical identification task: Stimulus properties

Complexity

Table 4.7 shows mean response times and mean correct response rates for the low and high complexity *kanji*.

Table 4.7 Mean response times and mean correct response rates of the L1 readers in the radical identification task for low and high complexity *kanji*

	Radical identification task					
	Do the two figures share a common component? –Yes					
	Low complexity			High complexity		
Group (N)	S1 - S2 Ex	RT (ms) SD	CR (%) SD	S1 - S2 Ex	RT (ms) SD	CR (ms) SD
L1 (16)	背 - 肯	762 229	90 16.3	散 - 敷	838 314	83.8 16.7

RT = response times in milliseconds; CR = correct response rate in %; N= the number of participants; SD = standard deviation

Although the L1 readers' performance on the low complexity *kanji* appeared to be quicker and more accurate than on the high-complexity *kanji*, the statistical analyses showed that there was no significant difference between the two groups in response speed, $t(15)=1.79$, $p>0.05$, or accuracy, $t(15)=1$, $p>0.05$. The high SDs showed that the performance was highly variable, particularly for the high complexity *kanji*, and this was the likely reason that the large difference between the means did not produce a statistically significant difference.

Character Frequency

Table 4.8 presents mean response times and mean correct response rates for the low and high frequency *kanji*.

Table 4.8 Mean response times and mean correct response rates of the L1 readers in the radical identification task for low and high frequency *kanji*

	Radical identification task					
	Do the two figures share a common component? –Yes					
	Low character frequency			High character frequency		
Group (N)	S1 - S2	RT (ms)	CR (%)	S1 - S2	RT (ms)	CR (ms)
	Ex	SD	SD	Ex	SD	SD
L1 (16)	胎 - 胆	812	95	彼 - 後	855	81.3
		214	8.9		305	17.1

RT = response times in milliseconds; CR = correct response rate in %; N= the number of participants; SD = standard deviation

There was no significant difference in response time between the low and high frequency *kanji*, t(15)<1, p>0.05. However, the L1 readers performed significantly more accurately on the low frequency *kanji* than on the high frequency *kanji*, t(15)=2.91, p<0.05. Also, the high SDs for the high frequency *kanji* showed that the responses of the L1 readers varied considerably. The fact that the L1 readers were less accurate in the high frequency *kanji* compared to the low frequency *kanji* is contrary to the pattern

traditionally subsumed under the term 'frequency effect'.

Radical Frequency

Table 4.9 shows mean response times and mean correct response rates for the low

and high radical frequency *kanji*.

Table 4.9 Mean response times and mean correct response rates of the L1 readers in the radical identification task for low and high radical frequency *kanji*

	Radical identification task					
	Do the two figures share a common component? –Yes					
	Low radical frequency			High radical frequency		
Group (N)	S1 - S2 Ex	RT (ms) SD	CR (%) SD	S1 - S2 Ex	RT (ms) SD	CR (ms) SD
L1 (16)	延 - 建	971 480	75 22.5	渋 - 混	772 222	91.3 10.2

RT = response times in milliseconds; CR = correct response rate in %; N= the number of participants; SD = standard deviation

L1 readers responded to the *kanji* with rare main radicals significantly more slowly than

to the ones with main radicals of high frequency, t(15)=2.09, p=0.05. Also, the L1

readers made significantly more errors in the low radical frequency *kanji* than for the

high radical frequency *kanji*, t(15)=2.15, p<0.05. Indeed, the correct response rate of the

L1 readers in the *kanji* with a low frequency main radical was rather low (75%).

Moreover, the large SDs (480ms for the response time and 22.3% for the correct response rate) showed that the L1 readers' performances on the low radical frequency *kanji* was very variable.

Homophone size

Mean response times and mean correct response rates for the low and high homophone size *kanji* are shown in Table 4.10.

Table 4.10 Mean response times and mean correct response rates of the L1 readers in the radical identification task for low and high homophone size *kanji*

	Radical identification task					
	Do the two figures share a common component? –Yes					
	Low homophone size			High homophone size		
Group (N)	S1 - S2 Ex	RT (ms) SD	CR (%) SD	S1 - S2 Ex	RT (ms) SD	CR (ms) SD
L1 (16)	卒 - 卓	913 341	77.5 21.8	祉 - 祥	807 229	81.3 13.6

RT = response times in milliseconds; CR = correct response rate in %; N= the number of participants; SD = standard deviation

Despite the difference in means, no significant differences were found between the two groups of *kanji* that differed in homophone size either in response speed, $t(15)=1.53$, $p>0.05$, or accuracy, $t(15)<1$, $p>0.05$. The L1 readers might have read some of the *kanji* in its *kun*-reading rather than its *on*-reading, in which case it would be possible that homophone size did not affect the L1 readers' performance significantly, as Japanese homophones consist mainly of *on*-readings (Tamaoka, 2005).

4.2.5 Comparison between the results of the character-ness judgment and radical identification tasks

Both the character-ness judgment and radical identification tasks were devised as an index associated with the orthographic processing of *kanji* recognition. The notion that both tasks might tap orthographic processing should not be taken as indicating that response times or error rates on the two tasks must be similar. Indeed, the results of the paired samples t-test showed that the L1 readers performed the character-ness judgment task significantly faster than the radical identification task at $t(15)=3.20$, $p<0.05$ for the items for which a 'yes' response was required. Response times were also faster for those items requiring a 'no' response, $t(15)=4.38$ $p<0.05$. Moreover, the L1 readers performed significantly more accurately in the character-ness judgment task than in the radical identification task, $t(15)=9.48$, $p<0.05$ for the items that required a 'yes' response and $t(15)=3.02$, $p<0.05$ for those requiring a 'no' response.

4.2.6 Discussion of the results of the character-ness judgment and radical identification tasks

The results of the tasks showed that the L1 readers performed the character-ness judgment task significantly more quickly and accurately than the radical identification task. The L1 readers' performance in the character-ness judgment task was well-established across the participants, as shown in the fast and accurate responses with low SDs, indicating that (as expected) the L1 readers had well developed orthographic character recognition skills. In the radical identification task, the common component was in fact the same main radical shared by the two characters. Given the high scores of the L1 readers in this task, it is evident that they were able to identify functional components (the main radical of the *kanji* in this case).

Orthographic processing at multiple levels

In the character-ness judgment task, there were no significant differences in response speed and in accuracy between the real *kanji* and the non-real *kanji*. In this task, it might have been possible for the items to be categorised into either type (real *kanji* or non-*kanji*) without full analysis of their components. It has been claimed that word shape is an important variable in identifying familiar words (Healy and Cunningham, 1992). If so, the L1 readers could have judged anything that had legitimate character shapes as real *kanji*, otherwise, as non-*kanji*, as the non-*kanji* with two components in wrong locations must have looked very odd to them. The processing for the character shapes might have therefore involved feature analysis at the component level. It could be the case that the information such as whether or not components were identified in their legitimate locations was sent up to the character level.

In the radical identification task in which the L1 readers were required to analyse components, it was likely that the information necessary for a task response was generated at the component level. Nevertheless, the information generated at the character-level might have also affected responses even though the processing at the component level would have greatly contributed to a response.

Character-dominant processing for high frequency characters

In both the character-ness judgement and the radical identification tasks, both complexity and homophone size had no significant effects on the L1 readers' responses. The question arises as to how to interpret their performances on the high and low frequency *kanji* and on the high and low radical frequency *kanji,* which appear contradictory in the character-ness judgment and radical identification tasks. That is, the L1 readers responded more quickly to the high frequency *kanji* than to the low frequency *kanji* in the character-ness judgment task, but were not affected by radical frequency. In the radical identification task, on the other hand, the L1 readers made fewer errors on the low frequency *kanji* than on the high frequency *kanji*, and responded more quickly and accurately for the high radical frequency *kanji* than the low radical frequency *kanji* (with large variabilities in high frequency *kanji* and low radical frequency *kanji*).

It is a well-established finding that high frequency words are recognised more quickly than low frequency words, both in alphabetic languages (Harley, 1995; Taft and Zhu, 1995; Nagy, Anderson, Schommer, Scott and Stallman, 1989; McClelland and Rumelhart, 1981; Morton, 1980; Taft and Forster, 1975) and in character-based languages (Hong, 1998; Tamaoka and Htsuzuka, 1995; Taft and Zhu, 1995; Tan, Hoosain and Peng, 1995). If high frequency *kanji* are identified faster than low frequency *kanji* at the character level, as recent models and research findings suggest, then how can the L1 readers' reversed frequency effect in the radical-identification task be accounted for?

Healy (1994) has put forward the Unitisation Model that is based upon the findings that individuals searching for target letters in a prose passage make a greater proportion of detection errors (i.e., MLE - missing letter effects) on high frequency words than on low frequency words. The model explains MLE by postulating that skilled readers process high frequency words mainly at a familiar larger-unit level, whereas they process low frequency words mainly at a smaller-unit level (Healy, 1994). The higher level processing does not preclude the processing of any lower levels, but successful completion of processing at a higher level would discourage any further processing at lower levels even if it has not yet been completed (Drewnowski and Healy, 1977). It is plausible then that the L1 readers identified the frequently appearing characters before their components had been fully processed. For the low frequency *kanji*, on the other hand, as the identification of the low frequency *kanji* would be slower, the processing of the component might be completed rapidly enough to affect the decision.

The above scenario however, does not account for the non-significant response time difference between the low and high frequency *kanji* in the radical identification task. Since the task was to identify a common component between two *kanji*, the L1 readers had to process the components and make judgements at the component level regardless of the *kanji* frequency (hence there was no significant difference in response speed between the low and high frequency *kanji*). However, the L1 readers responded significantly more accurately to the low frequency *kanji* than to the high frequency *kanji*. It is reasonable to think that, for the high frequency *kanji*, the output of the early character level processing might have interfered with the component processing, whereas it was less likely for the low frequency *kanji*.

Component level processing for high frequency radicals

In the character-ness judgment task, radical frequency had no significant effect on the L1 readers' performance. On the other hand, it had an impact on their performance in the radical identification task, which required them to focus on components of the *kanji*; the L1 readers performed better on the high frequency main radicals than the low frequency main radicals.

The more a reader sees a word, the more easily they recognise it (Share, 1995). The same might be true for a component. It could be that some frequently-seen main radicals might have formed fixed representations at the component level as independent units in the majority of the L1 readers. In addition, position symbols might be included in these independent units, as Taft and Zhu (1997a) argue. If it were the case, for a pair of characters with a high frequency main radical, an independent representation of the main radical of the first character may be identified in a brief time together with its positional information. For example, when the first character, 柱 is presented, the main radical 木 may be identified at the component level, and the information including the positional information (that this main radical usually appears on the left-hand side of a character) may be passed up to the character level. If this process indeed took place, it is reasonable to think that the common main radical in the second character 杯 can be identified fast and accurately. On the other hand, some lower frequency main radicals might not have been identified as independent units by some of the L1 readers.

The results might be accounted for by the notion of 'lemma', which was proposed by Taft (2004) in his Multilevel Interactive Activation Model. Lemma is defined as a layer of concept units that connect form, meaning and sound (pronunciation) (Taft, 2004). According to this model, any orthographic unit that is consistently associated with a semantic feature has a lemma. All words are represented by a lemma, and most characters also have their own lemma. The characters can stand alone as single-character words (free morphemes) have a strong lemma representation while the ones that need to take another character to form a word (bound morphemes) have a representation, but the link may not be strong. Therefore a free morpheme that has a stronger link to its lemma representation can be recognised much faster (and more accurately) than a bound morpheme that has a weaker link to its lemma representation. In this regard, it could be hypothesised that some high frequency main-radicals (which carried semantic information) might have formed weak lemma representations.

In relation to the above, it is also plausible to think that the L1 readers made use of the information conveyed from the names of the high frequency main radicals. As discussed in Chapter 1 Section 3, most main radicals have names, which may indicate their semantic categories and locations in characters. For example, the aforementioned main radical 木 is called *kihen*, and the *ki* of the *kihen* shows that this main radical represents the semantic category of 'tree', and the *hen* of the *kihen* shows that this radical usually appears on the left-hand side of the character. As this example illustrates, the information in the radical names can be very useful for the identification of the main radicals. However, not all the radical names were known to readers, as uncommon main radicals are not taught at school. The variability in the low frequency radicals could be because some of the L1 readers did not know the names of some of the low frequency main radicals.

Possible semantic processing

As discussed above, componential processing was vital for the radical identification task. Nevertheless, the information generated at the character-level also seemed to have affected the responses as indicated by the reverse frequency effect. If both the kanji and their main radicals were indeed processed, it is plausible to think that the relatively low correct response rate for the common-component items in the radical identification task might be attributed to inconsistent semantic information induced by the characters and their main radicals through their lemma representations. For the pairs with no common main radical, because the two *kanji* with different main radicals would usually have no semantic relations (see Chapter 1 Section 3 for details), the two distinct pieces of semantic information retrieved from the characters might have assisted the L1 readers in deciding that the two *kanji* had no common main radical. However, for the pairs with a common main radical, character identification did not always assist the component level identification, as some *kanji* with the same main radical may have only weak semantic relations. When the meanings of the *kanji* in a pair were only weakly

177

related, the information from the character and from the component would have been inconsistent. For example, one of the pairs that attracted the highest error rate was 普 (prevalence) and 暫 (temporary) with the 'sun/day' radical. In this case, it is unlikely that the meanings of the *kanji* have assisted in identifying a common main radical. On the other hand, one of the pairs that all the L1 readers responded correctly to was 礎 (foundation) and 硬 (hardness) with the 'stone' radical, in which the meanings of the *kanji* could be related to the meaning of the radical. This may also account for the lower correct response rate (83.9%) for the pairs with a common main radical compared to that for the pairs without a common main radical.

Orthographic processing by identification and comparison

Lastly, that the L1 readers' response times were slower in the radical identification task than in the character-ness judgement task needs to be discussed. At one level, this result might appear counter-intuitive, since the characters themselves are composed of radicals which would presumably need to be processed as part of the process of character recognition. This apparent puzzle occurs because the processes involved in the identification of stimuli are presumed to be the same as those that give rise to a response to the task. However, if a distinction is made between the processes involved in analysing the form properties of the stimulus and those that are involved in producing a response to the task, then the results look less mysterious.

The idea of different processes contributing to a response can be made clearer by considering an analysis proposed by Chambers and Forster (1975). They developed a 'multi-level' analysis of the recognition process that proposed that both the speed of feature analysis and subsequent comparisons determine response times. According to this model, (based upon an analysis of English) the process of word recognition can be viewed in terms of three levels of analysis (letter, letter cluster, and word) that operate simultaneously, and as soon as the identification required in the task is completed at any one of these levels, comparisons of the available information occur in order to reach a decision. Now, consider the two tasks in terms of the operations required to give a correct response. In the radical identification task, two *kanji* needed to be compared for a common component (main radical). On the other hand, no comparisons were required in the character-ness judgment task. The longer response times for the radical identification task might have been due to the additional process needed for comparing rather than identifying the stimuli.

In the radical identification task, the information generated at the component level, as well as at the character level, was used for the comparison. If the skilled readers had realised that it was the main radical that they had to look for, then the comparison could have been made just once for the pairs with a common main radical. For the pairs with no common main radical, on the other hand, in order to claim that there was no common main radical between the two *kanji*, all the (non-functional) radicals had to be compared. Therefore, one would expect that the no-common-component items would have required a longer processing time. However, the results showed that there was no significant difference in the response times between the two types of items. There are two possible explanations: first, all the radicals were compared regardless of item type, and second, the comparison was made only once both in the common-component items and no-common-component items because the L1 readers knew where to focus.

The fact that the L1 readers responded more accurately to the no-common-component items than to the common-component items may suggest that the second explanation (the comparison was made only once both in the common-component items and no-common-component items) is more likely. The significant difference in accuracy between the two types of items seems to be due to the relatively low correct response rate for the pairs with a common component (main radical). There were a few characters whose main radicals appeared in less common positions. For example, the main radical of the *kanji* 炭 is 火, which is at the bottom of the *kanji*. If the reader mistook the top part 山 as the main radical, and compared it against the top part of the second *kanji* 災, then s/he could mistakenly reject the second *kanji* as not sharing the same main radical.

In the following section, a summary of the interview data will be presented followed by discussion.

4.2.7 Character-ness judgement task: Interview data

Nine of the 16 participants did not have much to say about this task (see Example 1), probably because they performed the task with ease (see Example 2).

Example 1: I found it easy to do this task.

Example 2: I got into a rhythm while doing this task. And because I did that, I didn't get tired.

Six out of the remaining seven participants found it easy to reject the non-*kanji* which violated the locations of components (see Example 3). One participant mentioned that the ones with the left and right components swapped were easier than the ones with the top-bottom swapped, but another thought that it was the other way around. Two participants said that the non-*kanji* with a line added or subtracted were also easy (see Example 4) and two others said the non-*kanji* of this type were harder to judge than the ones with components in wrong positions. (see Example 5).

Example 3: Those (non-) *kanji* with their components swapped around were very easy to reject.

Example 4: The (non-) *kanji* that had an additional line or a line missing were easy.

Example 5: Additional or missing line was more difficult to judge.

4.2.8 Radical identification task: Interview data

11 out of 16 participants commented on the patterns of the characters and/or the locations of main radicals (see Example 1-2). Eight participants remarked that they

focused on the left or top part of the *kanji*, where the main radical of *kanji* often appears (see Example 3).

Example 1: Those characters that can be divided into right and left are easier than other types. For the other ones, I didn't know where I should focus on.

Example 2: It was easy to detect difference in *hen* (left main radical) in the two *kanji*, but wasn't easy to compare *tsukuri* (right main radical) as I didn't have enough time to look at the right hand side of the *kanji*. Those *kanji* that are segmented into top and bottom are more difficult to make judgement than are those with left and right parts.

Example 3: I mainly looked at the left or top parts of the character because that's where you usually find the main radical.

In the interview, the names of the main radicals were often mentioned, which suggested that the participants might have used a strategy of naming the main radicals for making their judgement (see Example 4).

Example 4: I checked if the two *kanji* had a common main radical by saying the names of main radicals, such as *ninben*, and *gyooninben* is 'no', or *shinnyoo* and *shinnyoo* is right.

Two participants mentioned the frequency of main radicals. It appears that high frequency main radicals were processed with ease. (see Example 5).

Example 5: *Kanji* with the same main radical in the same location were easy to identify, especially ones with the main radicals that you see frequently, such as *sanzui* (water radical).

Two other participants expressed the difficulty of distinguishing graphically similar radicals (see Example 6).

Example 6: Some similar ones like *hi* (日), *tsuki* (月), *kai* (貝), *me* (目), *miru*

(見) were hard to judge.

The remarks of five participants indicated that they sometimes remembered the *kanji* by reading them in the *kun*-reading, which showed the meaning of the *kanji* (see Example 7). A remark made by one of the participants suggested that the access to the meaning was automatic (see Example 8). From the meanings, they retrieved the graphic shapes of the *kanji* (see Example 7) and even at times by tracing out the *kanji* in the air (see Example 9), which is one of the techniques used in *kanji* teaching in Japan.

Example 7: For those ones, I usually remembered the meaning of *kanji* by reading them in the *kun*-reading, and had to retrieve the forms from memory to compare with the second *kanji*.

Example 8: Occasionally the meaning (the *kun*-reading) of the *kanji* were accessed automatically.

Example 9: when I saw the second *kanji*, I recalled its form (the first *kanji*) by quickly writing it out by moving my finger in the air.

4.2.9 Discussion of the interview about the character-ness judgement and radical identification tasks

Routinely-practiced processing

Apparently, the L1 readers felt that the character-ness judgement task was simple to perform. With abundant experience with *kanji*, they were able to say whether the *kanji* was real, or not real by observing the locations of the constituent components. The L1 readers did not have much to say about the task, probably because it was 'natural' and they did not need to bring their awareness into their consciousness.

The term 'natural' needs further consideration. Given the fact that the L1 readers could not verbalise what they were thinking while doing the character-ness judgement task, it is reasonable to think that they performed this task at an attention-free level. The Bilingual Interactive Activation Plus (BIA+) Model proposes that word recognition is a product of a specialised identification system, which operates over linguistic representations, and a task/decision system, which utilises non-linguistic task schema specifications (Dijkstra and Van Heuven, 2002). Although this model was developed to account for the word processing mechanism of bilinguals, the notions of an identification and a task/decision system are applicable to word recognition in general. This model emphasises the view that basic linguistic processes are carried out by the identification system whereas process such as instructions, task demands and participant strategies affect the task/decision system (Dijkstra and Van Heuven, 2002). The BIA+ Model proposes that the identification system operates early on in the processing hierarchy at the preconscious level, and provides continuous output to the task/decision system, which uses the information at an attention-sensitive level.

Conceivably, in the character-ness judgement task, there were fewer burdens on the task/decision system compared to the radical identification task. That is, in the character-ness judgement task the L1 readers might not have had to control the output from the identification system in order to respond to the task, resulting in shorter response times (see Chapter 4 Section 1) and less retrospective reports, compared to the case in the radical identification task. On the other hand, performance on the radical identification task was likely to be determined by the task/decision system, where information that had become available in the preconscious identification system was selectively used for the decision making.

Semantic and phonological processing

One might think that both the character-ness judgement and the radical identification tasks could be performed without accessing the phonological and semantic domains, as it is logically possible to perform these tasks without requiring such information. Nevertheless, the interview data suggested that the L1 readers utilised phonological (and in some cases semantic) information in order to compare two characters in the radical identification task.

Under standard models of short-term memory (e.g., Baddeley, 2000), phonological processing would be required for storing stimuli in the short-term memory. It has been claimed that phonologically encoded information is better retained in the

STM regardless of different orthographic types (Koda, 1993; Mou and Anderson, 1981; Tzeng and Hung, 1980). Moreover, semantic activation seems to take place as the phonological information is accessed. For example, in a study investigating phonological and semantic processing in two-*kanji* compound words, Morita and Matsuda (2000) found evidence of phonological activation in a synonym judgement task and semantic activation in a homophone judgement task, suggesting that both forms of information were routinely employed in performing these tasks even though they were not specifically required. Thus, it appears that phonological and semantic activation is mandatory in the preconscious identification system for L1 readers. This suggests that lemmas (representations that connect the three major aspects of a lexical item: form, pronunciation and meaning) have been formed in L1 readers' recognition network (see Chapter 2 Section 2 for details).

Processing in a meaningful unit

When the phonological information of the *kanji* becomes available, according to the Multilevel Interactive Activation Model (Taft and Zhu, 1995), other *kanji* characters with the same pronunciation become activated. In this regard, homophone size could affect the L1 readers' performances on these tasks. Tamaoka (2005) found that the homophone size of the left-hand side *kanji* of two-*kanji* compound words affected the performance of his participants in the lexical decision and naming tasks, as it was speculated that the participants had to suppress these homophones in order to perform the task. However, in the present study, there was no significant effect of the homophone size. This might be due to the fact that Japanese homophones consist of, mainly, *on*-readings (Tamaoka, 2005). In Tamaoka's study, two-*kanji* compound words (which are usually read in the *on*-reading) were used as the stimuli, and therefore, the participants were likely to have read them in the on-reading. On the other hand, as can be seen in the interview data summary, the participants in the current study seemed to have read the stimuli in the *kun*-reading whenever available. This might account for why the participants were not affected by the homophone size.

It appears that the meaning of the *kanji* was accessed via its *kun*-reading if the *kanji* had one, as the *kun*-reading is usually closely related to the meaning (see Chapter 1 Section 3). It may be more reasonable to say however, that the kanji were read in a meaning-bearing reading, because although a meaning-bearing reading is in most cases a *kun*-reading, it can be an *on*-reading on rare occasions (see Chapter 1 Section 3). The interview data suggest that the L1 readers usually read the *kanji* in the meaning-bearing readings. However, in the case where there was no meaning-bearing reading, it seems that the L1 readers put the *kanji* in a meaningful compound word, from which the meaning of individual *kanji* was probably accessed. And from that meaning, they might have retrieved or re-accessed the graphic form of the *kanji* (i.e., a cluster of radicals), in order to compare it with the second *kanji*.

In this regard, some L1 readers remarked that they read some main radicals by their names in order to remember their graphic forms for comparison, and that they had difficulty remembering the main radicals when they did not have names (although all the main radicals have names, some of them are not well-known).

There were other comments made in the interviews suggesting that low frequency main radicals were harder to judge than high frequency main radicals. The results of the analysis of the effect of the stimulus properties indeed showed that the L1 readers responded to the high frequency main radicals more quickly and more accurately than to the low frequency main radicals (see above). Taking the above together, it is plausible to think that the high frequency main radicals had a status as a functional component (main radical) whereas the low frequency main radicals might have been identified merely as one of the radicals. It might be the case then that only the high frequency main radicals holding a status as a functional component have their lemma representations (and therefore these main radicals can be read by their names).

Different task/decision strategies

The above remarks from the L1 readers that they focused on the main radicals may seem to suggest that processing may be limited to the component level. The various remarks given in the interviews for the radical identification task clearly showed that the L1 readers were aware of components and their positions and combinations. The L1 readers showed that they were able to segment a *kanji* into the main radical and non-main-radical parts. Moreover, it seems that they also knew that the main radical would often appear at the left-hand side or at the top of the *kanji*. In other words, they were most likely to know where to focus.

However, this interpretation that some L1 readers focused on the main radicals may be inconsistent with recent models such as the Multilevel Interactive Activation

Model for characters (Taft and Zhu, 1995) that assumes simultaneous activation at different levels. It may be more reasonable to think that, although multiple levels were active, the output of one was chosen by the task/decision system. The interview data indeed indicated that there were various processing strategies employed by the L1 readers. Although in some respects basic orthographic processing (the output from the preconscious identification system) was similar among the L1 readers, some could have used the information from the component level more than the information from the character level, or vice versa. These variations could be due to the readers' individual differences and/or the distinctive graphical features of each character. Dijkstra and Van Heuven (2002) claim that variant response patterns in different tasks, or even within the same task, are due to different uses of task/decision strategies, as the processing pattern in the identification system itself always stays the same. If word recognition is indeed a product of an identification system and a task/decision system, the variant strategies controlled by the task/decision system could have affected the *kanji* recognition performance of the L1 readers.

4.3 L2 readers of Japanese: Objectives and Methods

4.3.1 Objectives

As a comparison to the L1 results just discussed, a large-scale study was conducted to investigate the orthographic processing skills and awareness of L2 readers. At the broadest level, L2 readers were expected to develop their *kanji* recognition skills and awareness as their *kanji* vocabulary grew. To this end, L2 readers were assessed for their *kanji* vocabulary size using a *kanji* knowledge test (see Chapter 3 for details), and according to the results of this test, the participants were divided into three broad categories: beginner, intermediate and advanced. Two orthographic processing tasks and a retrospective interview (see Chapter 3 for details) were used to examine their orthographic processing skills and awareness.

This section reports the L2 readers' performance on the two orthographic tasks (the character-ness judgement and radical identification tasks) and the participants' reflective accounts. Firstly, the ability to judge 'character-ness' was compared across the three groups. The effects of four stimulus properties (complexity, character frequency, radical frequency and homophone size) were also examined. Secondly, the L2 readers' ability to identify a common main radical in two characters was compared across the groups. The effects of the four stimulus properties were also examined. Then, their performances in the two different tasks were compared. The last section reports the L2 readers' spoken accounts.

4.3.2 Methods

Participants

109 graduate and undergraduate university students participated in this study. The 109 L2 readers were grouped into 39 beginner, 40 intermediate and 30 advanced L2 readers of *kanji* according to their *kanji* vocabulary level. Among them, 32 beginner, 20 intermediate and 17 advanced readers did the character-ness judgement task, and 30 beginner, 20 intermediate and 17 advanced readers undertook the radical identification

task. The beginner group was larger compared to the other groups. This was because most of the beginner participants were asked to take the relatively easy orthographic tasks first in order to give some initial satisfaction prior to the start of the other difficult tasks (see Chapter 3 Section 2 for details).

Materials

In order to assess the *kanji* knowledge of the L2 readers, a *kanji* knowledge test that consisted of three lists of *kanji* from beginner, intermediate and advanced levels was used (see Chapter 3 Section 2 for details).

For assessing the L2 readers' *kanji* processing skills, the same two orthographic tasks used for the L1 readers were utilised.

Procedure

The L2 readers were first shown lists of *kanji* and asked if they were familiar with the group of *kanji* in each of the three lists. After they were asked to identify the list they were most familiar with (beginner, intermediate or advanced), they were required to tick all the *kanji* that they knew. Their kanji knowledge level was determined according to the number of the kanji ticked.

The procedure of administering the tasks was the same as for the previous study with the L1 readers.

4.4 L2 readers: Results and discussion

The mean values shown in this section are all adjusted means. As mentioned in Chapter 3 Section 3, all means were adjusted by weighting for the number of observations. The results of the analyses are presented in terms of LSD statistic instead of F-values or t-values. The correct 'no' responses for the items that required a 'no' response ('no' items) were excluded from the analyses (see Chapter 3 Section 3 for details).

4.4.1 Character-ness judgement task: Reaction times and correct response rates

In the character-ness judgement task, each participant (beginner, intermediate and advanced) was asked to judge whether or not the stimulus (e.g. 励) was a real character. Table 4.11 shows mean reaction times on the correct responses and correct response rates for the real-*kanji* items ('yes' items).

Table 4.11 Mean reaction times and correct response rates of the beginner, intermediate and advanced L2 readers in the character-ness judgement task for the real-*kanji* items

	Character-ness judgement task 励	
	Is the figure a real *kanji* character?- Yes	
Group	RT (ms)	CR (%)
Beg	1423	58.5
Int	1251	79.6
Adv	923	85.8

Beg = L2 readers of Japanese who knew 50-300 *kanji*; Int = L2 readers of Japanese who knew 300 - 1,000 *kanji*; Adv = L2 readers of Japanese who knew more than 1,000 *kanji*; RT = reaction times in milliseconds; CR = correct response rate in %.

In this task, the reaction times decreased as the level of *kanji* knowledge increased. The Advanced L2 readers responded to the real-*kanji* items significantly faster than the intermediate readers, (923 - 1251 = -328, LSD = 186), and the intermediate readers were faster than the beginner readers although the difference was only just significant, (1251 - 1423 = -172, LSD = 172). With regard to accuracy, there was no significant difference between the advanced and intermediate readers, (85.8 - 79.6 = 6.2, LSD = 11.1). The intermediate readers however, performed significantly more accurately than the beginner readers (79.6 - 58.5 = 21.1, LSD = 9.7).

4.4.2 Character-ness judgement task: Stimulus properties

Complexity

Differences in response to *kanji* that differed in complexity were analysed both in terms of mean reaction time and correct response rate (see Chapter 3 Section 3 for details). Table 4.12 shows mean reaction times and mean correct response rates for the low and high complexity *kanji*.

Table 4.12 Mean reaction times and mean correct response rates of the L2 readers in the character-ness judgement task for low and high complexity *kanji*

	Character-ness judgement task			
	Is the figure a real *kanji* character?- Yes			
	Low complexity 栄		High complexity 願	
Group	RT (ms)	CR (%)	RT (ms)	CR (%)
Beg	1333	57.5	1500	60.0
Int	1232	75.0	1242	79.0
Adv	851	85.9	1098	87.1

Beg = L2 readers of Japanese who knew 50-300 *kanji*, Int = L2 readers of Japanese who knew 300 - 1,000 *kanji*, Adv = L2 readers of Japanese who knew more than 1,000 *kanji*, RT = mean reaction times in milliseconds, CR = mean correct response rate in %.

For reaction time, the main effects of both complexity (p = 0.003) and kanji knowledge (p = 0.001) were observed. No significant interaction effect was observed (complexity x kanji knowledge: p = 0.135). For the correct response rate, only the main effect of kanji knowledge (p < 0.001) was significant. Neither the main effect of complexity nor interaction was significant (complexity: p = 0.425; complexity x kanji knowledge: p = 0.951).

Reaction time - complexity effect

The beginner and advanced groups responded to the low complexity *kanji* significantly more quickly than to the high complexity *kanji* (beginner: 1333 - 1500 = -167, LSD = 156; advanced: 851 - 1098 = -247, LSD= 173). However, the intermediate readers showed no significant difference in reaction time between the low and high complexity *kanji* (1232 - 1242 = -10. LSD = 169).

It was interesting to find that *kanji* complexity affected the reaction times of the L2 readers at both ends of the skill continuum: the beginner and advanced groups responded to the low complexity *kanji* significantly faster than to the high complexity *kanji*.

Reaction time - kanji knowledge effect

The reaction time of the advanced readers to the low complexity *kanji* was significantly quicker than that of the intermediate readers (851 - 1232 = -381. LSD = 287). However, there was no significant difference between the intermediate and beginner groups (1232 - 1333 = -101. LSD = 258). For the high complexity *kanji*, the difference between the advanced and intermediate groups was not significant (1098 - 1242 = -144. LSD = 285). However, the beginner group was significantly slower than the intermediate group (1500 - 1242 = 258, LSD = 256).

Correct response rate - kanji knowledge effect

The intermediate group performed significantly more accurately than the beginner group both for the low complexity (75 - 57.5 = 17.5, LSD = 12) and the high complexity *kanji* (79 - 60 = 19, LSD = 12). On the other hand, there was no significant difference between the advanced and intermediate groups for either the low complexity (85.9 - 75 = 10.9. LSD = 13.9) or the high complexity *kanji* (87.1 - 79 = 8.1. LSD = 13.9).

Character frequency

Mean reaction times and correct response rates of the L2 readers for the low and high frequency *kanji* are presented in Table 4.13.

Table 4.13 Mean reaction times and mean correct response rates of the L2 readers in the character-ness judgement task for low and high frequency *kanji*

| | Character-ness judgement task
Is the figure a real *kanji* character?- Yes | | | |
| | Low character frequency 娯 | | High character frequency 移 | |
Group	RT (ms)	CR (%)	RT (ms)	CR (%)
Beg	1569	38.8	1306	75.0
Int	1448	50.0	1056	97.0
Adv	1118	69.4	893	98.8

Beg = L2 readers of Japanese who knew 50-300 *kanji*, Int = L2 readers of Japanese who knew 300 - 1,000 *kanji*, Adv = L2 readers of Japanese who knew more than 1,000 *kanji*, RT = mean reaction times in milliseconds, CR = mean correct response rate in %.

The main effects of character frequency ($p < 0.001$) and kanji knowledge ($p = 0.002$) were significant, and no significant interaction effect was observed (character frequency x kanji knowledge: $p = 0.439$) for reaction time. Likewise, for correct response rate, the main effects of character frequency ($p < 0.001$) and kanji knowledge ($p < 0.001$) were significant, and there was no interaction effect (character frequency x kanji knowledge: $p = 0.09$).

Reaction time - character frequency effect

All the three groups responded to the *kanji* that are frequently seen (the high frequency *kanji*) more quickly than to the *kanji* that are rarely seen (the low frequency *kanji*). The differences were all significant: for the beginner (1306- 1569 = -263, LSD = 178), intermediate (1056 - 1448 = -392, LSD = 195) and advanced groups (893 - 1118 = -225, LSD= 191).

Reaction time - kanji knowledge effect

The advanced L2 readers responded to the low frequency *kanji* significantly faster than the intermediate readers (1118 - 1448 = -330. LSD = 301), but there was no significant difference in reaction time between the intermediate and beginner readers (1448 - 1569 = -121. LSD = 282). For the high frequency *kanji*, there was no significant difference between the advanced and intermediate readers (893 - 1056 = -163. LSD = 266). The intermediate readers responded to the high frequency *kanji* significantly faster than the beginner readers (1056 - 1306 = -250, LSD = 237).

Correct response rate - character frequency effect

All three groups performed more accurately for the high frequency *kanji* than the low frequency *kanji*. The differences were all significant: for the beginner (75 - 38.8 = 36.2, LSD = 8.8), intermediate (97 - 50 = 47, LSD = 11.1) and advanced groups (98.8 - 69.4 = 29.4, LSD = 12).

Correct response rate - kanji knowledge effect

The L2 readers' correct response rates showed exactly the same pattern as their reaction times. The advanced readers performed significantly more accurately than the intermediate readers (69.4 - 50 = 19.4, LSD = 13.4) for the low frequency *kanji*, but the difference between the intermediate and beginner readers was not quite significant (50 - 38.8 = 11.2. LSD = 11.6). For the high frequency *kanji*, the advanced readers were not significantly more accurate than the intermediate readers (98.8 - 97 = 1.8. LSD = 13.4). However, the intermediate readers performed significantly more accurately than the beginner readers (97 - 75 = 22, LSD = 11.6).

Radical frequency

Table 4.14 presents mean reaction times and mean correct response rates for the low and high radical frequency *kanji*.

Table 4.14 Mean reaction times and mean correct response rates of L2 readers in the character-ness judgement task for low and high radical frequency *kanji*

Group	Character-ness judgement task Is the figure a real *kanji* character?- Yes			
	Low radical frequency 耐		High radical frequency 板	
	RT (ms)	CR (%)	RT (ms)	CR (%)
Beg	1339	46.3	1353	77.5
Int	1318	72.0	1099	97.0
Adv	902	84.7	777	95.3

Beg = L2 readers of Japanese who knew 50-300 *kanji*, Int = L2 readers of Japanese who knew 300 - 1,000 *kanji*, Adv = L2 readers of Japanese who knew more than 1,000 *kanji*, RT = mean reaction times in milliseconds, CR = mean correct response rate in %

For reaction speed, the main effects of both radical frequency (p = 0.01) and kanji knowledge (p < 0.001) were significant. The interaction effect was not significant (p = 0.062). Significant main effects of radical frequency (p < 0.001) and kanji knowledge (p < 0.001) and interaction effect (p = 0.014) were observed also for accuracy.

Reaction time - radical frequency effect

The intermediate readers responded to the *kanji* with a frequently appearing main radical (high radical frequency *kanji*) significantly more quickly than to the *kanji* with a less frequently appearing main radical (low radical frequency *kanji*) (1099 - 1318 = -219, LSD = 143). However, for the beginner and advanced readers, reaction times between the two groups of *kanji* that differed in radical frequency were not significant (beginner: 1353 - 1339 = 14, LSD = 138; advanced: 777 - 902 = -125, LSD = 149).

Reaction time - kanji knowledge effect

The advanced L2 readers responded to the low radical frequency *kanji* significantly more quickly than the intermediate readers (902 - 1318 = -416, LSD = 262), but there was no significant difference between the intermediate and beginner readers (1318 - 1339 = -21, LSD = 242). For the high radical frequency *kanji*, the advanced readers responded to the *kanji* significantly faster than the intermediate readers (777 - 1099 = -322, LSD = 253) and the intermediate readers were significantly faster than the beginner readers (1099 - 1353 = -254, LSD = 223).

Correct response rate - radical frequency effect

The beginner and intermediate readers performed significantly more accurately on the high radical frequency *kanji* than on the low radical frequency *kanji* (beginner: 77.5 - 46.3 = 31.2, LSD = 8.3; intermediate: 97 - 72 = 25, LSD = 11.4), but the difference in the advanced readers' correct response rates between the low and high radical frequency *kanji* was not significant (95.3 - 84,7 = 10.6, LSD = 11.4).

Correct response rate - kanji knowledge effect

There was no significant difference in accuracy between the advanced and intermediate readers (84.7 - 72 = 12.7, LSD = 13.6) for the low radical frequency *kanji*. On the other hand, the intermediate readers responded to the low radical frequency *kanji* significantly more accurately than the beginner readers (72 - 46.3 = 25.7, LSD = 11.7). Likewise, for the high radical frequency *kanji*, no significant difference was observed between the advanced and intermediate readers (95.3 - 97 = -1.7, LSD = 13.6), but the intermediate readers' performance was significantly more accurate than that of the beginner readers (97 - 77.5 = 19.5, LSD = 11.7).

Correct response rate - interaction effect

Radical frequency impacted the most on the beginner readers' correct response rate (77.5 - 46.3 = 31.2, LSD = 8.3). As the kanji knowledge level increased, the effect became smaller. As illustrated above, the radical frequency did not affect advanced readers' performance significantly.

Homophone size

Table 4.15 presents mean reaction times and mean correct response rates for the low and high homophone size *kanji*.

Table 4.15 Mean reaction times and mean correct response rates of the L2 readers in the character-ness judgement task for low and high homophone size _kanji_

	Character-ness judgement task			
	Is the figure a real _kanji_ character?- Yes			
	Low homophone size 敏		High homophone size 将	
Group	RT (ms)	CR (%)	RT (ms)	CR (%)
Beg	1603	55.0	1447	58.1
Int	1277	86.0	1496	77.0
Adv	883	83.5	910	85.9

Beg = L2 readers of Japanese who knew 50-300 _kanji_, Int = L2 readers of Japanese who knew 300 - 1,000 _kanji_, Adv = L2 readers of Japanese who knew more than 1,000 _kanji_, RT = mean reaction times in milliseconds, CR = mean correct response rate in %.

Only the main effect of kanji knowledge was significant for reaction time ($p < 0.001$). The main effect of homophone size ($p = 0.706$) and the interaction effect ($p = 0.054$) were not significant. Also for correct response rate, only the main effect of kanji knowledge was significant ($p < 0.001$). The main effect of homophone size ($p = 0.85$) and interaction effect ($p = 0.213$) were not significant.

The homophone size had no significant effect on the L2 readers' performance at any *kanji* knowledge level either in terms of speed or accuracy.

Reaction time - kanji knowledge effect

The advanced L2 readers responded to the *kanji* with few homophones (low homophone *kanji*) significantly more quickly than the intermediate readers (883 - 1277 = -394, LSD = 314), and the intermediate readers responded significantly faster than the beginner readers (1277 - 1603 = -326, LSD = 288). The advanced readers also responded to the *kanji* with many homophones (the high homophone size *kanji*) significantly faster than the intermediate readers (910 - 1496 = -586, LSD = 318), but there was no significant difference between the intermediate and beginner readers (1496 - 1447 = 49, LSD = 292).

Correct response rate - kanji knowledge effect

The intermediate readers performed significantly more accurately than the beginner readers on the low homophone size *kanji* (86 - 55 = 31, LSD = 13.2) and on the high homophone size *kanji* (77 - 58.1 = 18.9, LSD = 13.2). However, there were no significant differences between the advanced and intermediate readers for the low (83.5 - 86 = -2.5, LSD = 15.3) and the high homophone size *kanji* (85.9 - 77 = 8.9, LSD = 15.3).

4.4.3 Radical identification task: Reaction times and correct response rates

In the radical identification task, each participant (beginner, intermediate and advanced) was required to judge whether or not the two stimuli (e.g. 礎 and 硬) shared a common component (e.g. 石). Table 4.16 presents mean reaction times for the correct responses and correct response rates of the beginner, intermediate and advanced L2 readers in the radical identification task for the common-component items ('yes' items).

Table 4.16 Mean reaction times and mean correct response rates of the beginner, intermediate and advanced L2 readers in the radical identification task for the common-component

| | Radical identification task 礎 - 硬 | |
| | Do the two figures share a common component?- Yes | |
Group	RT (ms)	CR (%)
Beg	923	72.0
Int	895	81.9
Adv	879	82.5

Beg = L2 readers of Japanese who knew 50-300 *kanji*; Int = L2 readers of Japanese who knew 300 - 1,000 *kanji*; Adv = L2 readers of Japanese who knew more than 1,000 *kanji*; RT = reaction times in milliseconds; CR = correct response rate in %.

Although the pattern of response times was predictable, no significant differences in reaction speed were found between the groups (between advanced and intermediate: 879 - 895 = -16, LSD = 187; between intermediate and beginner: 895 - 923 = -28, LSD = 167; between advanced and beginner: 879 – 923 = -44, LSD = 174). The analysis of the mean correct response rates showed that the intermediate groups performed the task significantly more accurately than the beginner group (81.9 - 72.0 = 9.9, LSD = 9.8). There was no significant difference between the advanced and intermediate readers (82.5 - 81.9 = 0.6, LSD = 11.1).

4.4.4 Radical identification task: Stimulus properties

Complexity

Table 4.17 shows mean reaction times and mean correct response rates for the low and high complexity *kanji*.

Table 4.17 Mean reaction times and mean correct response rates of the L2 readers in the radical identification task for low and high complexity *kanji*

	Radical identification task			
	Do the two figures share a common component? – Yes			
	Low complexity 背 - 肯		High complexity 散 - 敷	
Group	RT (ms)	CR (%)	RT (ms)	CR (%)
Beg	872	76.0	910	59.3
Int	843	91.0	835	78.0
Adv	824	94.1	844	77.7

Beg = L2 readers of Japanese who knew 50-300 *kanji*, Int = L2 readers of Japanese who knew 300 - 1,000 *kanji*, Adv = L2 readers of Japanese who knew more than 1,000 *kanji*, RT = mean reaction times in milliseconds, CR = mean correct response rate in %.

Neither the main effects nor the interaction effect of complexity and kanji knowledge were significant for response speed (complexity: p = 0.472; kanji knowledge: p = 0.644; complexity x kanji knowledge: p = 0.73). For accuracy, the main effects of both complexity (p < 0.001) and kanji knowledge (p < 0.001) were significant, but the interaction effect between them was not (complexity x kanji knowledge: p = 0.855).

Correct response rate - complexity effect

The analysis of the mean correct response rates showed that the L2 readers performed significantly more accurately on the low complexity *kanji* than the high complexity *kanji* in all three groups: beginner (76 – 59.3 = 16.7, LSD = 8.9), intermediate (91 – 78 = 13, LSD = 10.8) and advanced (94.1 – 77.7 = 16.4, LSD = 11.7).

The character complexity affected the L2 readers across the *kanji* level groups, although their reaction times did not differ significantly.

Correct response rate - kanji knowledge effect

Although there were no significant differences between the advanced and intermediate groups both for the low complexity *kanji* (94 - 91 = 3, LSD = 13.2) and high complexity *kanji* (77.6 - 78 = -0.4. LSD = 13.2), the intermediate readers' performance was significantly more accurate than the beginner readers on the low complexity *kanji* (91 – 76 = 15, LSD = 11.5) and the high complexity *kanji* (78 – 59.3 = 18.7, LSD = 11.5).

The intermediate and advanced readers were able to identify the main radicals of the *kanji* more accurately than the beginner readers.

Character Frequency

Table 4.18 presents mean reaction times and mean correct response rates for the low and high frequency *kanji*.

Table 4.18 Mean reaction times and mean correct response rates of the L2 readers in the radical identification task for low and high frequency *kanji*

| | Radical identification task Do the two figures share a common component?- Yes | | | |
| | Low character frequency 胎 - 胆 | | High character frequency 彼 - 後 | |
Group	RT (ms)	CR (%)	RT (ms)	CR (%)
Beg	946	66.7	948	72.7
Int	865	86.0	860	70.0
Adv	824	91.7	903	74.1

Beg = L2 readers of Japanese who knew 50-300 *kanji*, Int = L2 readers of Japanese who knew 300 - 1,000 *kanji*, Adv = L2 readers of Japanese who knew more than 1,000 *kanji*, RT = mean reaction times in milliseconds, CR = mean correct response rate in %.

For reaction time, neither the main effects nor the interaction effect of kanji knowledge and character frequency were significant (character frequency: $p = 0.558$; kanji knowledge: $p = 0.447$; character frequency x kanji knowledge: $p = 0.622$). For correct response rate, there were significant main effects of character frequency and kanji knowledge (character frequency: p = 0.043; kanji knowledge: p = 0.015). The interaction of character frequency and kanji knowledge was also significant (p = 0.002).

Correct response rate - character frequency effect

The beginner readers did not show a significant performance difference between the low and high frequency kanji (66.7 - 72.7 = -6, LSD = 9.7). On the other hand, the intermediate (86 - 70 = 16, LSD = 11.9) and advanced readers (91.8 - 74.1 = 17.7, LSD = 12.9) performed significantly more accurately on the low frequency kanji than on the high frequency kanji.

Correct response rate - kanji knowledge effect

All of the three groups did fairly well for the high frequency *kanji*, and there were no significant differences in correct response rate between the advanced and intermediate (74.1 - 70 = 4.1, LSD = 13.6) and between the intermediate and beginners (70 - 72.7 = -2.7, LSD = 11.9). On the other hand, a large difference was observed in performance on the low frequency *kanji* for the beginner group compared to the intermediate group. The intermediate readers identified the main radical of the low frequency *kanji* significantly more accurately than the beginner readers (86 - 66.7 = 19.3, LSD = 11.9). However, there was no significant difference between the advanced and intermediate readers (91. 8 - 86 = 5.6, LSD = 13.6).

Correct response rate - interaction effect

The results indicated that the (advanced and intermediate) L2 readers found a common component between two *kanji* more accurately in the low frequency *kanji* than in the high frequency *kanji*. On the other hand, those with only a limited amount of kanji knowledge (i.e., the beginner readers) did not show a significant difference between the low and high frequency *kanji*.

Radical Frequency

Table 4.19 presents mean reaction times and correct response rates for the low and high radical frequency *kanji*.

Table 4.19 Mean reaction times and mean correct response rates of the L2 readers in the radical identification task for low and high radical frequency *kanji*

	Radical identification task Do the two figures share a common component? - Yes			
	Low radical frequency 延 - 建		High radical frequency 渋 - 混	
Group	RT (ms)	CR (%)	RT (ms)	CR (%)
Beg	895	76.7	972	78.0
Int	952	76.0	919	86.0
Adv	919	68.2	820	94.1

Beg = L2 readers of Japanese who knew 50-300 *kanji*, Int = L2 readers of Japanese who knew 300 - 1,000 *kanji*, Adv = L2 readers of Japanese who knew more than 1,000 *kanji*, RT = mean reaction times in milliseconds, CR = mean correct response rate in %.

209

Neither the main effects nor the interaction effect of kanji knowledge and radical frequency were significant for reaction speed (radical frequency: p = 0.948; kanji knowledge: p = 0.608; radical frequency x kanji knowledge: p = 0.083). For accuracy, the main effect of kanji knowledge was not significant (kanji knowledge: p = 0.518). A main effect of radical frequency (p = 0.004) for correct response rate was found, and there was a significant interaction effect of radical frequency and kanji knowledge (radical frequency x kanji knowledge: p = 0.018)

Correct response rate - radical frequency effect

Both the beginner and intermediate readers performed fairly well for the low and high radical frequency *kanji*, and there were no significant differences between the two groups of *kanji* (beginner: 76.7 – 78 = -1.3, LSD = 10.4; intermediate: 76 – 86 = -10, LSD = 12.8).

On the other hand, the advanced L2 readers were significantly more accurate on the high radical frequency *kanji* than on the low radical frequency *kanji* (94.1 – 68.2 = 25.9, LSD = 13.8).

Correct response rate - interaction effect

While the frequency of main radicals did not impact on the performance of the L2 readers with beginner or intermediate levels of kanji knowledge, it significantly affected the advanced readers, who had been exposed to a number of main radicals.

Homophone size

Table 4.20 presents mean reaction times and mean correct response rates for the low and high homophone size *kanji*.

Table 4.20 Mean reaction times and mean correct response rates of the L2 readers in the radical identification task for low and high homophone size *kanji*

	Radical identification task			
	Do the two figures share a common component? - Yes			
	Low homophone size 卒 - 卓		High homophone size 祉 - 祥	
Group	RT (ms)	CR (%)	RT (ms)	CR (%)
Beg	1015	72.0	793	74.7
Int	1006	84.0	880	87.0
Adv	947	76.5	917	84.7

Beg = L2 readers of Japanese who knew 50-300 *kanji*, Int = L2 readers of Japanese who knew 300 - 1,000 *kanji*, Adv = L2 readers of Japanese who knew more than 1,000 *kanji*, RT = mean reaction times in milliseconds, CR = mean correct response rate in %.

Only the main effect of homophone size ($p < 0.001$) was significant, and neither the main effect for kanji knowledge nor the interaction of homophone size and kanji knowledge was observed for reaction time (kanji knowledge: $p = 0.885$; homophone size x kanji knowledge: $p = 0.063$). For correct response rate, there was a significant a kanji knowledge main effect (kanji knowledge: $p = 0.015$). Neither the main effect of homophone size nor the interaction effect of homophone size and kanji knowledge was significant (homophone size: p = 0.09; homophone size x kanji knowledge: p = 0.643).

Reaction time - homophone size effect

Both the beginner (793 - 1015 = -222, LSD = 102) and intermediate L2 readers (880 - 1006 = -126, LSD = 117) responded to the high homophone size *kanji* significantly faster than to the low homophone size *kanji*. However, the advanced L2 readers showed no significant difference between the low and high homophone size *kanji* in terms of their reaction times (917 - 947 = -30, LSD = 130).

The finding that the beginner and intermediate groups responded significantly more quickly to the high homophone size *kanji* than to the low homophone size *kanji* was unexpected.

Correct response rate - kanji knowledge effect

The intermediate readers performed significantly more accurately than the beginner readers both on the low homophone size *kanji* (84 – 72 = 12, LSD = 10.4) and the high homophone size *kanji* (87 – 74.7 = 12.3, LSD = 10.4), but there was no significant difference between the advanced and intermediate groups.

4.4.5 Comparison between the results of the character-ness judgement and radical identification tasks

The results of the comparison between the character-ness judgement and radical identification tasks revealed that there were significant differences in the reaction times between the two tasks in the beginner and intermediate groups. The beginner readers took significantly longer to perform the character-ness judgement task than the radical identification tasks (1423 - 923 = 500, LSD = 135) and so did the intermediate readers (1251 - 895 = 356, LSD = 182). By contrast, there was no significant difference in the reaction times of the advanced L2 readers between the two tasks (923 - 879 = 44, LSD= 180). With regard to accuracy, the beginner group's performance in the character-ness judgement task was significantly more error-prone than in the radical identification task (58.5 – 72 = -13.5, LSD = 7.6). There were no significant differences between the two tasks in the accuracy of the intermediate (79.6 – 81,9 = -2.3, LSD = 10.2) and advanced L2 readers' performances (85.8 – 82.5 = 3.3, LSD = 10.8).

4.4.6 Discussion of the results of the character-ness judgement and radical identification tasks

Gradual development of character-dominant processing

In summary, the beginner group performed the character-ness judgement task significantly more slowly and less accurately than the radical identification task. The intermediate group also performed slowly in the character-ness judgement compared to the radical identification task, but their mean correct response rate on the two tasks did

213

not differ significantly. The advanced L2 readers performed the two tasks with similar speed and accuracy.

The beginner L2 readers had very limited *kanji* knowledge. They had to scan all the constituent radicals and strokes in order to say whether or not the stimulus was a real *kanji*. However, their lack of kanji knowledge meant that they often could not make correct judgements. In comparison with the beginner readers, the intermediate readers had more knowledge of *kanji* and components. Nevertheless, their slow response in the character-ness judgement task suggested that the intermediate readers might have heavily relied on the component identification. The advanced readers' improved response speed may be taken as evidence of their superior skill in character-level identification. Overall, these results indicated gradual development of the character-based recognition across the groups.

As described in Chapter 4 Section 2, the L1 readers performed the character-ness judgement task significantly more quickly and accurately than the radical identification task. In the character-ness judgement task (when the stimuli were real *kanji*), the decision on the character was made as soon as it was identified at the character level. Also in this task only one decision was required for the character, and no comparisons were needed. On the other hand, in the radical identification task, after the completion of the character identification, further identification of the component was required in order to perform the task. Moreover, the comparison of the two stimuli for each pair was also necessary in order to examine whether or not there was a common component between them, hence it was slower and more errors were made.

The processing difference, which accounts for the finding of no differences in the reaction times and correct response rates in the advanced L2 readers, suggests that unlike the L1 readers, the advanced L2 readers might have at times needed the information from the component-level analysis to assist in their decision making. In other words, the results suggest that the advanced L2 readers orthographic processing skills have not yet become character-dominant, although these skills appear to be approaching the level of those of the L1 readers.

These findings may suggest that, with the growth of *kanji* vocabulary, the developing reader becomes able to focus on character level processing. That is, L2 readers gradually develop efficient character level dominant processing. However, the automatic character level operation that was seen in the L1 readers appears to take time to develop and they were not be seen in the L2 readers who took part in this study. This was the case even among the advanced readers who knew more than 1,000 *kanji*. It may be concluded that a substantial amount of exposure to *kanji* is required before character-dominant identification processes have become established.

A factor that hinders the orthographic processing – graphical complexity

The results of the analyses of the stimulus properties showed that the beginner L2 readers whose correct response rates were significantly lower than the intermediate and advanced readers, were heavily affected by the complexity of the *kanji*. In the character-ness judgement task, their responses to the low complexity *kanji* were significantly faster than to the high complexity *kanji*, and in the radical identification task, their performance on the low complexity *kanji* was significantly more accurate than on the high complexity *kanji*. These findings suggest that due to their limited vocabulary, novice readers of *kanji* cannot identify most characters, and that there are some components that they cannot identify as a unit. If this were the case, the beginner readers would need to focus on constituent radicals and secondary radicals, and even strokes that compose the *kanji*. Comprehending the intricate graphical features of the high complexity *kanji* would be taxing for the beginner L2 readers because of the large number of features needed to be considered without having a schema into which they could be chunked.

As expected, the intermediate readers who knew 300-1,000 characters performed significantly more accurately than the beginner readers on both low and high complexity *kanji* in the character-ness judgement task as well as in the radical identification task. In the character-ness judgement task, the intermediate readers could have recognised some *kanji* at the character-level. However, given the stimuli used in the task were selected from the list of 1,945 characters, roughly speaking, about a half or more *kanji* that appeared in the task were unfamiliar to them. It is therefore reasonable to think that these readers examined the constituent components of the stimuli in order to judge whether the stimuli were real or non-real. If indeed these readers relied on the component level processing, one might expect that the complexity of the *kanji* might have affected the intermediate readers' performance. Unexpectedly, the results showed no significant difference between the low and high complexity *kanji* in the character-ness judgement task for the intermediate readers. In the radical identification task on the other hand, the readers performed significantly more accurately on the low complexity *kanji* than on the high complexity *kanji*. Those readers were able to identify the main radicals of the low complexity *kanji* correctly at a rate of over 90%. These findings suggest that L2 readers with an intermediate level of *kanji* knowledge may be able to identify functional components (at least main radicals) accurately as long as the graphical features of the *kanji* are not too complex. It should be noted however, that being able to identify some components in the less complex *kanji* would not contribute to improved performance in the character-ness judgement task, since having real components did not mean that the stimulus was a real character. It could be that the performance of intermediate readers in the character-ness judgement task did not significantly differ between the low and high complexity kanji because they could not judge the character-ness of the stimuli at the character level for a large number of the stimuli. Even if they had found components in the low complexity *kanji*, finding them may not have assisted their decisions at the character level (as both the real and non-real *kanji* in this task consisted of real components) .

The advanced readers were significantly quicker in responding to the low complexity *kanji* than to the high complexity *kanji* in the character-ness judgement task, and they performed significantly more accurately on the low complexity *kanji* than on the high complexity *kanji* in the radical identification task. In the main, their response pattern was the same as the beginner readers. However, given that the advanced readers' accuracy was significantly higher than that of the beginner readers, it is unlikely that the recognition of the advanced readers had been hindered by the intricate graphical

217

features of the high complexity *kanji*. With the knowledge of 1,000 or more *kanji*, the advanced readers were likely to process *kanji* both at the character and component levels. However, because their character level processing may not be as fast and accurate as the L1 readers, it is plausible to think that, for some characters, their identification decision on the character (in the character-ness judgement task) was made only after a decision was made on the components, upon which character complexity may have had an effect. The complexity effect found in the radical identification task suggests that these readers were affected by the graphic complexity in identifying a component.

As described above, an improvement was observed in the L2 readers' orthographic processing skills as their *kanji* knowledge increased. However, the processing difference between the L1 and L2 readers was undeniable. The complexity of the *kanji* did not affect the L1 readers' performance significantly (see Chapter 4 Section 1) yet as the current results attest, even at the advanced level, L2 readers' performance was affected by the graphical complexity of characters.

Stronger network for high frequency characters

With regard to the effect of character frequency on the performance of the L2 readers, in every L2 group, performances on the high frequency *kanji* were significantly stronger in the character-ness judgement task both in terms of speed and accuracy.

The beginner readers' low correct response rate for the low frequency *kanji* was probably caused by their limited *kanji* sight vocabulary. That is, the low frequency *kanji* and their components were outside the range of their vocabulary. The intermediate and advanced readers appear to have developed a stronger recognition network for the *kanji* that they have often seen compared to those rarely seen.

Most of the so called neural network models, such as the Interactive Activation and Parallel Distributed Processing models (see Chapter 2 Section 2 for further descriptions about the models) describe network formation in terms of exposure and learning, which operates by adjusting weights of connections between units. In short, the more a particular form is processed, links between the representation of that form with relevant information become stronger in the network. Obviously, the L2 readers had more opportunities to see high frequency *kanji* compared to low frequency *kanji*. It is therefore reasonable to think that L2 readers have formed a stronger network for high frequency *kanji* than for low frequency *kanji*.

On the other hand, the L1 readers did not differ significantly in their correct response rates between the low and high frequency *kanji*. Although the L1 readers' performance was equally accurate for the low and high frequency *kanji*, they responded to the high frequency *kanji* significantly more quickly than the low frequency *kanji*, suggesting that the L1 readers are able to recognise the *kanji* that appear very frequently in print with great efficiency. The L2 readers' poorer performance on the low frequency *kanji* suggests that L2 readers may need extensive exposure to *kanji* characters before attaining the level of the L1 readers.

Development of character-dominant processing for high frequency characters

In the radical identification task, in comparison with the beginner L2 readers whose performance did not differ significantly for the low and high frequency *kanji*, the intermediate and advanced readers were able to identify the main radical of the *kanji* more accurately in the low frequency *kanji* than in the high frequency *kanji*. The L1 readers also found it easier to identify the main radicals in the low frequency *kanji* than in the high frequency *kanji*, indicating their sensitivity to the frequency of *kanji*.

This apparent superiority in low frequency *kanji* in the radical identification task seems to go against what might be expected in terms of the well-accepted frequency effect. In fact, that the components were missed more in the high frequency *kanji* than the low frequency *kanji* might reflect character-level dominance in the L1 readers' processing of high frequency *kanji*. In the radical identification task, a decision had to be generated at the component level, as the task was to identify a common component between two characters. For the high frequency kanji, as the L1 and L2 readers with intermediate to advanced *kanji* knowledge would have recognised those high frequency *kanji* at the character level at an early stage of processing, the outcome of the early character level processing might have negatively affected the identification of the components. For the low frequency *kanji* on the other hand, there seemed to be less interference from the character level probably because the recognition of low frequency *kanji* was slow. This might be a reason why the skilled readers identified a main radical more accurately in the low frequency *kanji* than in the high frequency *kanji*. The interference from the character level suggests character-level dominant processing.

Development via componential analysis stage

An effect of radical frequency was seen in the beginner and intermediate readers in the character-ness judgement task. The beginner readers' extremely low correct response rate for the low radical frequency *kanji* can be simply explained by their lack of knowledge of main radicals. Both the character and the main radical of the low radical frequency *kanji* were likely to have been unfamiliar to the beginner readers.

When judging the character-ness of the *kanji*, the intermediate readers performed significantly more quickly and accurately on the *kanji* with a high frequency main radical than on the *kanji* with a low frequency main radical, indicating that they might have relied on the information from the components. This suggests that the information from the high frequency main radicals facilitated quicker and more accurate character-ness judgements. The positive effect of radical frequency on character judgments implies that these readers referred to the components of the *kanji* in order to judge the character-ness because their character level identification had not yet been developed. In other words, the radical frequency effect on the performance of the intermediate readers in the character-ness judgement task appears to indicate their reliance on an analysis of the components of the *kanji* for recognition.

In contrast, the advanced readers did not differ significantly in their reaction times and correct response rates between the low and high radical frequency *kanji*. This was consistent with the response pattern of the L1 readers. When the task was simply to differentiate real *kanji* from non-*kanji*, the radical frequency did not affect the advanced readers' performance significantly probably because the task decisions were made at the character level although the information from sub-character features were also considered.

Development of component level processing for high frequency radicals

In the radical identification task, unlike the beginner and intermediate readers, the advanced readers performed the task significantly more accurately on the high radical frequency *kanji* than on the low radical frequency *kanji*, The L1 readers also found it easier to find the main radical in the *kanji* with a high frequency main radical, indicating their sensitivity to the frequency of main radicals. The findings suggest that the advanced L2 readers had developed recognition skills that are similar to the L1 readers, at least in terms of finding the main radicals in *kanji*.

No homophone size effects on orthographic processing

Regarding homophone size *kanji* in the character-ness judgement task, the L2 readers at all three *kanji* knowledge levels did not differ significantly in their reaction times to the low and high homophone size *kanji*. There was also no significant difference in their correct response rates between the two groups of *kanji* that differed in homophone size. These findings were consistent with the response pattern of the L1 readers.

In the radical identification task, on the other hand, the beginner and intermediate readers who had limited *kanji* knowledge responded to the high homophone size *kanji* significantly faster than to the low homophone size *kanji*. One would expect that the homophone size of the *kanji* would not affect the less-skilled L2 readers who had limited knowledge of *kanji* that they could read. However, the homophone effect was identified only in the beginner and intermediate groups and not in the advanced group. Moreover, these readers' reaction times to the high homophone size *kanji* were surprisingly fast (793ms and 880ms). These findings appear mysterious unless there were some other factors besides that of homophone size affecting the less skilled readers. Such a factor could be that the high homophone size *kanji* had their main radicals in 'conspicuous' positions. Indeed, inspection of the low and high homophone size *kanji* revealed that the high homophone size *kanji* had their main radicals on the left, or top, more often than the low homophone size *kanji* did (high - 80% vs low - 40%). As the low homophone size *kanji* tended not to have their main radicals on the left, or top, the beginner and intermediate L2 learners might have found it harder to find a common main radical in the *kanji* when the main radicals did not appear in these positions.

The advanced readers were not affected significantly by the homophone size. Likewise, homophone size did not impact upon the L1 readers' performance either in terms of their reaction time or their correct response rate. The results of this part of the study indicated that the recognition skills of the advanced L2 readers were close to those of the L1 readers.

The following section reports a summary of the interviews.

4.4.7 Character-ness judgement task: Interview data

Beginner L2 readers

The majority of the beginner L2 readers were able to tell how non-*kanji* were created in the character-ness judgement task. 21 out of the 32 participants in this group commented on recomposed components (see Example 1). About half of the 21 participants were able to explicitly express why they had rejected the non-*kanji* (see Example 2). The other half of the 21 made comments that were not as clear or focussed (see Example 3). Besides the *kanji* with the components swapped around, at least seven participants knew that there was another type of non-*kanji*, which had a line added or subtracted from correct *kanji* (see Example 4).

Example 1: The ones that weren't *kanji* had their components in the wrong places. For example, the component that should be on the left-hand side was on the right-hand side, or the top one was at the bottom.

Example 2: If I saw, for example, the roof radical (宀) on the bottom of the *kanji*, or the person radical (亻) on the right, I assumed that it was wrong.

Example 3: I wasn't really sure. So I just had to go by whether it looked right or not.

Example 4: I think some were easy to tell because they looked like the *kanji* that I already knew, but with some extra lines.

On the other hand, six participants reported that they could not distinguish *kanji* from non-*kanji* (see Example 5) and five participants admitted that there was a certain amount of guesswork involved in their judgements (see Examples 6-8).

Example 5: For a lot of the *kanji* that came up, I couldn't tell whether they were correct or not, because I didn't know them.

Example 6: If the left side was narrower than the right side, then I tended to say that was real *kanji*.

Example 7: When I saw too many separate parts, it raised my suspicion, and I automatically pressed the no key.

Example 8: If the *kanji* looked ugly or it didn't have some symmetry to it, or looked awkward to what I've seen before, then I would tend to give it as not correct.

It was difficult for the beginners to make judgements, because they could never tell confidently wether the wrongly-shaped *kanji* were non-*kanji* or real *kanji* that they had not seen before (see Examples 9-10).

Example 9: I thought it was difficult in that it's very possible that some *kanji* could exist but I just don't know them.

Example 10: Some of the ones I knew were reversed, but I thought it could be possible, maybe it was a real *kanji*, but just one backwards

Intermediate L2 readers

Most intermediate L2 readers claimed to be able to detect non-*kanji* without much difficulty. 17 out of the 20 participants explicitly or implicitly commented on the locations of main radicals (see Examples 11-12). Five of them also mentioned that there was another type of non-*kanji* in the task: *kanji* with an added or subtracted line (see Example 13).

> Example 11: Pattern of components was mainly what I was looking at, where the components were, whether or not they were acceptable.
>
> Example 12: I didn't know a lot of the *kanji*, but I could tell whether they were wrong or not by the radicals, like some radicals, you know they have to sit at the top, or on the left or right side of the character, but if they were in a wrong spot, then I could tell that it wasn't a real *kanji*.
>
> Example 13: The simple ones were easy to tell that they weren't real *kanji* because they just looked strange, and they had extra strokes that you could just tell.

The remark made by one participant suggests that L2 readers might have developed the ability to judge character-ness due to the years of study of Japanese *kanji* (see Example 14).

> Example 14: Because I've been learning *kanji* for a few years, so I know what looks like a *kanji* even if I don't understand the meaning of it.

Apparently, the intermediate L2 readers already knew many of the *kanji*. It was not too difficult to make judgement if the *kanji* used in the task was familiar to them:

they judged by the positions of the components. For the ones that were unfamiliar to them, they used their knowledge of the patterns of *kanji* (see Examples 15-16).

Example 15: Some of them I knew, if they had the radical in one place when it was supposed to be on the other side, I picked it easily. For others, I just used my knowledge from what I used to see.

Example 16: For the ones that I didn't know, I looked through the patterns that I would expect to see. When I didn't see the pattern, then I pressed the 'no' button.

Advanced L2 readers

For the advanced L2 readers, most of the *kanji* used in this task were familiar: at least they had seen them before somewhere. Eight out of the 17 advanced L2 readers found it easy to make judgements (see Example 17). Some advanced readers were even aware of some subtle features of the *kanji*, such as the difference in shape between left components and right components (see Examples 18-19).

Example 17: You could easily recognise what the *kanji* were meant to be, but their parts were in the wrong places. And some of them seemed to have just one or two strokes in silly places.

Example 18: You could tell because of the stroke, if the *kanji* had a left hand radical with the last stroke at the bottom going up on the right-hand side, it looked funny.

Example 19: For example, the radical *taberu* (the eating radical) with the stroke pointing upwards should be on the left but instead it was on the right hand side, or something like that.

One thing that was quite distinct from the other groups was that some participants in this group were able to account for their judgement using terms such as *hen* (the main radicals that appear on the left hand side of the *kanji*) and *kanmuri* (the main radicals that appear at the top), as were the L1 readers (see Example 20). The use of *kanji* dictionaries might have helped them learn the terms and their locations (see Example 21).

Example 20: The components might be in different positions, like *kanmuri* could appear at the bottom, and *hen* could be on the right-hand side.

Example 21: I quite like *kanji* dictionary, so I often look up different *hen* and have a look at what goes with each, and different readings and things....So I kind of learnt through that, different ways of making characters, and learnt what could go on the sides and what could go down at the bottom, and that kind of thing.

4.4.8 Radical identification task: Interview data

Beginner L2 readers

The results of the statistical analysis implied that the beginner L2 readers appeared not to have had adequate knowledge of components (main radicals) to perform this task. The interview data indicated that about a quarter of the beginner participants did not have a clear idea of what to look for (see Example 1). Five participants tried to look at the whole *kanji* (see Example 2), but found it hard. 12 out of the 30 beginner participants felt that they needed more time (see Examples 3-4).

Example 1: I used a grid square to try and divide the *kanji* into four parts to look for similarities. But it became difficult, when the *kanji* was quite detailed, to take every thing at once.

Example 2: That was really hard. I tried to look at the whole thing, but it was hard.

Example 3: I found the task very hard because I didn't have enough time to look at all the different elements. So a lot of time, if I thought I saw similar shapes, I said 'yes'.

Example 4: Just such a short time between the first one and the second one, I had time to imprint only part of the character. I mean I saw the whole character, and there was a visual image in my mind, but it faded away fast, so in order to memorise it, I probably needed to scan again.

A few participants expressed the physical discomfort they experienced during this task (see Examples 5-6), which indicated the intense concentration the beginners required. It appears that subtle features such as the font difference or the circle between the two *kanji* (mask) could affect the participants' processing procedure (see Examples 7-8).

Example 5: My eyes started to get sore by the end of the task.

Example 6: I got tired and my brain stopped.

Example 7: Because the fonts were different, sometimes they were hard to tell.

Example 8: Having the little round spot in between each one makes it difficult to look at the next one, because the round spot is so easy to recognise.

Three participants said that they looked for familiar shapes, and five participants remarked that it was easier to do the task when they could find any familiar shape(s) in the *kanji* (see Examples 9-10). 11 participants seemed to know where they could usually find the familiar main radicals in the *kanji* (see Example 11).

Example 9: I just found myself looking for familiar *katakana* or something I knew, and I just held on to that, or some pieces that I knew how to write.

Example 10: When I found some shapes that were familiar to me, it was easier to remember.

Example 11: I tended to look at the top or the side because those parts were where you would find differences.

Radicals that looked similar were also confusing for the beginner L2 readers (see Example 12). Another three participants reported that graphically complex *kanji* were hard to deal with (see Example 13). The results of the statistical analysis indeed showed the character complexity effect, although this variable affected not only the beginner level but all the L2 readers (see Chapter 4 Section 1 for details).

Example 12: It was difficult because there were radicals that were very similar, so it was difficult to tell which one came up first and which one came up second.

Example 13: If it was a complex *kanji* that had lots of components, then obviously I thought that was too hard.

Intermediate L2 readers

Seven out of the 20 intermediate L2 readers thought the speed of the task was very fast although none of them expressed any sort of discomfort due to the speed (see Example 14). Four participants reported that they tried to look at the whole *kanji* (see Example 15). However, three participants expressed the difficulty of paying attention to all radicals of the *kanji* (see Example 16), particularly of the first *kanji* (see Example 17).

Example 14: I thought that characters flashed up too quickly. I sometimes pressed the wrong button.

Example 15: The way I did the task was I tried to keep the image of the whole *kanji* in my mind, like for a few seconds, and sort of tried to superimpose the other one on top of it.

Example 16: It was hard to see all the components, it was hard to try to take a picture of each component.

Example 17: As soon as the second *kanji* was displayed, I felt as if I'd forgotten the previous *kanji* as there was nothing to cling to.

Nevertheless, quite a few participants knew where to focus. 10 participants commented on locations of the components (see Examples 18-19). Four participants remarked that it was easier to remember when the *kanji* or the main radical of the *kanji* was familiar to them (see Example 20).

Example 18: I looked specifically for the main radical. Usually, the main one is located on the left part of the *kanji*, but sometimes it can come at the top or other parts.

Example 19: If the common component was on the left-hand side or at the top, then I could recognise it easily, but it was a bit hard if the component was in any other places.

Example 20: Some of the *kanji*, I actually knew. So for those ones, it was not hard to find the radical, and I kind of expected that I would see that in the next *kanji*.

However, the difficulty of judgement varied depending on complexity of the *kanji* (see Example 21-22).

Example 21: For the complex ones, it was hard to tap. Sometimes, I couldn't remember what the first one was.

Example 22: If there was a complicated *kanji* with many components, I only looked at the few that stood out, like *ninben* (イ, the person radical) or *kihen* (木, the tree radical).

Components with similar graphic shapes were also confusing according to at least three participants (see Examples 23-24)

Example 23: When comparing two characters, I found it hard to say for certain if they shared the same part, or simply resembled each other in shape or form.

Example 24: I wasn't sure if the elements were not exactly the same but very similar…For example, when you got a *katakana* /ka/ (力, she meant the power radical), and if I saw the one that missed a bit at the top (刀, here, she meant the sword radical), I wasn't sure if they counted as the same or not.

Advanced L2 readers

What distinguished the advanced group from the other groups was that there were at least three participants who used the phonological code to remember shapes of the *kanji* (see Examples 25-26). Although in most cases, whether they were reading the characters or the main radicals, and whether it was in Japanese or in English were not clear, one participant remarked that he remembered the main radicals by naming them in English (see Example 27).

Example 25: I was trying to read the *kanji* out in my head.

Example 26: I would try to recognise it and say it in my head because I needed to remember and compare it with the second one.

Example 27: It was better if I could name the first *kanji* because I couldn't remember it visually, but I was able to remember it if I could give a name to the main radical, like the 'mouth radical' or 'sickness radical'.

11 out of the 17 advanced L2 readers reported that they focused on the main radical of the *kanji* (see Example 28). Among them, five participants reported that they looked mainly at the left-hand side, and in some cases other parts as well (see Example 29).

Example 28: I tended to focus on the main radical because I thought it might be the part that would be the same for the next one.

Example 29: I mainly looked at the left-hand side for *hen* (main radicals on the left side of *kanji*) although sometimes the bottom section of the *kanji*, I could see the similarity there.

Three advanced L2 readers referred to the difficulty of making judgement on the main radicals with similar graphical features (see Examples 30-31)

Example 30: When the two main radicals were similar, for instance, like *ninben* (亻, the person radical) and *gyouninben* (彳, the steps radical), I said that they were different, but in fact, they had a common component in them, so it really depends on what you think is the same and what is different.

Example 31: There were some elements, for instance, the difference between *nichi* or *hi* (日) and *shiro* (白), when one had *nichi* and another had *shiro*, I think I said they were different. For example, the difference between the main radical of *nani* (何 - with 亻, the person radical) and the main radical of *iku* (行 - with 彳, the steps radical), they were easier to differentiate because they were in the same position. But there were other ones, for instance, either in the middle, at the bottom or at the top, because I had to move the positions, it was harder to see the difference.

4.4.9 Discussion of the interview about the character-ness judgement and radical identification tasks

Development of component awareness

The interview data revealed a clear relationship between the amount of exposure to *kanji* and the development of awareness of functional components.

In the character-ness judgement task, although their *kanji* knowledge was very limited, it appears that most beginner readers were able to tell which ones were not real *kanji* by identifying some familiar graphical features in unusual locations. However, the grounds for their judgements varied widely. While some beginner readers seemed to know where frequently recurring main radicals should appear, others had no concrete idea except for a feeling of 'not looking right'. Conceivably, the beginner readers were at the stage of beginning to form their awareness of component locations. Nevertheless, the task could not be performed without enough knowledge of components. Indeed, the low correct response rates of the beginner readers in the character-ness judgement (see Chapter 4 Section 1 for details) showed that the beginner readers rejected a number of real *kanji* as not real. It could be that a combination of unfamiliar radicals looked 'not real' to them.

The intermediate readers remarked that they could tell real *kanji* from non-real by examining where the components were and whether or not they were acceptable. They also mentioned that they looked at the patterns of the component combinations. Clearly, sufficient exposure to *kanji* and their components is essential for the development of awareness of component locations and combinations.

The advanced readers obviously had many *kanji* that were familiar to them, and probably knew the expected locations of *kanji* components. They also seemed to have some insight into the size and shapes of main radicals, which would help determine the locations of radicals, such as that the bottom stroke of a left main radical usually goes up.

In order to find a common component in the radical identification task, the beginner readers clung to familiar shapes that they could identify. When they could not find any familiar shape in the *kanji*, there were at least two strategies that they could use. One, which was impossible to perform within the limited exposure time of the first *kanji*, was to examine all the separate graphical constituents of the *kanji*. The second, which was also impracticable, as the beginner readers did not have any phonological information to help them keep the graphic image in their short term memory, was to try and superimpose the holistic image of the first *kanji* onto the second *kanji*.

The intermediate readers' remarks indicated that they knew at least some, probably high frequency main radicals (as indicated in Chapter 4 Section 1). It appears that most readers sensed that they should focus on the main radicals of the characters whereas a few readers tried to look at all the radicals. This may suggest that generally, the concept of a component had been consolidated although it was still vague for a few. However, the intermediate readers had to purposefully search through all the parts when there were no familiar main radicals in the *kanji*.

The advanced readers, on the other hand, appeared to be more aware of main radicals, and to have known that the main radicals were the ones that they were required to look at. They were able to segment a *kanji* into the main radical and non-main-radical components, although it appears that similar main radicals were sometimes confusing.

No semantic processing in orthographic tasks

What was not mentioned in the interviews with the L2 readers were the meanings of the *kanji*. Some L1 readers commented that when they were presented with a *kanji*, the meaning of the *kanji* appeared to be automatically accessed via the meaning-bearing reading (usually, *kun*-reading) of the *kanji*. On the other hand, the interview data of the L2 readers showed that most of them paid attention merely to the graphical features of the *kanji*, suggesting that lemma representations (that connect the three major aspects of a lexical item: form, pronunciation and meaning) have not yet been formed in most L2 readers. However, a few advanced L2 readers appear to have read the *kanji* although there were no statements suggesting the access to the semantic information was automatic. There were also remarks indicating that a few participants read the main radicals by their names. These may possibly suggest that a few advanced readers possess at least some weak lemma representations. However, there was simply not enough evidence to support this argument.

4.5 Chapter four Summary

The analysis on the results of the L1 readers' performance on the two orthographic tasks showed that they were capable of very fast and accurate character-ness judgement and radical identification. Their faster recognition of the higher frequency *kanji* over the lower frequency *kanji*, and the character level dominant processing were all consistent with recent word recognition models (see Chapter 2 Section 2 for details).

The interview data provided clear evidence that the L1 readers were equipped with the orthographic knowledge (i.e., component positions and combinations, and names of main radicals), and they were able to draw upon it if required. The L1 readers' reflective accounts also suggested that the phonological and semantic processing appeared to be readily available even in the orthographic tasks.

The results of the tasks for the L2 readers suggest that L2 readers' orthographic processing skills improve as the knowledge of *kanji* (characters and their components) increases: 1) the L2 readers with limited *kanji* knowledge (less than 300 *kanji*) processed characters by using any graphical information available to them, but due to their lack of experience, their processing was hindered by graphical complexity; 2) the L2 readers who knew 300-1,000 *kanji* processed characters by relying heavily on the information of the components; and 3) L2 readers with more than 1,000 *kanji* were able to use the information from both characters and their components, with priority for character-level information.

The interview data suggest that the awareness of components and awareness of component locations and combinations develop as knowledge of *kanji* increase: 1) the L2 readers with limited *kanji* knowledge lacked the orthographic awareness required for character recognition, and therefore had no choice but to rely on any familiar graphic shapes; 2) the L2 readers whose *kanji* knowledge was between 300-1,000 characters were aware of locations and combinations for some functional components; and 3) the L2 readers with more than 1,000 *kanji* seemedd to possess this awareness for most functional components. The interview data further suggest that extensive exposure to *kanji* is required for developing native-like orthographic processing skills, which involve automatic access to phonological and semantic information (i.e., the formation of lemma).

5 Phonological processing skills and awareness

5.1 L1 readers of Japanese: Objectives and Methods

5.1.1 Objectives

Research suggests that once orthographic information is appropriately processed, phonological and morphological information also becomes automatically available for skilled readers (see Chapter 2 Section 3 for details). In an orthographically opaque script like Japanese *kanji* characters, simple grapheme to phoneme conversion at the sub-character level is not possible. However, research suggests that the phonological information of phonetic components of *kanji* becomes available to skilled readers at a very early stage of identification, and that this information mediates a link between the character and its meaning and/or pronunciation (see Chapter 2 Section 3 for details). In this regard, to be a skilled reader is to have the skills to extract the relevant phonological information from *kanji*. Readers of Japanese *kanji* are likely to gradually develop the skilled phonological processing skills. In the process of attaining them, readers are likely to develop awareness of the links between the characters and their phonetics (i.e., phonetic components) and awareness of the limitations of the phonological information that phonetics can contribute.

Two phonological tasks and a retrospective interview were used in order to investigate the development of phonological processing in character recognition among readers of Japanese with different levels of character knowledge. The tasks used were a phonological judgement task and a phonological matching task (see Chapter 3 for detailed description). The tasks were designed to tap the phonological processes used in character recognition and to determine the associated response patterns of readers. The interview questions were designed to supplement this data in order to gain greater insight into the readers' phonological awareness. These tasks and the interview were administered to a group of L1 readers first, and then to three groups of L2 readers. The results of the study of L1 readers provide a benchmark against which L2 readers' development in the phonological processing will be compared.

This section will report the results of the L1 readers' performance on the two phonological tasks and their reflective accounts. Their response patterns to the two tasks were examined separately first and then compared with each other. The effects of four stimulus properties (complexity, character frequency, radical frequency and homophone size) were also examined. The L1 readers' spoken accounts were then examined.

5.1.2 Methods

Participants

The same 16 native speakers of Japanese who participated in the orthographic tasks participated in this study (see Chapter 3 Section 2 for details).

Materials

The two phonological tasks used were a phonological judgement task and a phonological matching task. The phonological judgement task assessed how quickly and accurately the participants could decide whether or not the two *kanji* had a common on-reading. The two *kanji* were either with or without a common phonetic. The phonological matching task assessed how quickly and accurately the participants could decide whether or not a target *kanji* had the *on*-reading that was provided. One type of the *kanji* and *on*-reading pairs was a *kanji* with a 'valid' phonetic (i.e., consistent phonetic) and the on-reading of the *kanji* (which was also the sound represented by the phonetic). An example of such a pair was 祖 and /so/ (the sound of the *kanji* and of the phonetic). The other type of pair was a *kanji* with an 'invalid' phonetic (i.e., either an inconsistent phonetic or a non-main-radical component that had an identical graphic figure as a phonetic) and the reading of another *kanji* with the invalid phonetic. One of those pairs for example was 快 (the on-reading of this *kanji* was /kai/) and /ketsu/ (the on-reading of another *kanji*, 決). All the *kanji* used in this task had their phonetics highlighted (by shading other parts of the *kanji* leaving the phonetics intact). This

241

unusual condition was created in order to examine if any change in processing would occur in the 'explicit' condition. In each task, eight types of characters with different stimulus properties were included: low and high complexity, low and high frequency of occurrence, low and high radical frequency, and low and high homophone size (see Chapter 3 Section 2 for detailed descriptions of the tasks). Two versions of the tasks with differently-ordered items were prepared in order to avoid any effect of a particular order of presenting items.

Procedure

The participants were randomly grouped into two. Half of the participants undertook the phonological judgement task before the phonological matching task, and the other half did the tasks in reverse order. After taking the warm-up same-different judgement task, one group undertook one of the orthographic tasks, one of the semantic tasks (see Chapter 6), and the phonological judgement task, in that order. They then did the other orthographic task, the other semantic task and the phonological matching task. The other group did the same, except the order of the orthographic, semantic and phonological tasks was reversed. In each task, three practice items were provided. The participants were given the results of their performance on the practice items, and were asked if they would like to move on or redo the practice in order to make sure they understood the instructions for the task.

In the phonological judgement task, each of 120 pairs was displayed on the computer monitor one *kanji* at a time, one after the other, each for 500 ms. Prior to the first *kanji*, an eye-fixation mark (double circles) was displayed for 600 ms, and between the two *kanji*, a brief blank frame was inserted for 200ms. In the phonological matching task, instead of two *kanji* characters, a *kanji* and an *on*-reading of a *kanji* written in *romaji* (Roman letters) were shown. In both tasks, the second stimulus was presented until a response was made, but in order to encourage a quick decision the time for the response was limited to five seconds.

The participants were tested individually on one of the two scrambled versions of the test. The versions were selected randomly by the computer. The participants were asked to respond as quickly and as accurately as possible by pressing the 'yes' key for acceptance of the task questions (e.g., can the two characters be read in the same way?), the 'no' key for rejection of the question, or the 'skip' key if they could not make a decision. No feedback was given except for the first three practice items.

After each task, a short interview session was held where the participants were asked to talk about how they performed the tasks. The retrospective reports were audio-taped, and were later transcribed for qualitative description.

.

5.2 L1 readers of Japanese: Results and discussion

In this study, the results of the items for which a 'yes' was the correct response ('yes' items), and those for which a 'no' was the correct response ('no' items) are both shown (see Chapter 3 Section 2 for details). However, as described in the analysis section (Chapter 3 Section 3), the results of any analysis of the 'no' items should be interpreted cautiously. Only the correct responses in the 'yes' items were analysed for further discussion.

5.2.1 Phonological judgement task: Reaction times and correct response rates

In the phonological judgement task, each participant was required to judge whether or not the two characters (e.g., 符 and 府) shared a common reading (pronunciation). A 'yes' response was expected for the pairs that shared a common reading (hereafter, common-reading items) and a 'no' response was expected for the pairs that did not have a common reading between them (hereafter, no-common-reading). Mean response times and mean correct response rates of the L1 readers in the phonological judgement task for the common-reading items ('yes' items) and no-common-reading items ('no' items) are presented in Table 5.1.

Table 5.1 Mean response times and mean correct response rates of the L1 readers in the phonological judgement task for the common-reading items and no-common-reading items

Phonological judgement					
Can the two characters be read in the same way?					
	Correct Yes responses to the common-reading items			Correct No responses to the no-common-reading items		
Group (N)	S1 - S2	RT (ms) SD	CR (%) SD	S1 - S2	RT(ms) SD	CR (ms) SD
L1 (16)	符 -府 /fu/-/fu/	729 186	90.8 8.5	郊 - 洞 /koR/-/doR/	804 147	97.8 3.1

RT = response times in milliseconds; CR = correct response rate in %; N= the number of participants; SD = standard deviation

The L1 readers responded to the common-reading items significantly faster than to the no-common-reading items, t(15)=2.51, p<0.05. On the other hand, for accuracy, the L1 readers performed the no-common-reading items significantly more accurately than the common-reading items, t(15)=3.91, p<0.05, which could be due to a 'speed-accuracy' trade-off.

5.2.2 Phonological judgement task: Stimulus properties
Complexity

Table 5.2 shows mean response times and mean correct response rates for the low and high complexity *kanji*.

Table 5.2 Mean response times and mean correct response rates of the L1 readers in the phonological judgement task for low and high complexity *kanji*

	Phonological judgement					
	Can the two characters be read in the same way?-Yes					
	Low complexity			High complexity		
Group (N)	S1 - S2	RT (ms) SD	CR (%) SD	S1 - S2	RT (ms) SD	CR (ms) SD
L1 (16)	吸 - 級 /kyuR/-/kyuR/	695 143	85 17.1	陽 - 揚 /yoR/- /yoR/	815 314	90 14.6

RT = response times in milliseconds; CR = correct response rate in %; N= the number of participants; SD = standard deviation

Despite the substantial difference in means, the difference in the response times between the low and high complexity *kanji* was not quite significant t(15)=2, p=0.06, probably due to the large variability in the responses for the high complexity *kanji*. There was no significant difference in correct response rate between the low and high complexity *kanji*, t(15)=1.29, p>0.05.

Character Frequency

Table 5.3 presents mean response times and mean correct response rates for the low and high frequency *kanji*.

Table 5.3 Mean response times and mean correct response rates of the L1 readers in the phonological judgement task for low and high frequency *kanji*

	Phonological judgement					
	Can the two characters be read in the same way?-Yes					
	Low character frequency			High character frequency		
Group (N)	S1 - S2	RT (ms) SD	CR (%) SD	S1 - S2	RT (ms) SD	CR (ms) SD
L1 (16)	胴 - 洞 /doR/-/doR/	671 180	96.3 8.1	時 - 持 /ji/-/ji/	726 187	95 8.9

RT = response times in milliseconds; CR = correct response rate in %; N= the number of participants; SD = standard deviation

There were no significant differences either in speed, t(15)=1.31, p>0.05, or in accuracy, t(15)<1, p>0.05, between the low and high frequency *kanji*. Unlike in the orthographic tasks, character frequency did not affect the L1 readers' performance significantly in the phonological judgement task.

Radical Frequency

Table 5.4 shows mean response times and mean correct response rates for the low and high radical frequency *kanji*.

Table 5.4 Mean response times and mean correct response rates of the L1 readers in the phonological judgement task for low and high radical frequency *kanji*

	Phonological judgement					
	Can the two characters be read in the same way?-Yes					
	Low radical frequency			High radical frequency		
Group (N)	S1 - S2	RT (ms)	CR (%)	S1 - S2	RT (ms)	CR (ms)
		SD	SD		SD	SD
L1 (16)	孤 - 弧	714	95	沿 - 鉛	771	88.8
	/ko/-/ko/	183	11.5	/eN/-/eN/	368	17.8

RT = response times in milliseconds; CR = correct response rate in %; N= the number of participants; SD = standard deviation

For response speed, there was hardly any difference[1] between the low and high radical

---

[1]Note that in the pair in which the radical frequency was the key property, their homophone size was also significantly different (see Chapter 3 Section 2). Although each pair of the *kanji* was selected to vary only in one critical property, it was found that there was an unexpected difference. The low and high radical frequency *kanji* also differed significantly in their homophone sizes. The results of the independent samples t-test showed that this set of pairs was also significantly different in their homophone size, t(18) =3.51, p<0.05, which indicated that homophone size might have had a significant bearing on the effect of radical frequency on the percentage of correct responses.

frequency *kanji*, and indeed the statistical test of the difference was not significant, $t(15)<1$, $p>0.05$. However, analysis of the accuracy data indicated that the L1 readers were significantly more accurate in their responses for the low radical frequency *kanji* than for the high radical frequency *kanji*, $t(15)=2.61$, $p<0.05$.

Homophone size

Mean response times and mean correct response rates for the low and high homophone size *kanji* are shown in Table 5.5.

Table 5.5   Mean response times and mean correct response rates of the L1 readers in the phonological judgement task for low and high homophone size *kanji*

	Phonological judgement					
	Can the two characters be read in the same way?-Yes					
	Low homophone size			High homophone size		
Group (N)	S1 - S2	RT (ms)	CR (%)	S1 - S2	RT (ms)	CR (ms)
		SD	SD		SD	SD
L1 (16)	郡 - 群	744	81.3	砲 - 抱	700	95
	/guN/-/guN/	260	15.4	/hoR/-/hoR/	139	11.5

RT = response times in milliseconds; CR = correct response rate in %; N= the number of participants; SD = standard deviation

There was no significant difference in response time between the low and high homophone size, $t(15)<1$, $p>0.05$. In the accuracy data, the L1 readers performed significantly more accurately for the high homophone size *kanji* than the low homophone size *kanji*, $t(15)=2.71$, $p<0.05$.

5.2.3 Phonological matching task: Reaction times and correct response rates

In the phonological matching task, each participant was asked to judge whether or not the character had the reading that was presented (e.g., 祖 and /so/). A 'yes' response was expected for the pairs that included a character with a valid phonetic and its reading (hereafter, valid-phonetic items) and a 'no' response was expected for the pairs that contained a character with an invalid phonetic and a non-matching reading (hereafter, invalid-phonetic items). Table 5.6 presents the mean response times and mean correct response rates of the L1 readers in the phonological matching task for the valid phonetic items and invalid phonetic items.

Table 5.6 Mean response times and mean correct response rates of the L1 readers in the phonological matching task for the valid-phonetic items and invalid-phonetic items

	Phonological matching					
	Can the character be read as shown?					
	Correct Yes responses to the valid-phonetic items			Correct No responses to the invalid-phonetic items		
Group (N)	S1 - S2	RT (ms) SD	CR (%) SD	S1 - S2	RT(ms) SD	CR (ms) SD
L1 (16)	祖 - so	749 230	95.2 3.7	快 - ketsu	982 281	83.9 11.3

RT = response times in milliseconds; CR = correct response rate in %; N= the number of participants; SD = standard deviation

The L1 readers responded to the valid-phonetic items significantly faster than to the invalid-phonetic items, $t(15)=7.04$, $p<0.05$, and they responded to the valid-phonetic items significantly more accurately than to the invalid-phonetic items, $t(15)=4.43$, $p<0.05$. These results were not surprising because the *kanji* used in the invalid-phonetic items in the phonological matching task were phonologically opaque (i.e., not transparent).

5.2.4 Phonological matching task: Stimulus properties

Complexity

Table 5.7 shows mean response times and mean correct response rates for the low and high complexity *kanji*.

Table 5.7 Mean response times and mean correct response rates of the L1 readers in the phonological matching task for low and high complexity *kanji*

	Phonological matching					
	Can the character be read as shown? - Yes					
	Low complexity			High complexity		
Group (N)	S1 - S2	RT (ms)	CR (%)	S1 - S2	RT (ms)	CR (ms)
		SD	SD		SD	SD
L1 (16)	固 - ko	823	90	博 - haku	765	92.5
		240	14.6		228	12.4

RT = response times in milliseconds; CR = correct response rate in %; N= the number of participants; SD = standard deviation

There was no significant differences in speed between the low and high complexity *kanji*, t(15)=1.45, p>0.05. Likewise, the difference in accuracy was also not significant, t(15)<1, p>0.05. As was the case in the orthographic tasks, complexity had no significant impact on the L1 readers' performance in the phonological matching task.

Character Frequency

Table 5.8 presents mean response times and mean correct response rates for the low and high frequency *kanji*.

Table 5.8 Mean response times and mean correct response rates of the L1 readers in the phonological matching task for low and high frequency *kanji*

	Phonological matching					
	Can the character be read as shown? - Yes					
	Low character frequency			High character frequency		
Group (N)	S1 - S2	RT (ms) SD	CR (%) SD	S1 - S2	RT (ms) SD	CR (ms) SD
L1 (16)	符 - fu	645 235	96.3 8.1	副 – fuku	673 184	98.8 5.0

RT = response times in milliseconds; CR = correct response rate in %; N= the number of participants; SD = standard deviation

There was no significant difference between the mean response times of the low and high frequency *kanji*, t(15)<1, p>0.05. The same outcome was found for correct response rate, t(15)=1, p>0.05. As was the case in the phonological judgement task, character frequency did not affect the L1 readers' performance significantly in the phonological matching task.

Radical Frequency

Table 5.9 presents mean response times and mean correct response rates for the low and high radical frequency *kanji*.

Table 5.9 Mean response times and mean correct response rates of the L1 readers in the phonological matching task for low and high radical frequency *kanji*

	Phonological matching					
	Can the character be read as shown? - Yes					
	Low radical frequency			High radical frequency		
Group (N)	S1 - S2	RT (ms)	CR (%)	S1 - S2	RT (ms)	CR (ms)
		SD	SD		SD	SD
L1 (16)	版 - han	818	95	拒 - kyo	825	97.5
		552	11.5		381	6.8

RT = response times in milliseconds; CR = correct response rate in %; N= the number of participants; SD = standard deviation

In this task, the L1 readers performed equally well on the low and high radical frequency *kanji* as indicated by no significant difference in their response times, $t(15)<1$, $p>0.05$, or correct response rates, $t(15)<1$, $p>0.05$.

Homophone size

Table 5.10 presents mean response times and mean correct response rates for the low and high homophone size *kanji*.

Table 5.10 Mean response times and mean correct response rates of the L1 readers in the phonological matching task for low and high homophone size *kanji*

	Phonological matching					
	Can the character be read as shown? - Yes					
	Low homophone size			High homophone size		
Group (N)	S1 - S2	RT (ms) SD	CR (%) SD	S1 - S2	RT (ms) SD	CR (ms) SD
L1 (16)	徒 - to	676 236	95 8.9	剣 - ken	796 349	96.3 8.1

RT = response times in milliseconds; CR = correct response rate in %; N= the number of participants; SD = standard deviation

No significant differences in responses to the *kanji* that differed in homophone size were found either in terms of response time, t(15)=1.79, p>0.05, or correct response rate, t(15)<1, p>0.05.

5.2.5 Comparison between the results of the phonological judgement and phonological matching tasks

The results of the analysis on the difference in the response times for the items with expected 'yes' responses ('yes' items) showed that there was no significant difference between the two tasks, t(15)<1, p>0.05. However, for the items with expected 'no' responses ('no' items), the L1 readers responded to the phonological judgement task significantly faster than to the phonological matching task, t(15)=3.15, p<0.05. In the analysis of correct response rates, the L1 readers performed significantly more accurately on the phonological matching task than on the phonological judgement tasks for the 'yes' items, t(15)=2.15, p<0.05. In contrast, the participants performed significantly more accurately in the phonological judgement task than in the phonological matching tasks for the 'no' items, t(15)=5.06, p<0.05

5.2.6 Discussion of the results for the phonological judgement and phonological matching tasks

The comparison of the two phonological tasks showed results that were not straightforward to interpret, as shown in the above section. These results may need to be interpreted in terms of Chambers and Forster's (1975) 'multi-level' analysis that proposes that both the speed of identification and subsequent comparisons determine response times. According to this model, as mentioned in Chapter 4 Section 1, multiple levels of identification operate almost simultaneously, and as soon as the identification required in the task is completed at any one of these levels, comparisons of the available information occur in order to reach a decision. Now consider what processes were required in the phonological judgement and phonological matching tasks. Although both tasks might tap phonological processing, the processes contributing to a response appear to be dissimilar in the two phonological tasks, as follows.

Phonological processing by identification and comparison

In order to make a decision in the phonological judgement task, two characters needed to be identified at the character level (which activated multiple readings for each character), and the output of the character-level identification had to be compared. In this task, the processing at the component level was probably not as crucial as that at the character level (this will be further discussed later). On the other hand, in the phonological matching task, although the identification was needed for only one character, the identification of its phonetic at the component level was also likely to have occurred, as the phonetic was highlighted. Moreover, the reading provided in the Roman alphabet had to be decoded. The output of the character and component levels then needed to be compared with the phonological information of the provided reading.

It seems that approximately the same amount of time was required to reach a 'yes' response in the two phonological tasks although the processes undergone were different, as illustrated above. However, the L1 readers responded to the phonological matching task (i.e., a *kanji* and a reading) significantly more accurately than to the phonological judgement task (i.e., two *kanji*). The difference in accuracy between the tasks may be attributed to the multiple readings of the *kanji* characters. Given that each *kanji* can have more than one reading, the possibility of retrieving a common reading for both of retrieving characters for the first time is not high. In this regard, there seems to be more chance to retrieve a common reading between two stimuli in the phonological matching task (in which the required reading was provided) than in the phonological judgement task (in which the required reading was not provided). Furthermore, in the matching task, the phonological information retrieved at the character level was supported by the phonological information derived from the valid phonetic. It is likely that the phonology of the valid phonetic was accessed and compared with the reading of the *kanji* in the L1 readers' skilled phonological processing.

For a 'no' response, the L1 readers took longer and made more errors in deciding that the *kanji* did not have the reading provided (i.e., phonological matching task) than in deciding there was no common reading between the two *kanji* (i.e., phonological judgement task). Given that the highlighted component in the phonological matching task was an invalid phonetic, the output of the component level identification and the phonological information accessed via the reading were inconsistent. To describe this further, in the phonological matching task the invalid-phonetic items consisted of *kanji* with an invalid phonetic, and the reading shown after the *kanji* was not the reading of the *kanji* but the reading of another *kanji* that shared the same invalid phonetic with the target *kanji*. For example, one of the pairs was 快 and /ketsu/. The *on*-reading of this *kanji* 快 was /kai/, but the given reading /ketsu/ was the *on*-reading of another similar but different *kanji*, 決. The interference due to this inconsistent information in the comparison phase appears to be a reason for the slower response time and lower correct response rate in the phonological matching task compared to the case in the phonological judgement task.

Strong links between high frequency characters and meaning-bearing readings

It is widely acknowledged that high frequency words are recognised more quickly than low frequency words (in fact character frequency effects were observed in the orthographic tasks). Given that high frequency *kanji* are recognised faster than low frequency *kanji*, and that the phonological information attached to the high frequency *kanji* would be accessed automatically without waiting for the componential analysis (see Chapter 4 Section 1 for details), character frequency effects should have been observed in the phonological tasks as well. However, in the two phonological tasks, character frequency did not affect the L1 readers' performance significantly.

The fact that there are two types of readings, *kun*-reading and *on*-reading, may suggest a clue to the reasons for this unexpected finding. As described in the 'Japanese *kanji* characters' section (Chapter 1 Section 3), the *kun*-reading is the reading of native Japanese words, and represents the concept of the words. On the other hand, the *on*-reading is the reading of Chinese origin words, and usually does not hold any semantic information in itself, except for a few that are used for single-character words (e.g., /eki/ for 駅 (station) and /niku/ for 肉 (meat)). According to the lemma-version of the Multilevel Interactive Activation Model (see Chapter 2 Section 2 for details), the characters that would be a single-character word have a strong lemma representation. In the case of kanji characters, it means that the kanji that can be a single-character word are strongly linked to the meaning-bearing readings via their lemma representations. Given that single-character words are read in the meaning-bearing reading, then, based on assumptions common to most learning models of word recognition (e.g., the Parallel Distributed Processing model), it is reasonable to think that the more frequently the *kanji* appear in a single form, the stronger the link between the *kanji* and its *kun*-reading would become. If this were the case, the *kun*-reading (meaning-bearing reading) of *kanji* would be activated more strongly in high frequency *kanji* than in low frequency *kanji*. In the current phonological tasks however, the L1 readers were required to access the *on*-reading (non-meaning-bearing reading) of the *kanji*. Under such task conditions, then, it is conceivable that the L1 readers would need some extra time to inhibit the strong activation of the meaning-bearing reading in the high frequency *kanji* in order to access the non-meaning-bearing reading instead. This could be a reason why they did not show any character frequency effect in the phonological tasks.

Inhibitory effect of high frequency main radicals on processing of phonetics

In the phonological judgement task, the L1 readers responded to the low radical frequency *kanji* significantly more accurately than to the high radical frequency *kanji*. This radical frequency effect suggests that the L1 readers processed the *kanji* not only at the character level but also at the component level. The radical frequency effect also suggests that, at the component level, while the phonetics had been identified, the main radicals, which were also components of the *kanji*, had also been identified. The results that the low frequency radicals facilitated the identification of phonetics suggest that the activation of main radicals may be stronger than the processing of phonetics. In relation to this, the findings of a study in Chinese word recognition (Ho, Ng and Ng, 2003) suggest that knowledge of the location of main radicals, but not of the position of phonetics, is important for learning to read in Chinese characters. That is because compared to phonetics, main radicals have greater positional regularities (i.e., many main radicals have their fixed locations in the characters), and the position of the main radicals provides good information for identification of the corresponding characters (Ho, Ng and Ng, 2003). In the case of the present study, the high frequency main radicals appear to have been processed more quickly than the low frequency main radicals due to frequency effects. The quick processing of the high frequency main radicals might have inhibited the processing of the phonetics, which might have resulted in less contribution from the phonetics to the processing of the reading of the *kanji* (*on*-reading).

In the phonological matching task, on the other hand, the readers did not show any difference between the low and high radical frequency *kanji*. A possible reason for this would be that because the phonetics were highlighted in this task, interference from the main radicals was reduced. The idea behind this manipulation whereby the phonetics of the *kanji* were made conspicuous was to make the phonetics more accessible than the main radicals. This might be a reason why the radical frequency did not affect the readers' performance in the phonological matching task.

Possible phonetic frequency effect on phonological processing

The L1 readers responded to the high homophone size *kanji* more accurately than to the low homophone size *kanji* in the phonological judgement task. The study by Tamaoka (2005), however, suggests that *kanji* with many homophones require a longer time for naming than *kanji* with fewer homophones. Tamaoka accounted for this finding by positing an inhibitory effect generated by the homophones, which competed with the target *kanji*. Given this situation, it was expected the low homophone size *kanji* would facilitate the performance of the L1 readers. However, the results indicated that this was not the case.

If the homophones of the *kanji* were accessed when the *kanji* was recognised, then it is plausible to think that *kanji* that shared a common phonetic with the target *kanji* were accessed as well. The question arises as to whether other *kanji* with a common phonetic facilitate or inhibit the access to the phonology of the *kanji*. In the orthographic task where the L1 readers were asked to find a common main radical in two characters, the main radicals that appeared in many *kanji* were identified more quickly and accurately than the main radicals that were used in few *kanji* (see Chapter 4 Section 1 for details). Indeed, the meta-analysis of previous studies conducted by Andrews (Andrews, 1997) suggested that larger neighbourhoods would almost always be associated with better performance in tasks such as naming tasks.

It could be then that the frequency of the phonetic (in terms of the neighbourhood size of the phonetic), rather than the homophone size per se, had an impact on the L1 readers' performance. Unfortunately, the *kanji* database does not provide the frequency of phonetics. I therefore counted the number of *kanji* (in the list of the 1,945 *kanji*) that shared the same phonetics for each of the phonetics of the *kanji* used in the task. It was revealed that the average number of *kanji* that shared the same phonetic as the phonetics of the high homophone size *kanji* was approximately twice the average of the low homophone size *kanji* (5:2.4). It could be that it was not the homophone size but the type frequency of the phonetics (phonetic neighbourhood size) that affected the L1 readers' performance in this task. The strong contribution from the component (phonetic) might have supported the access to the *on*-reading of the character for the high homophone size (i.e., high phonetic neighbourhood size) *kanji*.

For the low homophone size (i.e., low phonetic neighbourhood size) *kanji*, the phonological information of the component (phonetic) did not facilitate the access to the phonology of the character as much as it did in the other type of the *kanji*. Given that the identification of the characters typically dominates over the identification of the smaller units, the retrieved phonology of the *kanji* without much contribution from the phonetic would probably be the *kun*-reading (as single-character words are often read in the *kun*-reading), which would have led to incorrect responses.

In the phonological matching task however, the L1 readers did not differ either in speed or accuracy between the two groups of *kanji* that differed in homophone size. It seems plausible to propose that the specially highlighted phonetics of the *kanji* (which indicated the *on*-reading of *kanji*) facilitated the access to the phonology of the characters regardless of homophone size (phonetic neighbourhood size). This could have inhibited the retrieval of the *kun*-reading and facilitated the access to the *on*-reading, which was the required reading in this task.

5 2.7 Phonological judgement task: Interview data

In the phonological judgement task, at least two participants remarked that they selectively read the *kanji* in the *on*-reading, and one of them thought he did not access the meaning of the characters (see Example 1). However, some participants reported that they were not able to suppress the *kun*-reading of *kanji* from automatically entering to their minds, and that this adversely affected their judgements (see Examples 2). It seems that the *kun*-reading sometimes comes to the readers' minds prior to (or at least appears to be more salient than) the *on*-reading even when they knew that the task required an *on*-reading (see Example 3). Five participants said that they resorted to the phonetics of the *kanji* (see Example 4), when they could not retrieve the *on*-reading from the *kanji*.

Example 1: In this task, I read the *kanji* in the *on*-reading. I don't think I've given a thought to the meaning of the *kanji*.

Example 2: Sometimes it wasn't easy to recall the *on*-reading of *kanji*. For example, I read the *kanji kyuu* (吸) as /su-u/ in *kun*-reading, and I thought it wasn't the same as the reading of the second *kanji*.

Example 3: I only needed to recall the *on*-reading of *kanji* for this task, but sometimes the *kun*-reading came to mind. When I saw /dai/ (題) in *mondai* followed by /da-ku/ (抱 in *kun*-reading), I thought it might be 'yes', and my response was delayed because of this. I think the reading that has an actual meaning would come out first.

Example 4: When the *on*-reading of the characters didn't come up in my head, I'd tentatively press the 'yes' key if there was a common phonetic component in the two characters.

10 of the 16 participants directly or indirectly mentioned that *kanji* with multiple readings were harder to process (see Example 5). It seems that only one reading would come to mind at a time (see Example 6), and that reading could be a wrong one, i.e., not the one that was required in this task. Six participants said that they sometimes pressed the 'no' key if they thought that the second *kanji* had a sound different from the first *kanji*, where the first *kanji* actually had another reading that was the same as the second one (see Example 7).

> Example 5: The *kanji* that had many readings were hard. For example, the character *kare* (彼) could be read as /kare/, /kano/, and /hi/. I didn't know which one would be useful to remember for the matching.
>
> Example 6: I couldn't think of all the readings. I could only have one reading at a time. So if the reading that came to my head was not one of the readings of the other character, then I had to try and think of the other readings (of the first character),
>
> Example 7: There was a *kanji* that could be read as /dai/, but I read it as /tai/ because one of its readings was /tai/ as in the word *taifuu* (台風) When I saw the screen showing the second *kanji dai* (題) of *mondai,* I accidentally pressed the 'no' key.

The results of the statistical analysis showed that the participants' 'yes' responses to the common-reading pairs were faster than their 'no' responses to the no-common-reading pairs. This was supported in the interview (see Example 8).

Example 8: It is easy to say 'yes', but I'd hesitate to say 'no' when I couldn't come up with the same pronunciation (reading) for the two *kanji*, as I thought there might be other readings as well.

5 2.8 Phonological matching task: Interview data

Five L1 readers referred to the *kanji* with multiple readings (see Example 1). One of them said that when the first reading was not the required reading, she had difficulty getting the other readings, as she could not recall the graphic representation of the first *kanji* (see Example 2).

Example 1: I'd remember the *kanji* in one of the readings, and I'd press the 'no' key when I saw/heard a different sound (reading). And then I'd usually realise that I had made an error immediately after pressing the key.

Example 2: I remembered the target *kanji* by one of its readings, not by its shape. So when the sound for the second *kanji* was different from the sound I had on my mind, I couldn't recall the shape of the *kanji* even if I tried to remember it. So I pressed 'no' for those ones. Sometimes, however, the shape of the *kanji* came back to my mind after a short while, and I realised that I had made a mistake.

The remarks made by three participants suggest that a word, not a character, was the unit of their recognition (see Examples 3-4).

Example 3: It was hard to perform the task, as I usually see *kanji* as part of words, and I don't pay attention to individual *kanji*.

Example 4: When I saw *kanji*, I usually tried to remember a compound word that contained the target *kanji*, but sometimes I had trouble recalling any compound word. I found it hard to make a decision when I heard the sound that was the reading of the other *kanji* of the two *kanji* of the compound word.

Because the *kanji* had been half-shaded, the phonetics were conspicuous to the participants, which sometimes caused the disturbance. Two participants mentioned that the reading of the highlighted phonetics affected their reading of the *kanji* (see Example 5)

Example 5: I sometimes found myself remembering only the highlighted parts, and had trouble remembering the other parts. And that made reading the *kanji* harder.

5.2.9 Discussion of the interview about the phonological judgement and phonological matching tasks

Problem of multiple readings

It appeared that the L1 readers knew that they had to retrieve the *on*-reading in the phonological tasks. When the *kanji* in the item had only one *on*-reading, the task was not difficult. However, there were some *kanji* that had more than one *on*-reading, and in some cases, one or more *kun*-readings as well. If the reading that was retrieved was different from the one being asked for in the task, the participants could make an incorrect judgement. In this respect, factors such as frequency of occurrence of *kanji* with a particular *on*-reading or the ratio of *on*-reading to *kun*-reading might have

265

affected the L1 readers' performances. This is a separate property from the stimulus properties that were considered in the current study. The collators of the *kanji* database indeed found no correlation between the *on*-reading ratio and the number of *kanji* homophones (Tamaoka, Kirsner, Yanase, Miyaoka and Kawasaki, 2002).

In both tasks, the L1 readers tended to take more time on the 'no' items, which seems to be logical. In the interview, for example, in the phonological judgement task, the L1 readers remarked that they had to reconsider their immediate response before pressing the 'no' key, to check if there was definitely no common reading between the two stimuli, as there might have been other readings as well. In the common-reading items, apparently, they had to take this second step only when they could not come up with the same reading. Judging from the L1 readers' remarks in the interview, it seems that recalling multiple readings simultaneously was not possible, and therefore they had only one or two readings in their minds at a time. It appears that only after finding out that the reading was not the same as that of the other stimulus, did they go and find other readings to see if there were any that were the same as the reading of the other one. Sometimes, however, the L1 readers found it difficult to retrieve other readings because the graphic image of the target *kanji* had disappeared from their minds after remembering the stimulus (*kanji*) by one of its readings.

The activation models such as the Multi-level Interactive Activation Model (Taft and Zhu, 1995) explain simultaneous activation at the word, morpheme (character), sub-morpheme (component) and feature (stroke) levels. However, as described above, the interview data suggest that the 'consciously-guided' aspect of decision making is serial. That is, even though the identification process may be parallel and multiple options may be sent to the decision making program, there is a processing 'bottle-neck' at a very late stage of processing.

Processing in a meaning-bearing unit

Although the L1 readers knew that they were required to retrieve the *on*-reading, it seems that they sometimes could not help reading the *kanji* in its *kun*-reading. Judging by their remarks, they tended to read a single character that can be a (single-character) word in its *kun*-reading, which had a meaning attached. On the other hand, if the character was not able to be a word in its own right, the L1 readers would put it into a meaningful compound word before reading the character in its *on*-reading (unlike single-character words, *kanji* in a compound word are often read in their *on*-readings). That is, the L1 readers automatically put the *kanji* in a meaningful unit: either as a single-character word or in a compound word. It appears that it was not simple a task to read an individual *kanji* in an *on*-reading (which was a non-meaning-bearing reading).

Making a compound word when the target *kanji* has no meaning-bearing reading seems to be a natural processing strategy even for L1 children. For instance, Yamada (1998) asked Japanese middle school and high school students to name *kanji* on their own. The results of error analyses showed that visual and visual-semantic errors abounded, suggesting a very weak association between *kanji* and the reading. The most interesting error type was that when they could not read the *kanji* in its meaning-bearing reading, the children sometimes gave a reading of another *kanji* that was the other constituent of the compound word in which the target *kanji* was embedded. For example, 写 /sha/ was read as /shiN/ because 真 /shiN/ is the other constituent of the word 写真 /shashiN/ (photograph).

The above finding suggests that the reading of a compound word may be stored at some level as a single reading, instead of two readings of two independent characters. It was interesting that there was a remark also in the interview that the reading of one of the *kanji* in a compound word was almost mistaken as the reading of the other *kanji* of the word. Research suggests that recognition units are formed at the word level rather than the individual character level (Kess and Miyamoto, 1997). If this were the case, then the reading of *kanji* can only be accessed via the identification of a word in which the *kanji* is found. On the other hand, Taft (2004) claims that a character is pronounced only via the mediation of a lemma. It might be that anything that has a lemma (a concept) is linked to a single reading that indicates the concept, regardless of the orthographic status. Further evidence to support this argument may be found in the fact that L1 readers read some *kanji* as if these characters were *words*. The *kanji* mentioned in the interview were 抱 and 吸. The participants read them as /da-ku/ and /su-u/, both of which were their *kun*-readings (meaning-bearing readings), despite the fact that く /ku/ in 抱く and う /u/ in 吸う did not appear on the screen.

Component awareness indicated in component-level processing

In the cases where the L1 readers could not instantly come up with any reading, they seemed to resort to the phonetics of the *kanji*. By looking at the phonetic of the *kanji*, it seems that they were able to infer the reading, suggesting that they were aware of the phonetics of *kanji*. However, as mentioned above, the participants remarked that they felt distracted by the reading of the highlighted phonetics in the cases of *kanji* with invalid phonetics. This certainly suggests that the participants were aware of the limitations of phonetic information. The interview data indicated that the phonology of the characters and the phonetics might not necessarily be made available on a conscious level at the same time. The L1 readers mentioned that they used the phonetics when they could not read the characters. It appears that the phonology of phonetics becomes a focus when the output of phonological processing of the characters does not help to solve the task. Overall, the findings suggest that certain levels of processing are more routinely considered (probably due to experience in considering the properties of stimuli at the level) for decision making. It could also be because the characters, but not the phonetics, had lemmas: that is, the phonology of the kanji would have been accessed through their lemma at the preconscious level whereas the phonology of the phonetics would have had to be retrieved strategically.

5.3 L2 readers of Japanese: Objectives and Methods

5.3.1 Objectives

The phonological aspects of the *kanji* recognition skills and awareness of L2 readers were investigated for comparison with the L1 results just discussed. Two phonological processing tasks and a retrospective interview (see Chapter 3 for details) were used to examine their skills and awareness. As in the study with the L1 readers, the materials used were a phonological judgement task and a phonological matching task. Likewise, the effects of the four stimulus properties were also examined. The main aspects of awareness examined in the interview were awareness of information in components and awareness of the limitations of component information (see Chapter 3 for detailed selections of the tasks, stimulus properties and awareness).

5-3-2 Methods

Participants

Out of the 109 participants, 21 beginner, 19 intermediate and 27 advanced readers undertook the phonological judgement task, and 18 beginner, 21 intermediate and 26 advanced readers did the phonological matching task. However, because of the use of the option to skip a trial, in some cases the number of valid trials in a participant's responses was very limited. In cases where the responses (yes or no) of a participant were less than 10, the data of that participant were excluded from the analyses. For example, 21 beginner learners were originally asked to do the phonological judgement task, but the analysable number of observations in this task fell to 10 after the exclusions. The final numbers of analysable observations were 10 beginner, 16 intermediate and 27 advanced readers in the phonological judgement task, and 8 beginner, 19 intermediate and 26 advanced readers in the phonological matching task.

Materials

The same two phonological tasks used for the L1 readers were used for the L2 readers.

Procedure

The procedure of administering the tasks was the same as for the previous study with the L1 readers.

5.4 Test results and discussion

The mean values shown in this section are all adjusted means. The results of the analyses are shown in LSD statistics instead of F-values or t-values. Only the correct responses for the expected 'yes' items are reported here (see Chapter 3 Section 3).

5.4.1 Phonological judgement task: Reaction times and correct response rates

In the phonological judgement task, each participant (beginner, intermediate and advanced) was required to judge whether or not the two *kanji* (e.g., 符 and 府) shared a common reading (e.g., /fu/). Table 5.11 presents mean response times and mean correct response rates of the beginner, intermediate and advanced L2 readers in the phonological judgement task for the common-reading items ('yes' items).

Table 5.11 Mean response times and mean correct response rates of the beginner, intermediate and advanced L2 readers in the phonological judgement task for the common-reading items

	Phonological judgement task 符 - 府 /fu/ - /fu/ Can the two characters be read in the same way? –Yes	
Group	RT (ms)	CR (%)
Beg	1328	25.9
Int	1420	47.7
Adv	1311	57.9

Beg = L2 readers of Japanese who knew 50-300 *kanji*; Int = L2 readers of Japanese who knew 300 - 1,000 *kanji*; Adv = L2 readers of Japanese who knew more than 1,000 *kanji*; RT = response times in milliseconds; CR = correct response rate in %.

In this task, no significant differences in response time were identified across the groups (between advanced and intermediate: 1311 - 1420 = -190, LSD = 295; between intermediate and beginner: 1420 - 1328 = 92, LSD = 358).

However the accuracy increased as the *kanji* knowledge levels of the groups increased. The difference between the advanced and intermediate readers was significant (57.9 - 47.7 = 10.2, LSD = 10.2) at the 0.05 level. The intermediate group performed the task significantly more accurately than the beginner group (47.7 - 25.9 = 21.8, LSD = 10.7). The increase in accuracy clearly indicated the development of *kanji* recognition in the L2 readers.

The extremely low correct response rate of the beginner readers was most likely to be the result of the fact that the L2 readers who knew less than 300 characters actively skipped or pressed the 'no' button for most of the items. The intermediate and advanced readers had more correct responses, but they were still very low. The poor correct response rates showed that the L2 readers had scant knowledge of *kanji* phonology: the advanced readers were still inaccurate in terms of finding a common reading in two *kanji*, not to mention the beginner and intermediate readers.

5.4.2 Phonological judgement task: Stimulus properties

Complexity

Differences in the responses to *kanji* that differed in complexity were statistically analysed both in terms of mean response time and correct response rate (see Chapter 3 Section 3 for details). Table 5.12 shows mean response times and mean correct response rates for the low and high complexity *kanji*.

Table 5.12 Mean response times and mean correct response rates of the L2 readers in the judgement task for low and high complexity *kanji*

	Phonological judgement task			
	Can the two characters be read in the same way? -Yes			
	Low complexity 吸 - 級 /kyuR/-/kyuR/		High complexity 陽 - 揚 /yoR/- /yoR/	
Group	RT (ms)	CR (%)	RT (ms)	CR (%)
Beg	1368	40.0	1297	33.0
Int	1386	60.0	1403	51.6
Adv	1311	54.8	1506	56.3

Beg = L2 readers of Japanese who knew 50-300 *kanji*, Int = L2 readers of Japanese who knew 300 - 1,000 *kanji*, Adv = L2 readers of Japanese who knew more than 1,000 *kanji*, RT = mean response times in milliseconds, CR = mean correct response rate in %

For response time, the main effect of complexity, the main effect of *kanji* knowledge, and the interaction effect of complexity and *kanji* knowledge were all non-significant (complexity: p = 0.175; *kanji* knowledge: p = 0.905; complexity x: *kanji* knowledge: p = 0.167). For accuracy, neither the main effect of complexity nor the interaction effect was significant (complexity: p = 0.236; complexity x: *kanji* knowledge: p = 0.394), but the main effect of *kanji* knowledge was significant (*kanji* knowledge: p = 0.041).

Correct response rate - kanji knowledge effect

The results of individual comparisons showed that the advanced L2 readers responded to the high complexity *kanji* significantly more accurately than the beginner readers (56.3 – 33 = 23.3, LSD = 18.5), but no other comparisons showed a significant difference. For the high complexity *kanji*, the differences between the beginner group and the intermediate group (33 - 51.6 = -18.6, LSD = 20.1) and between the intermediate group and the advanced group (51.6 – 56.3 = -4.7, LSD = 18.8) were non-significant. Likewise, for the low complexity *kanji*, the differences between the beginner group and the intermediate group (40 - 60 = -20, LSD = 20.1) and between the intermediate group and the advanced group (60 – 54.8 = 5.2, LSD = 18.8) were all non-significant.

Character Frequency

Table 5.13 presents mean response times and mean correct response rates for the low and high frequency *kanji*.

Table 5.13 Mean response times and mean correct response rates of the L2 readers in the judgement task for low and high frequency *kanji*

	Phonological judgement task Can the two characters be read in the same way? -Yes			
	Low character frequency 胴 - 洞 /doR/-/doR/		High character frequency 時 - 持 /ji/-/ji/	
Group	RT (ms)	CR (%)	RT (ms)	CR (%)
Beg	1756	21.0	1669	22.0
Int	1625	40.0	1564	57.9
Adv	1339	44.4	1256	73.3

Beg = L2 readers of Japanese who knew 50-300 *kanji*, Int = L2 readers of Japanese who knew 300 - 1,000 *kanji*, Adv = L2 readers of Japanese who knew more than 1,000 *kanji*, RT = mean response times in milliseconds, CR = mean correct response rate in %.

For response speed, neither the main effect nor the interaction effect of character frequency and *kanji* knowledge was significant (character frequency: $p = 0.251$; *kanji* knowledge: $p = 0.135$; character frequency x *kanji* knowledge: $p = 0.987$). On the other hand, for accuracy, the main effects of character frequency ($p < 0.001$) and *kanji* knowledge ($p < 0.001$), and the interaction of character frequency and *kanji* knowledge ($p = 0.004$) were all significant.

Correct response rate - character frequency effect

For accuracy, the beginner readers, who were able to read very few *kanji*, did not differ significantly between the low and high frequency *kanji* ($21 - 22 = - 1$, LSD = 12.6), but significant differences were observed between the two groups of *kanji* in the intermediate and advanced readers. The intermediate readers performed on the high frequency *kanji* significantly more accurately than on the low frequency *kanji* ($57.9 - 40 = 17.9$, LSD = 12.9). They must have found some *kanji* that they could read among the high frequency *kanji* although a large proportion of the *kanji* was probably phonologically unfamiliar to them. The difference between the two groups of *kanji* was even larger for the advanced readers, who performed significantly more accurately on the high frequency *kanji* than on the low frequency *kanji* ($73.3 - 44.4 = 28.9$, LSD = 10.9). The correct response rates of the L2 readers at all the *kanji* knowledge levels for the low frequency *kanji* were very low (under 50%).

Correct response rate - *kanji* knowledge effect

The beginner readers' performance on the low frequency *kanji* was particularly poor, and was significantly worse than the intermediate (21 – 40 = -19, LSD = 17.9). There was no significant difference in accuracy between the intermediate and advanced readers (40 – 44.4 = -4.4, LSD = 16.8). The response pattern was the same for the high frequency *kanji*. The correct response rate of the beginner readers was very low, and was significantly lower than the intermediate (22 - 57.9 = -35.9, LSD = 17.9). The difference between the intermediate and advanced readers was not significant (57.9 - 73.3 = -15.4, LSD = 16.8).

Correct response rate - interaction effect

As shown above, when the knowledge of *kanji* was very limited such as in the case of the beginner readers, the frequency of the *kanji* used in the task had no significant impact on their performance. For the intermediate and advanced readers, the reading of the high frequency *kanji* was much more accurate than the low frequency *kanji*, and the difference was even larger for the advanced readers than for the intermediate readers.

Radical Frequency

Table 5.14 presents mean response times and mean correct response rates for the low and high radical frequency *kanji*.

Table 5.14 Mean response times and mean correct response rates of the L2 readers in the judgement task for low and high radical frequency *kanji*

| | Phonological judgement Can the two characters be read in the same way? -Yes | | | |
| Group | Low radical frequency 孤 - 弧 /ko/-/ko/ | | High radical frequency 沿 - 鉛 /eN/-/eN/ | |
	RT (ms)	CR (%)	RT (ms)	CR (%)
Beg	1339	24.0	1505	28.0
Int	1384	44.2	1492	45.3
Adv	1338	55.6	1426	57.0

Beg = L2 readers of Japanese who knew 50-300 *kanji*, Int = L2 readers of Japanese who knew 300 - 1,000 *kanji*, Adv = L2 readers of Japanese who knew more than 1,000 *kanji*, RT = mean response times in milliseconds, CR = mean correct response rate in %.

Neither the main effect nor the interaction effect of radical frequency and *kanji* knowledge was significant (radical frequency: $p = 0.090$; *kanji* knowledge: $p = 0.934$; radical frequency x: *kanji* knowledge $p = 0.905$) for response speed. For accuracy, only the main effect of *kanji* knowledge ($p < 0.001$) was significant. Neither the main effect of radical frequency (p = 0.529) nor the interaction effect (radical frequency x: *kanji* knowledge: p = 0.933) was significant.

Correct response rate - *kanji* knowledge effect

For the low radical frequency *kanji*, although there was no significant difference between the advanced and intermediate readers (55.6 - 44.2 = 11.4, LSD = 17.3), the intermediate readers performed significantly more accurately than the beginner readers (44.2 - 24 = 20.2, LSD = 18.5). On the other hand, no significant differences in accuracy were observed for the high radical frequency either between the advanced and intermediate readers (57 - 45.3 = 11.7, LSD = 17.3) or between the intermediate and beginner readers (45.3 - 28 = 17.3, LSD = 18.5).

Homophone size

Table 5.15 presents mean response times and mean correct response rates for the low and high homophone size *kanji*.

Table 5.15 Mean response times and mean correct response rates of the L2 readers in the judgement task for low and high homophone size *kanji*

	Phonological judgement			
	Can the two characters be read in the same way? -Yes			
	Low homophone size 郡 - 群 /guN/-/guN/		High homophone size 砲 - 抱 /hoR/-/hoR/	
Group	RT (ms)	CR (%)	RT (ms)	CR (%)

	RT	CR	RT	CR
Beg	1540	29.0	1370	30.0
Int	1435	44.2	1577	47.4
Adv	1333	51.9	1080	66.7

Beg = L2 readers of Japanese who knew 50-300 *kanji*, Int = L2 readers of Japanese who knew 300 - 1,000 *kanji*, Adv = L2 readers of Japanese who knew more than 1,000 *kanji*, RT = mean response times in milliseconds, CR = mean correct response rate in %.

For response time, neither the main effect nor the interaction effect of homophone size and *kanji* knowledge was significant (homophone size: p = 0.118; *kanji* knowledge: p = 0.124; homophone size x *kanji* knowledge: p = 0.104). For correct response rate, the main effects of homophone size (p = 0.007) and *kanji* knowledge (p < 0.001) were significant. The interaction of homophone size and *kanji* knowledge was not significant (p = 0.066).

Correct response rate - homophone size effect

For accuracy, the advanced readers performed significantly more accurately on the high homophone size *kanji* than on the low homophone size *kanji* (66.7 – 51.9 = 14.8, LSD = 8.5). No significant differences between the two groups of *kanji* that differed in homophone size were observed in the intermediate (44.2 – 47.4 = -3.2, LSD = 10.1) and in the beginner readers (29 – 30 = -1, LSD = 9.8). No significant differences were observed in the beginner or intermediate readers probably because these readers had scant knowledge of homophones.

Correct response rate - *kanji* knowledge effect

With regard to the *kanji* with few homophones (the low homophone size *kanji*), there was no significant difference either between the advanced and intermediate readers (51.9 - 44.2 = 7.7, LSD = 14.8) or between the intermediate and beginner readers (44.2 - 29 = 15.2, LSD = 15.8). For the high homophone size *kanji*, on the other hand, the advanced readers performed significantly more accurately than the intermediate readers (66.7 - 47.4 = 19.3, LSD = 14.8), and the intermediate readers significantly more accurately than the beginner readers (47.4 - 30 = 17.4, LSD = 15.8). These results indicated that the L2 readers might have been able to read high homophone size *kanji* before low homophone *kanji*.

5.4.3 Phonological matching task: Reaction times and correct response rates

In the phonological matching task, each participant was asked to judge whether or not the character had the reading presented (e.g., 祖 and /so/).

Table 5.16 shows mean response times and mean correct response rates of the beginner, intermediate and advanced L2 readers in the phonological matching task for the 'yes' items.

Table 5.16 Mean response times and mean correct response rates of the beginner, intermediate and advanced L2 readers in the phonological matching task for the valid-phonetic items

	Phonological matching task 祖 so	
	Can the character be read as shown? - Yes	
Group	RT (ms)	CR (%)
Beg	1349	21.7
Int	1001	42.3
Adv	1060	66.9

Beg = L2 readers of Japanese who knew 50-300 *kanji*; Int = L2 readers of Japanese who knew 300 - 1,000 *kanji*; Adv = L2 readers of Japanese who knew more than 1,000 *kanji*; RT = response times in milliseconds; CR = correct response rate in %.

The L2 readers' response pattern was similar to the phonological judgement task. No significant differences in response speed were identified between the advanced and intermediate groups (1060 - 1001 = 59, LSD = 281) or between the intermediate and beginner groups (1001 - 1349 = 348, LSD = 363).

However, the advanced group performed the task significantly more accurately than the intermediate group (66.9 - 42.3 = 24.6, LSD = 10), and the intermediate group performed significantly more accurately than did the beginner group (42.3 - 21.7 = 20.6, LSD = 10.8). These results indicated the growth of the knowledge of *kanji* phonology.

5.4.4 Phonological matching task: Stimulus properties

Complexity

Table 5.17 shows mean response times and mean correct response rates for the low and high complexity *kanji*.

Table 5.17 Mean response times and mean correct response rates of the L2 readers in the matching task for low and high complexity _kanji_

| | Phonological matching Can the character be read as shown? - Yes | | | |
| | Low complexity 固 - ko | | High complexity 博 - haku | |
Group	RT (ms)	CR (%)	RT (ms)	CR (%)
Beg	1200	20.0	1342	22.2
Int	1014	39.1	1095	30.5
Adv	1086	68.5	1378	54.6

Beg = L2 readers of Japanese who knew 50-300 _kanji_, Int = L2 readers of Japanese who knew 300 - 1,000 _kanji_, Adv = L2 readers of Japanese who knew more than 1,000 _kanji_, RT = mean response times in milliseconds, CR = mean correct response rate in %.

For response speed, only the main effect of complexity was significant ($p = 0.007$), and neither the main effect of _kanji_ knowledge ($p = 0.397$) nor the interaction effect (complexity x _kanji_ knowledge: $p = 0.484$) was significant. For accuracy, a significant main effect of complexity ($p = 0.019$) and a significant main effect of _kanji_ knowledge (p < 0.001) were observed. The interaction effect (complexity x *kanji* knowledge: p = 0.138) was not significant.

Response time - complexity effect

The advanced L2 readers' responses to the low complexity *kanji* were significantly faster than to the high complexity *kanji* (1086 - 1378 = -292, LSD = 205), but there was no significant difference between the low and high complexity *kanji* either for the intermediate readers (1014 - 1095 = -81, LSD = 305) or for the beginner readers (1200 - 1342 = -142, LSD = 431).

Correct response rate - complexity effect

The advanced readers performed the low complexity *kanji* not only significantly more quickly but also significantly more accurately than the high complexity *kanji* (68.5 - 54. 6 = 13.9, LSD = 10.4). No significant differences in accuracy were observed between the low and high complexity *kanji* in either the intermediate (39.1 - 30. 5 = 8.6, LSD = 11.5) or the beginner readers (20 - 22.2 = 2.2, LSD = 12.5).

Correct response rate - *kanji* knowledge effect

In comparisons between the groups of L2 readers, for the low complexity *kanji*, the advanced readers responded significantly more accurately than the intermediate readers (68.5 - 22.2 = 46.3, LSD = 14.4), and the intermediate readers were significantly more accurate than the beginner readers (39.1 - 20 = 19.1, LSD =15.7). The advanced group was also significantly more accurate than the intermediate groups (54.6 - 30.5 = 24.1, LSD = 14.4) for the high complexity *kanji*. However, there were no significant differences between the intermediate and beginner readers for the high complexity *kanji* (30.5 - 22.2 = 8.3, LSD = 15.7).

Character frequency

Mean response times and mean correct response rates of the L2 readers for the low and high frequency *kanji* are presented in table 5.18.

Table 5.18 Mean response times and mean correct response rates of the L2 readers in the matching task for low and high frequency *kanji*

	Phonological matching Can the character be read as shown? - Yes			
	Low character frequency 符 - fu		High character frequency 副 - fuku	
Group	RT (ms)	CR (%)	RT (ms)	CR (%)
Beg	1394	13.3	1083	35.6
Int	1069	23.8	874	74.3
Adv	1162	59.2	761	92.3

Beg = L2 readers of Japanese who knew 50-300 *kanji*, Int = L2 readers of Japanese who knew 300 - 1,000 *kanji*, Adv = L2 readers of Japanese who knew more than 1,000 *kanji*, RT = mean response times in milliseconds, CR = mean correct response rate in %.

For response time, only the effect of character frequency was significant ($p < 0.001$), and neither the main effect of *kanji* knowledge ($p = 0.209$) nor interaction (character frequency x *kanji* knowledge: p = 0.518) was observed. For accuracy, the main effects of character frequency (p < 0.001) and *kanji* knowledge (p < 0.001) were significant as was the interaction effect (character frequency x *kanji* knowledge: p = 0.002).

Response time - character frequency effect

The advanced L2 readers responded to the high frequency *kanji* significantly faster than to the low frequency *kanji* (761 - 1162 = -401, LSD = 192). On the other hand, neither the intermediate (1069 - 874 = 195, LSD = 308) nor the beginner readers (1394 - 1083 = 311, LSD = 456) showed a significant difference in their response times between the low and high frequency *kanji*.

Correct response rate - character frequency effect

As far as accuracy is concerned, however, the frequency of *kanji* impacted significantly upon all the three L2 groups. The advanced readers responded to the high frequency *kanji* significantly more accurately than to the low frequency *kanji* (92.3 - 59.2 = 33.1, LSD = 10), and so did the intermediate readers (74.3 - 23.8 = 50.5, LSD = 11.1). Even in the beginners, the difference was significant (35.6 - 13.3 = 22.3, LSD = 12).

Correct response rate - *kanji* knowledge effect

The advanced readers performed on the low frequency *kanji* significantly more accurately than did the intermediate readers (59.2 - 23.8 = 35.4, LSD = 12.1). The

286

correct response rates of the intermediate and beginner readers for the low frequency *kanji* were extremely low, and there was no significant difference between them (23.8 -13.3 = 10.5, LSD = 13.2). The development in phonological processing ability was only evident in the L2 readers' performance on the high frequency *kanji*. The advanced readers were able to match the high frequency *kanji* with their readings very accurately. Their accuracy was significantly higher than that of the intermediate readers (92.3 - 74.3 = 18, LSD = 12.1). The difference between the intermediate and beginner readers was even larger, with the intermediate readers performing significantly more accurately than the beginner readers (74.3 - 35.6 = 38.7, LSD = 13.2). Apparently, for the beginner readers, reading the low frequency *kanji* was simply not possible.

Correct response rate - interaction effect

Although the character frequency effect was significant for the L2 readers at all *kanji* knowledge levels, it had its clearest impact on the intermediate readers (74.3 - 23.8 = 50.5, LSD = 11.1).

Radical frequency

Table 5.19 presents mean response times and mean correct response rates for the low and high radical frequency *kanji*.

Table 5.19 Mean response times and mean correct response rates of the L2 readers in the matching task for low and high radical frequency _kanji_

| | Phonological matching
Can the character be read as shown? - Yes | | | |
| | Low radical frequency
版 - han | | High radical frequency
拒 - kyo | |
Group	RT (ms)	CR (%)	RT (ms)	CR (%)
Beg	1278	15.6	1305	24.4
Int	888	21.9	1234	41.9
Adv	1170	44.6	1136	70

Beg = L2 readers of Japanese who knew 50-300 _kanji_, Int = L2 readers of Japanese who knew 300 - 1,000 _kanji_, Adv = L2 readers of Japanese who knew more than 1,000 _kanji_, RT = mean response times in milliseconds, CR = mean correct response rate in %.

The main effects of radical frequency, of _kanji_ knowledge, and the interaction effect were all non-significant for response speed (radical frequency: $p = 0.426$; _kanji_ knowledge: $p = 0.724$; radical frequency x _kanji_ knowledge: $p = 0.170$). For accuracy, the main effects of radical frequency ($p < 0.001$) and _kanji_ knowledge ($p < 0.001$) were significant. The interaction effect (radical frequency x _kanji_ knowledge: $p = 0.127$) was not significant.

Correct response rate - radical frequency effect

Radical frequency affected the accuracy of the advanced and intermediate readers' performances. The advanced readers responded to the high radical frequency *kanji* significantly more accurately than to the low radical frequency *kanji* (70 - 44.6 = 25.4, LSD = 10.4). The intermediate readers also processed the high radical frequency *kanji* significantly more accurately than the low radical frequency *kanji* (41.9 - 21.9 = 20, LSD = 11.6).

The finding that the radical frequency affected the L2 readers' performance in the phonological task was unexpected, as the main radicals had no function in bearing the phonological information of the *kanji*.

Correct response rate -*kanji* knowledge effect

A comparison between the groups indicated that the advanced readers performed the low radical frequency *kanji* more accurately than the intermediate readers (44.6 - 21.9 = 22.7, LSD = 13.9). However, there was no significant difference for this measure between the intermediate and beginner readers (21.9 - 15.6 = 6.3, LSD = 15.2). Accuracy differences between the groups were larger for the high radical frequency *kanji*. The advanced readers performed significantly more accurately than the intermediate readers (70 - 41.9 = 28.1, LSD = 13.9), and the intermediate readers were significantly more accurate than the beginner readers (41.9 - 24.4 = 17.5, LSD = 15.2).

Homophone size

Table 5.20 presents mean response times and mean correct response rates for the low and high homophone size *kanji*.

Table 5.20 Mean response times and mean correct response rates of L2 readers in the matching task for low and high homophone size *kanji*

| | Phonological matching
Can the character be read as shown? - Yes | | | |
| | Low homophone size
徒 - to | | High homophone size
剣 - ken | |
Group	RT (ms)	CR (%)	RT (ms)	CR (%)
Beg	1309	17.8	1187	27.8
Int	985	38.1	950	60.0
Adv	1205	75.4	866	66.9

Beg = L2 readers of Japanese who knew 50-300 *kanji*, Int = L2 readers of Japanese who knew 300 - 1,000 *kanji*, Adv = L2 readers of Japanese who knew more than 1,000 *kanji*, RT = mean response times in milliseconds, CR = mean correct response rate in %.

For response speed, only the main effect of homophone size was significant ($p = 0.002$). Neither the main effect of *kanji* knowledge ($p = 0.308$) nor the interaction effect of homophone size and *kanji* knowledge ($p = 0.168$) was significant. For accuracy, the main effect of homophone size ($p = 0.039$), of *kanji* knowledge ($p < 0.001$), and the interaction effect of homophone size and *kanji* knowledge ($p < 0.001$) were all significant,

Response time - homophone size effect

For response speed, the advanced L2 readers responded to the high homophone size *kanji* significantly more quickly than to the low homophone size *kanji* (866 - 1205 = -339, LSD = 193). The differences between the two groups of *kanji* were not significant in the intermediate (985 – 950 = 35, LSD = 272) and beginner groups (1309 – 1187 = 122, LSD = 442).

Correct response rate - homophone size effect[2]

The intermediate readers responded to the high homophone size *kanji* significantly more accurately than to the low homophone size *kanji* (60 - 38.1 = 21.9, LSD = 11). No significant differences were observed between the low and high homophone size *kanji* in the advanced group (75.4 - 66.9 = 8.5, LSD = 9.9) or in the beginner group (17.8 - 27.8 = -10, LSD = 11.9).

---

[2]Note that in the pair in which the homophone size was the key property, their complexity was also significantly different (see Chapter 3 Section 2). Although each pair of the *kanji* was selected to vary only in one critical property, it was found that there was an unexpected difference. The low and high homophone size *kanji* also differed significantly in their complexity. The results of the independent samples t-test showed that this set of pairs was also significantly different in their complexity, t(8)=2.36, p<0.05. The high homophone size *kanji* had less complexity than the low homophone size *kanji*. It indicated that complexity might have had a significant bearing on the effect of homophone size on the response times and percentage of correct responses.

Correct response rate - *kanji* knowledge effect

The advanced readers performed significantly more accurately than the intermediate readers on the low homophone size *kanji* (75.4 - 38.1 = 37.3, LSD = 12.8), and the intermediate readers were significantly more accurate than the beginner readers (38.1 - 17.8 = 20.3, LSD = 14). For high homophone size *kanji*, the intermediate readers performed significantly more accurately than the beginner readers (60 - 27.8 = 32.2, LSD = 14). However, the difference between the advanced and intermediate readers was non-significant (66.9 - 60 = 6.9, LSD = 12.8).

Correct response rate - interaction effect

The L2 readers showed gradual improvement in processing for the low homophone size *kanji*. As shown above, the intermediate readers were significantly more accurate than the beginner readers, and the advanced readers were significantly more accurate than the intermediate readers. On the other hand, for the high homophone size *kanji*, there was a considerable difference in the correct response rates between the beginner readers and the intermediate readers (60 - 27.8 = 32.2, LSD = 14), but no significant difference between the intermediate and advanced readers.

5.4.5 Comparison between the results of the phonological judgement and phonological matching tasks

In terms of overall magnitude, there was no significant difference in response time between the phonological judgement and phonological matching tasks for the beginner group (1328 - 1349 = -21, LSD = 271). On the other hand, the intermediate (1420 - 1001 = 419, LSD = 320) and advanced groups (1311 - 1060 = 251, LSD = 87) performed the phonological matching task significantly more quickly than the phonological judgement task. With regard to accuracy, there were no significant differences between the tasks in the beginner group (25.9 - 21.7 = 4.2, LSD = 10.3) or in the intermediate group (47.7 - 42.3 = 5.4, LSD = 10.3). However, the difference in accuracy between the two tasks was significant in the advanced group, with the mean correct response rate of the phonological matching task being higher than that of the phonological judgement task (66.9 - 57.9 = 9, LSD = 8).

5.4.6 Discussion of the results of the phonological judgement and phonological matching tasks

The results of the comparison of the phonological judgement and phonological matching tasks showed that the beginner group showed no significant difference either in terms of the response times or the correct response rates (except for the property of character frequency in the phonological matching task). Judging from their extremely low correct response rates, showing no significant difference between their response times to the two tasks probably means that these phonological tasks were simply beyond their capacity. The fact that a number of the beginner readers refused to perform the tasks or skipped a considerable number of task items also indicated their inability to perform the phonological tasks. Hence, only the results of the intermediate and advanced readers will be discussed here.

Exposure to characters and development of phonological processing

The intermediate and advanced groups responded to the phonological matching task (i.e., a *kanji* and a reading) significantly more quickly than to the phonological judgement task (i.e., two *kanji)*. Given that in both tasks the phonology of two stimuli had to be decoded and compared, the difference in response time between the two tasks implies that the two comparisons have different degrees of ambiguity. In the phonological judgement task, the readings of two *kanji* had to be compared. However, as each *kanji* can have more than one reading, in some cases the readers had several combinations to compare before finding the common reading between them. On the other hand, in the phonological matching task, at least the phonology of the given reading was unambiguous unlike that of the *kanji*. The readers only needed to find the same reading within the multiple readings of the *kanji*. The L2 readers' faster response times for the phonological matching task was probably due to the fewer combinations for comparison required by the task.

If it is the different degree of ambiguity that is producing the different response times, then one would expect that the L1 readers would also respond to the phonological matching task faster than to the phonological judgement task. On the contrary, there was no significant difference in response time between the two tasks. It appears that the L1 readers' relatively slow responses to the phonological matching task was likely to be attributed to the decoding of the unfamiliar Roman alphabet, which was used for providing the readings. Certainly this would not be the case with the L2 readers who were familiar with the alphabet.

The advanced readers responded to the phonological matching task, not only more quickly but also more accurately than to the phonological judgement task. The L1 readers also performed the phonological matching task significantly more accurately than the phonological judgement task. In the phonological matching task, the participants only needed to match the given reading with one of the readings of *kanji*, which was assisted by the valid phonetic of the *kanji* (that indicated the required *on*-reading). If the participants successfully accessed the required on-reading of the *kanji* and confirmed the reading using the information from the valid phonetic, there should have been few errors. This would have been the case with the L1 readers. On the other hand, the phonological judgement task attracted more errors, as there were many possible reading combinations of the given two *kanji*.

In the case of the L2 readers, however, their relatively low correct response rates in these phonological tasks may suggest that for these readers the links between the *kanji* and the phonology were inefficient (i.e., slow and inaccurate) when they had to find the potential readings of the *kanji* without any reading cues (i.e., when the required reading was not provided), but they sometimes managed to tell that the given reading was (or was not) the reading of the *kanji* (i.e., when the required reading was provided). It should be pointed out that the intermediate readers made numerous errors in both tasks, and as it turned out, there was no significant difference in their low correct response rates between the tasks, suggesting the links between the *kanji* and their phonology were not yet well-established. That is, unlike the L1 readers, the L2 readers had not yet formed a full phonological network due to their lack of sight *kanji* vocabulary.

Complexity effect on component level processing

The results of the analyses of the stimulus properties showed that, in the phonological matching task, (i.e., a *kanji* and a reading) the advanced readers performed on the high complexity *kanji* not only more slowly, but also less accurately than on the low complexity *kanji*. However, the complexity effect was not observed in the phonological judgement task (i.e., two *kanji*). On the other hand, the intermediate readers were not affected by the complexity of *kanji* in either task.

Chapter 4 Section 3 reported that orthographic complexity impacted on the performances of the advanced L2 readers significantly in the orthographic tasks). In general, this was interpreted by postulating that the advanced readers' identification decisions on the characters were usually made after a decision was generated on the components, upon which character complexity had an effect (see Chapter 4 Section 3). The finding that there was no significant complexity effect on the advanced readers' performance in the phonological judgement task suggests that in this task the decision might have been made at the character level without much contribution from componential analysis, suggesting that they might not have used the information conveyed by the phonetics (except some familiar frequently appearing phonetics). The fact that the advanced readers showed a complexity effect in the phonological matching task suggests that, given the phonetics of the *kanji* were highlighted in this task, these readers might have identified the phonetics as phonetics, upon which character complexity had probably had an effect.

On the other hand, the complexity had no significant impact on the intermediate readers. This result might appear counter-intuitive. Since more than half of the *kanji* used in the tasks were unfamiliar to these readers, one might think that they would try to find some familiar components in the unfamiliar *kanji,* upon which complexity should have an effect. However, in the phonological tasks, which required the participants to read the *kanji*, identifying familiar components would not have improved their performance in the tasks, unless the phonological function of the components were utilised for retrieving the phonology of the *kanji.* It was probably the case that the intermediate readers could not make use of the familiar components due to their lack of knowledge of phonetics.

Likewise, the L1 readers were not affected by the complexity of the *kanji.* In the main, their response pattern was the same as that of the intermediate L2 readers. However, given their exposure to and experience with *kanji*, it is more likely that the L1 readers and made decisions at the character level regardless of the graphical complexity of the *kanji* (see Chapter 5 Section 2 for detailed discussion).

No evidence of strong links between high frequency characters and meaning-bearing readings

In the analysis of character frequency, in both the phonological judgement and phonological matching tasks the intermediate and advanced readers responded to the high frequency *kanji* more accurately than to the low frequency *kanji*. Moreover, in the phonological matching task, the advanced readers responded to the high frequency *kanji* not only more accurately but also significantly faster than to the low frequency *kanji*. These findings were consistent with previous findings on L2 readers' phonological processing (Wang and Koda, 2005).

On the other hand, however, no effect of character frequency was observed in the L1 readers. It is assumed that the meaning-bearing reading (usually, *kun*-reading) was activated faster in high frequency *kanji* than in low frequency *kanji* due to the frequency effect, and that the fast-activated meaning-bearing reading (which was, in most cases, a *kun*-reading) interfered with the retrieval of the *on*-reading, which was the required reading in the tasks (see Chapter 4 Section 2 for details). The L1 readers therefore needed some extra time to inhibit the strong activation of the *kun*-reading in the high frequency *kanji* in order to access the *on*-reading instead. The interview data suggested that in some cases the readers had to put the *kanji* in a compound word in order to get the on-reading of the constituent *kanji*. In other words, although high frequency *kanji* were processed faster than low frequency *kanji,* this time advantage was cancelled out because of the time required for the inhibition of *kun*-readings.

In the case of the L2 readers, the results of their task performance suggested that the frequency effect was not cancelled out. In other words, the dominance of the meaning-bearing reading (usually *kun*-reading) over the non-meaning-bearing reading (usually *on*-reading) that was observed in the L1 readers was not evident in the L2 data. Clearly, for the L2 readers, the links between *kanji* and *kun*-readings were no stronger than the links between *kanji* and *on*-readings. The Interactive Activation Model (McClelland and Rumelhart, 1981) suggests that lexicons are modified continuously over time by learning, which change the strength of links between units (see Chapter 2 Section 2 for details). In the developing network of the intermediate and advanced readers, higher frequency characters have formed stronger links with their readings compared to lower frequency characters (hence there was a character frequency effect). However, it appears that there was little difference in the strength of links for *kun*-readings and *on*-readings (hence there was no interference effect of *kun*-readings).

No inhibitory effect of high frequency main radical on component level processing

In the phonological judgement task, neither the speed nor the accuracy was affected by the radical frequency for both the intermediate and advanced readers. In order to interpret these results, it is again necessary to reflect upon the results for the L1 readers. In the phonological judgement task, a reverse radical frequency effect was observed in the L1 readers, i.e., they responded to the low radical frequency *kanji* more accurately than to the high radical frequency *kanji*. This result suggested that the L1 readers tried to use the information conveyed from the component level processing, but that the processing of high frequency main radicals interfered with the processing of phonetics, which resulted in a smaller contribution from the phonetics to the decision making at the character level. In other words, the information from phonetics may be less salient in items with high frequency main radicals because the information from high frequency main radicals becomes available to the readers at a very early stage of processing. As phonetics are helpful for the *on*-reading, less information from phonetics means less information for *on*-readings. The L1 readers could have then read the *kanji* with high frequency radicals in their *kun*-readings, which was not the required reading in the task.

Returning to the results of the advanced L2 readers, the finding of no significant effect of radical frequency in the phonological judgement task might be because they made decisions at the character level without much contribution from the component level processing probably due to the limited knowledge of phonetics. Although sub-character features might have also been processed, it seems that there was no competition between the main radicals and phonetics. In other words, it is plausible to think that the main radicals and phonetics may not have been clearly separated in the advanced readers' network in terms of their functions (i.e., the components mainly had links to semantic domains).

For the intermediate readers who had less sight *kanji* vocabulary, they had no choice but to rely on the component level processing. However, in the phonological judgement task, which required the participants to read the *kanji*, identifying familiar

300

components (which were main-radicals in most cases) would not have assisted them in retrieving the phonology of the *kanji*.

Possible radical frequency effect on identification of phonetics

In the phonological matching task, on the other hand, the advanced readers were affected by radical frequency. They performed significantly more accurately on the high radical frequency *kanji* than on the low radical frequency *kanji*. The identification of high frequency main radicals might have helped them decide that the highlighted components were in fact phonetics, as phonetics are always on the non-main-radical side. With the reading provided, they might have been able to identify the phonology of some of the phonetics, which would have assisted in reading the *kanji*.

The intermediate readers also produced more correct responses for the *kanji* with a higher frequency radical than for the *kanji* with a lower frequency radical. In rare cases, the intermediate readers might have been able to use the phonetics for retrieving the phonological information when they successfully recognised them. However, the extremely low correct response rate for the low radical frequency *kanji* indicated that the intermediate readers might have skipped many of these *kanji*, which could have resulted in the better performance in the high radical frequency *kanji*. Presumably, as the low frequency radicals were not familiar to them, and as most phonetics were also unfamiliar to them, they had no choice but to skip them unless they knew the readings of the *kanji*. When the intermediate readers responded correctly to the low radical frequency, they did so with an average response speed that was very similar to the L1 readers' (888ms). These comparatively rapid response times possibly indicate that the participants occasionally adopted a strategy of guessing.

Possible homophone size (phonetic frequency) effect on orthographic and phonological processing

With respect to the variable of homophone size, the intermediate readers did not show any differences either in terms of response speed or accuracy in the phonological judgement task. However, in the phonological matching task these readers responded more accurately to the high homophone size *kanji* than to the low homophone size *kanji*. As discussed in Section 2 of this chapter, *kanji* that have a high homophone size tend to also have a large phonetic neighbourhood size (i.e., the *kanji* with high homophone size are likely to have a phonetic that is used in many other *kanji*). Apparently, the intermediate readers occasionally accessed the phonological information of some of the phonetics that had high neighbourhood sizes. Because some of the commonly used phonetics are legitimate *kanji* in their own right, the intermediate readers might have guessed the reading of the high homophone size *kanji* using the phonology of these 'embedded *kanji*' (that were in fact the *phonetic* components of the target kanji) as a guide, probably without knowing that they were the phonetics. It is plausible that the intermediate readers did not show any significant difference between the low and high homophone size *kanji* in the phonological judgement task because they did not identify the phonetics as the phonetics. Only when the reading was provided, did they identify the phonology of the phonetics.

The advanced readers were affected by homophone size, or rather by phonetic neighbourhood size both in the phonological judgement and in the phonological matching tasks. In the phonological judgement task, they performed significantly more accurately on the high homophone size *kanji* than on the low homophone size *kanji*. As mentioned above, high homophone size *kanji* tend to have a phonetic that is used in many other *kanji* (large phonetic neighbourhood). The advanced readers probably utilised those commonly appearing familiar phonetics to name the *kanji*. In the phonological matching task, they responded to the high homophone size *kanji* significantly faster than to the low homophone size *kanji*. The strength of links between the phonetic and its phonology would have been enhanced by practice (i.e., more exposure), which resulted in the faster access of the phonology of the phonetic with a large neighbourhood. Indeed Andrews (1997) found that larger neighbourhoods would produce better performances in tasks such as naming tasks. It should be pointed out that, in this task, the advanced readers did not differ in terms of the accuracy between the low and high homophone size *kanji*. As the phonetics of the *kanji* in this matching task were highlighted, the advanced readers' attention was most likely drawn to the phonetics regardless of their neighbourhood size. This then would have given them equal access to the phonology of the components, with no resulting difference in their performance in terms of accuracy between the low and high homophone size *kanji*.

The L1 readers also performed significantly more accurately on the high homophone size *kanji* than on the low homophone size *kanji*. Although it is tempting to consider that the same processes were operative for the L1 and advanced L2 readers, there may, in fact, be two separate causes for their performance. That is, the reason why the L2 advanced readers' better performance on the high homophone size *kanji* could be due to the neighbourhood size of phonetics, whereas the cause for the effect in the L1 readers might be more complicated. In the phonological judgement task, because the low homophone size *kanji* did not facilitate the phonological processing of the components as much as it did in the high homophone size *kanji*, the retrieved phonology of the *kanji* could be at the character level, and therefore the *kun*-reading (i.e., meaning-bearing reading) instead of the *on*-reading could be retrieved. This should have induced some errors in the low homophone size *kanji*. On the other hand, in the phonological matching task, the highlighted phonetics facilitated the access to the on-readings of the characters regardless of homophone size (phonetic neighbourhood size) (see Chapter 5 Section 2 for detailed discussion).

5.4.7 Phonological judgement task: Interview data

Beginner L2 readers

This task was not possible for most of the beginner readers due to their lack of knowledge of the reading of *kanji*. For instance, 15 out of the 21 beginner L2 readers reported that they could not read most of the *kanji* (see Example 1). Nine participants admitted that they skipped many of the task items (see Example 2), and a few readers refused to continue the task after trying a couple of the items (see Example 3).

Example 1: It was really difficult because I didn't know the reading of most of the *kanji*, which just made it practically impossible to do this task.

304

Example 2: I had to skip a lot. I tried to guess on a slight recognition of familiar parts, but it was hard.

Example 3: Because I didn't know most of the *kanji*, I thought it was pointless to do this task, because you had to know how to read them, so it didn't make sense to try and read new *kanji*.

For the beginner readers who did not have any knowledge of phonetics, they had no way of making judgements but simply guessed based on the recognition of familiar parts (see Example 2). While four participants thought that the two *kanji* had the same reading if there was a common graphical feature between the two *kanji* (see Example 4), six participants expressed their hesitancy in accepting the phonological relationship between the two *kanji* sharing similar graphical features (see Example 5).

Example 4: if I saw the same portion, I thought they might have the same reading, so I put 'yes'.

Example 5: I've come to the conclusion that the *kanji* looking similar does not necessarily mean that they would have similar readings. I don't believe that it could be correct, I don't know. It just sounds too simple that it would be correct.

Intermediate L2 readers

The majority of the intermediate L2 readers found the task difficult, as they did not know the reading of most of the *kanji* used in the task. 15 out of the 19 participants reported that they guessed the phonological relationship of the *kanji* on the basis of whether there was a common radical between the two *kanji* (see Example 6). Four of them, however, claimed that such a strategy would not always work (see Example 7). One participant made the decision based on her assumption that there was no relationship between the radicals and readings (see Example 8). Two participants mentioned the positions of the radicals (see Examples 9-10)

Example 6: Occasionally I tried to make guesses by using the radicals, if the major radicals of the two *kanji* were the same, then I tended to say 'yes'.

Example 7: Sometimes the reading could be the same if the two had the same component, but it's not always the case. If you don't know the reading, it's hard to guess.

Example 8: If they had the same component in them, I thought they wouldn't have the same sound because they might be related and so probably they wouldn't have the same sound.

Example 9: When the same figure came up in the same spots, I'd say that they did have the same reading.

Example 10: I guessed them based on whether or not they had the same component on the right hand side.

At least two participants knew that there were main radicals and phonetics although they seemed not to know how to distinguish between them (see Example 11).

Example 11: I think I just relied on the radicals. But probably that was not the best idea because I know that the *kanji* could have sound radicals (phonetics)

306

and meaning radicals (main radicals). So if you were relying on the meaning radical, it doesn't necessarily mean that the reading would be the same.

With more knowledge of *kanji*, some of the intermediate readers seemed to have managed to read some *kanji*. However, six participants mentioned the difficulty of having multiple readings in a *kanji* (see Example 12).

Example 12: It was difficult to think of all the readings of the *kanji* before the next *kanji* came up. If you couldn't remember a reading, particularly an *on*-reading, then it was hard to match them up properly.

Advanced L2 readers

13 out of the 27 advanced L2 readers felt that the task was difficult due to the multiple readings of *kanji* (see Examples 13-14) particularly when only a brief period of time was given for a response (see Example 15).

Example 13: That one was quite difficult because a lot of *kanji* have more than one reading. So you have to work out whether there is one between the two characters that actually matches or not.

Example 14: The first reading that would come to mind might not be the one that they (the two *kanji*) had in common. There might be another reading because all the readings don't always come straight to mind all at once.

Example 15: One reading comes to mind before another reading, and you have to try and remember what the other readings are, but you don't have much time, so it's really tricky.

Moreover, the advanced readers sometimes had difficulty retrieving the *on*-reading from individual *kanji*. Three participants said that although they knew that the reading required in the task was the *on*-reading, they sometimes retrieved the *kun*-reading before the *on*-reading (see Example 16). One of the strategies the advanced readers used in this task was to put the *kanji* in a compound word (see Example 17). However, even when they could remember the *on*-reading of *kanji*, sometimes differentiating 'short and long vowels' was not easy (see Example 18).

> Example 16: Because when I saw the second one, I remembered *kun-yomi*, and then tried to remember *on-yomi*, and by the time I worked that out, I forgot what the first one was, because I was busy concentrating on the second one.

> Example 17: Another thing I did was, when I saw the first character, oh this was all very very quickly, I tried to think of a word, which the character that I don't know would appear in.

> Example 18: The length of sounds was a bit confusing. I wasn't sure if one was /ko/ and the other one was /koR/.

The remarks that nine participants made suggest that words are stored in a unit of a word, and remembering a reading for each character is not something they routinely do (see Examples 19-20).

> Example 19: The way I learnt *kanji* was remembering them in words, but not so much the *kanji* by themselves, so it was pretty hard. I usually thought of a word that had the *kanji* in it to get the reading of the *kanji*.

Example 20: I was really slow getting the reading when it was out of context. Just remembering it by itself is a bit hard. I kept thinking like a word. There was one that was *ten* and *kai*. One was 'heaven' and the other one was 'turn' or 'circulate'. I found it easy to do because it was a word. There was also *kai* and *chuu*. I thought of *kaichuu-denntoo* (torch). I thought of things that were parts of words.

The participants were able to respond quickly if they knew both *kanji*, When they knew how to read only one of the two *kanji*, it seemed that the degree of difficulty varied depending on which of the two *kanji* they knew (see Examples 21-22).

Example 21: If you know the first *kanji*, then it's not too bad because you have the reading in your head, and you just have to think whether the next one can be read that way.

Example 22: The hardest thing was when you didn't know the first *kanji*, and you had to try and remember what it was even though you didn't know it....the reading of the next one could be the same as the one you didn't even know.

When the participants encountered two unfamiliar *kanji*, at least 15 participants made use of the phonetics. Although some of them might not have known clearly which ones were phonetics, six of them seemed to know where to look (see Examples 23-25).

Example 23: Sometimes I guessed the reading by looking at the non-main-radical part of the *kanji*.

Example 24: Sometimes if the components on the right, well sometimes on the left but usually on the right-hand side, were the same, I assumed that they had the same reading.

Example 25: I understand that the components on the right-hand side give more influence on the sounds.

Apparently, some of them knew that only some phonetics were reliable. One advanced participant told me that unusual phonetics were more reliable in terms of phonetic information (see Example 26).

Example 26: I took a guess when there was, like the component (she meant 'the phonetic') on the *noo* (悩), I think, and the *kanji* 'brain' (脳) came up, and there was the same component on the right hand side. I just guessed that they would probably be pronounced the same because it's a kind of funny component, like it's a little bit unusual, I think, for all of those to be together.

5.4.8 Phonological matching task: Interview data

Beginner L2 readers

This task was not possible for the beginner readers as they did not know most of the *kanji*. Nine out of the 18 beginner L2 readers reported that they did not know most of the *kanji* and/or had to skip them (see Example 1). Also, they probably had no way of making an educated guess without knowing any phonetics. It appears that the majority of the beginner readers were not aware of the existence of and the function of the phonetics (see Example 2). Four participants mentioned that they tried to find a familiar radical in the *kanji* and link it to the sound (see Examples 3-4). However, the radicals they referred to were usually main radicals rather than phonetics, which did not have any phonetic information.

Example 1: I skipped a lot because I didn't know most of them. It was too hard.

Example 2: I tried to pick up some pictures from the *kanji* to get the meaning to get the reading, but within five seconds, it was almost impossible.

Example 3: The part showing was something to do with 'fire' (the fire radical) for example, and then could it be pronounced /ka/ (i.e., the reading of the *kanji* 'fire')? A couple of them I recognised part of *kanji* maybe read like that.

(Note: the fire radical itself has no phonological information attached, although the character that has an identical graphic figure as the fire radical has the reading /ka/).

Example 4: For example, when I saw the water radical, I assumed it would be read /sui/ (i.e., the reading of the *kanji* 'water').

Moreover, the task was simply impossible for them to perform due to lack of knowledge of multiple readings (see Example 5)

Example 5: Even for the *kanji* that I knew, usually I only knew one of the pronunciations, so I couldn't tell if the pronunciation shown on the screen was 'yes' or 'no'. Even if it wasn't the one I knew, it doesn't necessarily mean that it was 'no'. It could be the other pronunciation that I didn't know.

As described in Chapter 3 Section 2, in this task, the *kanji* was accompanied by a line either before or after it, to indicate that the *kanji* was one of the two *kanji* in a compound word (which indicated that the *kanji* should be read in its *on*-reading). One beginner reader realised that there were some lines before or after the *kanji* (see Example 6). Unfortunately, however, this participant's observation did not help her find the correct reading.

Example 6: I wasn't sure when you had a line and the *kanji*, or the *kanji* and a line, whether you meant it to be part of a word so it would be the *on*-reading, but I didn't know the *on*-reading anyway.

Intermediate L2 readers

One of the intermediate L2 readers described the complex processes required in this task (see Example 7).

Example 7: You see the character, and try to remember what sound you associate it with, and you pick one, then the sound card comes up. It (the reading displayed on the sound card) might be the one you thought of or a different one. If a different one is displayed, you think, is that another alternatives? You need a little bit of time to think.

When the *kanji* was familiar, at least three participants were able to read it very quickly (see Example 8). However, as suggested in the above remark (see Example 7), the reading might have been different from the one required in the task (see also Example 9).

312

Example 8: All the ones that I knew, I could tell what the readings were as soon as I saw them.

Example 9: For the ones I knew, sometimes I knew the reading straight away, but sometimes I had to think of the other readings, for example, that's /hana/ but it's also /ka/ or something.

One of the strategies that the participants employed was to put the *kanji* in a compound word (see Examples 10-11). However, retrieving the required reading of the *kanji* from a compound word was not so easy (see Example 12).

Example 10: If the reading that came up to my head was a *kun*-reading of the *kanji*, I had to put it together with another *kanji* to get an *on*-reading.

Example 11: I tried to think of a word that had the character in it, and whether that could be read in that way.

Example 12: when I saw one of the *kanji* in the word *kaisha*, I immediately knew this *kanji* meant 'company', but I had to think how it was pronounced, and a minute later I thought it was /kai/.

As suggested in this remark (see Example 12), the reading of *kanji* may be best triggered by considering the word as a whole, and retrieval of a reading for each constituent *kanji* of the word may not be so simple. Probably for this reason, at least 10 participants remarked that they chose to make use of the components to infer the readings of the *kanji*. Among these 10, three participants indicated that they knew of the phonetics (see Example 13). There was at least one participant who knew of the different functions of the main radicals and phonetics (see Example 14).

313

Example 13: If you've got (the part) *koo* in it, you actually read the whole *kanji* /koR/'.

Example 14: I know that there are sound symbols (phonetics), for example, /kaN/ and /haN/. Usually I find them on the right-hand side of the *kanji*, they are different from the meaning symbols (main radicals). I know that there are also some *kanji* where there are no sound symbols at all.

On the other hand, the other seven participants might not have been aware of the difference (see Example 15). One participant thought that the main radical could be used for getting the *on*-reading (see Example 16).

Example 15: Sometimes I saw part of the character that looked like another character I knew the reading of, I just went by that.

Example 16: I did sometimes look at the radical, like when it was 'water' (the water radical), I would say /sui/ (i.e., the reading of the *kanji* 'water') was the reading (of the *kanji* on the screen)'.

Three participants reported that they did not have any way of guessing (see Example 17).

Example 17: If I didn't know the *kanji*, I had absolutely no idea. I couldn't even guess. I don't know whether there is any particular way you know, or whether a certain part of *kanji* tells you.

Two participants reported that sometimes the pronunciation card assisted them in remembering the reading of the *kanji*. The remarks made by these participants indicated that some participants performed the task in the reverse order. Instead of retrieving a

314

reading of the *kanji* and checking it against the displayed pronunciation, they tried to find the part that could be read as the pronunciation shown by the computer (see Example 18).

> Example 18: I was trying to recognise the part of the *kanji* that sounded like what the computer pronounced. Like the character 'open' had the 'gate' and the middle part, I think that the middle part means 'to open' and has the pronunciation /kai/.

Advanced L2 readers

Seven out of the 26 participants expressed that the task was easy whereas five participants said that it was hard. The majority of the seven participants who said that it was not too hard, pointed out that having the pronunciation displayed after the *kanji* made this task easy (see Example 19).

> Example 19: I found that with the sound actually being given, it was easy to tell whether or not it suited the character.

The remarks made by three participants suggest that the reading of the *kanji* is stored, not as individual *kanji*, but in a unit of a word (see Example 20). Two participants said that they thought of a word that contained the *kanji* in order to get the required reading (see Example 21)

> Example 20: There was *tei* from the word *hootei*. I was familiar with it. I knew how to read it, but I wasn't really sure that the *kanji* was the first *kanji* or the second *kanji* of the two *kanji* combination of the word. There were some *kanji*

that I knew what they meant, but if you just put them themselves, I can't read them, but if you put them with another *kanji* in a word, I can tell 'that's right. That's the *kanji* from blah blah blah'.

Example 21: So you had to kind of think of a word which the character could be in and think what the reading would be. It's not that I thought of a word every time I saw a character, but sometimes when I wasn't sure I had to think of a word specifically. Kind of putting it into context and work out what the pronunciation was.

Two participants did not appreciate the use of *romaji* (Roman letters) to represent the pronunciation (see Example 22).

Example 22: Initially I found it a little bit strange to see the Romanised pronunciation. I was expecting it to be *hiragana*.

Also, having someone else's voice (the voice-over reading out the pronunciations of the *kanji*) was not welcomed (see Example 23).

Example 23: I normally say it in my head, and so having someone else's voice was distracting for me. It slowed me down. When I read Japanese, I used to read it by saying it aloud, but I don't do that any more. I just sub-vocalise in my head, sometimes when I don't have to vocalise it, I just go faster. Having someone else's voice just slows the whole process down for me.

Furthermore, remarks made by two participants suggest that not having the *kanji* at the centre of the screen (due to the lines showing the position of the *kanji* in a word)

316

might have had an adverse effect. The position of the *kanji* on the screen affected the recognition processes of a few of the readers (see Examples 24-25)

Example 24: It was easier when the *kanji* appeared on the left-hand side (of the screen).

Example 25: I had to think if I could pronounce it that way depending on where the *kanji* was.

19 participants referred to the particular components of the *kanji* that could be used for retrieving the reading of *kanji*. However, having many *kanji* that they could read, the advanced L2 readers did not need to rely on the component information so often. They only used the phonetic to get the reading of unfamiliar *kanji*. What was distinct from the participants in the other groups was that at least seven participants knew that phonetics were separate components from main radicals (see Examples 26-27).

Example 26: I have a feeling that there are some rules where one side of the character gives the meaning and the other side gives the pronunciation, but sometimes it's the other way around.

Example 27: I have, in my head, a hypothesis about certain radicals (presumably, he meant 'components') that are used a lot of the time, therefore, you can rely on them for meanings or sounds. Some of them I have come across for the reading rather than for the meaning, like *hoo* (方) is often the sound one.

At least four participants were aware of the limitations of the use of the phonetics (see Example 28). One of them seemed to have come to know what phonetics would be more reliable or less reliable (see Example 29).

Example 28: A lot of the time, you can't rely on that (the phonetic of the *kanji*).

Example 29: It was easy if you saw ones, like *doo* in *doo kutsu* (meaning 'cave'), the ones with strong phonetic things like *doo* nearly always have the same sound. So you can really bank on. But some are weaker than others, some get changed more.

Three participants remarked that they tried to see the whole *kanji* instead of just seeing the phonetic. However, it seemed that the highlighted phonetics affected their performances (see Examples 30-31).

Example 30: The fading out of some of the parts of the *kanji* made the identification of the reading a little bit difficult.

Example 31: Sometimes the bits that faded out led me to believe that it was a different *kanji*, like I said /kai/ for the character 'plum' (梅). Because the left-hand side of this *kanji* (木) which represents 'tree' was faded out, and it looked like 'water' (氵). If it's 'water', then it's read as /kai/ meaning 'ocean (海)'.

5.4.9 Discussion of the interview about the phonological judgement and phonological matching tasks

Weak links between characters and phonology

The interview data showed beyond doubt that the phonological tasks were difficult for the L2 readers, particularly for the beginner and intermediate readers. These tasks were thought to be hard even by the L1 readers despite their satisfactory performance. Lack of *kanji* knowledge was the obvious cause of the difficulty for the beginner L2 readers.

The intermediate L2 readers knew more *kanji* than did the beginner readers, but it seems that they tended to know the reading of *kanji* only in the words that they learnt from textbooks, and therefore experienced difficulty in retrieving readings of individual characters. Although a few of the intermediate readers seemed to know of the phonological function of components, generally they could not distinguish phonetics from main radicals.

Sources of confusion for the advanced L2 readers appeared to be diverse, but it seems that the slow access to the phonology, presumably due to the weak linkage between characters and their phonology, was one of the main causes of the difficulty. Judging from their remarks in the interviews, they were aware of the multiple readings of the *kanji*, and they also knew that they were required to retrieve the *on*-reading of the *kanji*. Nevertheless, they often could not access the reading required within the limited time.

The L1 readers also mentioned that because the single characters tended to be linked closely to the *kun*-reading, the expected *on*-reading was not easy to obtain. However, as evidenced in their performance results, the L1 readers were in fact able to access the required reading within the set time.

Exposure to characters and development of phonological awareness

There were two strategies that the L1 readers employed in order to perform the phonological tasks. One strategy often used was to make a compound word that contained the *kanji*. Many intermediate and advanced readers also tried to get the *on*-reading of the *kanji* by making a compound word that contained the *kanji*, suggesting that the characters were stored as part of words (not separately). However, this method was useful only when the *kanji* was familiar to them.

Another strategy was the use of the phonetics of the *kanji*. It appears that the L1 readers resorted to the phonetic of the *kanji* when the *on*-reading of *kanji* was not readily available. However, evidently, their use of the phonetic was restricted to the times that it was valid. The majority of the advanced L2 readers also tried to make use of this functional component. The interview data showed that the advanced readers had some knowledge of phonetics, and that they were also aware of the limitations of the use of phonetic information. The intermediate readers on the other hand, seemed not to be very aware of phonetics. Evidently, most knew that the main radicals of the *kanji* would give semantic information. However, it appears that the function of the phonetics was not well known to most of them. Therefore, some of them concluded that the *kanji* with a common main radical had the same reading, whereas others thought they had different readings, as the *kanji* with similar meanings should not have the same reading. It seems that as most *kanji* were unfamiliar, most beginner readers relied on any radicals that they knew how to read in order to get a reading. Needless to say, their efforts were in vain.

Slow development of awareness of phonetics

Conceivably, awareness of phonetics develops more slowly than awareness of main radicals. There are at least three reasons for the slow development of phonetic awareness. A large number of the *kanji* that learners learn at the beginning stage are single-component characters, which do not have a phonetic. Moreover, although they learn a few compound *kanji* (*kanji* made of two components) that have a phonetic, the reading of *kanji* introduced in classrooms tends to be in a meaning-bearing reading, which in most cases is a *kun*-reading. Also, the *kanji* that are introduced at an early stage tend to be high frequency *kanji*, which have more than one reading (Shu and Anderson, 1998). For these reasons, it is unlikely that beginner learners notice the phonological links between the *kanji* and the phonetics. An analysis of 2,557 characters that Chinese children are expected to learn during the 6 years of elementary school (Shu and Anderson, 1998) shows that the majority of characters introduced after the first grade are compound characters (characters consisting of two components), and the percentage of compounds with a regular pronunciation increases through the fourth grade and then levels off. A relatively small percentage of the characters introduced in the first grade are compounds with a predictable structure and a regular pronunciation. This implies that first graders have limited opportunities to acquire insight into the internal structure of Chinese characters. The same is true for L2 readers who are at a beginning stage of *kanji* learning. They have limited opportunities to be aware of phonetics.

5.5 Chapter five summary

In the present study, the L1 readers displayed response patterns that indicated that they read the *kanji* that can be single-character words in the *kun*-reading in the phonological tasks. The evidence gathered suggests that in L1 readers' recognition network, the access to the *kun*-reading, which is linked closely to the semantic property of characters, may dominate over the access to the *on*-reading, at least when the visual stimuli are single characters. In relation to this, the finding that the L1 readers' reading of characters was inhibited by the high frequency main radicals suggest that the access to main radicals may dominate over the access to phonetics. The results of the tasks also suggest that the widely-accepted frequency effect may not apply to the retrieval of the *on*-reading from individual *kanji* characters when they appear on the screen on their own. At least in the current phonological tasks, which required the L1 readers to access the *on*-reading of the *kanji*, the character frequency did not produce a significant effect on their performance.

Overall, the L1 readers' reflective accounts supported the findings from the phonological processing tasks. They felt that that they could not help reading the *kanji* in the *kun*-reading although they knew that the required reading was the *on*-reading. In order to retrieve the *on*-reading, the L1 readers employed two strategies. One was to put the character in a compound word and read it in the meaningful reading. Apparently the L1 readers were aware that the readings of the constituent characters of compound words were more likely to be in *on*-readings. The other strategy was to use the phonetic of the *kanji*. Evidently, the L1 readers were aware of the function of phonetics. At the same time, they were aware of the limitations of the phonological information that phonetics could convey. The interview data indicated that the L1 readers resorted to the phonetics of the characters only when there were no other means to retrieve the phonology of the *kanji*. Taking these findings together, it was suggested that the phonology of the kanji would have been accessed through their lemma at the preconscious level while the phonology of the phonetics would have to have been retrieved strategically.

The L2 readers demonstrated poor phonological processing skills across the board. Those with limited *kanji* knowledge had few characters that they could read. Those whose *kanji* knowledge was between 300 and 1,000 characters certainly displayed better phonological skills than the novice L2 readers. Nevertheless, the results of their performance on the two phonological processing tasks indicated that they could not use the information from the components of the *kanji*. However, the evidence gathered from the interviews suggests that they sometimes relied on the main radicals. This might have resulted in many errors. The L2 readers with more than 1,000 *kanji* were able to read the high frequency *kanji* reasonably well. However, even the fairly skilled readers did not demonstrate skilled phonological processing. There was no evidence of either the

323

dominance of the *kun*-reading over the *on*-reading or the competition between a main radical and a phonetic.

The interview data indicated that L2 readers who knew 300-1,000 characters had only a vague awareness of phonetics, and could not distinguish the phonetics from the main radicals. Learners of Japanese seem to become aware of the phonological function of phonetics when they have learnt about 1,000 *kanji*.

However, a large difference still exists between advanced level learners and native speakers of Japanese. Koda (1999b) suggests that what really separates native from non-native performance is the ability to detect component information validity and to incorporate 'valid' information selectively into on-going character processing. In accord with this proposal, the present study indicated that only several very advanced L2 readers had the ability to use phonetics selectively.

6 Semantic processing skills and awareness

6.1 L1 readers of Japanese: Objectives and Methods

6.1.1 Objectives

People read words or sentences to comprehend the meaning. Research suggests that reading ability is closely related to the ability to use semantic-category information (Koda, 2002). Investigation of such ability is indeed interesting and worthwhile. However, this is the most difficult aspect of the study. Up until now, it has been possible to design sets of information processing tasks that had definitive answers (i.e., judgement of whether or not two characters share a common reading). These previous tasks probed for the way that language users processed structural information about graphical and phonological forms and used the time it took to make a correct positive decision (and the percentage of correct decisions made) as data. When it comes to probing a language-user's semantic structure, the same approach is unlikely to succeed. This is because, unlike the presence or absence of form-based features, the association between semantic bearing elements is not as clear-cut. That is, people may have different opinions over the semantic relatedness of two characters. For example, I believe that most people would agree that the *kanji* 頭 (head) and 顔 (face) are semantically related. On the other hand, 宝 (treasure) and 宮 (palace) may or may not be seen as related. Even though these two pairs of *kanji* both have a common main radical between the two *kanji*, the strength of semantic relatedness varies considerably. The study of how variously skilled language-users process semantics therefore required a different approach.

The purpose of this part of the study is to ascertain a performance profile of L1 readers' semantic processing in *kanji* recognition and to thereby establish a norm for competent language users' processing. As discussed in Chapter 3 Section 2, the statistical analysis performed on the results of two semantic processing tasks (see Appendix H) revealed that the approach that was taken for orthographic and phonological processing would not be useful for the study of semantic processing. The participants' semantic processing was therefore examined using a normative approach.

Three examinations were conducted in order to gauge effects of semantic properties in *kanji* recognition: two of these used timed processing *kanji* recognition tasks and the other one employed a non-timed pen and paper task. In order to assess their semantic processing, a group of L1 readers was asked to undertake two semantic processing tasks. These tasks were designed to elicit the readers' skills in processing *kanji* semantically (see Chapter 3 Section 2 for details). Separately, a semantic relatedness rating task, which had pairs of the stimuli used in the timed processing tasks, was conducted on another group of L1 readers (see Chapter 3 Section 2 for details). The rating task aimed at establishing a profile of how L1 readers would judge the strength of semantic connectedness of the experimental items. The items were then grouped into several categories of different strength of semantic relationship using the mode values of the rating (see Chapter 3 Section 3).

In order to obtain a normative response pattern among the skilled readers, the results of the timed semantic processing tasks (the mean percentage of affirmative/negative responses and the mean response time of each participant) for each category of the items with a different strength of relatedness (which was established as the results of the semantic relatedness rating task) were calculated. These response patterns of the L1 readers serve as a benchmark against which the response patterns of the L2 readers will be compared. In this study, the effects of the four stimulus properties of *kanji* were not examined, as the number of items in each modal category was too small for any meaningful analysis. Thus, what is important in interpreting the data of these experiments is the description of the way the data from each of the participant groups hangs together. That is, data interpretation will be based upon patterns of mean reaction times and errors along with indications of their variability.

An interview was conducted after each of the timed processing tasks. The aim of the interview was to examine the L1 readers' awareness of information in components (main radicals and phonetics) and their awareness of the limitations of component information (see Chapter 3 Section 2 for details) in developing a semantic interpretation. The interview data also serves as complementary data to the quantitative study.

6.1.2 Methods

Participants

16 native speakers of Japanese participated in the timed semantic tasks. These 16 participants were the same people who undertook the orthographic and phonological tasks referred to in the previous chapters. These 16 participants also participated in the interview sessions. A different group of 45 native speakers of Japanese undertook the semantic relatedness task (see Chapter 3 Section 2 for details). No participants performed both the timed semantic processing tasks and the non-timed semantic relatedness task.

Materials

Two timed semantic processing tasks, interview questions and a semantic relatedness rating task, were prepared (see Chapter 3 Section 2 for details). The timed semantic tasks were designed to elicit the L1 readers' online semantic processing skills. The tasks used were a semantic judgement task and a semantic categorisation task.

The semantic judgement task was designed to examine the participants' judgement of the semantic relationship between two *kanji*. The stimuli were *kanji* pairs with or without a common main radical (hereafter common-radical items and no-common-radical items) and fillers. All the common-radical items had some potential semantic (at least etymological) connection between the two *kanji* via a common main radical that showed a semantic category. In the no-common-radical items, two *kanji* did not have a common main radical and were likely to be semantically unrelated. For the fillers, half were *kanji* pairs that were semantically related and the other half were *kanji*

pairs that had no semantic relationship between them. Sample *kanji* pairs are shown on

Table 6.1.

Table 6.1 Sample *kanji* characters used in the semantic judgement task

Types of stimuli in the semantic judgement task	Samples	
	1st *kanji*	2nd *Kanji*
Pairs of *kanji* with a common main radical	砂 (sand)	- 砕 (crush)
Pairs of *kanji* without a common main radical	狩 (hunt)	- 鉄 (steel)
Fillers	上 (up)	- 中 (middle)

Note: The English translations in parentheses did not appear in the task.

The second task, the semantic categorisation task, was designed to examine the

participants' judgement of the semantic relationship between a *kanji* character and a

semantic category. As described in the 'Japanese *kanji* characters' section (Chapter 1

Section 3), all *kanji* have one main radical, and each main radical represents a semantic

category. For example, the main radical イ represents the category of 'people'. The

semantic category names that were used in the task were English translations of the

categories that main radicals represented. As this task was intended also to be

administered to groups of English-speaking learners of Japanese, English instead of

Japanese was used for the category names. The task consisted of *kanji* characters and

the category names of their main radicals in English (hereafter radical-category items),

kanji and the category names of unrelated main radicals (hereafter no-radical-category items), and fillers. In this task, the main radicals were highlighted (more precisely, other parts of the *kanji* were shaded leaving the main radicals intact) to draw the reader's attention to the main radicals. For the fillers, half were *kanji* with a semantically related category name and half were *kanji* with a category name that does not have a semantic relationship with the *kanji*. Table 6.2 presents sample *kanji* and semantic category names.

Table 6.2 Sample *kanji* characters and category names used in the semantic categorisation task

Types of stimuli in the semantic categorisation task	Samples	
	Kanji	Category name
Pairs of *kanji* and the category names of their main radicals	雪 (snow)	- rain
Pairs of *kanji* and the category names of unrelated main radicals	貸 (lend)	- gate
Fillers	子 (child)	- person

Note: The English translations in parentheses did not appear in the task

For both the semantic judgement and the semantic categorisation tasks, two versions with differently-ordered items were prepared in order to avoid any effect of a particular order of presenting items (see Chapter 3 Section 2 for details).

To create a normative profile of L1 readers, a semantic relatedness rating task, which had pairs of the stimuli used in the timed processing tasks, was prepared. This task consisted of two lists: The first list consisted of the above-mentioned common-radical items (e.g., 雪 and 霜), and the second list consisted of the radical-category items (e.g., 雪 and 'rain'). For the purpose of rating, a scale of 0-5 was provided next to each item (see Chapter 3 Section 2 for details).

Procedure

Two timed semantic processing tasks and an interview were conducted on the 16 L1 readers, and a semantic relatedness rating task was administered to another group of 45 L1 readers.

Timed semantic processing tasks

For the timed semantic processing tasks, the 16 L1 readers were randomly allocated into two groups. Half of the participants undertook the semantic judgement task before the semantic categorisation task, and the other half did the tasks in reverse order. After taking the warm-up same-different judgement task, one group undertook one of the orthographic tasks, the semantic judgement task, and one of the phonological tasks, in that order. They then did the other orthographic task, the semantic categorisation task and the other phonological task. The other group did the same, except the order of the orthographic, semantic and phonological tasks was reversed. In each task, three practice items were provided. The participants were given feedback on the correctness of their performance for the practice items, and were asked if they would like to move on or redo the practice in order to make sure they understood the instructions for the task.

In the semantic judgement tasks, each of the 120 pairs was displayed on the computer monitor one character at a time, one after the other each for 500 ms. Prior to the first *kanji*, an eye-fixation mark (double circles) was displayed for 600 ms, and between the two *kanji*, a blank frame was inserted for 200ms. In the semantic categorisation task, instead of two *kanji* characters, a *kanji* and the name of a semantic category in English appeared. In both tasks, the second stimulus was presented until a response was made, but the time for the response was limited to five seconds in order to encourage a quick decision.

The participants were tested individually on one of the two scrambled versions of the tasks. In the semantic judgement task, the participants were instructed to judge whether or not the two *kanji* belonged to the same meaning category, and in the semantic categorisation task, to judge whether or not the *kanji* belonged to the meaning category shown by the English word (these task questions raised a methodological issue, which will be discussed towards the end of this section). The participants were required to respond as quickly as possible by pressing the 'yes' key for acceptance of the task questions (e.g., Are the two characters in the same meaning category?), the 'no' key for rejection of the question or the 'skip' key if they could not make a decision. No feedback was given except for the first three practice items.

Interview

After each task, a short interview session was held where the participants were asked to talk about how they performed the tasks. The retrospective reports were audio-taped, and were later transcribed for qualitative analysis.

Semantic relatedness rating task

For the semantic relatedness rating task, the 45 native speakers were shown a list of the 40 common-radical items (e.g., 砂 - 砕) and the 40 radical-category items (e.g., 雪 - rain). They were then asked to rate them for their semantic relatedness using numbers 0 - 5 (0 being totally unrelated and 5 being strongly related). The participants were instructed to circle one of the six numbers indicating how much they thought each pair was semantically related (see Chapter 3 Section 2 for details). While most participants printed the lists out and worked on paper, some preferred to perform the task on a computer monitor. Strictly speaking, taking a task on paper and on the computer might not have produced exactly the same responses. However, as the participants were allowed to spend as much time as they wished in either situation - i.e., there was no time limit for responding to the items in this task, the differences were assumed to be minimal.

A mode value of the rating was calculated for each of the 40 pairs of *kanji* (the common-radical items that were taken from the semantic judgement task) and 40 pairs of *kanji* and a semantic category name (the radical-category items that were taken from the semantic categorisation task). The two sets of 40 items were then grouped into several categories of different strength of semantic relationship according to the mode values of the rating judgement.

6.2 L1 readers: Results and discussion

6.2.1 Semantic relatedness rating task: ratings

The results of the semantic relatedness rating task will be presented first.

As shown in Table 6.3, out of the 40 common-radical items from the semantic judgement task, seven items were rated as 5 (the mode value showing that the stimuli were semantically strongly related), nine items as 4, another nine items as 3, seven items as 2 or 1 (mode category '2' and mode category '1' items were combined, as the number of items in each mode category was very small), and eight items as 0.

Table 6.3 Different strength of semantic relatedness (shown in mode values) rated by the L1 readers for the common-radical items

Semantic relatedness		Common-radical items	
Mode value of rating	No of items	Samples	
5 (strongly related)	7	顔 (face)	- 頭 (head)
4	9	鎖 (chain)	- 鉄 (steel)
3	9	菜 (plant)	- 芋 (potato)
2	7	砂 (sand)	- 砕 (crush)
1		宝 (treasure)	- 宮 (palace)
0 (not related)	8	昇 (rise)	- 星 (star)

Note: The English translations of the *kanji* did not appear in the task.

If the L1 readers had depended only on the information from the main radicals, then they would have rated all the items as related. However, their ratings on the common-radical items were spread across the scale. Although all the items had a common main radical between the two *kanji*, the readers seemed to have formed judgements about the semantic relatedness of the characters without specifically relying on the information from the main radical.

For the 40 radical-category items (see Table 6.4), six items were rated as '5', 14 items as '4', another 14 items as '3', and six items as '2', '1' or '0' (mode category '2', mode category '1' and mode category '0' items were combined, as the number of items in each mode category was very small).

Table 6.4 Different strength of semantic relatedness (shown in mode values) rated by the L1 readers for the radical-category items

Semantic relatedness		Radical-category items	
Mode of rating	No of items	Samples	
5 (strongly related)	6	雪 (snow)	- rain
4	14	秋 (autumn)	- grain
3	14	動 (move)	- power
2		従 (follow)	- steps
1	6	畑 (field)	- fire
0 (not related)		素 (element)	- thread

Note: The English translations of the *kanji* did not appear in the task.

For the radical-category items, the ratings skewed towards 'related' (mode categories '5', '4' and '3'). Only six out of the 40 items were rated lower than '3'. Apparently, the L1 readers tended to see the semantic relatedness between the *kanji* and the category name when the main radical was explicitly indicated.

6.2.2 Semantic judgement task: Percentages of affirmative responses and reaction times

In the above section, the 40 common-radical items and 40 radical-category items were categorised into different mode categories according to their rated degree of semantic relatedness. In this section, for the purpose of obtaining a normative response pattern for the skilled readers, the results of the timed processing tasks (i.e., semantic judgement and semantic categorisation) were organized using the modal relatedness divisions obtained from the results of the non-timed semantic rating task.

In order to examine how the L1 readers responded to the items in each mode category in the timed environment, firstly, the mean percentage of affirmative responses and the mean response time of the L1 readers to the common-radical items (in the semantic judgement task) were calculated for each mode category of different strength of relatedness. Table 6.5 shows mean percentages of 'yes' responses (i.e., the participants judged that the two characters belonged to the same semantic category) and mean response times of the 16 L1 readers to the common-radical items in each mode category. Here the variables of most interest are the percentage of affirmative responses and the spread of these (SDs), and not necessarily only the response times. This is because the response times calculated on few affirmative responses (e.g., mode category '0' had only 16.4% affirmative responses) may not be very reliable.

336

Table 6.5 Mean percentages of affirmative responses (i.e., the participants judged that the two characters belong to the same semantic category) and associated mean response times of the L1 readers for the common-radical items (the semantic judgement task)

Group (No. of subjects)		Semantic judgement task — Are the two characters in the same meaning category? -Yes				
		Mode value of rating for semantic relatedness (No. of items)				
		Highly related		Moderately related		Not related
		5 (7)	4 (9)	3 (9)	2+1 (7)	0 (8)
L1 (16)	Affirm%	95.5	68.1	69.4	48.2	16.4
	SD	8.6	16.7	20.5	30.4	11.8
	RT	849	1055	1133	1262	1117
	SD	222	284	265	638	267

Affirm% = % of affirmative responses to the task question; SD = Standard deviation; RT = response time

The response pattern of the L1 readers in the semantic judgement task was consistent with the ratings. The items that were rated as highly related in the non-timed semantic rating task were the ones that attracted affirmative responses in the timed processing task. For the pairs of *kanji* that were rated as 'highly related' by the group of 45 L1 readers (i.e., mode category '5'), nearly all of the 16 L1 readers thought the characters were in the same semantic category (95.5%). On the other hand, the percentage of affirmative responses was very low (16.4 %) for the items that were rated as 'not related' (i.e., mode category '0'). Overall, the percentages of the affirmative responses in the semantic judgement task were very much in accord with the semantic relatedness ratings. The standard deviations for the most highly related items (i.e., mode category '5') and for the no relationship items (i.e., mode category '0') were relatively low (8.6 and 11.8). This indicated that the L1 readers made a similar semantic relatedness judgement for these items. Conversely, the relatively high standard deviation (30.4) for the marginally related items (i.e., mode category '2 + 1') indicated the L1 readers' semantic judgement on these items was variable.

For the response times, the L1 readers responded quickly (849 ms) to the items that were rated as most related (i.e., mode category '5'), and the relatively low standard deviation (222) shows that their responses were fairly homogeneous. The items rated as marginally related (i.e., mode category '2 + 1'), which induced the highest standard deviation for the affirmative response percentage, recorded the slowest responses (1262 ms), and its standard deviation for the response time was also the highest of all (638). It should be noted however that this response time and its standard deviation were based on relatively few responses.

6.2.3 Semantic judgement task: Percentages of negative responses and reaction times

Table 6.6 shows the mean percentages of 'no' responses (i.e., the participants judged that the two characters do not belong to the same semantic category) and associated mean response times of the 16 L1 readers to the common-radical items for each mode category of different strength of relatedness.

Table 6.6 Mean percentages of negative responses i.e., the participants judged that the two characters do not belong to the same semantic category) and associated mean response times of the L1 readers to the common-radical items (the semantic judgement task)

Group (No. of subjects)		Semantic judgement task Are the two characters in the same meaning category? -No				
		Mode value of rating for semantic relatedness (N of items)				
		Highly related		Moderately related		Not related
		5 (7)	4 (9)	3 (9)	2+1 (7)	0 (8)
L1 (16)	Neg%	4.5	31.9	30.6	51.8	83.6
	SD	8.6	16.7	20.5	30.4	11.8
	RT	1121	1117	1267	1085	1034
	SD	486	391	456	332	276

Neg% = % of negative responses to the task question, SD = Standard deviation; RT = response time

The items that were rated as having only marginal or no semantic relationship in the non-timed semantic rating task (i.e., mode categories '2 + 1' and '0') were by and large the ones that attracted a negative response in the timed processing task. The percentage of negative responses was very low (4.5 %) in the highly related items (i.e., mode category '5'). The percentages of negative responses were in inverse proportion to the mode values of the semantic relatedness rating.

One would think that the response speed might also align with the response speed of the affirmative responses. Unexpectedly, however, the response times of the negative responses were relatively flat across the different mode categories, although the means for the response times of highly to moderately related items must be observed cautiously due to the low (negative) response rates.

6.2.4 Semantic categorisation task: Percentages of affirmative responses and reaction times

Table 6.7 shows mean percentages of 'yes' responses (i.e., the participants judged that the character belong to the presented semantic category) and associated mean response times of the 16 L1 readers to the radical-category items (in the semantic categorisation task) for each mode category of different strength of relatedness.

Table 6.7 Mean percentages of affirmative responses (i.e., the participants judged that the character belongs to the presented semantic category) and associated mean response times of the L1 readers for the radical-category items (the semantic categorisation task)

Group (No. of subjects)		Semantic categorisation task Is the character in the meaning category shown? -Yes			
		Mode value of rating for semantic relatedness (N of items)			
		Highly related 5 (6)	Moderately related 4 (14)	3 (14)	Marginally related 2+1+0 (6)
L1 (16)	Affirm%	88.5	75.9	57.1	16.7
	SD	11.7	18.4	17.5	26.5
	RT	1087	1212	1293	1317
	SD	260	338	323	441

Affirm% = % of affirmative responses to the task question; SD = Standard deviation; RT = response time

As was the case in the semantic judgement task, the responses of the 16 L1 readers in the semantic categorisation task were directly related to the ratings of semantic relatedness. The items that were rated as highly related in the non-timed semantic rating task (mode categories '5' and '4') were the ones that attracted affirmative responses in the timed processing task. The items that were rated as marginally or not related in the non-timed rating task (i.e., mode category '2 + 1 + 0') attracted the least number of affirmative responses in the timed processing task. Unlike in the semantic judgement task, in the semantic categorisation task only the most highly related items (i.e., mode category '5') showed a relatively low standard deviation (11.7). The marginally or not related items (i.e., mode category '2 + 1 + 0') had the highest standard deviation (26.5), indicating that the L1 readers varied in their judgement on these items.

For the response times of the affirmative responses, the L1 readers responded relatively quickly (1,087 ms) to the items that were rated as the most highly related (i.e., mode category '5'), and the relatively low standard deviation (260) shows that their responses were fairly homogeneous. The items rated as marginally related or not related (mode category '2 + 1 + 0'), which induced the highest standard deviation for the percentage of affirmative responses, were the slowest to be responded to (1,317 ms), and the standard deviation for the response time was also the highest of all (441), although it should be noted this response time and the associated measure of standard deviation were based on only a few responses.

6.2.5 Semantic categorisation task: Percentages of negative responses and reaction times

Table 6.8 shows mean percentages of 'no' responses (i.e., the participants judged that the character would not belong to the presented semantic category) and associated mean response times of the 16 L1 readers to the radical-category items for each mode category of different strength of relatedness.

Table 6.8 Mean percentages of negative responses (i.e., the participants judged that the character does not belong to the semantic category) and associated mean response times of the L1 readers to the radical-category items rated (the semantic categorisation task)

		Semantic categorisation task			
		Is the character in the meaning category shown? -No			
		Mode value of rating for semantic relatedness (N of items)			
		Highly related	Moderately related		Marginally related
		5 (6)	4 (14)	3 (14)	2+1+0 (6)
L1 (16)	Neg%	11.5	23.7	42.4	83.3
	SD	11.7	18.9	18.4	26.5
	RT	1702	1446	1352	1213
	SD	888	818	486	351

Neg% = % of negative responses to the task question, SD = Standard deviation; RT = response time

As can be seen in the table, the percentages of negative responses were inversely related to the mode values of the semantic relatedness ratings, which was a pattern that was the reverse of the percentages of the affirmative responses. The pattern of responses for the items in the semantic categorisation task was similar to those observed in the results of the semantic judgement task in terms of the percentage of negative responses.

The response times for the negative responses also showed a reversed pattern compared to the affirmative responses. This was quite different from the pattern shown by the response times of the negative responses in the semantic judgement task, which was essentially flat across the mode categories. The items that were rated as marginally related or not related (i.e., mode category '2 + 1 + 0') were the quickest to be responded to (1,213 ms) and the standard deviation was the lowest (351) among the four mode categories, although it should be noted this response time and its standard deviation were based on only a few responses. The negative responses to the most highly related items (i.e., mode category '5') were the slowest (1,702 ms) and the standard deviation was extremely high (888).

6.2.6 Discussion of the results of semantic judgement and semantic categorisation tasks

Character-level dominant processing

Overall, the results of the tasks suggest that the ultimate judgement about the meaning of a character is not necessarily determined by the component level processing. As stated before, if the L1 readers had used the information from the main radicals, then they would have rated all the items as 'in the same category'. This was certainly not the case. Even when the main radicals were made conspicuous, as in the semantic categorisation task, the L1 readers did not rely solely on the semantic information of the

343

main radicals. This might have been because the L1 readers had formed strong lemma representations for the *kanji* at the character level (i.e., the lemma representations have well-established links to orthographic, phonological and semantic representations of the kanji).

This notion that L1 adult readers did not rely on the main radical, however, may not mean that they did not process this information at all. Indeed, there is evidence from studies, such as the one by Shu and Anderson (1997), that even child L1 readers of Japanese process the information conveyed by the semantic radical. This was demonstrated by the finding that semantic information from the main radicals became more prominent as character familiarity decreased and it was suggested that L1 children are able to decompose characters into informative parts, and use the semantic information when necessary (Shu and Anderson, 1997). It is therefore reasonable to think that the L1 readers in the present study who were skilled adult readers had lemma representations formed at least for high frequency main radicals through repeated access to them. Nevertheless, their final judgement was based on the semantic information from the characters probably because for the skilled adult readers, all the characters would have been familiar and as such, information from the character level would have predominated over the information from the components at the time of decision-making.

Processing both at the character and component levels

The L1 readers indeed seemed to have been affected by the semantic information conveyed by the main radicals. The results showed that, in both tasks, the response times for the affirmative responses tended to be faster in judging the more related items than in judging the less related items. The study by Yamada and Takashima (2001) may be of help in interpreting this trend. These researchers presented words written in *hiragana* one by one to Japanese children, and asked them to say aloud the name of the main radical of the would-be *kanji* that corresponded to the *hiragana* words. The responses of the participants were quicker and more accurate when the main radicals were semantically closely related to the target *kanji*, and slower responses and higher error rates were observed where the meanings of the *kanji* and its main radical were not closely related. The researchers concluded that the inconsistency between the information from the whole *kanji* and from the main radical was likely to have been the cause of the slower responses and higher error rates. The study suggests that Japanese children consider the information both from the character and the main radical. The idea that the determination of the meaning of a kanji can be influenced by information from both the character and main radical, is consistent with the finding from the current study with adult L1 Japanese language users that faster response times were recorded in judging the more related items and the slower response times in judging the less related items.

For the negative responses, different patterns of response speed were observed in the two tasks. This might have been due to the conspicuousness of the components in the semantic categorisation task. The relatively flat response times of the negative responses in the semantic judgement task suggest that the participants applied a response deadline after which they would default to the position that the two kanji were not related. It appears that, after about 1,000 ms, if they did not see any connections in the two *kanji*, they pressed the 'no' button. Thus, when the main radicals were not highlighted, the decisions seemed to have been made mainly based on the information from the character level processing although the common main radical shared by the two characters was also likely to have been processed.

On the other hand, the slower response times of the negative responses to the more strongly related radical-category pairs in the semantic categorisation task might suggest that the semantic information generated at the component level interfered with the information from the character level. For example, one of the strongly related pairs was 雪 (snow) and 'rain'. Those participants who did not think 'snow' and 'rain' were related have pressed the 'no' button, but their responses were slow. The slow decision-making was probably due to the interference caused by the activation of the highlighted main radical (the rain radical), which indicated the given semantic category (rain). The findings suggest that while semantic information is processed both at the character and component levels, decisions are made mainly at the character level with some input from the component level processing.

6.2.7 Semantic judgement task: Interview data

In the interview, two out of the 16 participants remarked that it was sometimes confusing because the information from the two sources (i.e., the character and the main radical) was inconsistent (see Example 1).

> Example 1: I considered information both from the main radical and *kanji* as a whole. Sometimes the answer was yes for one, but not for the other one, so it was very confusing.

However, for the majority, it was not the inconsistent information that troubled them. Seven participants referred to the difficulty of making judgements based on semantic categories (see Example 2). It seems that the participants tended to relate *kanji* by random or arbitrary word association (see Examples 3-4).

> Example 2: Some of them were tricky. For example, *miru* (看 - look after) and
>
> *yome* (嫁 - bride) were related in some ways, but are not in the same meaning group.
>
> Example 3: I wasn't sure of the difference between being in the same category and being able to associate the two characters. For example, *iwa* (岩 - rock) and *kishi* (岸 - shore) are not the same kind of things, but I could easily associate one with the other.

Example 4: For example, mise (店 - shop) and *ko* (庫 - part of the word 'storage') in *sooko* (storage) could be associated, but I was not sure whether these two were in the same category.

One of the participants remarked that making judgements was hard also because a category could only be decided after seeing two *kanji* characters (see Example 5).

Example 5: This task was much harder than the others. I guess that's because I can't identify what category the *kanji* is in until I see the second *kanji*. You have to remember the first *kanji* without knowing what to expect, and only when you view the second *kanji*, would you decide whether or not both of them belong to the same category.

In order to remember the *kanji*, six participants reported that they used phonological information to get the meanings of the *kanji* (see Example 6).

Example 6: I've always read the *kanji* in its *kun*-reading so that I could get the meaning of it. I was comparing the meanings.

(Note: the relationship between the *kun*-reading and the meaning will be discussed later)

Where the *kanji* did not have a *kun*-reading, the participants gave the *kanji* some context by placing the *kanji* in a compound word (see Example 7), from which they accessed the meaning of the *kanji*.

Example 7: I think I was reading the *kanji* out in its *kun*-reading. For those ones that I was not sure how to read in *kun*-reading, I quickly made compound words using the *kanji*.

The *kanji* that the L1 readers could not read in their *kun*-reading tended to have an obscure meaning. Five participants mentioned that, occasionally, the meaning of the individual *kanji* as a single character was not clear to them (see Example 8)

Example 8: There were some cases where I didn't know the meaning of the *kanji* per se. For example, the *kanji so* (素) usually comes with other *kanji*. I don't know what this *kanji* means when this is used on its own.

6.2.8 Semantic categorisation task: Interview data

Apparently, English was a stumbling block for some of the L1 readers of Japanese. Although all of the participants were fluent speakers of English and had been reading English regularly, seven participants reported some problems with the category names written in English (see Examples 1-2) including errors in the recognition of the English words (see Example 3).

Example 1: It was hard as I had to translate the English word into Japanese.

Example 2: Cognitive load was heavy, as I had to read English and hear the word at the same time. For me, it was hard to switch from Japanese to English.

Example 3: I at first took 'flesh' as 'fresh' and pressed the wrong one, and then after doing that a couple times, I realised that it was actually 'flesh'.

However, it seemed that viewing the English category names was sometimes helpful in remembering the main radicals (see Example 4).

Example 4: For some *kanji*, I could not find any main radical in the first place, but after seeing the category name in English, I remembered what the main radical of the *kanji* was. For example, only when I saw the English word, 'knife', did I remember the main radical *rittoo* (the name of the knife radical in Japanese).

The remarks made in the interview suggest that the L1 readers performed this task by reading the *kanji* in its *kun*-reading. Although this was not explicitly pointed out, most of the example *kanji* given during the interviews were in the *kun*-reading (see Example 5). The interview data, on the other hand, showed that at least two participants tried to remember the *kanji* by naming the main radicals (see Example 6).

Example 5: Is *iwa* (岩) related to 'mountain'? Is *osu* (押) related to 'hand'?

Example 6: Usually I could recall the name of the matching main radical, such as *sanzui* for the category name 'water'.

Three participants referred to the confusion caused by the inconsistent information from the character and the main radical (see Example 7).

Example 7: Sometimes I wasn't sure whether I should make a decision based on the meaning of the main radical or the meaning of the whole character.

Six participants commented on the ambiguity of the term, 'category' (see Examples 8-10)

Example 8: Sometimes I couldn't make a quick decision, as I wasn't sure whether the *kanji* was simply associated with or was in the same category shown in English. For instance, *iwa* (岩) is surely related to 'mountain', but I'm not sure it is in the category of 'mountain'. Similarly, the relationship between *yuki* (雪) and 'rain' is not clear.

Example 9: You may say that 秋 (autumn) is associated with 'grain' as autumn is the season of harvest, but the word 'autumn' does not have anything to do with 'grain',

Example 10: I wasn't sure which button to press when I saw something like *shimaru* (閉) and 'gate', because one is a verb and the other is a noun.

Two participants remarked that the *kanji* with multiple meanings and those that do not have meanings on their own were hard to process (see Examples 11-12)

Example 11: This task was really hard. There are some *kanji* that have multiple meanings, and other ones that have no meaning by themselves.

Example 12: I encountered some *kanji*, of which I don't know the meaning. For example, what is the meaning of the *kanji kin* (均) in *heikin* (average)?.

6.2.9 Discussion of the interview about the semantic judgement and semantic categorisation tasks

Component awareness

The L1 readers were aware of the structures and functions of the main radicals. They were also aware of the limitations in utilising the semantic information of the main radicals for making semantic judgement. However, it is not that the L1 readers were aware of the main radical and its limitations in every character. The interview data indicated that the participants did not access the semantic information of some low frequency main radicals. For example, the main radical *ritto* (knife radical) was identified only after the English word 'knife' was presented. The information of high frequency main radicals such as *sanzui* (water radical) might become available more readily than less frequent main radicals such as *ritto* (knife radical). It is plausible to think that high frequency main radicals such as *sanzui* have stronger lemma representations than less frequency main radicals such as *ritto*. Moreover, the strength of the lemma may be affected by the semantic relationship between the main radical and the characters sharing the main radical. The interview data suggest that the L1 readers utilise the information of the main radical provided that the main radical actually proves useful in the character recognition. This suggests that more useful main radicals are more 'frequently utilised'. It may be therefore hypothesised that the frequency of utilisation, rather than the frequency of occurrence in print, determines the strength of lemma representations.

Processing at multiple levels

The interview data suggest that *kanji* recognition involves more than the processing of characters and components. In this study, even though the stimuli were individual characters, recognition decisions were made at the word level for some characters (i.e., some characters had to be integrated into a word in order to retrieve the meaning of the characters). To discuss this further, the issues of multiple readings need to be considered.

Some L1 readers remarked that they accessed the meaning of the *kanji* by reading it in its *kun*-reading (that was the meaning-bearing reading). When they could not read the *kanji* in its meaning-bearing reading (either because the *kanji* did not have any *kun*-reading or it had a rarely used *kun*-reading), they formed a compound word using the *kanji* and then inferred the meaning of the *kanji* by reference to the word. For example, as 庫 does not have a meaning-bearing reading, a participant could have thought of a word such as 倉庫 (storage), and then guessed that this *kanji* might have had a meaning related to 'storage'.

As described in the 'Japanese *kanji* characters' section, the *on*-reading shows the pronunciation of Chinese words that have been introduced to Japan (see Chapter 1 Section 3 for detailed explanations). Today, *kanji* with an *on*-reading are often found in compound words, and the *on*-reading of individual *kanji* often does not mean anything on its own (Tamaoka, 2003). Also, because an *on*-reading can be represented by a great number of *kanji*, it is usually not reliable for accessing the semantic information of the *kanji* (Tamaoka, 2005). The *kun*-reading is more closely connected to semantics than is the *on*-reading, as the *kun*-reading is the pronunciation of native Japanese words. Therefore, when the *kanji* cannot be read in its *kun*-reading (meaning-bearing reading), the *kanji* needs to be placed into a compound word in order to get the semantic information. In essence, the L1 readers read the stimuli as a meaning-bearing unit. When the *kanji* did not have a meaning-bearing reading, it appears that the L1 readers had to access the meaning of a compound word with the target *kanji* in it in order to retrieve the meaning of the *kanji*.

Routinely considered level for decision making

According to the lemma-version of the Multilevel Interactive Activation Model (see Chapter 2 Section 2 for details), the characters that could be a single-character word (free morphemes) have a strong lemma representation while the ones that need to take another character to form a word (bound morphemes) have a representation, but the link between those *kanji* and their lemma representations may not be strong. Judging from the L1 readers' remarks in the interviews, they appear to have read the *kanji* in its meaning-bearing reading, whenever it was possible, to access the lemma representations of the *kanji*. However, Taft (2004) claims that a character is pronounced only via the mediation of a lemma. If this were the case, it was not that the readers read the *kanji* in its meaning-bearing reading *in order to* access the lemma representations, but it was rather that they read the *kanji* in its meaning-bearing reading *because* those *kanji* had their lemma representations. According to the model, a character that has a strong lemma can be read by itself, whereas a character that has no lemma or a weak lemma (i.e., bound morpheme) needs to be put into a form of a compound word from which the reading of the character can be retrieved. As a case in point, Taft and Zhu (1995) reported that the first-position character of a two-character binding word (i.e., the first character is always followed by the second character and the second character always follows the first character) was named faster than the second-position character. Also, the second character was sometimes given the pronunciation of the first character. These findings suggest that, when a character has a very weak lemma representation, readers need to activate the lemma representation at the whole word level in order to determine the pronunciation of the character.

However, Taft and Zhu (1995) propose that not all compound words are stored in a binding form (i.e., not having lemma representations for individual characters). They asked L1 Chinese readers to name two types of *hanzi*: 1) *hanzi* that have only one possible combination with another *hanzi* (Type 1), and 2) *hanzi* with several possible partners to form different words (Type 2). The results showed that, for Type 1, the *hanzi* that comes in the first position (i.e., the first *hanzi* of the two-*hanzi* compound word) was read faster than the second position *hanzi*. On the other hand, for the Type 2 *hanzi*, there was no significant difference between the times required for reading the first position *hanzi* and for the second position *hanzi*. Taft and Zhu propose that individual characters have lemma representations when they can be combined with other characters to form different compound words.

In the current study, the interview data suggested that the strength of the link between a *kanji* (orthographic representation) and its lemma representation may vary even among multiple combination characters. For example, both 昨 and 素 are bound morphemes that can form various compound words, and do not have a meaning-bearing, *kun*-reading. However, when comparing these characters, the *kanji* 昨 has a more clear meaning whereas the meaning of the *kanji* 素 may be more obscure. 昨 is used in words such as 昨日 (yesterday), 昨夜 (last night) and 昨年 (last year), and so the meaning of the *kanji* 'last' or 'previous' is not hard to infer. On the other hand, the meaning of 素 that can be found in words such as 素材 (raw material), 素質 (aptitude), 要素 (factor), and 酸素 (oxygen) would appear to be much harder to retrieve.

One of the remarks made by a participant suggests that the *kanji* that have multiple meanings and the ones that have no meaning by themselves are hard to process. In the main, having many meanings and having no clear meaning can be considered to be the same. As shown in the above example of the *kanji* 素, when the character does not have a meaning-bearing reading, its meaning needs to be inferred from several compound words containing the character; hence the character may be given many meanings but no particular meaning by itself. On the other hand, it might be the case that some bound morphemes representing clear meanings such as 昨 have established their positions as quasi-free morphemes. This may suggest that lemma representations of characters exist not because they can be linguistically divided into such units, but because they are simply established by frequent visual encounters.

Interestingly, when the L1 readers' attention was drawn to the main radicals (semantic categorisation task), some readers read the main radicals by their names (e.g., *sanzui*) to access the concept of the category (e.g., 'water-related') shown by the main radical. This indeed suggests that some main radicals may have lemma representations at the component level. The L1 readers might have read some main radicals because they had their lemma representations. Taking these together, it may be proposed then, that semantic processing is constrained by lemma representations.

The above-described findings suggest that when the stimulus has a lemma representation, phonological and semantic information linked to the representation would be activated almost simultaneously. However, when there is no (or only a weak) lemma representation (e.g., a constituent character of a compound word that does not have a meaning-bearing reading on its own), the stimulus may be required to be put into a larger unit (e.g., a character into a compound word) before being processed via the mediation of a lemma. When the stimulus has lemma representations at different levels (e.g., there are lemma representations both at the character and component levels), the information activated through the stronger lemma representation would be sent to the decision system before the information linked to the other lemma.

Lastly, there were two issues that highlighted problems of the study. One of them concerned the instructions given to the participants in the tasks. For both the semantic judgement and semantic categorisation tasks, the participants were required to make judgements on whether the stimuli belonged to the same semantic category rather than whether the stimuli could be associated. However, the L1 readers mentioned that making their judgement was not simple, as being able to associate two stimuli and seeing the two in the same semantic category were not easily separable criteria for them. In this regard, it is worth commenting that the manner in which a person comes to develop a meaning (or semantic) network may be in part formed thorough social and personal experiences. The association between 看 (look after) and 嫁 (bride) is a classic example. Some participants judged these two *kanji* as being semantically related, as the meaning of the *kanji* 嫁 could be extended to 'wife', 'daughter-in-law', and to 'someone who is expected to look after all members of the family including the sick and elderly' depending on how you see '嫁'. In this regard, the instructions were devised in order to emphasise that the judgement should be made on the basis of whether or not the two stimuli could be in the same semantic category; this was done to avoid the consideration of far-fetched associations. However, even though the instruction's emphasis was on the semantic category, the participants sometimes could not avoid relating the two *kanji* or the *kanji* and the category name by word association.

The interview data have also thrown light on the difficulty of dealing with two different languages, in this case Japanese and English. The link between *kanji* and their meanings may be weaker in English for Japanese readers. The L1 readers' responses to the stimuli might have been slowed down because of the need to determine precisely how the Japanese and English examples could be related.

6.3 L2 readers of Japanese: Objectives and Methods

6.3.1 Objectives

The purpose of this part of the study is to investigate and categorise the development of semantic processing skills and awareness of L2 readers. To this end, the same tasks (semantic judgement and semantic categorisation) and interview that were used in the L1 readers' study were administered to three groups of L2 readers (beginner, intermediate and advanced groups), and the response patterns of the L2 readers were compared with those of the L1 readers.

The results of the previous study with the L1 readers indicated that the skilled readers' semantic processing measured in the semantic judgement and semantic categorisation tasks was primarily constrained at the character level or even higher (see Chapter 6 Section 1 for details). That is, the L1 reader typically used the information of the main radicals only when the main radicals were reliable (i.e., when the meaning of the target kanji was in the semantic domain indicated by the main radical).

This part of the study examines if this bias towards using higher level representation exists and if the selective use of main radicals is observed for the L2 readers. Along with the tasks, an interview was conducted after each of the semantic tasks. The main aim of the interview was to investigate whether the L2 readers were aware of information in main radicals and of the limitations of the information from main radicals (see Chapter 3 Section 1 for details).

6.3.2 Methods

Participants

20 beginner, 40 intermediate, and 17 advanced readers undertook the semantic judgement task, while 18 beginner, 40 intermediate and 16 advanced readers did the semantic categorisation task (see Chapter 3 Section 1 for details).

Materials

The same two semantic tasks used for the L1 readers were used.

Procedure

The procedure of administering the tasks was the same as for the previous study with the L1 readers.

6.4 L2 readers of Japanese: Results and discussion

As described in the 'analysis' section (Chapter 3 Section 3), the results of the semantic judgement and semantic categorisation tasks were not subject to statistical analysis as were the orthographic and phonological data. Instead, in order to characterise the response patterns of the L2 readers, the responses were compared against those of the L1 readers and also across the three groups of L2 readers.

6.4.1 Semantic judgement task: Patterns of affirmative responses and reaction times

For the 40 common-radical items (e.g., 砂 - 砕) in the semantic judgement task, the participants were required to judge whether two characters that had a common main radical were from the same meaning category. Figure 6.1 presents the L2 readers' patterns of response results for affirmative responses (those accepting the semantic relationship of the common-radical items). To enable ready comparison with the response results of the L1 readers, these data are also included in the figure as norm values (see Chapter 6 Section 1 for a detailed explanation). In keeping with the previous section that reported the L1 results, mean percentages of affirmative responses of the L2 readers for the common-radical items are reported according to the degrees of relatedness as assessed by separate L1 raters (i.e., mode values). Mode category '5' means the most highly related items, and mode category '0', the least related items (see Chapter 6 Section 1 for a detailed explanation). Note that the mean values are raw means, not adjusted means. Statistical analyses were not performed, as the sample size in each category was too small. Due to lack of reliability in the L2 readers' negative responses, only affirmative responses accepting the semantic relations are reported here (see Chapter 3 Section 3 for discussion).

Figure 6.1 Mean percentage and 95% Confidence Intervals of affirmative responses (i.e., the participants judged that the two characters were members of the same semantic category) of the L2 readers for the 40 common-radical items

Semantic judgement task

Are the two characters members of the same meaning category?

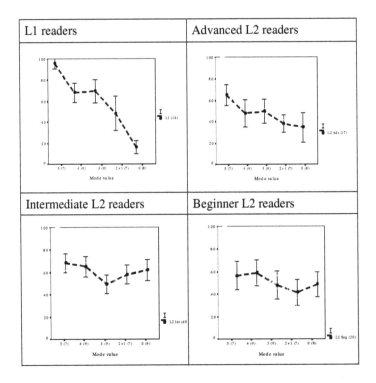

Note: The filled squares show mean values. The whiskers indicate 95% Confidence Intervals for the means. The numbers in parentheses show the numbers of participants (right) or the numbers of items (bottom).

The response pattern of the advanced L2 readers showed the most similarity with the L1 readers' as both showed a trend for fewer affirmative responses as the modal values decreased; on the other hand, the curves of the intermediate and beginner L2 readers were distinct from that of the L1 readers. The items that were rated as 'highly related' by the L1 readers (mode category '5') were the ones that attracted the most affirmative responses (i.e., the participants judged that the two characters were members of the same semantic category) from the advanced L2 readers, and the items that were rated as 'not related' by the L1 readers (mode category '0') attracted the least. Generally, the percentages decreased as the strength of relatedness decreased, although the difference between the highest percentage (in mode category '5') and the lowest percentage (in mode category '0') for the advanced L2 readers was smaller than for the L1 readers. By contrast, the response patterns of the intermediate and beginner readers did not show a descending curve. The intermediate readers demonstrated a U-shape response pattern, and the beginner readers showed a rather flat pattern. The 95% confidence intervals of the means of the intermediate and beginner readers were constant across the items with different strengths of semantic relationships. This was in marked contrast to the varied 95% confidence intervals of the advanced readers.

Figure 6.2 shows patterns of response times of the L2 readers' affirmative responses for accepting the semantic relationship of the common-radical items.

**Figure 6.2 Mean response times and 95% Confidence Intervals of the L2 readers'
affirmative responses (i.e., the participants judged that the two characters were
members of the same semantic category) to the 40 common-radical items**

Semantic judgement task

Are the two characters members of the same meaning category?

s

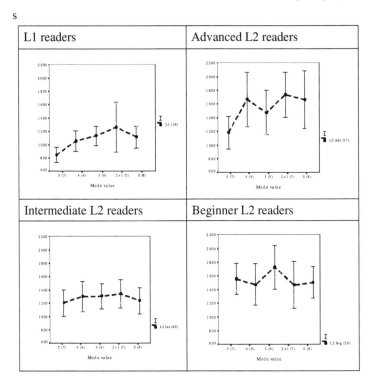

Note: The filled squares show mean values. The whiskers indicate 95% Confidence Intervals for
the means. The numbers in parentheses show the numbers of participants (right) or the numbers
of items (bottom).

Given that the advanced L2 readers knew more *kanji* than did the readers of the other

groups, the advanced readers might have been expected to demonstrate the fastest

response times among all the L2 participants. Interestingly however, the response times of the advanced readers were generally longer than those of the intermediate readers. In fact, the intermediate readers showed consistently shorter response times across the items from the different modal ratings of semantic relationships (from mode category '5' to mode category '0'). The intermediate readers took less time on the judgement than the advanced readers, except for their response to the most related items (mode category '0').

6.4.2 Semantic categorisation tasks: Patterns of affirmative responses and reaction times

For the 40 radical-category items (e.g., 雪 - rain) in the semantic categorisation task, the participants were required to judge whether the character was a member of the semantic category shown. Figure 6.3 presents the L2 readers' patterns of affirmative responses (accepting the semantic relationship between a character and a semantic field).

Figure 6.3 Mean percentage and 95% Confidence Intervals of affirmative responses (i.e., the participants judged that the character was a member of the semantic category shown) of the L2 readers for the 40 radical-category items

Semantic categorisation task

Is the character a member of the meaning category?

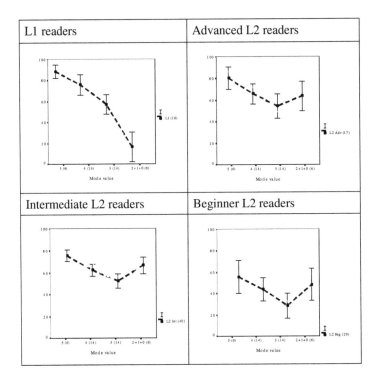

Note: The filled squares show mean values. The whiskers indicate 95% Confidence Intervals for the means. The numbers in parentheses show the numbers of participants (right) or the numbers of items (bottom).

For the radical-category items, the response pattern of the advanced L2 readers did not follow the trend of the L1 readers. Remember that the items that were judged as 'highly related' (mode category '5') were the ones that attracted affirmative responses (i.e., the participants judged that the character was in the category), and the items that were rated as 'not related' (mode category '0') attracted the least percentage of responses from the L1 readers. The pattern of the L2 readers stands in marked contrast to that just described. Although the items that were rated as highly related by the L1 readers (mode category '5') attracted the highest percentage of affirmative responses from the advanced readers, the rest of the items also attracted many affirmative responses. Moreover, the response patterns of the intermediate readers overlapped considerably with the response pattern of the advanced readers. Furthermore, the beginner readers, who had only a few *kanji* that they could identify, followed the same response pattern as the other two groups of L2 readers, although the percentages of their affirmative responses were all low. The number of L2 readers' affirmative responses reduced as the semantic relatedness of the items decreased from mode category '5' items to mode category '3' items, but their affirmative responses rose for the marginally or not related items (mode category '2 + 1 + 0') (see Figure 6.3).

Figure 6.4 presents patterns of response times of the L2 readers' affirmative responses in accepting the semantic relationship (between the *kanji* and the semantic field) of the main radical category items.

Figure 6.4 Mean response times and 95% Confidence Intervals of the L2 readers' affirmative responses (i.e., the participants judged that the character was a member of the semantic category shown) to the 40 radical-category items

Semantic categorisation task

Is the character a member of the meaning category?

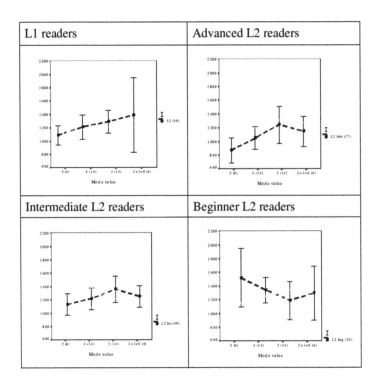

Note: The filled squares show mean values. The whiskers indicate 95% Confidence Intervals for the means. The numbers in parentheses show the numbers of participants (right) or the numbers of items (bottom).

The advanced readers and the intermediate readers were similar in their patterns of response times. Their response times increased (in a fairly linear fashion) as the strength of semantic relatedness decreased from mode category '5' to mode category '3', and

368

then their response times to the marginally or not related items (mode category '2 + 1 + 0') dropped to the level of mode category '3'. In this regard, the advanced and intermediate readers differed from the L1 readers who demonstrated a steady increase in the response times from highly related to least related. The response times of the beginner readers did not show any systematic pattern. Another interesting phenomenon observed was that the advanced readers showed shorter response times than those of the L1 readers.

6.4.3 Discussion of the results of the semantic judgement and semantic categorisation tasks: patterns of affirmative responses and reaction times
Development of character-dominant processing

Generally, the results of the common-radical items (i.e., two characters had a common main radical) showed that the advanced readers have developed a semantic network that at least partially resembles that of the L1 readers. The higher percentage of affirmative responses to the more related items and lower percentage to the less related items indicated that the semantic processing of the advanced readers was not dependent on the main radicals. Given their exposure to a number of radicals (particularly as main radicals), it is unlikely that they did not process the main radicals. Nevertheless, the results indicated that they did not rely on the semantic information from the main radicals when making semantic judgements. This less dependence on the main radicals may be taken as evidence for the development of the dominance of character level information over that of the components, which was also evident in the other aspects of processing for skilled readers (see Chapters 4 and 5 for details).

Limited links between characters and meaning

Nevertheless, there were differences in the response pattern between the advanced L2 readers and the L1 readers. These differences might be because 'words in the second language would activate semantic representations less deeply and do so for a shorter duration', as Segalowitz (1986:16) has claimed. It is plausible to think that the advanced readers had access to only one aspect of the semantic information of the characters, and made their judgement on the limited information. If this were the case, they were less likely to say 'yes' to the task question (Do the two *kanji* characters belong to the same semantic category), as they often did not find any overlapping meanings between the two *kanji*. This could be why the percentages of affirmative responses of the advanced readers for related items were relatively lower than those of the L1 readers.

The response pattern of the intermediate readers for the common-radical items showed a U-shaped curve, which was distinct from that of the L1 readers. This will be further discussed later (see Chapter 6 Section 4.4). The beginner readers' rather flat response pattern (indicating a lack of sensitivity to the rated connectedness of *kanji* in a pair) was also very different from that of the L1 readers. The beginner L2 readers' affirmative response rate was generally lower than the rates of the readers from the other groups. However, it was not as low as one would anticipate from their limited *kanji* knowledge. It could be that these readers tackled this task orthographically, simply looking for some common graphic features in the two *kanji,* in which case, all of the

370

kanji that shared a common radical would be possible 'yes' response candidates; a response strategy that would led to a flat curve like the one exhibited by the beginner readers.

Character-level processing and component-level processing

Unexpectedly, the response speed of the intermediate readers to the common-radical items was generally faster than that of the advanced readers, and was closer to that of the L1 readers. One would anticipate faster response times for the advanced readers, who were presumably more skilled than the intermediate readers. However, as it turned out, the less-skilled readers took less time in making the judgement than the more-skilled readers, except for the responses to the most related items. Also their response speed was relatively constant across the different mode categories of sematic relatedness. A possible interpretation of this might be that the intermediate readers largely relied on the semantic information from the main radicals whereas the advanced readers might have attempted to use the information both from the characters and the main radicals, which resulted in the slower response times, as more time was required for the comparison of the information from the two sources. However, the advanced readers' longer 95%CIs compared to those of the intermediate readers indicated that their response speed was very variable, which suggests that some lower-skilled advanced readers responded to the items in a manner similar to that demonstrated by the intermediate readers (i.e., relying largely on the component level processing).

Stronger component-level processing for conspicuous main radicals

The results of the semantic categorisation task suggested a completely different picture. In the semantic categorisation task that had pairs consisting of a character and a semantic category name, the response patterns of the L2 readers, even the advanced readers, differed from that of the L1 readers, as described below. In this task, the main radicals of the *kanji* were highlighted, and the semantic field shown by the category name was what the main radical of the *kanji* represented (radical-category items). The L1 readers' responses in the semantic categorisation task were consistent with the non-timed semantic relationship ratings, as was the case in the semantic judgement task (i.e., the L1 readers judged the highly related items as 'judged to be in the category', and the marginally or not related items as 'judged to be not in the category'). In other words, as expected, the L1 readers made semantic judgements based on the information from the characters even when the main radicals of the *kanji* were highlighted.

The L2 readers, on the other hand, did not follow this pattern. Their patterns of responses were more or less similar among all the three groups with all showing a U-shape. The percentages of the affirmative responses judging that the character belonged to the semantic category decreased from the highly related items to the moderately related items. However, the marginally or not related items attracted more affirmative responses than the moderately related items.

The results of the advanced L2 readers for the radical-category items in the semantic categorisation task are particularly worth noting. These readers, who showed a similar response pattern to the L1 readers in the semantic judgement task, showed a very similar response pattern to the intermediate readers in the categorization task both in terms of the percentage of their affirmative responses and response times. The advanced readers' performance might have been affected by the highlighted main radicals. That is, the emphasis on the main radical might have produced a bias for component-level processing. This will be discussed further later (see Chapter 6 Section 4.4).

For the beginner readers, the percentages of affirmative responses were relatively lower than the other L2 readers with more *kanji* knowledge. However, although the percentages of their affirmative responses were lower than the intermediate and advanced readers across the mode categories, the beginner readers' response pattern was not as flat as the one for the semantic judgement task. It could be because the beginner readers identified familiar parts in some of the *kanji*, and that they tried to match those familiar parts with the semantic category names shown in English, and that the degree of familiarity of the main radicals might have affected their responses.

In order to further examine the mode of processing (character level, component level or both levels) of the L2 readers, their response patterns were compared with the percentages of *kanji* and main radicals that were considered to be in the range of the L2 readers' *kanji* knowledge, and therefore 'recognisable' (the selection of 'recognisable' *kanji* and main radicals will be discussed in the next section).

6.4.4 Exploration of the response patterns: Comparisons with recognisable kanji and main radicals

In this section, the response patterns of the advanced and intermediate readers and the proportion of 'recognisable' (i.e., within the range of familiarity) main radicals and characters were compared. The response patterns of the beginner readers were not included in the comparisons because the findings from the results of the orthographic tasks (see Chapter 4 Section 2 for details) suggested that these readers were relying on graphic elements that were familiar to them rather than the functional components (i.e., main radicals in this case).

For the selection of recognisable main radicals and characters, the *kanji* database (Tamaoka, Kirsner, Yanase, Miyaoka, and Kawakami, 2002) containing the data from the standardised Japanese Proficiency Test was once again used (see Chapter 3 Section 2 for details). As described in the 'Japanese *kanji* characters' section (Chapter 1 Section 3), some main radicals can be legitimate *kanji* with a slight change in their size and shape while other main radicals cannot. The former may be more familiar than the latter to L2 readers, as the same radicals can be seen as characters as well as main radicals. In relation to this, Ho, Ng, and Ng, (2003) found that Chinese children were able to use lexical radicals (i.e., the main radicals that may be legitimate characters) earlier than non-lexical radicals (i.e., the main radicals that cannot be legitimate characters on their own).

Given that the lexical main radicals were likely to be recognised more than the non-lexical, firstly, the main radicals that could be single-component *kanji* were selected

374

as 'recognisable main radicals' from levels four and three of the *kanji* database. The *kanji* listed in levels four and three are considered to be beginner *kanji* in the standardised Japanese Proficiency Test (see Chapter 3 Section 2 for details). Secondly, using the same *kanji* database, all the *kanji* that were listed in levels four and three were selected as 'recognisable *kanji*'. The *kanji* listed in level two might have been recognisable for advanced readers. However, for the current analysis, only the beginner level *kanji* were chosen as recognisable *kanji*. This was because to be able to semantically process the *kanji* in less than five seconds, the readers had to have consolidated knowledge of the *kanji*.

Common-radical items: Relationship between the intermediate readers' responses and recognisable main radicals

In Section 4.3 of this chapter it was argued that the intermediate readers may have relied on the semantic information from the main radicals of the *kanji* when making semantic judgements. If this were the case, the percentage of the intermediate readers' affirmative responses to the common-radical items would be in accordance with the proportion of the recognisable main radicals, as they may have judged that the two characters were members of the semantic category when they found a recognisable main radical between them.

In order to examine the relationship between the intermediate readers' affirmative responses and the proportion of recognisable main radicals, a mean percentage of recognisable main radicals was calculated for each mode category. For example, seven common-radical items were rated as 'highly related' by the L1 readers (see Chapter 6 Section 1 for details). As each item in the 'highly related' category (i.e., mode category '5') was a pair of characters, there were 14 characters. Each of these characters was examined as to whether they had any of the recognisable main radicals, and a mean percentage of the recognisable main radicals was calculated for this mode category. The same procedure was followed for the other four mode categories. The mean percentages of the recognisable main radicals across the items in mode category '5' was 57%, 44% in mode category '4', 33% in mode category '3', 43% in mode category '2 + 1', and 38% in mode category '0'.

The pattern of the percentages of the recognisable main radicals in the items with mode categories 5-0 was then compared with the affirmative response pattern of the intermediate readers for the mode categories. Figure 6.5 shows the relationship between the response pattern of the intermediate readers for the common-radical items and the pattern of the percentages of the recognisable main radicals across the mode categories.

Figure 6.5 The relationship between the pattern of mean percentages of the intermediate readers' affirmative responses to the common-radical items and the pattern of mean percentages of the recognisable main radicals

Semantic judgement task

Are the characters members of the same semantic category?

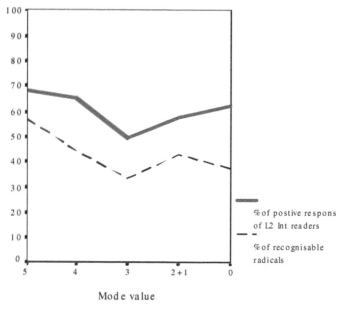

Note: Int = intermediate learners; AffirmR = affirmative responses; Rec-Radical = recognisable main radicals

Although the percentages of the affirmative responses of the intermediate readers were higher overall than the percentages of the recognisable main radicals, the patterns were parallel to each other. This suggests that the intermediate readers may have largely relied on the familiar main radicals in making their semantic judgements. The higher percentages of the intermediate readers' affirmative responses compared to the percentages of the recognisable main radicals might suggest that the intermediate readers were able to recognise more main radicals than those identified as 'recognisable'. Some high frequency main radicals that cannot be legitimate *kanji* such as *sanzui* (water radical) and *tehen* (hand radical) may have also been recognised by the intermediate readers.

Common-radical items: Relationship between the advanced readers' responses and recognisable characters and main radicals

As discussed in Section 4.3 of this chapter, the results of the advanced readers for the common-radical items suggested that they may have made their judgements based on the information from the characters rather than on the information from the main radicals. Therefore, the response pattern of the advanced readers was expected to resemble the pattern of the percentages of the recognisable characters. To examine this relationship, the mean percentage of recognisable *kanji* was calculated for each mode category in the common-radical group. The mean percentages of the recognisable *kanji* were 21% in mode category '5', 6% in mode category '4', 17% in mode category '3', 14% in mode category '2 + 1', and 6% in mode category '0'.

These percentages of the recognisable *kanji*, however, were overall too low to account for the response pattern of the advanced readers. It must be that the advanced readers had more information to use for their judgement than just the recognisable *kanji*. It is plausible to think that when the advanced readers could not recognise the *kanji*, or when they could not retrieve the meaning of the *kanji* immediately, they might have relied on the familiar main radical of the *kanji*. Therefore, along with the recognisable *kanji*, the recognisable main radicals were also included in the examination. The percentages of the recognisable *kanji* and recognisable main radicals increased to 64% in mode category '5', 50% in mode category '4', 50% in mode category '3', 43% in mode category '2 + 1', and 44% in mode category '0'.

The pattern of the percentages of the recognisable *kanji* and main radicals for the items in mode categories 5-0 was then compared with the affirmative response pattern of the advanced readers. Figure 6.6 shows the relationship between the two patterns.

Figure 6.6 The relationship between the pattern of mean percentages of the advanced readers' affirmative responses to the common-radical items and the pattern of mean percentages of the recognisable *kanji* and main radicals

Semantic judgement task

Are the characters members of the same semantic category?

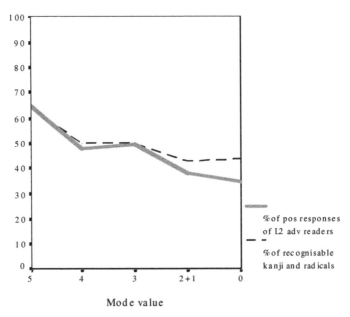

Mode value

Highly related   Moderately related   Not related

Note: Adv = advanced learners; AffirmR = affirmative responses; Rec-*kanji*-radical = recognisable *kanji* and main radicals

Across all the mode categories except the mode category '0', the pattern of the advanced readers' affirmative responses to the common-radical items almost mirrored with the pattern of percentages of recognisable *kanji* and main radicals. The percentages of affirmative responses to mode categories '2 + 1' and '0' were only slightly lower than the percentages of the recognisable *kanji* and main radicals. This suggests that the advanced readers were able to correctly judge the weak relationship of these pairs.

Radical-category items: Relationship between the advanced and intermediate readers' responses and recognisable main radicals

For the radical-category items (used in the phonological matching task), the results of the advanced and intermediate readers were very similar. In Section 4.3 of this chapter, it was argued that these L2 readers might have relied on the main radicals when making judgements on the semantic relationship between *kanji* and semantic categories because the main radicals of the *kanji* were highlighted. In this section, therefore, the response patterns of the advanced and intermediate readers were compared with the proportion of recognisable main radicals. In order to examine the relationship, the percentage of recognisable main radicals was calculated for each mode category.

One extra procedure, the exclusion of any main radicals that had different meanings when they were in the form of characters, was undertaken for this examination. It is important to keep in mind that the recognisable main radicals were main radicals that can be legitimate single-component characters. For the radical-category items, if the L2 readers used recognisable main radicals for their judgement, it can be assumed that they must have used the semantic information of the main radicals to match the category names presented. Therefore, the semantic information conveyed by the main radicals had to be the same even when they were in the form of characters, otherwise, the use of the main radicals would not have been helpful when making judgements. To this end, two radicals were excluded from the group of recognisable main radicals, as they had different meanings as characters and as main radicals (月 has the meaning of 'moon' as a character, but 'flesh' as a main radical: 小 has the meaning of 'small' as a character, but 'feeling' as a main radical).

After the exclusion of these two main radicals, the percentages of recognisable main radicals was 50% in mode category '5', 29% in mode category '4', 36% in mode category '3', and 33% in mode category '2 +1 + 0'. The pattern of percentages of recognisable main radicals for the radical-category items in mode categories 5-0 was then compared with the affirmative response patterns of the advanced and intermediate readers (Figure 6.7)

Figure 6.7 The relationship between the patterns of mean percentages of the advanced and intermediate readers' affirmative responses to the radical-category items and the pattern of mean percentages of the recognisable main radicals

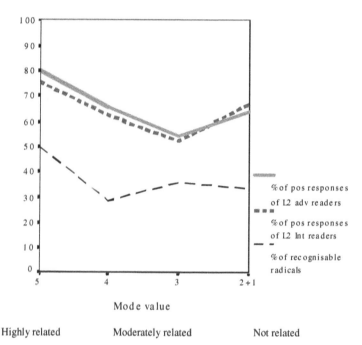

Semantic categorisation task

Is the character a member of the semantic category shown?

Mode value

Highly related   Moderately related   Not related

Note: Int = intermediate readers; Adv = advanced readers; Affirm R = affirmative responses; Rec-Radical = recognisable main radicals

As can be seen in the figure, it appears that there is no clear relationship between the affirmative responses of the advanced and intermediate readers and the percentage of recognisable main radicals. This suggests that the advanced and intermediate readers did not rely solely on the recognisable main radicals. In the following section, the response patterns of the advanced and intermediate readers are compared with the pattern of the percentages of the recognisable main radicals and characters combined.

Radical-category items: Relationship between the advanced and intermediate readers' responses and recognisable *kanji* and main radicals

The mean percentage of recognisable *kanji* was calculated for radical-category items in each mode category. These percentages were 50% in mode category '5', 21% in mode category '4', 14% in mode category '3', and 17% in mode category '2 + 1 + 0'. After combining the recognisable *kanji* with the recognisable main radicals, the relevant percentages were 83% in mode category '5', 50% in mode category '4', 36% in mode category '3', and 50% in mode category '2 + 1 + 0'. This pattern was then compared with the pattern of the percentages of the affirmative responses of the advanced and intermediate readers (Figure 6.8).

Figure 6.8 The relationship between the patterns of mean percentages of the advanced and intermediate readers' affirmative responses to the radical-category items and the pattern of mean percentages of the recognisable *kanji* and main radicals

Semantic categorisation task

Is the character a member of the semantic category shown?

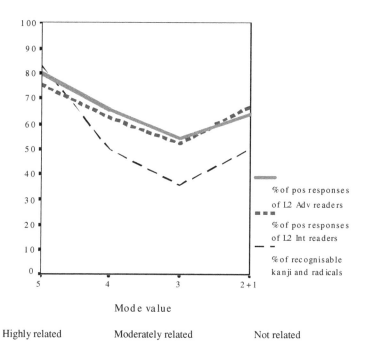

Mode value

Highly related   Moderately related   Not related

Note: Int = intermediate readers; Adv = advanced readers; Affirm R = affirmative responses; Rec-*kanji*-radical = recognisable *kanji* and main radicals

The response patterns of the advanced and intermediate readers were similar to the patterns of the percentages of recognisable *kanji* and main radicals although the percentage of recognisable *kanji* and main radicals curve was lower. In other words, the advanced and intermediate readers might have used not only the information from the component level, but also the semantic information generated from the character level for the radical-category items. The difference between the two factors suggests that the L2 readers were able to recognise more *kanji* and main radicals than those that were 'recognisable' ones.

In the semantic judgement task where the participants were required to judge whether the two characters were members of the same semantic category, the advanced readers were able to judge the weak relationship of the 'not related' pairs. However, in the semantic categorisation task, the advanced readers did not show any evidence that they judged the weakly related pairs in the same way as the L1 readers did. If the advanced readers had subordinated the information from the main radicals to the information from the characters, then the percentage of their affirmative responses for the low mode category items (e.g., mode category '2 + 1+ 0') should have been lower than the percentage of the recognisable *kanji* and main radicals. That is, if they had accessed the meanings of the 'recognisable' *kanji* or the *kanji* with the 'recognisable' main radical and compared them with the semantic categories presented, then they would have rejected their semantic relationship, recording a lower percentage of affirmative responses than the percentage of recognisable *kanji* and main radicals. However, unlike their performance on the common-radical items, this was not the case for the radical-category items. This suggests that the advanced readers, like intermediate readers, were still heavily affected by the semantic information from the main radicals.

6.4.5 Discussion of the results of the comparisons with the recognisable kanji and main radicals

The L1 readers showed similar response patterns in the two semantic tasks. In general, these skilled readers identified the semantic relationship between pairs of highly related stimuli (two characters, or a character and a category name), and rejected any relationship between pairs of non-related stimuli, regardless of the conspicuousness of the main radicals of the *kanji*. However, unlike the L1 readers, the response patterns of the L2 readers differed for the semantic judgement and semantic categorisation tasks. The possible basis of this difference will be considered in the following section.

The development of character-dominant processing

The results of the comparisons of the response patterns of the advanced and intermediate readers with regard to the proportion of the recognisable *kanji* and main radicals confirmed some of the response patterns and revealed some interesting findings about the performance of these readers.

For the semantic judgement task, the results of the comparisons suggested that the intermediate readers are likely to have made their judgements by chiefly relying on the main radicals that they recognised (probably because they were not able to recognise the whole *kanji*), whereas the advanced readers seem to have considered the semantic information of both the characters and main radicals in their judgements. The results of the comparisons further indicated that the advanced readers judged the rated weakly related pairs as weakly related. These findings suggest that at least for some advanced

329

readers, character level information predominated over component level information in determining semantics.

A factor affecting character level processing – the conspicuousness of the main radicals

For the semantic categorisation task, the results of the comparisons suggested that the advanced and intermediate readers might have used the semantic information of both the recognisable characters and main radicals. However, the advanced readers' prioritisation of the character level over the component level information, which was identified in their performance on the common-radical items, was not observed for the radical-category items. This difference might have been because the advanced readers' judgement was affected by the highlighting of the main radicals. That is, the advanced readers' attention might have been drawn more to the information from the main radicals because they were conspicuous.

For the intermediate readers, they appeared to have relied heavily on the main radicals when they performed the semantic judgement task. When the main radicals were highlighted, one would expect that the intermediate readers would rely on the main radicals even more than when the main radicals were not highlighted. However, the results of the comparison of their response patterns and the proportion of the recognisable *kanji* and main radicals suggest that it was more likely that the intermediate readers used not only the main radicals but also the characters as a whole, which was an interesting finding. This issue will be discussed in the following section.

6.4.6 Semantic judgement task: Interview data

Beginner L2 readers

10 out of the 20 beginner L2 readers expressed difficulty in performing the semantic judgement task. Nine participants commented on their lack of *kanji* knowledge (see Example 1), and three participants referred to the limited time for responses (see Example 2).

> Example 1: This was very difficult for me because I didn't know most of the *kanji*.
>
> Example 2: Most of my answers were guesses because in such a short amount of time I couldn't really take a look at the *kanji* hard enough to try and get any meaning.

It seems most of the beginner L2 readers simply matched the two *kanji* by their graphical features. 13 participants remarked that they looked for visually similar parts in the two *kanji* (see Examples 3-4).

> Example 3: I had difficulty recognising what the *kanji* meant. I sometimes used similar parts for guessing.
>
> Example 4: If I didn't know the *kanji*, I thought if they had similar figures, they might be related.

Seven participants mentioned 'radical'. A few of them might have known a few main radicals, but it seems that their knowledge of main radicals was limited (see Example 5).

Example 5: I could try and pick the meaning by the radicals, like the one for 'water' or the one for 'strength'. But even for the ones that I didn't know, if there was a common radical I just assumed that they would have similar meanings.

On the other hand, at least four participants were hesitant about making judgements based on common radicals although they seem to have noticed that some of the pairs shared a common main radical between the characters (see Example 6).

Example 6: Just because they had the same radical on the side, doesn't necessarily mean that they were in the same semantic group, even though the constructed meaning within the character might be part of the meaning.

Intermediate L2 readers

One participant in the intermediate group described how demanding this task was (see Example 7)

Example 7: Number one, I had to try and get the meaning of the *kanji*, and number two, try and remember the first one when I saw the second, and at the same time try and see if they were in the same category.

25 out of the 40 intermediate L2 readers reported that they used the radicals for their judgements. There was evidence that at least four participants were looking particularly at the main radicals (not any radicals) (see Example 8).

Example 8: With important radicals like 'fire' and 'rain' and things like that, and if they were there, I thought that they (the *kanji*) were probably in the same category.

On the other hand, nine participants expressed their hesitancy in relying only on the radicals (see Example 9). At least one of them knew some radicals were more reliable than the others (see Example 10).

> Example 9: I'd think about in what word I'd seen it, and think if the one was related to the other one at all. I'd think about the context of the words because you can't always rely on the radicals.

> Example 10: I know that there are some radicals that always give you the same meaning, like 'community', but, for example, the radical for 'tree', I know some *kanji* with this radical that don't have the meaning 'tree'.

Two intermediate L2 readers remarked that they sometimes forgot what the first *kanji* was. One of them remarked that she named the first *kanji* by their categories (see Example 11).

> Example 11: Sometimes, I forget the first one when I was looking at the second one. I tried to say the category, like 'number', 'colour', when I saw the first character. It was harder when I couldn't think of the category in the first place. I tended to forget those ones that I couldn't name.

Advanced L2 readers

Compared to the L2 readers at the lower levels, the advanced L2 readers recognised many *kanji*. However, four out of the 17 advanced readers felt that putting the *kanji* into a semantic category was difficult (see Example 12). One of them raised a question regarding the definition of 'the same semantic category' (see Example 13), as the definition could vary from person to person.

> Example 12: It was hard to tell whether the characters were in the same category or not. Sometimes if the radical was the same, you would kind of assume that they were in the same category, but sometimes they could have different meanings.

> Example 13: But what exactly is similar anyway? And who thinks or who regards the same things to be similar? It could be very different between different people?

Furthermore, two of the participants remarked that they tended to connect the *kanji* by word association (see Examples 14-15).

> Example 14: I think I was trying to match them by semantic operation. If they went together in any sort of form, then I'd click 'yes' even though I knew that I was not supposed to do so. I had lots of trouble. I think I got better towards the end. I had trouble separating the meaning from the semantic association. For example, I was thinking a way to connect the two characters *yasumi* (holiday) and *umi (sea)*, like *natsu-yasumi*' 'summer holidays' and at the 'beach'.

> Example 15: Sometimes there were things that were not really related, like the one that was 'north' and the other one was 'country', but I said 'yes'. I think because I was thinking of this Japanese movie called *Kita no kuni kara* (From the northern country). It was a semantic thing for me, but that's probably not what you were looking for.

Two participants said that they read the *kanji* out to remember the meaning of the first *kanji* and then compared it with the next *kanji* (see Example 16). Remarks made by two other participants suggested the advanced L2 readers had a bilingual semantic network (see Example 17).

Example 16: I sort of read it to myself to remember the meaning of the *kanji*.

Example 17: I thought of the meaning of the *kanji* in English sometimes, and other times, Japanese meanings came to my mind.

Four out of the 17 participants expressed the difficulty of processing *kanji* out of context (see Examples 18-19)

Example 18: It was hard to think of the meanings just on their own without any *hiragana* or context at all.

Example 19: a lot of the *kanji* that came up, I didn't know the meanings of or only recognised them in a compound, which didn't really tell me the meaning of the character. There was *hai* from *haikei* (background), and I know it means *senaka*, 'back', but when I was doing the test, I couldn't tell the meaning of the first part of the word *haikei*.

. When they could not retrieve the meaning of the *kanji* on its own, eight participants remarked that they sometimes used the (main) radicals (see Example 20). However, at least four out of these eight participants were aware of the limitations of the use of the (main) radicals (see Example 21).

Example 20: Sometimes I went by the radical. If they had the same radical, you could generally say that they had something to do with each other.

Example 21: I've noticed of course that there are a couple pairs of *kanji* with the same radical, but the meanings are not always the same, so you can't always think that they are connected.

6.4.7 Semantic categorisation task: Interview data

Beginner L2 readers

Seven out of the 18 beginner readers found the semantic categorisation task very difficult, as they didn't know most of the *kanji* displayed (see Example 1).

Example 1: It wasn't just that I didn't know the *kanji*, but I didn't know any *kanji* that related to a particular category. Like the category 'stone', I didn't know any *kanji* for 'stone', so it was pretty difficult.

Despite what was intended to be the processing order (that the participants would look at the *kanji*, access the meaning of the *kanji* and then compare it with the English word), some participants appear to have done the task in the reverse order (see Example 2). Three participants tried to see if there were any parts that looked like what the English word indicated (see Example 3).

Example 2: When the English word came up, I thought if I knew a *kanji* that related to..... if it said 'colour', and if I knew any *kanji* for colour, and if the *kanji* didn't match with what I knew, I pressed 'no'.

Example 3: Usually you can sort of picture the word in the *kanji*, like yeah, that's the 'plant', or like that because you can connect the *kanji* with some of the words sometimes.

When the *kanji* was unfamiliar, two participants remarked that they guessed its meaning from the meaning of a graphically similar *kanji* (see Example 4). Six participants reported that they made their judgement based on familiar parts that they recognised. At least for three of these participants, the familiar parts were the main radicals (see Example 5) although the number of familiar main radicals was extremely limited (see Example 6).

Example 4: I tried to remember a similar *kanji* to the *kanji* on the screen, and guessed from the meaning of the *kanji* that I knew.

Example 5: When I saw the 'water' radical, I guessed that it was related to water. So I did make guesses in that way.

Example 6: Other things like 'grain', 'hill' or 'cloth', I had no idea what the symbol (main radical) would look like.

Three participants said that they tried to look at the whole *kanji* (see Example 7).

Example 7: I tended to see not only just part of the *kanji* but also the rest of the *kanji*. And in some of the answers, I think I gave for what the *kanji* was as opposed to not necessarily what the part was involved. I might be picking what the *kanji* was rather than what the specific semantic was that time.

Intermediate L2 readers

Even though the intermediate L2 readers had more *kanji* vocabulary, there were still many *kanji* that they did not know. When they did not know the meaning of the *kanji*, 18 out of the 40 participants reported that they had used the main radical to guess the semantic category (see Examples 8-9). However, eight participants remarked that it was not easy because there were some main radicals that they didn't know (see Example 10).

> Example 8: For those ones that I didn't know, I guessed based on their radicals. When I saw the radicals, I just assumed that the characters would have the meaning something similar to that.
>
> Example 9: For the ones I didn't know, I looked for the part of the *kanji* that I knew like 'fire' and 'heart' and things. I thought that it might have a chance because they were important parts of *kanji*, and they might influence what the meaning of the *kanji*.
>
> Example 10: There were a couple that I wasn't sure like 'flesh'. It wasn't easy to guess if I didn't know the radical.

At least four participants remarked that they tried to see the whole *kanji* (see Example 11), although it was hard to see the parts other than the main radicals (see Example 12).

> Example 11: There were some (main radicals) that I didn't know like 'bamboo' or 'flesh'. In those cases, I looked at other parts of the *kanji* as well to see if there was anything that I could get the meaning from.
>
> Example 12: I found it hard because I couldn't see the whole character, like most of the time, I just saw the radical. It flashed so quickly, so it was hard to see the whole character.

The intermediate readers seemed to have attempted to access information from various aspects. Three participants reported that they tried to get the meaning of the *kanji* in context (see Examples 13-14).

Example 13: I think I'd guess based on the radicals and my experience with where I thought it (the *kanji*) would go in, context or something like that.

Example 14: But I tried more to associate the *kanji* with any words that I knew, and tried to figure out the meaning of the character from the word.

There was another group who did the task in a way that was not intended. Instead of processing the *kanji* and then comparing it with the category name, six participants reported that they sometimes used the category names to connect with the *kanji* (see Example 15).

Example 15: I used the English words. For example, when it said 'fire', I looked for the part which meant 'fire' in the character. If I found the part, and I said 'yes', but if I didn't, then I said 'no'.

Three participants found having the English category names made the task easier (see Example 16). However, one participant pointed out the problem of going between the languages (see Example 17).

Example 16: This one was easier than the other tasks because of English, hearing it, so it was easier for the brain.

Example 17: When you take the test in English, there could be a problem in between the languages. It's always difficult to go between the languages. Especially when you take the meaning of *kanji*, and try to translate it in English, and try to explain it. Because *kanji* has a number of meanings, and also a word English could have a number of meanings based on context.

Six participants felt that the category names were sometimes confusing (see Example 18).

Example 18: It was a bit hard to know what category to put the *kanji* in. For example, I think there was the *kanji* for 'face' and the category was 'head' or 'neck', and I put 'no' because it wasn't a head, but actually it was in that region. So it was a bit confusing.

Advanced L2 readers

Four participants referred to the ambiguity of the term 'category' (see Examples 19-20).

Example 19: This was quite difficult because there were some that the *kanji* popped up, and I knew the meaning of them, but I wasn't quite sure whether they did fit in that sort of category or not. For example, one question was 'stomach', and I wasn't sure it was 'flesh' or not, and another one........ I can't remember the *kanji*, but I understood the meaning, but didn't quite know if it would fit in the semantic field or not.

Example 20: Some of the semantic categories were a bit, not vague, but whether some words were going into or not depends on how big you want to make them. You can see how it was trying to trick, like having 'tree' for *hen* (on the left) and it says 'tree' even though the actual meaning isn't. So you had to watch for that.

Six out of the 16 advanced L2 readers reported that they tried to look at the whole *kanji* rather than just the main radicals (see Example 21).

Example 21: Sometimes it was not clear-cut, and you could have gone the other way. For example, *sake* (酒 - liquor) came up as a counter of 'water'. Initially, I went 'no', but I then thought there was a liquid connotation, so I might have been wrong. There was a few like that. Some *kanji* had a radical related to 'hand', but the actual meanings of the characters didn't fit in. I just said 'no' to those ones. You look at the whole character, and think what that actually means, and what sort of words you use it in, rather than seeing individual radicals.

On the other hand, when the *kanji* were unfamiliar, five participants reported that they used the semantic information of the main radicals (see Example 22).

Example 22: I sometimes guessed based on the radicals, like when I saw *nikuhen*, and it said 'flesh', then even when I didn't know what the *kanji* really was, but that's what vaguely I thought it was.

One participant reported that, prior to this task, she had never given meanings to the radicals (see Example 23).

Example 23: This was the first time I've ever translated the radicals into groups.
I've never thought of them like that.

6.4.8. Discussion of the interview about the semantic judgement and semantic categorisation tasks

Development of semantic processing

The interview data indicated that the L2 readers used whatever means they could in order to do the tasks. The findings suggest that many beginner L2 readers, due to their small *kanji* vocabulary, relied heavily on any familiar visual features of the *kanji* in order to perform the two semantic tasks. In the semantic judgement task, they seemed to look for a common shape (not necessarily a main radical) between the two *kanji* characters. Access to the meanings within five seconds was probably beyond the capabilities of most of these readers. The interview data indicated that some of the beginner readers performed the semantic judgement task in the same manner as the radical identification task (see Chapter 4 Section 4 for details), i.e., comparing two graphic figures without the mediation of meanings. In the semantic categorisation task, they seemed to have tried to find any familiar part in the *kanji* that could be connected to the meaning that the English words presented.

For the intermediate readers who knew at least 300 *kanji*, the interview data suggest that they were aware of most of the radicals (likely the main radicals) and their locations in the *kanji*. In Section 4.3 of this chapter, the intermediate readers' performance in the two semantic tasks indicated that they relied heavily on the main radicals for making judgements. The interview data indeed showed that the majority of the intermediate readers relied on the main radicals although the data also indicated that some of the readers tried to examine the whole *kanji* or to put the kanji in context to get the meanings. It seems that the intermediate readers had to rely heavily on the main radicals not because they chose the strategy of processing the *kanji* based on the information from the main radicals, but rather that they had no choice but to rely on the main radicals as their *kanji* knowledge was limited. However, making semantic judgements by relying on the main radicals was not simple in the semantic categorisation task, as the readers had to know the categories indicated by the main radicals in order to perform well in this task. As a result, the intermediate readers seemed to have used information from various aspects including the whole *kanji*, words that contain the target *kanji*, and contexts indicated by the English words. This may account for the results of the comparison of the intermediate readers' response patterns with the recognisable *kanji* and main radicals (see Chapter 6 Section 4.4), which indicated that these readers used not only the main radicals but also the characters in the semantic categorisation task.

The advanced L2 readers, who knew more than 1,000 *kanji*, were less reliant on the main radicals, as they had many *kanji* that they could recognise and whose meanings they knew. It seems however, that they used the main radicals of the *kanji* when they encountered unfamiliar *kanji*, or when the meaning of the *kanji* was vague or unclear. Overall, their semantic processing demonstrated some similarities to that of the L1 readers. Nevertheless, there was a considerable difference in the performance of these

343

two groups. The interview data of the L1 readers indicated that they were able to consciously compare the multiple pieces of information from the various levels, which became available from the results of processing of the stimuli via their lemma representations, and choose which to utilise for the task. This simultaneous handling of multiple pieces of information was not evident from the advanced readers' interview data, at least not at the conscious level. The advanced readers' processing appeared to be rather sequential; moving from the character level processing to the component level processing or to the word level processing when the information from the characters was not sufficient for performing the task.

Development of component awareness

Interestingly, the L2 readers from beginner to advanced were aware that the main radicals were not very reliable in retrieving the meanings of the *kanji*. Evidently, the intermediate and advanced L2 readers were aware of the limitations of the function of main radicals of *kanji*. Although the beginner L2 readers also seemed to be aware of the limitations of the radical information, their remarks should be taken as evidence of uncertainty of their judgement rather than an awareness developed from experience given that they only knew a limited number of *kanji* and their components.

Koda (2002) claims that with limited *kanji* processing experience, L2 readers become sensitive to the structural and functional properties of components. She adds that what discriminates L1 readers from L2 readers is that L1 readers are aware of the validity of component information. The interview data showed some evidence of the

344

advanced readers (and a few intermediate readers) being aware of the validity issue.

Similarly, Taft (1999) claims that an expert-like semantic processing system may be retarded in the absence of information about main radicals. It should be noted, however, that there was one case in the interview in which an advanced reader reported that she had never translated the main radicals. As can be seen in this case, it seems that one can have an advanced level of *kanji* knowledge even without the knowledge of main radicals.

Semantic processing and phonological processing

Also worth noting was whether the L2 readers used any phonological information to perform the semantic tasks. The L1 readers remarked that they accessed the meaning of *kanji* via their meaning-bearing readings. Moreover, some of the L1 readers remarked that they read the main radicals by their names and accessed to their semantic information.

The L2 interview data indicated that some advanced readers used the phonological information in order to remember the meanings of the *kanji*. Although whether or not the *kanji* were read in their meaning-bearing reading was not specified in most of the cases, there were remarks suggesting that at least a few advanced readers read the *kanji* in their *kun*-readings. There were also a few remarks suggesting that at least a few advanced readers read the main radicals by their names (in Japanese). These findings suggest that at least some advanced readers have begun to form some lemma representations.

Bilingual processing

English words in the semantic categorisation task assisted the performance of the L2 readers, particularly the less-skilled readers who could not access the meanings of the *kanji* within a brief period of time. There were some remarks indicating that the intermediate readers recognised the category names, which were presented after the *kanji*, prior to the recognition of the *kanji*, which were presented first. They remarked that they tried to find the meaning of the English word in the *kanji* or tried to look for the part in the *kanji* that meant what the category showed. It could be hypothesised that these less-skilled readers finished processing the English words before the completion of the processing of the *kanji*. The intermediate readers' remarks that they found it easier when there were English words, indicated their skilled processing of the alphabetic script. They might have been able to identify the meanings of some characters with the help of the English words. This might be a reason why the intermediate readers used the information from the characters as well as from the main radicals in the semantic categorisation task, as shown in Chapter 6 Section 4.4.

On the other hand, the evidence suggests that advanced readers were able to access the meaning of the characters or the semantic information of the main radicals, before the English words (semantic category names) appeared. Some remarks from the advanced readers indicated that they came up with the meanings of the *kanji* sometimes in Japanese and sometimes in English. This notion of semantic development in which either L1 or L2 processing contributes is consistent with bilingual models that propose that lexical items in two languages are independently stored in separate memory systems, but that these representations share a common representation at the abstract level, that is, a language-free conceptual system (Chen, 1992). Based on the results of his earlier studies, Chen claimed that skilled and less-skilled L2 readers use different routes to process words. At the initial stage of learning to read in L2, adult beginners are likely to use their L1 to acquire L2 words. Therefore, the recognition of words in an L2 requires translation between languages. For more skilled readers, on the other hand, L2 words can be recognised relatively independently, without mediation of the L1, indicating that they can directly access the meanings of words through the conceptual system (Chen, 1992). The advanced readers' remarks in the current study may suggest that the semantic information of stimuli (i.e., *kanji*) in English was at times retrieved via the lemma representations.

Lastly, the issue of how semantic relation is related to 'association' and 'categorisation' needs to be addressed. As discussed in the previous section (see Chapter 6 Section 1 for details), some L1 readers were confused as to whether they should analyse item pairs in terms of association or category. The advanced L2 readers also remarked that they tended to judge the relations by association, and whether or not they could link the two *kanji* or the *kanji* and the category name in any possible ways. This style of processing would suggest that semantic networks appear to be based on word association, which can be formed by individual experiences even for L2 readers who have learnt the language in a classroom situation.

347

6.5 Chapter six summary

This chapter dealt with the most interesting but difficult aspect of character recognition, namely semantic processing. In the first part of the study, a performance profile of L1 readers' semantic processing in *kanji* recognition was obtained by establishing the norms that competent language users used for processing semantic information. In the second part, the L2 readers' semantic processing as demonstrated in their response patterns to the semantic tasks was compared against the norm.

Overall, the competent Japanese readers' judgement of semantic relatedness seemed to be primarily constrained by the semantic information from characters rather than components. Evidence suggested that the L1 readers' final decisions were generally based on the information from characters (via their lemma representations) although they seemed to have accessed the semantic information of some commonly used main radicals as well.

Clearly, the L1 readers were aware and were able to use the information from most of the main radicals in semantic processing. However, it appears that these skilled readers made use of the information only when the main radicals had useful information for the recognition of the characters. These readers seemed to be aware of the limitations of the information from the main radicals with respect to the meaning of the entire characters.

Furthermore, when the character did not have a clear meaning on its own, the L1 readers remarked that they had to think of a compound word that contained the character. Judging from their remarks in the interview, when the target *kanji* did not have any meaning-bearing reading (i.e., usually a *kun*-reading), they needed to give the *kanji* a context (i.e., making a compound word using the *kanji*). Taking all these together, the semantic information of characters seems to have become available to the readers in the form of meaning-bearing units (i.e., concepts), which led the readers to name the units in the meaning-bearing readings. It could therefore be hypothesised that the L1 readers' semantic processing was executed mainly through lemma representations.

The L2 readers' response patterns were compared against the norm. The findings suggest that the L2 readers attempted to use any information available to them for semantic judgements.

The beginner readers seemed to have relied on any familiar graphic figures and the English words to find the relationships between the stimuli. Some beginner readers were aware of the function of main radicals, and they might have attempted to use the semantic information of the main radicals for their judgements. However, apparently their awareness per se did not help them perform the tasks, as they had only a few main radicals that they could recognise.

The intermediate readers appeared to have relied on the main radicals and the category names. Their extensive use of the main radicals was interpreted as the result of their inadequate *kanji* knowledge. It would be reasonable to think that the intermediate readers were able to recognise most of the recurrent main radicals, and therefore relied on them when they failed to retrieve the meanings of the characters. Judging from the interview data, these readers were aware of not only the function, but also the limitations of the semantic information that main radicals would convey. However, they

349

might have had no other choice but to rely on the main radicals, as their *kanji* knowledge was still limited. When the category names were given in English, the intermediate readers seemed to be able to remember the meaning of the *kanji* with the help of the words. It would therefore be plausible to think that they might have been able to access the meanings of the characters if they had had more time. In other words, they needed some cues to be able to access the meanings of the characters within a brief period of time. It seems that the intermediate readers sometimes made a compound word when they could not access the meaning of the *kanji*.

The advanced readers showed some evidence of using semantic information from various sources, which were also seen in the L1 readers' performances, although the process of which was sequential rather than simultaneous. The advanced readers seemed to be aware of the function and limitations of the information from the main radicals with respect to the meaning of the entire characters. The findings showed that when comparing two characters, the advanced readers' performance was similar to that of the L1 readers. However, unlike the L1 readers, who showed consistent performance across the tasks, the advanced readers seemed to have been affected by the main radicals when they were conspicuous, which suggests their unstable higher-level dominance processing.

7 Conclusions

7.1 Further discussion

The ability to recognise words is the bedrock of efficient reading comprehension. The review of the literature on word recognition indicated: 1) word recognition skills and awareness in L1 develop stage by stage regardless of the type of script; 2) the nature of L1 word recognition skills and awareness varies according to features of the script; 3) L1 word recognition skills and awareness affect L2 reading positively or negatively partly depending on the orthographic distance (in terms of orthographic depth) between the L1 and L2; and 4) L2 specific recognition skills and awareness gradually develop with increased exposure to the L2 script (see Chapter 2 for details).

If L1 word recognition skills and awareness affect L2 reading, and the influence can be positive or negative depending on the orthographic distance between the L1 and L2, then given the different orthographic features of English and Japanese, reading Japanese can be a serious challenge to English-speaking L2 learners. Indeed, the acquisition of *kanji* characters has long been recognised as one of the most difficult aspects of Japanese language learning for learners with alphabetic language backgrounds (e.g., Ishida, 1989). However, as mentioned above, research suggests that L2-specific recognition skills and awareness gradually develop as the exposure to the L2 script increases. It is reasonable then to expect that research into the character recognition processes of English-speaking learners may provide some instructional implications for enhancing the development of their character recognition ability.

The main aim of the study was to investigate changes in developing L2 readers' *kanji* recognition skills and awareness at different stages of L2 exposure (beginner to advanced learners). The approach undertaken was to attempt to compile a broad description of learners' developing character recognition processes. It was thus different from a highly constrained, model-testing approach, which characterises many psycholinguistic studies.

Since characters contain different kinds of linguistic information (orthographic, phonological and semantic), skills accessing each of these domains and awareness of such information were investigated. Orthographic, phonological and semantic processing skills were assessed by measuring the accuracy and speed of processing of visual representations along with the effects of stimulus properties of characters using a set of well-controlled experimental materials (tasks). Awareness was investigated through reflection on the processes using a verbal protocol method (interview). The results of the tasks were analysed quantitatively and the interview data were examined qualitatively (see Chapter 3 for details).

The following sections present a summary of the characteristics of orthographic, phonological and semantic processing of Japanese *kanji* characters employed by each group of L2 readers (beginner, intermediate and advanced learners of *kanji*) and the L1 readers (Japanese native speakers).

7.1.1 Summary of the study

The L2 reader participants were current or ex-university students who were learning or had learnt Japanese as a second language. These participants were divided into three levels of *kanji* knowledge, beginner, intermediate and advanced, according to their scores on the *kanji* knowledge test that was devised for the purposes of this study. The L1 readers participated in the study as representatives of fluent readers of *kanji*. The results of the orthographic, phonological and semantic tasks administered to the participants and the data from the interview sessions were compared across the three L2 groups (beginner, intermediate and advanced), and were also compared with the results of the L1 readers.

As a whole, the results suggested that the character recognition skills of the L2 readers of Japanese gradually developed (along with an accompanying increase in awareness) in a manner that was shaped by the processing demands imposed by *kanji*. A summary of the findings (from the task and interview results) for each group of participants is presented below in the order of less-skilled to skilled levels (see Chapters 4, 5, and 6 for details). Note that the following summary is intended to provide a broad overview of the developmental trajectory of L2 character recognition based upon what was ascertained from the tasks and the interview. The 'broad brush' style adopted in this summary is to illustrate major trends and should not be taken as an indication that there were no interesting individual differences within the same skill level.

Beginner readers

Orthographic domain

Overall processing skills: The beginner readers only recognised a limited number of high frequency *kanji*. It is clear that their orthographic processing for most *kanji* was restricted to the processing of shapes that were familiar to them. The task results indicated that there were times that the beginner readers could not segment the *kanji* into smaller units, suggesting that their performance was heavily affected by the complexity of the *kanji*.

Orthographic awareness: It appears that the beginner readers were at the stage of beginning to form their awareness of components. Some beginner readers were able to declare knowledge of at least a few frequently seen radicals and their typical locations.

Phonological domain

Overall processing skills: As the beginner readers knew few *kanji* that they were able to pronounce, the phonological tasks were simply beyond their capabilities. They were unable to use phonological information conveyed by phonetics (components that may give some indication of the pronunciation of the characters) for reading unfamiliar *kanji*.

Phonological awareness: There was no evidence that these readers were aware of the role of the phonetics in the *kanji*.

Semantic domain

Overall processing skills: The beginner readers seem to have connected the *kanji* with semantic categories (often wrongly) by relying on a few familiar shapes that held meaning for them (not necessarily radicals). Where there were English words (semantic category names), the beginner readers tried to find the part in the *kanji* that could be connected to the words.

Morphological awareness: Some of the readers were aware of the potential function of the main radicals of *kanji*. However, due to their limited knowledge of main radicals, their rudimentary awareness of main radicals did not help much in performing the character recognition tasks.

Intermediate readers

Orthographic domain

Overall processing skills: The intermediate readers identified some high frequency *kanji* at the character level. However, in general, there was evidence both in the task results and the interview data that the way they performed the orthographic tasks was primarily influenced by the recognition of familiar high frequency functional components (main-radicals and phonetics). These readers appeared to have made orthographic judgements by checking the locations and combinations of familiar functional components although in general they appeared to have great difficulty in distinguishing graphically similar components.

Orthographic awareness: It appears that most intermediate readers were aware of the typical locations and combinations of some high frequency main radicals and frequently seen non-main-radical components (i.e., components that are not main radicals).

Phonological domain

Overall processing skills: Although the intermediate readers had learnt a number of *kanji*, they made numerous errors in the phonological tasks, most likely because they did not know the required *on*-reading of the *kanji*, except in a few high frequency cases. Many intermediate readers tried to get the *on*-reading of the *kanji* by making a compound word that contained the *kanji*, but this method was useful only when the *kanji* was familiar to them. The intermediate readers' performance at this level appeared to be constrained by the use of only a limited number of familiar phonetics from which the readings of some unfamiliar characters might have been attempted.

Phonological awareness: Generally, intermediate readers were aware that they were required to read the *kanji* in the *on*-readings. It appears that a few intermediate readers were vaguely aware that the phonetics would help in reading the *kanji*. However, the results on the whole suggest that, generally, the intermediate readers had only a limited knowledge of phonetics, and could not reliably distinguish phonetics from main radicals. In some cases, because some of the commonly used phonetics are legitimate *kanji* in their own right, the intermediate readers might have guessed the reading of the *kanji* using the phonology of these 'embedded *kanji*' (which were in fact the *phonetic* components of the target *kanji*) as a guide, probably without knowing that they were the phonetics.

Semantic domain

Overall processing skills: The intermediate readers seem to have used information from various aspects including the whole *kanji,* words that contain the target *kanji,* and contexts indicated by the English words (semantic category names). However, it was evident from the pattern of the results that the intermediate readers extensively used the main radicals for connecting the *kanji* with the semantic categories. Judging from the remarks made in the interviews, it was not because they had confidence in this use of main radicals, but because they had no other choice when they did not know the meaning of the *kanji*.

Morphological awareness: As a broad categorisation, the intermediate readers were aware of the semantic function of some familiar main radicals. They were also aware that the semantic information conveyed by main radicals does not fully describe the meaning of the *kanji*.

Advanced readers

Orthographic domain

Overall processing skills: The overall results of the orthographic tasks indicated that the advanced readers did not rely solely on components when performing orthographic tasks, which suggested the development of character level processing. It appears that many *kanji* were identified at the character level. However, the data also suggest that the advanced L2 readers might have at times needed the information from the component-level analysis to assist in their decision-making. The interview data indicated that some advanced readers read (pronounced) the *kanji* to keep them in their working memories, suggesting that phonological information was utilised even in the orthographic tasks (where phonological information was not a prerequisite for performing the task).

Orthographic awareness: The interview data suggested that most advanced readers were aware of the typical locations and combinations of most functional components. They also seemed to have some insight into the size and shapes of main radicals (such as that the bottom stroke of a left main radical usually goes up), which would have helped them to determine the locations of radicals.

Phonological domain

Overall processing skills: The advanced readers often could not get the specific reading of the *kanji* required in the tasks within the brief period of time allowed, most likely because the links between the characters and their phonology were weak, particularly for the low frequency *kanji*. The results suggest that for these readers higher frequency characters had formed stronger links with their readings compared to lower frequency characters (hence there was a character frequency effect). However, it appears that there was little difference in the strength of links for *kun*-readings and *on*-readings (hence there was no interference effect of *kun*-readings). In order to get the required *on*-readings, the advanced readers often put the *kanji* into a compound word. At other times, they used the phonetics for reading the *kanji*. The task results indicated that the advanced readers generally performed more accurately on the high radical frequency *kanji* than on the low radical frequency *kanji*, suggesting that the identification of high frequency main radicals may have helped them find the phonetics, as phonetics are always on the non-main-radical side. The advanced readers were able to utilise some high frequency phonetics to name the *kanji*.

Phonological awareness: The advanced readers were aware that the *kanji* often have multiple readings, and they also knew that they were required to retrieve the *on*-reading of the *kanji*. However, most of them did not seem to be aware of the functional difference between the *kun*- and *on*-readings (that is, the *kun*-readings are usually meaning-bearing readings whereas the *on*-readings are not). The interview data indicated that the advanced readers had some knowledge of phonetics, and that they were also generally aware of the limitations of the use of phonetic information. However, due to their limited knowledge of phonetics, most advanced L2 readers did not have the ability to use phonetics selectively.

Semantic domain

Overall processing skills: The advanced readers had many *kanji* that they could recognise and whose meanings they knew. The results suggested that on the whole, the advanced readers primarily made their semantic judgements based on the information of the whole character with assistance from information from the main radical. When they could not readily access the meaning of the character on its own, they attempted to make a compound word that contained the target character in order to get its meaning. They used the main radicals only when they encountered unfamiliar *kanji* or when the meaning of the *kanji* was vague or unclear. However, when the main radicals were conspicuous (highlighted), it appears that the advanced readers could not repress the information from these, and so their judgement was affected by the component-level processing. The interview data suggest that the advanced L2 readers' processing appeared to be sequential, moving from character level processing to word level processing and to component level processing when the information from the characters was not sufficient for performing the task. It was reported by some readers at this level that the meanings of the characters came to them in English for some characters and in Japanese for others.

Morphological awareness: The advanced readers were aware of the functions and limitations of the semantic information conveyed by main radicals. Some of them were aware of the validity of main radicals, and therefore used them selectively.

As can be seen above, the L2 readers' gradual development in character processing skills and awareness was evident. By comparing the general pattern of their results with those of the L1 readers, similarities and differences between the advanced level L2 readers and L1 readers become apparent.

L1 readers

Orthographic domain

Overall processing skills: The results of the orthographic tasks suggested that a decision was in most cases made at the character level. Even in the task where componential processing was vital (i.e., the radical identification task), there was some evidence in the data that the information generated at the character level had affected the responses, particularly for high frequency *kanji*. These findings suggest that in general, character level information dominated over component level information. The findings from the interview data suggest that the L1 readers of Japanese processed the characters phonologically even for the orthographic tasks. At the moment when they identified the *kanji*, the L1 readers read the *kanji* in the meaning-bearing reading (in most cases it was the *kun*-reading of the *kanji*, which represents a meaning), and the meaning of the *kanji* was made available simultaneously. This suggests that the dominance of the meaning-bearing reading (usually, the *kun*-reading) over the non-meaning-bearing reading (usually, the *on*-reading) had been established for the L1 readers. When the *kanji* did not have a meaning-bearing reading, the L1 readers remarked that they put the *kanji* in a meaningful compound word, from which the meaning of individual *kanji* was probably inferred. Moreover, it was reported by a few L1 readers that some high frequency main radicals were read by their names, which indicated meaning categories.

Orthographic awareness: The L1 readers were able to judge the character-ness of the *kanji* at an attention-free level (that is, they did not need to bring their awareness into their consciousness). On the other hand, when they were required to focus on the components of the *kanji*, these readers were aware of how they performed the task. These findings suggest that well-practised processing may be attention-free, but more controlled information processing may be required when the readers need to execute non-routine practices (such as analysing the components of the *kanji*). The interview data (which were obtained after the radical identification task) suggest that the L1 readers were fully aware of constraint on the locations and combinations of components.

Phonological domain

Overall processing skills: In the phonological tasks, in which the L1 readers knew that the *on*-reading was the required reading, some of them could not help reading the *kanji* in the *kun*-reading (as it was the meaning-bearing reading). When the *kanji* did not have a meaning-bearing reading, the L1 readers usually put the *kanji* into a meaningful compound word and read the word in its meaning-bearing reading (which was usually the on-reading). It appears that the L1 readers automatically put the *kanji* in a meaningful unit: either as a single-character word or in a compound word. The findings suggest that certain levels of phonological processing are more routinely used for decision-making. When the reading accessed was a *kun*-reading, then the L1 readers consciously put the *kanji* into a compound word in order to retrieve the *on*-reading of the constituent *kanji* (which was the required reading for the phonological tasks). The L1 readers occasionally used phonetics, but only when they were reliable for retrieving the readings of the *kanji*. The task results also suggest the dominance of information obtained by the processing of main radicals over that obtained by the processing of phonetics. As a case in point, the data suggested that access to the phonological information conveyed by the phonetics interfered with the high frequency main radicals.

Phonological awareness: The L1 readers were aware of the multiple readings of *kanji*. They also knew the general functional difference between the *kun*- and *on*-readings. However, it seems the initial retrieval of a reading was not under their control. Often the *kanji* were read in their meaning-bearing readings. If the reading that was retrieved was different from the one being asked for, they had to take another step to get another reading. Judging from the L1 readers' remarks in the interview, it seems that recalling multiple readings simultaneously was not possible, and therefore they had only one of the readings in their minds at a time. In the cases where the L1 readers could not instantly come up with any reading, they seemed to resort to the phonetics of the *kanji*. The L1 readers were fully aware of the functions and limitations of phonetics. They also showed sensitivity to the validity of phonetics (that is, they only used reliable phonetics).

Semantic domain

Overall processing skills: The data obtained from the semantic tasks indicated that there was a general tendency for phonological and semantic information from the character level to predominate over the information from the components at the time of decision-making (most likely because character level information would be more routinely used). Apparently, this dominance of character level information was not affected by, for instance, the highlighted main radicals (the artificial marking of conspicuous aspects of the input). When the *kanji* had no meaning-bearing reading and no clear meaning on its own, a decision would be made based mainly on the phonological and semantic information retrieved from a compound word containing the target *kanji*. The interview data suggest that the L1 readers named the *kanji* in the meaning-bearing readings, that is, those indicating the broad meanings (or concepts) of the *kanji*. In the cases where the *kanji* did not have a reading that represented a concept, the readers accessed the concept of the character via the meaning-bearing reading of a compound word that had the target *kanji* in it. Sometimes, the L1 readers named the main radical (they knew the names of some commonly used main radicals) and processed information from the main radicals and took this into consideration when making a decision.

Morphological awareness: The L1 readers were aware of the functions and limitations of most main radicals. However, it is not that the L1 readers were aware of the main radical and its limitations in every character. The data indicated that the L1 readers were also aware of the validity of main radicals.

421

7.1.2 Proposal for developmental phases

The descriptions of the findings in the previous section suggest that L2 readers of *kanji* gradually make progress in their recognition skills and awareness on a continuum of development. Moreover, there were indications that the advanced L2 readers' *kanji* recognition was approaching that of the L1 readers. To some extent, it appears that the level of processing skills and the sophistication of awareness were interrelated, both of them being enhanced through increasing exposure to *kanji*. Based on the findings, I wish to propose four broad phases in the development of *kanji* recognition skills and awareness. I shall call these the partial, componential, synthetic and conceptual processing phases. It should be noted that some descriptions only apply to the recognition of compound characters that have a main radical and a phonetic. As Leck, Weekes and Chen (1995) found evidence for two distinctive recognition procedures for single-component characters and compound characters, single-component *kanji* (characters with only one component) do not require any componential processing.

Partial processing phase

This novice stage is characterised by readers simply looking at visual stimuli (i.e., *kanji* characters) holistically, but this process is limited and gives rise to an ability of only being able to identify familiar visual features in the stimuli. Readers gradually become aware of frequently seen radicals in *kanji* and then of the typical locations of the familiar radicals. The identification of *kanji* characters for the readers at this stage operates via the identification of the familiar visual features, which is mostly, but not always, at the level of the unit of a radical (not necessarily a functional radical). This style of processing is affected by the graphical complexity of *kanji*. The visual complexity at times hinders the identification of the familiar radicals.

The initial partial processing phase may last for only a short time for L2 readers who receive systematic instruction on the functional components of *kanji* in classrooms. Without explicit instruction in functional components and/or training for raising awareness of the functions of components, novice readers may persist in this phase.

Componential processing phase[1]

As they gain *kanji* knowledge, readers become able to recognise a few frequently seen, familiar *kanji* at the character level without necessarily relying on the information from the component level. Sometimes they attempt to recognise the *kanji* by accessing the phonological and semantic information of the compound word even though the information may be limited. For unfamiliar *kanji*, readers learn to process them analytically. The transition to this style of processing is governed by exposure. At the beginning of this phase, readers become able to identify frequently seen main radicals,

---

[1] This 'componential processing phase' is equivalent to the 'phonological phase' in Harris and Coltheart's (1986) model. As has been discussed in the previous chapters, the mechanism of grapheme-phoneme conversion is irrelevant in character recognition processing. What is critical is the analysis of components. Phonological processing in alphabetic scripts is in fact the analysis of functional elements: letters that carry phonological information. In this regard, the 'phonological processing phase' is in fact a 'componential processing phase'. The 'phonological processing phase' may need to be replaced by 'componential processing phase' in order to make the description of word recognition more universal.

and gradually, for most *kanji,* develop the ability to segment a character into the main-radical component and the non-main-radical component. With the help of formal instruction, readers become aware of the typical locations and combinations of high frequency main radicals. Readers also become aware of the function of main radicals in general, and start to strategically use the information from the functional component in order to recognise unfamiliar *kanji.* Although they are also aware of the limitations of the role of main radicals, they sometimes overgeneralise the information from the component level when they cannot recognise the *kanji* at the character level. Readers gradually become aware of the function of phonetics over time, and toward the end of this phase, readers become able to use a limited number of phonetics.

To reach this stage, an important change in the manner in which the processing system groups elements into a 'component' is required. For example, initially, the processing system of a developing reader might begin with a 'component' that might in effect be a 'familiar shape'. Progress in processing would facilitate the change of this unit into a 'radical'. The unit would eventually be a radical or a set of radicals that carry semantic or phonological information, namely a main radical or a phonetic. Only then would it be a 'functional component'. When a 'component' becomes a functional component, readers will be able to process semantic and phonological information at the component level.

Synthetic processing phase

This is a more sophisticated stage where readers make a recognition decision at the level of meaning by utilising information generated at different levels (word, character and component levels). By this stage, readers can recognise a number of *kanji* based mainly on the information generated at the character level (if the visual stimuli were *kanji*), as frequently appearing *kanji* have formed strong links between orthographic, phonological and semantic information, provided that they have a meaning in their own right. Readers intentionally use word level information to assist the decision-making at the character level when the *kanji* do not have clear meanings on their own. Readers also strategically use the component information to assist, but do not rely solely on the information from the component level unless the *kanji* is totally unfamiliar. When a familiar *kanji* is presented, the phonologically encoded information is retained in the short-term memory as the complex processing is performed. Readers become aware of the general difference between the *kun*-reading and the *on*-reading. However, in which reading the *kanji* is read depends purely on the familiarity of the reading, and not on the functional difference between the two types of the readings (that is, the *kun*-readings are usually the appropriate meaning-bearing readings whereas the *on*-readings are not). In this phase, readers become aware of the functions not only of the main radicals but also of the phonetics of *kanji*, and are able to use the information from both types of functional components to process unfamiliar *kanji*. At the same time, they are aware of the limitations of the roles of main radicals and phonetics in *kanji*.

However, due to their restricted knowledge, they are not aware of the validity of individual functional components, and therefore cannot use them selectively.

Conceptual processing phase

Readers make gradual developmental progression and eventually attain automaticity (i.e., attention-free processing) for most *kanji,* as conceptual (lemma) representations that connect orthographic, phonological and semantic information at the multiple (word, character and component) levels are being formed through learning (e.g., frequent exposure and practice). The formation of lemmas is crucial for information to cohere, which assists automatised processing. At this most refined stage, the *kanji* that are free or quasi-free morphemes have lemma representations, and therefore when the *kanji* are presented, the phonological and semantic information can be accessed automatically via their lemma representations. The *kanji* that have no clear concepts are recognised through lemma representations of the words that contain the target *kanji.* Some main radicals that have clear semantic information may have formed their lemma representations. Where there are lemma representations for the *kanji* and its main radicals for example, the information from whichever has a stronger lemma will become available faster. To a certain extent, readers can reflect on the information generated at the different levels (word, character and component), and are able to use the information selectively if necessary. They are aware of the functional difference between the *kun*-reading and the *on*-reading, and are able to use the information, although the processing of the *kun*-reading dominates over the *on*-reading. They are also aware of the

426

functional differences between the main radicals and the phonetics, as well as their validity, and can use this information, although the processing of the main radical dominates over the phonetic.

7.1.3 Universal and script-specific aspects of processing

The previous sections described the characteristic changes in developing English-speaking L2 readers' *kanji* recognition ability and proposed possible developmental phases. The overall findings suggest that the developmental phases of L2 readers may be fundamentally similar to those of L1 children, which have been found to be similar in both alphabetic scripts and morphographic scripts (see Chapter 2 Sections 2 and 3 for details). Given this, it could be concluded that the process of development characterised by a shift from partial processing to analytical processing and then to more integrated processing involves universal phases, regardless of types of orthography and whether reading in an L1 or L2. Simply put, the idea is that in processing a script readers make the best use of the linguistic knowledge that they have at the time. Processing begins with local and incomplete information, and progresses via the use of attention demanding intentional and analytical processing, into sophisticated attention-free processing.

In attempting to process new information, at any phase of learning to read, L2 readers make use of pre-existing internal knowledge, which would be L1 specific at the initial stage, but gradually incorporate L2-specific information over years. The findings of the present study suggest that this transformation is governed by frequency of exposure. At each developmental phase, the recognition of high frequency characters (and high frequency functional components) preceded the recognition of low frequency characters (and low frequency functional components), which supports the universality of the frequency effect that has been demonstrated in a number of studies (e.g., Akamatsu, 2002; Hong, 1998; Tamaoka and Hatsuzuka, 1995; Share, 1995; Tan, Hoosain and Peng, 1995; Taft and Zhu, 1995; McClelland and Rumelhart, 1981). Many existing word recognition models (such as the Interactive Activation Model and the Parallel Distributed Processing Model) account for the frequency effect by the strength of the links between units in the internal recognition system, which changes continuously over time according to exposure (see Chapter 2 Section 2.4 for details). Seidenberg and his associates (Harm and Seidenberg, 2004, Seidenberg and McClelland, 1989) particularly emphasise that the strength of the links changes continuously by learning, which occurs as a result of the comparison of the new information accumulated via the interactions of a number of processing units and previously stored information.

Given that the links between units in the network are shaped by the frequency of exposure, the development of recognition skills may seem to be better described as item-based rather than as stage-based (Share, 1995). The findings of the current study indeed suggest that the developmental phases for character recognition ability are, to some extent, item-based. It appears that the links between orthographic, phonological and semantic information for frequently appearing *kanji* are formed at an early stage of the development, whereas the formation of the links for rarely seen *kanji* tends to be

428

delayed. Moreover, the findings suggest that not only the rate of the development, but also the points of attainment may vary according to the features of items. For example, the rarely used *kanji* that do not have any meaning-bearing readings on their own seem to have weak links even in the skilled readers' network, suggesting that such weak links stay weak. Nevertheless, although the speed of development may vary according to the features of individual items, the item-based development seems to be on a trajectory of stage-based development: from local and incomplete processing to intentional and analytical processing, and then sophisticated attention-free processing.

Despite the universal developmental phases, L2 readers seem not to be able to simply transfer the recognition skills and awareness that they have acquired in their L1 to an L2 reading setting (see Chapter 2 Section 4 for details). It seems that the developmental phases have to be repeated when the L1 and L2 are orthographically dissimilar. The L2 participants in the present study were all skilled readers (of English) who had gone through the developmental phases in their L1. Nevertheless, their performance in the character processing tasks and the interviews indicated a gradual development in the L2, starting from the novice processing phase. Due to the very different features of the alphabetic script (English) and the morphographic script (*kanji*), the English-speaking L2 readers had to relearn how to process unfamiliar information. At the initial stage, L2 readers do not have any useful information processing network that can be used for *kanji* processing. In order for the existing network (that is of little use for character processing) to transform into a useful one, it appears that 'learning' has to take place. The transformation seems to occur according to two principles: link formation through learning corresponding information, and information processing based on the learnt information. Research suggests that the rate of the transformation may vary according to the orthographical distance between the L1 and the L2 (see Chapter 2 Sections 3 and 4 for details). In the present study, the English-speaking advanced readers who had studied *kanji* for at least five years were still far from proficient in character recognition. The script of the present study, Japanese *kanji*, is an orthographically deep script, and the participants had no prior experience of studying any other such script. These two factors might have contributed to the slow development of L2 processing skills.

In the case of character processing, by being frequently exposed to *kanji*, L2 readers would learn the positional and configurational constraints of the recurrent constituent radicals, and would soon learn that some radicals (or sets of radicals) carry semantic or phonological information. Using this component level information, L2 readers (orthographically, phonologically and semantically) would process *kanji*. With further exposure to *kanji*, the links between orthographic, phonological and semantic information in the *kanji* would become stronger, and L2 readers would gradually become able to process the *kanji* with the assistance of, but without relying on, such componential analysis. If the *kanji* frequently appears in print as a constituent element of a compound word rather than as a single-character word, then the links between the orthographic, phonological and semantic information of the word would become stronger than the links of such information of the *kanji* character. In those cases, L2 readers would learn to process the *kanji* (if the task so requires) via the information attached to the word. With extensive practice, a 'hub' that connects individual links would be formed, and L2 readers would eventually be able to efficiently process *kanji* using all the learnt information.

As illustrated above, some script-specific recognition skills and awareness would develop over time as the reader's internal network undergoes a transformation. Nevertheless, just as in the case of the processing of an alphabetic script (e.g., English) it appears that the processing of a morphographic script (e.g., *kanji*) is also influenced by frequency of exposure and amount of practice, which suggests some basic function is common to all: that is, the process of connecting different forms of available information and integrating this into appropriate actions may be universal.

7.1.4 Exposure and Instruction

It was found that the reader's internal processing system is shaped by the frequency of exposure (to the script) and the amount of practice (of processing the script), and that well-routined processing leads to attention-free processing. Indeed, there is abundant research to suggest that character processing ability develops as exposure to characters increases (e.g., Ku and Anderson, 2003; Nagy, Kuo-Kealoha, Wu, Li, Anderson, and Chen, 2002). Recent research has also indicated that established character processing skills can be undermined by lack of practice due to limited exposure to the script (Kim and Davis, 2001). Nevertheless, some researchers claim that skilled processing ability does not develop solely as a result of exposure to script (e.g., Carlisle, 2003). Familiarising learners with the functions of particular orthographic properties in the

431

target language appear to be extremely important for enhancing script-specific recognition ability (Carlisle, 2003; Nagy, Kuo-Kealoha, Wu, Li Anderson and Chen, 2002). To this end, explicit instruction on L2 specific structure and function may help learners develop awareness of features and may facilitate the development of recognition skills and awareness (Carlisle, 2003; Koda, 1997).

The timing of instruction, however, needs to be considered. It has been shown that inappropriate instruction at too early a stage leads to little success. For example, Peterson and Haines (1992) gave three groups (low, middle and high segmentation abilities) of English-speaking children the same amount of instruction in segmentation, letter-to-sound correspondences and reading words by analogy. The results showed that while children with low segmentation ability improved most in segmentation ability and a little in letter-to-sound matchings, middle and high segmenters showed the biggest improvement in reading by analogy and letter-to-sound matchings (Peterson and Haines, 1992). These results indicated that children at the early development phase were not ready for higher skills. It appears that there are multiple levels of skills, and they seem to be acquired step by step.

On the other hand, it seems that appropriate instruction at the right time can improve children's reading ability. For example, a study by Bradley and Bryant (1985) reports that instruction in the alphabetic letters at the right times assisted English-speaking children in developing their phonological skills, which facilitated the development of their reading and spelling abilities.

An example in a character-based language is a study by Nagy, Kuo-Kealoha, Wu, Li, Anderson and Chen (2002). These researchers implemented instruction for enhancing children's morphological skills through awareness-raising training in Chinese Grades 1 and 4 classes. The intervention focused on both character and word morphology. In daily lessons, when new words were introduced, children were encouraged to pay attention to individual constituent characters, and were told to analyse how the characters were semantically linked to the word. For each character that they learnt, if it was a compound character, the children were asked to segment it into the main radical and the non-main-radical component, and were assisted in analysing how the meaning of the main radical contributed to the meaning of the character. The children were exposed to many example characters and main radicals, and through them, they were taught the relationship of characters to words, and of main radicals to characters.

The results of a pre-test and a post-test in each grade level class showed that the effects of morphological intervention were significant on vocabulary growth in the Grade 4 children, but not in the Grade 1 children. The study suggests the right timing of morphological instruction may be around Grades 3-4 when regular compound characters account for a large proportion of vocabulary. Although this study only showed the intervention effect on vocabulary growth, and not on the development of word recognition skills, given the strong relationship between vocabulary and recognition skills (see Chapter 2 Section 1), the findings are worth considering.

The above studies suggest that instruction at the right time may enhance the development of word recognition ability. The following section discusses the possibility, based on the findings of the present study, of enhancing character recognition ability by explicit instruction at critical times.

7.1.5 Teaching kanji characters

Teaching of *kanji* has long been a neglected area in Japanese language teaching (Noguchi, 1995). The most popular method of teaching has been rote learning (Shimizu and Green, 2002). Teachers introduce *kanji* to learners one by one together with their reading and meaning without breaking them into smaller units, and tell the learners to practice reading and writing the *kanji* numerous times. Learners are generally left to their own devices in terms of how to learn and store the *kanji*. Such learning conditions do not provide a good opportunity for learners to understand the structure and function within and between characters. At the same time, the use of contextual information has been emphasised due to the belief that the reading and meaning of *kanji* words are highly context dependent (Shimizu and Green, 2002). However, although the use of contextual clues assists readers in inferring the meaning of unknown words when it is used in conjunction with semantic analysis of the constituent characters (Mori and Nagy, 1999), Mori (2003) found that context often provided syntactic information but not semantic information of the words.

Recently, the use of mnemonic devices has been introduced to *kanji* instruction due to the influence of research findings in cognitive psychology (Shimizu and Green,

2002). Mnemonic strategy often involves the analysis of smaller units of characters, that is, breaking a graphically complex *kanji* into manageable smaller units and making a short story by attaching meanings to the smaller units. This strategy has become one of the most widely used methods of teaching *kanji* (Shimizu and Green, 2002). However, while this method may assist readers in remembering the structure of individual *kanji*, it cannot give the readers semantic and phonological information of the *kanji*, and it does not help in developing the readers' internal processing system.

As we have seen, the findings of the present study suggest that a change in the manner in which the processing system groups elements into a 'component' occurs during the componential processing phase of development. Explicit instruction in the functional components may assist L2 readers in moving from the partial processing phase to the componential processing phase more quickly. Indeed research suggests that reader's belief in the effectiveness of using internal structural information facilitates *kanji* recognition (Mori, 2002). In the light of such research, there is a growing shift from rote memory to componential analysis in *kanji* teaching (Toyoda, 1998; Noguchi, 1995). On-line and off-line teaching materials focusing on teaching the functional components of *kanji* have become available (e.g., *Kanji* Clinic - http://www.*kanji*clinic.com/; Basic *Kanji* Book, 1991; and Intermediate *Kanji* Book, 1993). These teaching materials should help strengthen the links between characters and their constituent components. Evidence demonstrates that learners retain new *kanji* characters better using componential analysis (Kubota and Toyoda, 2001; Flaherty and Noguchi, 1998).

More teaching materials are needed for teaching relationships between characters. This does not necessarily mean that characters that share a common functional component should be taught together all at once. Indeed, evidence suggests that teaching related words may 'create competition between items, which in turn increases difficulty during learning and during memory retrieval' (Finkbeiner and Nicol, 2003:379). However, it may be helpful for adjusting the strength of links between characters as well as between characters and their functional components if each introduction of a new *kanji* were made in relation to already-introduced *kanji* with an emphasis on the common component.

Although knowledge of functional components is essential, the findings of the current study suggest that the skilled readers (L1 readers) do not know all the existing functional components and that they make use of only reliable functional components. As briefly discussed in Chapter 1 Section 3, the reliability of functional components must be assessed in terms of frequency, regularity and consistency. The main radicals and phonetics that appear rarely in *kanji* are of little use. If the semantic information conveyed by a main radical has no, or weak, relationship with the meaning of a *kanji*, or if the *kanji* that share a main radical have considerably different meanings, skilled readers would probably not use that main radical in character recognition. Likewise, if the phonological information conveyed by a phonetic does not give a clue to the pronunciation of a *kanji*, or if the *kanji* that share a common phonetic have varied pronunciations, skilled readers would not utilise the phonetic. It is therefore important that the readers be given an opportunity to find out which main radicals and phonetics are more useful than others, as not all main radicals and phonetics are equally helpful in *kanji* recognition.

The finding that some skilled readers read main radicals by their names to access the concept of the category shown by the main radical suggests that teaching L2 readers the names of reliable main radicals may be helpful. As described in Chapter 1 Section 3, the names of commonly-used main radicals often indicate their locations and semantic categories (e. g., the name *'tehen'* shows that this radical appears on the left-hand side, and indicates that the meaning of *kanji* with this radical may be related to the semantic category, 'hands').

The collective data of the present study suggest that the development of awareness of phonetics evolved much later than that of main radicals. However, research findings regarding this issue are not in uniform agreement. A study by Ho, Ng, and Ng (2003) found that Chinese children came to utilise phonetics prior to main radicals, whereas Shu and Anderson (1998) found that Chinese children became aware of main radicals earlier than phonetics. One reason for why there might not be a clear preference in the developmental sequence in Chinese could be that main radicals and phonetics are equally important and useful because in Chinese there is a large cohort of phonetic compound characters (characters consisting of a main radical and a phonetic). In Japanese *kanji*, however, the number of phonetic compound characters is much smaller and the phonetics are useful only for the retrieval of *on*-readings, i.e., one of the two types of readings (see Chapter 1 Section 3 for details). This could be a reason for the slow development of phonetic awareness in Japanese.

The trend from the holistic approach to the componential approach is likely to contribute to the development of character recognition ability in L2 readers. However, the findings of the present study suggest that focusing on the components alone is not sufficient. In fact, too much emphasis on components may encourage a microscopic approach, which would result in recognition errors. In order to help L2 readers move from the componential processing phase to the synthetic processing phase, L2 readers should be made aware that *kun-* and *on-*readings are not merely two types of readings, but that they are fundamentally different; that is, a *kun-*reading usually represents a word and its meaning whereas an *on-*reading is likely to be part of a word and does not have a meaning in itself (see Chapter 1 Section 3 for details). The data of the present study suggest that skilled readers read *kanji* in their meaning-bearing readings. There are numerous materials to teach *kun-*readings and *on-*readings of *kanji* on the market. However, it appears that most of them present the readings of *kanji*, sometimes together with the readings of compound words that contain the target *kanji*, without emphasising the difference between meaning-bearing readings and non-meaning-bearing readings. Some training to encourage L2 readers to read *kanji* at the meaning-bearing level may be beneficial for link formation (e.g., 認める /mito-meru/ for 認, as this is the meaning-bearing reading of this *kanji*, and 認識の識 /niNshiki no shiki/ ('*shiki*' as in '*ninshiki*') for 識 as this *kanji* only has a meaning-bearing reading as a compound word).

The findings of the present study suggest that fluent readers recognise most *kanji* efficiently due to automatic or attention-free processing. In order to bring L2 readers up to the most refined phase of character recognition development, repeated training for strengthening links between units may be necessary. For example, when new words (i.e., orthographic, semantic and phonological information at the word level) are introduced, L2 readers should be encouraged to pay attention to individual constituent characters (i.e., orthographic, semantic and phonological information at the character level) and to examine how the characters are linked to the word. For each of the constituent *kanji*, if it is a compound character, L2 readers should be assisted in analysing how the semantic information in the main radical is related to the meaning of the character and how the phonological information in the phonetic contributes to the pronunciation of the character. Needless to say, exposure to an extensive range of *kanji* vocabulary and some training in structuring and restructuring the vocabulary by categorising the words under several abstract concepts may be critical for further development in character recognition.

7.1.6 Limitations of the present study

When skilled readers read a text, they not only process the words efficiently, but they also use information from the sentence and discourse for comprehension. Research suggests that skilled readers can carry out higher-level processing because their word recognition is efficient and does not require a large portion of their working memory (see Chapter 2 Section 2 for details). Word recognition ability is one of the most important skills that needs to be developed for efficient reading. The present study has focused on investigating the development of character recognition ability among second language learners with alphabetic backgrounds at different levels of proficiency, and attempted to draw instructional implications for enhancing the development of L2 readers' character recognition ability. Character recognition skills were measured for accuracy and speed of processing of visual representations using behavioural tests, and awareness was assessed in terms of an ability to reflect on the processes using a verbal protocol method. Although the research was designed and conducted with great care, there were some compromises that needed to be made, as outlined below.

First of all, the ecological validity of the controlled experiments might be questioned. However, given the wide range of processes involved in reading, a restricted investigation in an experimental setting was essential for trying to distinguish word recognition processes from other more general cognitive dispositions and biases. Also, as my research focused on learners' on-line recognition of *kanji* characters, time-sensitive measurement such as computerised testing was essential.

Presenting *kanji* in isolation in the experiments was also potentially problematic. I am aware that success in the recognition of individual *kanji* does not necessarily guarantee successful word recognition, let alone reading comprehension. It is somewhat artificial to take individual *kanji* out of context, and results obtained from such a test do not necessarily apply to *kanji* recognition in all circumstances. However, the study of the recognition of individual *kanji* offers an opportunity to break down the complicated recognition processes of *kanji*-written words to something more manageable. That is, presenting *kanji* characters in isolation avoids manifest variables that would make the results hard to interpret.

There were also other reasons for using *kanji* characters and not *kanji* compound words in the test. Firstly, the efficient recognition of each *kanji* in a *kanji* compound word is essential (Okita, 1995). Secondly, while there is a corpus of 1,945 general-use characters already selected by the Ministry of Education in Japan, there are no guidelines to follow in the selection of so-called general-use *kanji* compound words. Given the strong correlation between *kanji* recognition skills and vocabulary knowledge found in the research literature, and given the abundant evidence that vocabulary knowledge and reading ability are related to each other (see Chapter 2 Section 1 for details), it can be safely assumed that a strong relationship exists between *kanji* recognition skills and reading ability more generally.

One of the major compromises in the design of the current study was the number of participants. Out of the initial pool of 224 volunteer participants, only 109 fulfilled the requirements for this study, which resulted in having 39 beginner, 40 intermediate and 30 advanced L2 readers of kanji altogether. Although each task involved different combinations of participants, because the total number was limited, the task performances of the few participants were analysed from various aspects.

Another major compromise was having only five items for the examination of the effects of each aspect of the stimulus properties. Ideally, many items are needed in each separate category of test in order to ensure appropriate response time distributions and generality over item types. As Chambers and Forster (1975) have remarked, at least 20

441

items should be included in each major condition. It is obvious that the current results would be more reliable with more items. However, in the current study, the number of the items had to be kept to five for the following critical reasons. One is that finding many items with the required combination of stimulus properties (e.g., *kanji* with a phonetic that had properties of low complexity, medium character frequency, medium radical frequency and medium homophone size) was not easy. Also, having more items for each property would have required the participants to spend more time on the experiments. In order to avoid errors due to fatigue, the number of items was kept down. This number was a compromise solution after considering the maximum number of items that the beginner readers may be able to handle in a task and the minimum number of items needed for statistical power in later analysis.

Another issue in relation to the stimulus properties was that although each pair of *kanji* was selected to vary only in one critical property, a few task items did in fact co-vary with another property. This was unavoidable due to a number of restrictions that were involved in the selection of the *kanji* (see Chapter 3 Section 2 for details). This co-variance was taken into consideration when interpreting the results of the analyses.

The results of the study have re-emphasised that the functional difference between the *kun*-reading and the *on*-reading is significant in Japanese character recognition processes. With the benefit of hindsight, a task should have been designed to demonstrate the development of skills and awareness of the two types of readings. The description of the development would be more precise with the results of such a task.

Other issues related to the nature of the tests used include the use of English for the *on*-readings and the semantic category names, and for one aspect of the instruction of the semantic tasks (i.e., that the assessment required in the semantic judgement task should be based on a common semantic category instead of semantic association). If *hiragana* instead of English had been used, it would still have raised a methodological issue, as less-skilled L2 readers might have needed longer processing times for the *hiragana*. If the task instruction had been to associate the two *kanji* characters, interpretation of the data would have been even harder, as there may have been some associations specific to individual readers' experiences.

In the present study, an interview was employed to elicit the participants' orthographic, phonological and morphological awareness. As talking about their performance required a conscious analysis of the automatic processes, it might have affected the participant's performances in the tasks that followed. In order to lessen the practice effect on particular tasks, a different set of tasks in a different order was allocated to each different group of participants.

There might be an argument that the interview should have taken a more guided form so that the results would have been able to be analysed quantitatively. However, the free structure of the interview provided invaluable information that could not have been obtained otherwise. I am aware that what was reported in the interview does not necessarily indicate a complete picture of the participants' state of awareness. However, it provided data about awareness that otherwise could be inferred only by inferences from the task performance.

443

7.2 Conclusions

The aim of my research was to investigate the development of L2 word recognition ability, one of the most important abilities that learners need to develop for efficient reading. The study outlined the development of *kanji* recognition skills and awareness among learners of Japanese by integrating psycholinguistic methods with an applied linguistic perspective. By analysing the results of behavioural tests and a verbal protocol administered to both L1 and L2 readers of Japanese, the study described the changes in developing L2 learners' *kanji* recognition skills and their awareness of the structure and function of characters at the different stages of L2 exposure.

The overall findings suggest that the changes in processing patterns demonstrated by the participants in the present study may be fundamentally similar to those of L1 children, which have been found to be similar regardless of the types of script involved. The changes in L2 readers' developing *kanji* recognition ability were accounted for by the transformation of the internal processing system: This transformation seems to occur by continuous link formation through learning corresponding information, and information processing based on the learned information. The process of transformation, which is affected by the frequency of exposure and the amount of practice, and therefore appears to be item-based, generally progresses on a stage-based developmental trajectory; the processing begins with local and incomplete information and progresses via intentional and analytical processing to develop into sophisticated attention-free processing.

Although the developmental trajectory may be universal, the findings of the present study suggest that, when L1 and L2 are orthographically distant, L2 readers repeat the developmental phases due to the lack of their ability to process script-specific information. L2 readers with alphabetic backgrounds cannot simply transfer the recognition skills and awareness acquired in their L1 in the new environment of character recognition. The findings of the study suggest that script-specific recognition skills and awareness develop over time as the L2 reader's internal processing system undergoes successive transformations. By identifying several critical skills and awareness, the present study has discussed the possibility of enhancing character recognition ability with the use of explicit instruction at critical moments.

To conclude, this book began with a simple research program: describing the development of *kanji* recognition ability among learners of Japanese. The book presented the findings of the study and proposed developmental phases of character recognition ability, and identified universal and script-specific aspects of written language processing. It has also made some recommendations for explicit instruction to enhance the development of character recognition ability, based on the findings of both current and previous studies. While the book is by no means comprehensive, it has provided a basis for determining, and insights into, the types of issues that might be usefully investigated in future research using more targeted and rigorous procedures. Such research may enable the formulation of comprehensive word recognition models that can account for developing script-specific recognition ability. These would serve as valuable resources for research pertaining to L2 word recognition ability and the teaching of L2 scripts.

References

Adams, M. J. (1990). *Beginning to Read: Thinking and Learning about Print.* Massachusetts: MIT press.

Akamatsu, N. (1999). The effects of first language orthographic features on word recognition processing in English as a second language. *Reading and Writing - An Interdisciplinary Journal, 11,* 381-403.

Akamatsu, N. (2002). A similarity in word-recognition procedures among second language readers with different first language backgrounds. *Applied Psycholinguistics, 23,* 117-133.

Akamatsu, N. (2003). The effects of first language orthographic features on second language reading in text. *Language Learning, 53*(2), 207-231.

Alderson, J. C. (2000). *Assessing Reading.* Cambridge: Cambridge University Press.

Alegria, J., & Morais, J. (1991). Segmental analysis and reading acquisition. In L. Rieben & C. A. Perfetti (Eds.), *Learning to Read: Basic Research and its Implications.* Hillsdale: Lawrence Erlbaum Associates.

Andrews, S. (1997). The effect of orthographic similarity on lexical retrieval: Resolving neighbourhood conflicts. *Psychonomic Bulletin & Review, 4*(4), 439-461.

Baddeley, A. (2000). The episodic buffer: A new component of working memory? *Trends in cognitive Sciences, 4*(11), 417-423.

Barron, R. W. (1981). Development of visual word recognition: A review. In T. G. Waller & G. F. Mackinnon (Eds.), *Reading Research: Advances in Theory and Practice* (Vol. 3): Academic Press, Inc.

Birdsong, D. (1989). *Metalinguistic Performance and Interlinguistic Competence.* Berlin: Springer-Verlag.

Bradley, L., & Bryant, P. E. (1985). *Rhyme and Reason in Reading and Spelling.* Ann Arbor: University of Michigan Press.

Brisbois, J. E. (1995). Connections between first- and second-language reading. *Journal of Reading Behavior, 27, 4,* 565-584.

Brown, T. L., & Haynes, M. (1985). Literacy background and reading development in a second language. In T. H. Carr (Ed.), *The Development of Reading Skills* (pp. 19-34). San Francisco: Jossey-Bass.

Campbell, R., & Sais, E. (1995). Accelerated metalinguistic (phonological) awareness in bilingual children. *British Journal of Developmental psychology, 13,* 61-68.

Caravolas, M., & Bruck, M. (1993). The effect of oral and written language input on children's phonological awareness: A cross-linguistic study. *Journal of Experimental Child Psychology, 55,* 1-30.

Carlisle, J. F. (2000). Awareness of the structure and meaning of morphologically complex words: Impact on reading. *Reading and Writing - An Interdisciplinary Journal, 12,* 169-190.

Carlisle, J. F. (2003). Morphology matters in learning to read: A commentary. *Reading Psychology, 24,* 291-322.

Carson, J. E., Carrell, P. L., Silberstein, S., & Kuehn, P. A. (1990). Reading-writing relationships in first and second language. *TESOL Quarterly, 24*(2), 245-266.

Castles, A., & Coltheart, M. (2004). Is there a causal link from phonological awareness to success in learning to read? *Cognition, 91,* 77-111.

Castles, A., & Davis, C. (1998). The use of a rapid priming technique 1: Word recognition development in children. *South Pacific Journal of Psychology, 10*(1), 9298.

Castles, A., Holms, V., Neath, J., & Kinoshita, S. (2003). How does orthographic knowledge influence performance on phonological awareness tasks? *The quarterly Journal of experimental Psychology, 56A*(3), 445-467.

Chambers, S. M., & Foster, K. I. (1975). Evidence for lexical access in a simultaneous matching task. *Memory & Cognition, 3*(5), 549-559.

Chen, H. C. (1992). Lexical processing in bilingual or multilingual speakers. In *Cognitive Processing in Bilinguals* (83 ed., pp. 253-264). Amsterdam: Elsevier Science Publishers.

Chen, H. C., & Shu, H. (2001). Lexical activation during the recognition of Chinese characters: Evidence against early phonological activation. *Psychonomic Bulletin & Review, 8*(3), 511-518.

Chen, X., Wu, N., & Anderson, R. C. (2003). Stages in learning to pronounce Chinese characters. *Psychology in the Schools, 40*(115-124).

Chen, Y. P., Allport, D. A., & Marshall, J. C. (1996). What are the functional orthographic units in Chinese word recognition: The stroke or the stroke pattern? *The quarterly Journal of Experimental Psychology, 49A*(4), 1024-1043.

Chikamatsu, N. (1996). The effects of L1 orthography on L2 word recognition: A study of American and Chinese learners of Japanese. *Studies in Second Language Acquisition, 18*, 403-432.

Chitiri, H. F., Sun, Y., Willows, D. M., & Taylor, I. (1992). Word recognition in second-language reading. In *Cognitive Processing in Bilinguals* (83 ed., pp. 283-297). Amsterdam: Elsevier Science Publishers.

Coltheart, M., Rastle, K., Perry, C., Langdon, R., & Ziegler, J. (2001). DRC: A dual route cascaded model of visual word recognition and reading aloud. *Psychological Review, 108*, 204 - 256.

Comeau, L., Cormier, P., Grandmaison, E., & Lacroix, D. (1999). A longitudinal study of phonological processing skills in children learning to read in a second language. *Journal of Educational Psychology, 91*(1), 29-43.

Crystal, D. (1987). *The Cambridge Encyclopedia of Language*: Cambridge University Press.

Cunningham, A. E., Stanovich, K. E., & Wilson, M. R. (1990). Cognitive variation in adult college students differing in reading ability. In T. H. Carr & B. A. Levy (Eds.), *Reading and its Development: Component Skills Approaches* (pp. 129-159): Academic Press.

Davis, C. (1999). *The self-organising lexical acquisition and recognition (solar) model of visual word recognition*. Unpublished Doctorate thesis, The University of New South Wales.

Davis, C., & Castles, A. (1998). The use of rapid priming technique 1: Adult language processing. *South Pacific Journal of Psychology, 10*(1), 85-91.

De Courcy, M. (1995). A Chinese puzzle-learning experiences of a class of adult beginners. *Babel, 30*(1), 32-37.

De Courcy, M. (1997). Four adults' approaches to the learning of Chinese. *Australian Review of Applied Linguistics, 20*(2), 67-93.

Dijkstra, T., & Van Heuven, W. (2002). The architecture of the bilingual word recognition system: From identification to decision. *Bilingualism: Language and Cognition, 5*(3), 175-197.

Dobson, A. (1997). Reading strategies of Japanese L2 learners. Paper presented at the 10th Japanese Studies Association of Australia, Melbourne, Australia.

Drewnowski, A., & Healy, A. F. (1977). Detection errors on *the* and *and*: Evidence for reading units larger than the word. *Memory & Cognition, 5*(6), 636-647.

Driscoll, M. P. (1994). *Psychology of Learning for Instruction*. Boston: Allyn and Bason.

Edwards, H. I., & Kirkpatrick, A. G. (1999). Metalinguistic awareness in children: A developmental progression. *Journal of Psycholinguistic Research, 28*(4), 313-329.

Ehri, L. C., & Bobbins, C. (1992). Beginners need some decoding skill to read words by analogy. *Reading Research Quarterly, 27*(1), 13-26.

Ellis, N. C., & Hooper, A. M. (2001). Why learning to read is easier in Welsh than in English: Orthographic transparency effects evinced with frequency-matched tests. *Applied Psycholinguistics, 22*, 571-599.

Ericsson, K. A., & Simon, H. A. (1984/1993). *Protocol Analysis: Verbal Reports as Data*. Cambridge, MA: MIT Press.

Ferrand, L., & Grainger, J. (2003). Homophone interference effects in visual word recognition. *Quarterly Journal of Experimental Psychology, Section A: Human Experimental Psychology, 56A*(3), 403-419.

Finkbeiner, M., & Nicol, J. (2003). Semantic category effects in second language word learning. *Applied Psycholinguistics, 24*, 369-383.

Flaherty, M., & Noguchi, M. S. (1998). Effectiveness of different approaches to kanji education with second language learners. *JALT Journal, 20*, 60-78.

Flores d'Arcais, G. B. (1992). Graphemic, phonological, and semantic activation processes during the recognition of Chinese characters. In H. C. Chen & O. J. L. Tzeng (Eds.), *Advances in Psychology-Language Processing in Chinese* (pp. 37-68). Amsterdam: Elsevier Science Publishers B. V.

Flores d'Arcais, G. B., & Saito, H. (1993). Lexical decomposition of complex kanji characters in Japanese readers. *Psychological Research, 55*, 52-63.

Flores d'Arcais, G. B., Saito, H., & Kawakami, M. (1995). Phonological and semantic activation in reading kanji characters. *Journal of Experimental Psychology: Learning, Memory, and Cognition, 21*(1), 34-42.

Foorman, B. (1994). Phonological and orthographic processing: Separate but equal? In V. W. Berninger (Ed.), *The Varieties of Orthographic Knowledge - Theoretical and Developmental Issues* (Vol. 1, pp. 321-358). Dordrecht: Kluwer Academic Publisher.

Fowler, C. A. (1981). Some aspects of language perception by eye: The beginning reader. In O. J. L. Tzeng & H. Singer (Eds.), *Perception of Print: Reading Research in Experimental Psychology* (pp. 171-196). Hillsdale: Lawrence Erlbaum Associates.

Frost, R., & Katz, L. (1992). *Orthography, Phonology, Morphography, and Meaning.* Amsterdam: North-Holland.

Gass, S. M. (2001). Innovations in second language research methods. *Annual Review of Applied Linguistics, 21*, 221-232.

Geva, E., & Siegel, L. S. (2000). Orthographic and cognitive factors in the concurrent development of basic reading skills in two languages. *Reading and Writing - An Interdisciplinary Journal, 12*, 1-30.

Geva, E., & Wang, M. (2001). The development of basic reading skills in children: A cross-language perspective. *Annual Review of Applied Linguistics, 21*, 182-204.

Gombert, J. E. (1992). *Metalinguistic Development* (T. Pownall, Trans.). London: Harvester Wheatsheaf.

Goswami, U., Ziegler, J. C., Dalton, L., & Schneider, W. (2003). Nonword reading across orthographies: How flexible is the choice of units? *Applied Psycholinguistics, 24*, 235-247.

Gottardo, A., Yan, B., Siegel, L. S., & Wade-Wooley, L. (2001). Factors related to English reading performance in children with Chinese as a first language: More evidence of cross-language transfer of phonological processing. *Journal of Educational Psychology, 93*(3), 530-542.

Gough, P. B. (1991). The first stages of word recognition. In L. Rieben & C. A. Perfetti (Eds.), *Learning to Read: Basic Research and its Implications* (pp. 47-56). Hillsdale: Lawrence Erlbaum Associates.

Grabe, W. (2004). Research on teaching reading. *Annual Review of Applied Linguistics, 24*(1), 44-69.

Harley, T. A. (1995). Visual word recognition. In T. A. Harley (Ed.), *The Psychology of Language - From Data to Theory* (pp. 67-100). East Sussex: Psychology Press.

Harm, M. W., & Seidenberg, M. S. (2004). Computing the meanings of words in reading: Cooperative division of labor between visual and phonological processes. *Psychological Review, 111*(3), 662-720.

Harris, M., & Coltheart, M. (1986). *Language Processing in Children and Adults: An Introduction*. London: Routledge & Kegan Paul.

Hatano, G. (1986). How do Japanese children learn to read? Orthographic and eco-cultural variables. In B. R. Foorman & A. W. Siegel (Eds.), *Acquisition of Reading Skills: Cultural Constraints and Cognitive Universals* (pp. 81-114): Lawrence Erlbaum Associates.

Hatch, E., & Lazaraton, a. (1991). *The Research Manual - Design and Statistics for Applied Linguistics*. New York: Newbury House Publishers.

Hatta, T., Hatae, T., & Kirsner, K. (1984). Orthographic dominance and interference effects in letter recognition among Japanese-English and English-Japanese bilinguals. *Psychologia, 27*, 1-9.

Hatta, T., Kawakami, A., & Tamaoka, K. (1998). Writing errors in Japanese kanji: A study with Japanese students and foreign learners of Japanese. In C. K. Leong & K. Tamaoka (Eds.), *Cognitive Processing of the Chinese and the Japanese languages* (Vol. 14, pp. 303-316). Dordrecht: Kluwer Academic Publishers.

Hayashi, O. (1982). *Zusetsu Nihongo [Graphic Japanese]*. Tokyo: Kadokawa Shuppan.

Hayes, E. B. (1987). The relationship between Chinese character complexity and character recognition. *Journal of the Chinese Language Teachers Association, 22*(2), 45-57.

Hayes, E. B. (1988). Encoding strategies used by native and non-native readers of Chinese mandarin. *The Modern Language Journal, 72*(2), 188-195.

Haynes, M., & Carr, T. H. (1990). Writing system background and second language reading: A component skills analysis of English reading by native speaker-readers of Chinese. In T. H. Carr & B. A. Levy (Eds.), *Reading and its Development: Component Skills Approaches* (pp. 375-421): Academic Press.

Healy, A. F. (1994). Letter detection: A window to unitization and other cognitive processes in reading text. *Psychonomic Bulletin and Review, 1*(3), 333-344.

Healy, A. F., & Cunningham, T. F. (1992). A developmental evaluation of the role of word shape in word recognition. *Memory & Cognition, 20*(2), 141-150.

Herriman, M. (1991). Metalinguistic development. *Australian Journal of Reading, 14*, 4(Nov.), 326-338.

Hirose, T. (1984). Kanji oyobi kana tango no imiteki shori ni oyobosu hyouki hindo no kouka [The effect of script frequency on semantic processing of kanji and kana words]. *The Japanese Journal of Psychology, 55*(3), 173-176.

Hirose, H. (1998). Identifying the on- and kun-readings of Chinese characters: Identification of on versus kun as a strategy-based judgment. In C. K. Leong & K. Tamaoka (Eds.), *Cognitive Processing of the Chinese and the Japanese Languages* (Vol. 14, pp. 221-240). Dordrecht: Kluwer Academic Publishers.

Ho, C. S.-H., Ng, T.-T., & Ng, W. K. (2003). A 'radical' approach to reading development in Chinese: The role of semantic radicals and phonetic radicals. *Journal of Literacy Research, 35*(3), 849-878.

Ho, C. S. H., & Bryant, P. (1997). Learning to read Chinese beyond the logographic phase. *Reading Research Quarterly, 32*(3), 276-289.

Holm, A., & Dodd, B. (1996). The effect of first written language on the acquisition of English literacy. *Cognition, 59*, 119-14

Hong, E.-L. (1998). The relationship between Chinese character frequency of occurrence and response latency: A direct prediction of the Forster's Search Model. *South Pacific Journal of Psychology, 10*(1), 68-75.

Hong, E. L., & Yelland, W. (1997). The generality of lexical neighbourhood effects. In H. C. Chen (Ed.), *Cognitive Processing of Chinese and Related Asian Languages* (pp. 187-203). Hong Kong: The Chinese University Press.

Hoosain, R. (1991). *Psycholinguistic Implications for Linguistic Relativity: A Case Study of Chinese*. Hillsdale: Lawrence Erlbaum Associates.

Horiba, Y., van den Broek, P. W., & Fletcher, C. R. (1994). Second-language readers' memory for narrative texts: Evidence for structure-preserving processing. In A. H. Cumming (Ed.), *Bilingual Performance in Reading and Writing* (pp. 43-71). Michigan: Research Club in Language learning.

Hsu, S. H., & Huang, K. C. (2001). Effects of minimal legible size characters on Chinese word recognition. *Visible Language, 35*(2), 178-191.

Huang, H. S., & Hanley, J. R. (1995). Phonological awareness and visual skills in learning to read Chinese and English. *Cognition, 54*, 73-98.

Ishida, T. (1989) Kanji no shidouhou [Kanji teaching methods]. *Kouza Nihongo to Nihongo Kyouiku [Japanese and Japanese Language Teaching]*, 8 Meiji Shoten.

Jackson, M. D., & McClelland, J. L. (1981). Exploring the nature of a basic visual-processing component of reading ability. In O. J. L. Tzeng & H. Singer (Eds.), *Perception of Print: Reading Research in Experimental Psychology* (pp. 125-136). Hillsdale: Lawrence Erlbaum Associates.

Jackson, N. E., Chen, H., Goldsberry, L., Kim, A., & Vanderwerff, C. (1999). Effects of variations in orthographic information on Asian and American readers' English text reading. *Reading and Writing - An Interdisciplinary Journal, 11*, 345-379.

Jackson, N. E., Lu, W.-H., & Ju, D. (1994). Reading Chinese and reading English: Similarities, differences, and second-language reading. In V. W. Berninger (Ed.), *The Varieties of Orthographic Knowledge - Theoretical and Developmental Issues* (Vol. 1, pp. 73-110). Dordrecht: Kluwer Academic Publisher.

Juffs, A. (2001). Psycholinguistically oriented second language research. *Annual Review of Applied Linguistics, 21*, 207-220.

Kaiho, H., & Nomura, Y. (1983). *Kanji Joho Shori no Shinrigaku [the psychology of kanji information processing]*. Tokyo: Kyoiku Shuppan.

Kawakami, A., Hatta, T., & Tamaoka, K. (1991). Reading processes of English sentences in Japanese and Canadian students. *Reading and Writing: An Interdisciplinary Journal, 3*, 31-42.

Kawakami, M. (2002). Kanji niji jyukugo no ruijigosuu to kousei moji shutugen hindo ga goi handan kadai no oyobosu kouka [Effects of neighbourhood size and kanji character frequency on lexical decision of Japanese kanji compound words]. *The Japanese Journal of Psychology, 73*(4), 346-351.

Ke, C. (1996). An empirical study on the relationship between Chinese character recognition and production. *The Modern Language Journal, 80*(3), 340-350.

Ke, C. (1998). Effects of language background on the learning of Chinese characters among foreign language students. *Foreign Language Annals, 31*(1), 91-100.

Kess, J. F., & Miyamoto, T. (1997). Accessing the Japanese mental dictionary through the Japanese writing system. *Occasional Paper, 15*.

Kim, J., & Davis, C. (2001). Loss of rapid phonological recoding in reading Hanja, the logographic script of Korean. *Psychonomic Bulletin & Review, 8*(4), 785-790.

Koda, K. (1989a). Effects of L1 orthographic representation on L2 phonological coding strategies. *Journal of Psycholinguistic Research, 18, 2*, 201-222.

Koda, K. (1989b). The effects of transferred vocabulary knowledge on the development of L2 reading proficiency. *Foreign Language Annals, 22*(6), 529-541.

Koda, K. (1990). The use of L1 reading strategies in L2 reading. *Studies in Second Language Acquisition, 12, 4*, 393-410.

Koda, K. (1992). The effects of lower-level processing skills on FL reading performance: Implications of instruction. *The Modern Language Journal, 76,* 502-512.

Koda, K. (1993). Transferred L1 strategies and L2 syntactic structure in L2 sentence comprehension. *The Modern Language Journal, 77, 4,* 490-499.

Koda, K. (1994). Second language reading research: Problems and possibilities. *Applied Psycholinguistics, 15,* 1-28.

Koda, K. (1995). Cognitive consequences of L1 and L2 orthographies. In Taylor, Insup, Olson & David (Eds.), *Scripts and literacy: Reading and Learning to Read Alphabets, Syllabaries and Characters* (pp. 311-326). Dordrecht, Netherlands: Kluwer Academic Publishers.

Koda, K. (1996). L2 word recognition research: A critical review. *The Modern Language Journal, 80*(4), 450-460.

Koda, K. (1997). Orthographic knowledge in L2 lexical processing: A cross-linguistic perspective. In J. Coady & T. Huckin (Eds.), *Second Language Vocabulary Acquisition* (pp. 35-51). Cambridge: Cambridge University Press.

Koda, K. (1999a). Development of L2 intraword orthographic sensitivity and decoding skills. *The Modern Language Journal, 83*(1), 51-64.

Koda, K. (1999b). Role of intraword awareness in kanji knowledge development. Paper presented at the AILA, Tokyo.

Koda, K. (2000). Cross-linguistic variations in L2 morphological awareness. *Applied Psycholinguistics, 21*(3), 297-320.

Koda, K. (2002). Writing systems and learning to read in a second language. In W. Li, J.

S. Gaffney & J. L. Packard (Eds.), *Chinese Children's Reading Acquisition* (pp. 225-248). Boston: Kluwer Academic Publishers.

Ku, Y-M., & Anderson, R. C. (2003). Development of morphological awareness in Chinese and English. *Reading and Writing - An Interdisciplinary Journal, 16*, 399-422.

Kubota, M., & Toyoda, E. (2001). Learning strategies employed for learning words written in kanji versus kana. *Australian Review of Applied Linguistics, 24*(2), 1-16.

Kuhara-Kojima, K., Hatano, G., Saito, H., & Haebara, T. (1996). Vocalization latencies of skilled and less skilled comprehenders for words written in hiragana and kanji. *Reading Research Quarterly, 31*(2), 158-171.

Leck, K. J., Weekes, B. S., & Chen, M. J. (1995). Visual and phonological pathways to the lexicon: Evidence from Chinese readers. *Memory & Cognition, 23*(4), 468-476.

Lee, S. Y., Stigler, J. W., & Stevenson, H. W. (1986). Beginning reading in Chinese and English. In B. R. Foorman & A. W. Siegel (Eds.), *Acquisition of Reading Skills: Cultural Constraints and Cognitive Universals* (pp. 123-150): Lawrence Erlbaum Associates.

Leong, C. K., & Tamaoka, K. (1995). Use of phonological information in processing kanji and katakana by skilled and less skilled Japanese readers. *Reading and Writing: An Interdisciplinary Journal, 7*, 377-393.

Li, H., & Chen, H-C. (1997). Processing of radicals in Chinese character recognition. In H-C. Chen (Ed.), *Cognitive Processing of Chinese and Related Asian Languages* (pp. 141-160). Hong Kong: The Chinese University Press.

Li, W., Anderson, R. C., Nagy, W. E., & Zhang, H. (2002). Facets of metalinguistic awareness that contribute to Chinese literacy. In W. Li, J. S. Gaffney & J. L. Packard (Eds.), *Chinese Children's Reading Acquisition* (pp. 87-106). Boston: Kluwer Academic Publishers.

Liu, Y., Peng, D. L. (1997). Meaning access of Chinese compounds and its time course. In H. C. Chen (Ed.), *Cognitive Processing of Chinese and Related Asian Languages* (pp. 219-232). Hong Kong: The Chinese University Press.

MacLaren, R., I. (1989). The distinction between linguistic awareness and metalinguistic consciousness: An applied perspective. *Rassegna Italiana di Linguistica Applicata, 21*(1-2), 5-18.

Mahony, D., Singson, M., & Mann, V. (2000). Reading ability and sensitivity to morphological relations. *Reading and Writing - An Interdisciplinary Journal, 12*, 191-218.

Martin, S. E. (1972). Nonalphabetic writing systems: Some observations. In J. F. Kavanagh & I. G. Mattingly (Eds.), *Language by ear and by eye: The relationships between speech and reading* (pp. 81-102). London: The MIT Press.

Masuda, H., & Saito, H. (1999). Two types of radical frequency effects on Japanese kanji character recognition. *Psychologia -An International Journal of Psychology in the Orient, 42*, 222-242.

McBride-Chang, C., & Ho, C. S-H. (2000). Developmental issues in Chinese children's character acquisition. *Journal of Educational Psychology, 92*(1), 50-55.

McBride-Chang, C., Shu, H., Zhou, A., Wat, C. P., & Wagner, R. K. (2003). Morphological awareness uniquely predicts young children's Chinese character recognition. *Journal of Educational Psychology, 95*(4), 743-751.

McClelland, J., & Rumelhart, D. (1981). An interactive activation model of context effects in letter perception: Part 1. An account of basic findings. *Psychological*

Review, 88, 375-407.

McDonough, S. (1995). *Strategy and skill in learning a foreign language*. London: Edward Arnold.

Meara, P., & Jones, G. (1987). Tests of vocabulary size in English as a foreign language. *Polyglot, 8*(1), 1-40.

Miller, K. F. (2002). Children's early understanding of writing and language: The impact of characters and alphabetic orthographies. In W. Li, J. S. Gaffney & J. L. Packard (Eds.), *Chinese Children's Reading Acquisition: Theoretical and Pedagogical Issues* (pp. 17-30). Boston: Kluwer Academic Publishers.

Moore, H. (1996). Word-attack skills in beginners' Japanese reading comprehension. *Australian Review of Applied Linguistics, 19, 1*, 73-88.

Mori, Y. (1998). Effects of first language and phonological accessibility on kanji recognition. *The Modern Language Journal, 82*(1), 69-81.

Mori, Y. (2002). Individual differences in the integration of information from context and word parts in interpreting unknown kanji words. *Applied Psycholinguistics, 23*, 375-397.

Mori, Y. (2003). The roles of context and word morphology in learning new kanji words. *The Modern Language Journal, 82*(3), 404-420.

Mori, Y., & Nagy, W. (1999). Integration of information from context and word elements in interpreting novel kanji compounds. *Reading Research Quarterly, 34*(1), 80-101.

Morita, A., & Matsuda, F. (2000). Phonological and semantic activation in reading two-kanji compound words. *Applied Psycholinguistics, 21*, 487-503.

Morton, J. (1980). The Logogen Model and orthographic structure. In U. Frith (Ed.), *Cognitive Processes in Spelling* (pp. 117-133). New York: Academic Press.

Morton, J., & Sasanuma, S. (1984). Lexical access in Japanese. In L. Henderson (Ed.), *Orthographies and Reading: Perspectives from Cognitive Psychology, Neuropsychology, and Linguistics* (pp. 25-42). London: Lawrence Erlbaum Associates.

Mou, L-C., & Anderson, N. (1981). Graphemic and phonemic codings of Chinese characters in short-term retention. *Bulletin of the Psychonomic Society, 17*((6)), 255-258.

Nagy, W., Anderson, R. C., Schommer, M., Scott, J. A., & Stallman, A. C. (1989). Morphological families in the internal lexicon. *Reading Research Quarterly, 24*(3), 262-279.

Nagy, W. E., Kuo-Kealoha, A., Wu, X., Li, W., Anderson, R. C., & Chen, X. (2002). The role of morphological awareness in learning to read Chinese. In W. Li, J. S. Gaffney & J. L. Packard (Eds.), *Chinese Children's Reading Acquisition* (pp. 59-86). Boston: Kluwer Academic Publishers.

Nation, P. (1993). Using dictionaries to estimate vocabulary size: Essential, but rarely followed procedures. *Language Testing, 10*, 27-40.

Noguchi, M. S. (1995). Component analysis of kanji for learners from non-kanji using countries. *The Language Teacher, 19*(10).

Nomura, M. (1981). Statistics on reading of zyoyo-kanji. *Keiryo Kokugo Gakkai/Mathematical Linguistics, 13*(1), 27-33.

Nomura, M. (1984). Kanji no tokusei wo hakaru [Measuring characteristics of kanji]. *Kanji wo Kagaku suru [Sciencing kanji]*, 1-33.

Okita, Y. (1995). Kanji learning strategies and student beliefs on kanji learning. *Japanese-Language Education around the Globe, 5,* 105-124.

Osaka, M., & Osaka, N. (1994). yomi to waakingu memori youryou - nihongo ban riidhingu supan tesuto niyoru sokutei [Working memory capacity related to reading: Measurement with the Japanese version of reading span test]. *The Japanese Journal of Psychology, 65*(5), 339-345.

Paradis, M., Hagiwara, H., & Hiderbrandt, N. (1985). *Neurolinguistic Aspects of the Japanese Writing System.* Orlando: Academic Press Inc.

Peng, D.-l., Li, Y.-p., & Yang, H. (1997). Orthographic processing in the identification of Chinese characters. In H-C. Chen (Ed.), *Cognitive Processing of Chinese and Related Asian Languages* (pp. 86-108). Hong Kong: The Chinese University Press.

Perfetti, C. A. (1986). Cognitive and linguistic components of reading ability. In B. R. Foorman & A. W. Siegel (Eds.), *Acquisition of Reading Skills: Cultural Constraints and Cognitive Universals* (pp. 11-40): Lawrence Erlbaum Associates.

Perfetti, C. A. (1991). Representations and awareness in the acquisition of reading competence. In L. Rieben & C. A. Perfetti (Eds.), *Learning to Read: Basic Research and its Implications* (pp. 33-44). Hillsdale: Lawrence Erlbaum Associates.

Perfetti, C. A. (2003). The universal grammar of reading. *Scientific Studies of Reading, 7*(1), 3-24.

Perfetti, C. A., Van Dyke, J., & Hart, L. (2001). The psycholinguistics of basic literacy. *Annual Review of Applied Linguistics, 21,* 127-149.

Perfetti, C. A., & Zhang, S. (1991). Phonological processes in reading Chinese characters. *Journal of Experimental Psychology; Learning, Memory and Cognition, 17,* 633-643.

Perfetti, C. A., & Zhang, S. (1995). Very early phonological activation in Chinese reading. *Journal of Experimental Psychology: Learning, Memory, and Cognition, 21,* 24-33.

Perkins, K., Brutten, S. R., & Pohlmann, J. T. (1989). First and second language reading comprehension. *RELC Journal, 20, 2,* 1-9.

Peterson, M. E., & Haines, L. P. (1992). Orthographic analogy training with kindergarten children: Effects on analogy use, phonemic segmentation, and letter-sound knowledge. *Journal of Reading Behavior, 24, 1,* 109-127.

Pressley, M., & Afflerback, P. (1995). *Verbal protocols of reading: The Nature of Constructively Responsive Reading.* New Jersey: Lawrence Erlbaum Associates, Publishers.

Read, J. (1993). The development of a new measure of L2 vocabulary knowledge. *Language Testing, 10*(3), 356-371.

Read, J. (2000). *Assessing Vocabulary.* Cambridge: Cambridge University Press.

Reynolds, B. (1998). *Phonological Awareness in EFL Reading Acquisition.* Paper presented at the JALT.

Rohl, M., & Milton, M. (1993). The importance of syntactic and phonological awareness to early literacy. *Australian Journal of Language and Literacy, 16, 2*(May), 157-168.

Saito, H. (1981). Kanji to kana no yomi ni okeru keitaiteki fugooka oyobi on'inteki fugooka no kentoo [Use of graphemic and phonemic encoding in reading kanji and kana]. *The Japanese Journal of Psychology, 52*(5), 266-273.

Saito, H., Kawakami, M., Masuda, H., & Flores d'Arcaise, G. (1997). Contributions of radical components to kanji character recognition and recall. In H.-C. Chen (Ed.), *Cognitive Processing of Chinese and Related Asian Languages* (pp. 109-140). Hong Kong: The Chinese University Press.

Sakuma, N., Sasanuma, S., Tatsumi, I., & Masaki, S. (1998). Orthography and phonology in reading Japanese kanji words: Evidence from the semantic decision task with homophones. *Memory and Cognition, 26*(1), 75-97.

Sarig, G. (1987). High-level reading in the first and in the foreign language: Some comparative process data. In J. Devine, P. L. Carrel & D. E. Eskey (Eds.), *Research in Reading in English as a Second Language* (pp. 107-123). Washington D. C.: TESOL.

Sayeg, Y. (1996). The role of sound in reading kanji and kana. *Australian Review of Applied Linguistics, 19*(2), 139-151.

Segalowitz, N. (1986). Skilled reading in the second language. In J. Vaid (Ed.), *Language Processing in Bilinguals: Psycholinguistic and Neuropsychological Perspectives* (pp. 3-19). Hillsdale: Lawrence Erlbaum Associates.

Seidenberg, M. S., & McClelland, J. L. (1989). A distributed, developmental model of word recognition and naming. *Psychological Review, 96*(4), 523-568.

Share, D. L. (1995). Phonological recoding and self-teaching: Sine qua non of reading acquisition. *Cognition, 55*(2), 151-218.

Shillaw, J. (1996, 17 Dec. 1996). The application of Rasch Modelling to yes/no vocabulary tests. *Vocabulary Acquisition Research Group Virtual Library.* Retrieved 12 March, 2002, from
http://www.swan.ac.uk/cals/calsres/vlibrary/js96a.htm

Shimizu, H., & Green, K. E. (2002). Japanese language educators' strategies for and attitudes toward teaching kanji. *The Modern Language Journal, 86*(2), 227-241.

Shimomura, M., & Yokosawa, K. (1991). Processing of kanji and kana characters within Japanese words. *Perception & Psychophysics, 30`*, 19-27.

Shu, H. (2003). Chinese writing system and learning to read. *International Journal of Psychology, 38*(5), 274-285.

Shu, H., & Anderson, R. C. (1997). Role of radical awareness in the character and word acquisition of Chinese children. *Reading Research Quarterly, 32*(1), 78-89.

Shu, H., & Anderson, R. C. (1998). Learning to read Chinese: The development of metalinguistic awareness. In J. Wang, A. Inhoff & H.-c. Chen (Eds.), *Reading Chinese Script: A cognitive Analysis* (pp. 1-18). Malwah, N.J.: Lawrence Erlbaum Association.

Shu, H., Anderson, R. C., & Wu, N. (2000). Phonetic awareness: Knowledge of orthography-phonology relationship in the character acquisition of Chinese children. *Journal of Educational Psychology, 92*(1), 56-62.

Shu, H., Chen, X., Anderson, R. C., Wu, N., & Xuan, Y. (2003). Properties of school Chinese: Implications for learning to read. *Child Development, 74*(1), 27-47.

Singer, M. H. (1982). *Competent Reader, Disabled Reader: Research and Application.* Hillsdale: Lawrence Erlbaum Associates.

Slobin, D., & Bever, T. G. (1982). Children use canonical sentence schemas: A crosslinguistic study of word order and inflections. *Cognition, 12*, 229-263.

Stanovich, K. E. (1980). Toward an interactive compensatory model of individual differences in the development of reading fluency. *Reading Research Quarterly, 16*, 32-71.

Stanovich, K. E. (1982). Word recognition skill and reading ability. In M. H. Singer (Ed.), *Competent Reader, Disabled Reader: Research and Application* (pp. 81-102). Hillsdale: Lawrence Erlbaum Associates.

Stanovich, K. E. (1991). Changing models of reading and reading acquisition. In L. Rieben & C. A. Perfetti (Eds.), *Learning to Read: Basic Research and its Implications* (pp. 19-31). Hillsdale: Lawrence Erlbaum Associates.

Stone, G. O., Vanhoy, M., & Van Orden, G. C. (1997). Perception is a two-way street: Feedforward and feedback phonology in visual word recognition. *Journal of Memory and Language, 36*(3), 337-359.

Taft, M. (1991). *Reading and the Mental Lexicon*. Hove: Lawrence Erlbaum Associates.

Taft, M. (2004). Processing of characters by native Chinese readers. In P. Li, L. H. Tan, E. Bates & O. J. L. Tzeng (Eds.), *Handbook of East Asian Psycholinguistics: Chinese*. Cambrige: Cambrige university Press.

Taft, M., & Chung, K. (1999). Using radicals in teaching Chinese characters to second language learners. *Psychologia - An international journal of psychology in the orient, 17*(4), 243-251.

Taft, M., & Forster, K. (1975). Lexical storage and retrieval of prefixed words. *Journal of Verbal Learning and Verbal Behaviour, 14*, 638-647.

Taft, M., & Zhu, X. (1995). The representation of bound morphemes in the lexicon: A Chinese study. In L. B. Feldman (Ed.), *Morphological Aspects of Language Processing* (pp. 293-316). Hove, H. K.: Lawrence Erlbaum, Associates.

Taft, M., & Zhu, X. (1997a). Submorphemic processing in reading Chinese. *Journal of Experimental Psychology: Learning, Memory, and Cognition, 23*(3), 761-775.

Taft, M., & Zhu, X. (1997b). Using masked priming to examine lexical storage of Chinese compound words. In H. C. Chen (Ed.), *Cognitive Processing of Chinese and Related Asian Languages* (pp. 233-341). Hong Kong: The Chinese University Press.

Takahashi, N. (1993). Nyuumonki no yominouryoku no jyukutatuka katei [Becoming skilful at reading in beginners]. *Japanese Journal of Educational Psychology, 41*(3), 264-274.

Tamaoka, K. (1991). Psycholinguistic nature of the Japanese orthography. *Studies in Language and Literature, 11*(1), 49-82.

Tamaoka, K. (1992). Eigo o bogo to suru nihongo gakushuusha no tangoshori no kooritsu [Lexical processing efficiency in native English learners of Japanese]. *ibunkakankyooiku [Intercultural/transcultural education], 6*, 99-113.

Tamaoka, K. (1997). Chuugokugo to eigo o bogo to suru nihongog akushuusha no kanji oyobi kanahyookigoi no shorihooryaku [The processing strategy of words presented in kanji and kana by Chinese and English speakers learning Japanese]. *Gengo Bunka Kenkyuu [Studies in Language and Literature], 17*(1), 65-77.

Tamaoka, K. (2003). Where do statistically-derived indicators and human strategies meet when identifying on-and kun-readings of Japanese kanji? *Cognitive Studies, 10*(4), 441-468.

Tamaoka, K. (2005). The effect of morphemic homophony on the processing of Japanese two-kanji compound words. *Reading and Writing - An Interdisciplinary Journal*, 1-22.

Tamaoka, K., & Hatsuzuka, M. (1995). Kanjinijijukugo no shori ni okeru kanjishiyouhindo no eikyou [The effects of kanji printed-frequency on processing Japanese two-morpheme compound words]. *The Science of Reading, 39*(4), 121-137.

Tamaoka, K., Kirsner, K., Yanase, Y., Miyaoka, Y., & Kawakami, M. (2002). A web-accessible database of characteristics of the 1945 basic Japanese kanji. *Behavior Research Methods, Instruments and Computers, 34*(2), 260-275.

Tamaoka, K., Leong, C. K., & Hatta, T. (1991). Processing numerals in Arabic, kanji, hiragana and katakana by skilled and less skilled Japanese readers in grades 4-6. *Psychologia, 34*, 200-206.

Tamaoka, K., & Yamada, H. (2000). The effects of stroke order and radicals on the knowledge of Japanese kanji orthography, phonology and semantics. *Psychologia Society, 43*(3), 199-210.

Tan, L. H., Hoosain, R., & Peng, D.-l. (1995). Role of early presemantic phonological code in Chinese character identification. *Journal of Experimental Psychology: Learning, Memory, and Cognition, 21*(1), 43-54.

Tan, L. H., Hoosain, R., & Siok, W. W. (1996). Activation of phonological codes before access to character meaning in written Chinese. *Journal of Experimental Psychology: Learning Memory and Cognition, 22*(4), 865-882.

Taylor, I. (1981). *Reading Research: Advances in Theory and Practice* (Vol. 2): Academic Press.

Taylor, I. (1997). Psycholinguistic reasons for keeping Chinese characters in Korean and Japanese. In H. C. Chen (Ed.), *Cognitive processing of Chinese and related Asian languages.* Hong Kong: The Chinese University Press, 299-322.

Taylor, I. (1998). Learning to read in Chinese, Korean and Japanese. In A. U. Durgunoglu & L. Verhoeven (Eds.), *Literacy Development in a Multilingual context: Cross-Cultural Perspectives* (pp. 225-248). Mahwah, N. J.: Lawrence Erlbaum Associations.

Taylor, I. (2002). Phonological awareness in Chinese reading. In W. Li, J. S. Gaffney & J. L. Packard (Eds.), *Chinese Children's Reading Acquisition* (pp. 39-58). Boston: Kluwer Academic Publishers.

Tollini, A. (1992). Hi-kanji-kei gakushuusha no tame no nyuumonki ni okeru kanji gakushuu shidou no ichi-kousatsu [Teaching of kanji for beginner learners from non-kanji backgrounds]. *Japanese Language Education around the Globe, 2,* 65-76.

Tomita, T., & Sanada, K. (1997). Shin-Hyouki [*New Orthography*]. Tokyo: The Japan Foundation.

Toyoda, E. (1998). Teaching kanji by focusing on learners' development of graphemic awareness. *Australian Review of Applied Linguistics, Series S*(15), 155-168.

Tunmer, W. E., & Bowey, J. A. (1984). Metalinguistic awareness and reading acquisition. In W. E. Tunmer, C. Pratt & M. L. Herriman (Eds.), *Metalinguistic Awareness in Children; Theory, Research, and Implications* (pp. 144-167): Springer-Verlag.

Tunmer, W. E., & Herriman, M. L. (1984). The development of metalinguistic awareness: A conceptual overview. In W. E. Tunmer, C. Pratt & M. L. Herriman (Eds.), *Metalinguistic Awareness in Children* (pp. 12-35). Berlin Heidelberg: Springer-Verlag.

Tunmer, W. E., & Hoover, W. A. (1992). Cognitive and linguistic factors in learning to read. In P. B. Gough, L. C. Ehri & R. Treiman (Eds.), *Reading Acquisition* (pp. 188-209). Hillsdale: Lawrence Erlbaum Associates.

Tunmer, W. E., & Rohl, M. (1991). Phonological awareness and reading acquisition. In D. J. Sawyer & B. J. Fox (Eds.), *Phonological Awareness in Reading; the Evolution of Current Perspectives* (pp. 1-29). New York: Spring-Verlag.

Tyler, A. L., & Nagy, W. (1990). Use of derivational morphology during reading. *Cognition, 36*(1), 17-34.

Tzeng, O. J. L., & Hung, D. L. (1980). Reading in a non-alphabetic writing system: Some experimental studies. In J. F. Kavanagh & R. L. Venezky (Eds.), *Orthography, Reading, and Dyslexia* (pp. 211-226). Baltimore, M.D.: University Park Press.

Tzeng, O. J. L., Zhong, H. L., Hung, D. L., & Lee, W. L. (1995). Learning to be a conspirator: A tale of becoming a good Chinese reader. In B. de Gelder & J. Morais (Eds.), *Speech and Reading: A Comparative Approach.* Hillsdale: Lawrence Erlbaum Associates.

Vellutino, F. R. (1991). Introduction to three studies on reading acquisition. *Journal of Educational Psychology, 83, 4*, 437-443.

Vellutino, F. R., & Scanion, D. M. (1991). The effects of instructional bias on word identification. In L. Rieben & C. A. Perfetti (Eds.), *Learning to Read: Basic Research and its Implications* (pp. 189-203). Hillsdale: Lawrence Erlbaum Associates.

Vermeer, A. (2001). Breadth and depth of vocabulary in relation to L1/L2 acquisition and frequency of input. *Applied Psycholinguistics, 22*, 217-234.

Wade-Woolley, L. (1999). First language influences on second language word reading: All roads lead to Rome. *Language Learning, 49*(3), 447-471.

Wagner, R. K., & Barker, T. A. (1994). The development of orthographic processing ability. In V. W. Berninger (Ed.), *The Varieties of Orthographic Knowledge - Theoretical and Developmental Issues* (Vol. 1, pp. 243-276). Dordrecht: Kluwer Academic Publisher.

Wagner, R. K., & Torgesen, J. K. (1987). The nature of phonological processing and its casual role in the acquisition of reading skills. *Psychological Bulletin, 101*(2), 192-212.

Wang, J. (1988). Kanji no oninshori to imishori wa dooji ni kanryoo suruka [Do phonological and semantic processings of kanji finish at the same time?]. *The Japanese Journal of Psychology, 59*(4), 252-255.

Wang, M., & Koda, K. (2005). Commonalities and differences in word identification skills among learners of English as a second language. *Language Learning, 55*(1). 71-98.

Wang, W. S. Y. (1981). Language structure and optimal orthography. In O. J. L. Tzeng & H. Singer (Eds.), *Perception of Print - Reading Research in Experimental Psychology* (pp. 223-236). Hillsdale, New Jersey: Lawrence Erlbaum Associates.

Wimmer, H., & Goswami, U. (1994). The influence of orthographic consistency on reading development: Word recognition in English and German children. *Cognition, 51,* `91-103.

Wydell, T. N., Patterson, K. E., & Humphreys, G. W. (1993). Phonologically mediated access to meaning for kanji: Is a rows still a rose in Japanese kanji? *Journal of Experimental Psychology: Learning, Memory, and Cognition, 19*(3), 491-514.

Yaden Jr, D. B., & Templeton, S. (1986). Introduction: Metalinguistic awareness-an etymology. In D. B. Yaden Jr & S. Templeton (Eds.), *Metalinguistic Awareness and Beginning Literacy-Conceptualizing -What it means to read and write-* (pp. 3-10): Heinemann Portmouth.

Yamada, J. (1998). Script makes a difference: The induction of deep dyslexic errors in logograph reading. *Dyslexia, 4,* 197-211.

Yamada, J., & Takashima, H. (2001). The semantic effect on retrieval of radicals in logographic characters. *Reading and Writing: An Interdisciplinary Journal, 14,* 179-194.

Yelland, G. W., Pollard, J., & Mercuri, A. (1993). The metalinguistic benefits of limited contact with a second language. *Applied Psycholinguistics, 14,* 4(Dec.), 423-444.

Zhang, B., & Peng, D. (1992). Decomposed storage in the Chinese lexicon. In H. C. Chen & O. J. L. Tzeng (Eds.), *Advances in Psychology-Language Processing in Chinese.* Amsterdam: Elsevier Science Publishers.

Appendix A   Kanji Knowledge Test

Please tick all the kanji that you know.

Beginner Level

後	校	国	時	父	安	店	先	前	半
円	外	午	千	車	年	食	分	新	週
間	高	毎	名	話	道	会	電	中	社
今	本	女	出	生	書	母	学	休	気
院	持	画	秋	開	作	待	映	昼	勉
動	堂	顔	界	習	貸	曜	菜	頭	服
運	計	教	試	世	体	病	台	方	特
音	事	写	料	所	産	洗	便	説	遠
族	地	注	度	不	文	洋	有	理	問
以	建	医	元	仕	場	題	発	用	物
朝	員	研	屋	漢	住	京	自	験	室
歌	旅	去	業	力	着	集	夕	私	銀
館	帰	悪	海	親	味	明	合	働	林
都	薬	近	英	真					

移	泳	奥	衣	介	岸	依	械	易	胃
貨	囲	害	願	限	押	誤	岩	吸	枯
塩	快	刷	固	妻	険	肩	散	祭	昨
延	賛	砂	情	吹	星	刺	順	省	宿
酒	祝	容	栄	掘	責	群	祖	腹	性
柔	折	庫	昔	硬	雪	徒	寺	席	常
腰	降	居	娘	到	混	翌	級	救	城
袋	脳	均	許	看	賃	畑	健	将	査
故	案	肯	勤	較	困	忘	婚	鈍	塗
埋	敗	刻	郵	悩	犯	郊	杯	背	帯
節	彼	脂	留	鉄	望	担	勇	炭	探
抱	暴	昇	倍	泊	薄	貧	届	疲	被
異	副	息	仲	宝	宙	柱	卒	陽	閉
板	版	般	販	底	庭	布	府	怖	負
復	婦	符	福	普	裏	陸	律	略	封

礼	戻

Advanced Level

郭	懐	桜	怪	狂	威	陥	尉	脅	郷
頑	契	筋	距	郡	芋	姻	陰	隠	屈
詠	剣	圏	窮	括	拠	宮	華	沿	炎
嫁	貢	孤	鉛	拒	顧	往	彩	劾	弧
索	舎	削	剤	砕	射	恨	架	鎖	祉
宗	従	銃	旬	盾	恒	渋	彰	暫	悟
庶	娯	尽	祥	昭	炊	陣	壊	唱	症
霜	促	窃	狩	宣	礎	衰	措	衷	逮
称	卓	垂	致	忠	租	耐	帝	勅	奏
是	貞	怠	邸	胎	胆	廃	討	梅	潜
脱	痘	胴	洞	稲	惜	博	迫	披	肥
素	卑	敏	染	剖	範	併	敷	房	柄
秘	妨	揚	盲	密	膨	朗	浪	励	某
猟	炉	砲	隆	郎	帥				

Appendix B   List of *kanji* used in the six tasks

Character-ness Judgment task

Real-kanji	Non-real-kanji	Fillers
	*Components were reversed	
励	(礼)	雨
宗	(快)	何
栄	(均)	外
陣	(昼)	学
犯	(勇)	間
順	(勤)	気
筋	(賛)	後
較	(塩)	語
願	(節)	校
奥	(裏)	国
劾	(宜)	左
窃	(姻)	時
恨	(往)	書

卑　　（狩）　　食
娯　　（砕）　　前
易　　（情）　　男
後　　（界）　　長
敗　　（従）　　電
責　　（動）　　読
移　　（常）　　南
舎　　（孤）　　聞
耐　　（祖）　　毎
素　　（致）　　友
故　　（祭）　　話
射　　（妻）　　右
板　　（括）　　円
柄　　（併）　　半
息　　（押）　　母
服　　（忠）　　金

背	(宙)	見
敏	(卒)	午
刷	(封)	行
律	(娘)	高
留	(堀)	今
堂	(密)	山
到	(祉)	子
契	(帝)	車
脅	(貞)	出
将	(昭)	女
称	(唱)	来

Radical Identification Task

Common-component		No-common-component		Fillers	
困	固	昔	寺	何	道
犯	狂	尽	旬	外	肉
郎	邸	寺	衣	学	売
背	肯	帯	庫	間	画
秘	称	柔	勇	気	買
散	敷	廃	奥	休	歩
普	暫	順	銃	後	旅
範	筋	膨	礎	語	用
礎	硬	鎖	救	行	夜
頑	顧	敷	勤	校	朝
府	庶	垂	宣	国	円
胎	胆	郭	尉	時	同
某	架	盾	卑	書	青
悟	惜	衷	胃	前	学
窃	窮	帥	往	男	草

481

害	容	望	袋	電	鳥
常	帯	庫	異	読	親
婚	婦	査	易	南	雨
彼	後	限	映	分	父
負	責	席	常	聞	悪
延	建	威	延	来	春
炭	災	版	彩	話	持
索	素	郵	故	英	着
袋	衰	般	孤	安	文
房	戻	朗	祖	音	習
迫	逮	併	泊	花	弟
拒	押	拠	械	兄	真
倍	促	息	宗	飲	読
柱	杯	促	浪	私	妹
渋	混	柄	酒	思	黒
届	居	是	留	紙	試

卒　卓　　　律　刷　　　終　族
封　射　　　隆　服　　　借　行
勉　勅　　　剤　郡　　　週　勉
埋　堀　　　徒　脱　　　体　待
祉　祥　　　底　肩　　　茶　究
看　省　　　郷　庭　　　昼　会
降　陥　　　肩　貞　　　店　病
症　痘　　　染　貨　　　冬　者
星　昇　　　奏　帝　　　動　切

Phonological Judgment Task

Common-reading		No-common-reading		Fillers	
吸	級	砲	級	五	後
犯	氾	彼	炊	円	園
祖	租	拒	租	用	洋
固	枯	悩	枯	語	午
彼	披	博	披	交	公
博	薄	郡	薄	字	時
陽	揚	案	揚	千	先
腹	復	徒	復	大	代
壊	懐	陽	懐	天	点
貧	袋	房	袋	半	反
胆	担	吹	担	会	回
胎	怠	忠	怠	京	教
胴	洞	郊	洞	工	高
娯	誤	版	誤	社	車
符	府	泳	府	以	医

484

昨	作	彩	作	院	員
時	持	堀	持	九	急
望	忘	時	忘	自	事
副	福	剣	福	台	題
界	介	吸	介	中	注
版	販	朗	販	自	後
孤	弧	昨	弧	以	園
房	防	邸	防	台	洋
彩	菜	腹	菜	社	午
朗	郎	符	郎	五	公
迫	泊	望	泊	工	時
拒	距	沿	距	語	先
泳	詠	娯	詠	京	代
忠	仲	界	仲	用	点
沿	鉛	胎	鉛	交	反
郡	群	胆	群	天	回

教　院　脳　迫　脳　悩
高　九　安　孤　安　案
車　会　屈　副　屈　堀
医　円　塗　星　塗　徒
員　字　底　祖　底　邸
急　千　性　固　性　星
事　半　校　壊　校　郊
題　中　抱　貸　抱　砲
注　大　険　胴　険　剣

Phonological Matching Task

Valid-phonetic		Not-valid-phonetic		fillers	
吸 _	kyuu_	礼 _	satsu_	雨 _	_u
犯 _	hi_	快 _	ketsu_	外 _	gai_
祖 _	so_	_ 刻	_gai	学 _	gaku_
固 _	ko_	_ 居	_ko	_ 間	_kan
彼 _	hi_	肥 _	ha_	休 _	kyuu_
博 _	haku_	廃 _	hatsu_	_ 行	_koo
陽 _	yoo_	暴 _	baku_	高 _	koo_
腹 _	fuku_	筋 _	jo_	_ 車	_sha
_ 壊	_kai	隠 _	on_	食 _	shoku_
貧 _	_tai	_ 較	_koo	山 _	san_
胆 _	tan_	往 _	chuu_	小 _	shoo_
胎 _	tai_	怪 _	kei_	水 _	sui_
胴 _	doo_	_ 砕	_sui	長 _	choo_
娯 _	go_	_ 剖	_bai	読 _	doku_
符 _	fu_	_ 郭	_jun	_ 名	_mei

昨 _	saku_	_ 待	_ji	_ 話	_wa
時 _	ji_	限 _	kon_	来 _	rai_
_ 望	_boo	_ 院	_kan	歌 _	ka_
_ 副	_fuku	情 _	sei_	開 _	kai_
_ 界	_kai	婦 _	soo-	帰 _	ki_
版 _	han_	岩 _	seki_	_ 売	_kyuu
孤 _	ko_	般 _	yaku_	動 _	ka_
致 _	chi_	_ 炭	_kai	_ 店	_shin
砂 _	sa_	郵 _	sui_	朝 _	shuu_
朗 _	roo_	異 _	kyoo_	_ 親	_mai
迫 _	haku_	梅 _	kai_	近 _	choo_
拒 _	kyo_	純 _	don_	花 _	sui_
_ 泳	_ei	許 _	go_	家 _	shin_
忠 _	chuu_	措 _	shaku_	牛 _	ki_
沿 _	en_	探 _	shin_	_ 強	_kin
郡 _	gun_	_ 略	_kaku	_ 古	_shoku

悩_	noo_	敏_	kai_	_止	_choo
案_	an_	埋_	ri_	_紙	_kai
_徒	_to	貧_	bun_	終_	kyoo_
_密	_mitsu	_脱	_etsu	住_	shi_
_邸	_tei	到_	chi_	新_	nyuu_
_星	_sei	陥_	kyuu_	_通	_ka
郊_	koo_	症_	sei_	_道	_shi
砲_	hoo_	恒_	sen_	入_	an_
剣_	ken_	_郷	_roo	_明	_tuu

Semantic Judgment Task

Common-radical		No-common-radical		Fillers	
吸	吹	従	吹	百	万
肥	脂	彩	脂	黒	青
砂	砕	怖	砕	牛	犬
帯	布	動	布	南	下
庫	店	刺	店	人	女
鎖	鉄	狩	鉄	赤	白
顔	頭	菜	頭	友	兄
雪	霜	宝	霜	北	東
閉	開	顔	開	上	外
節	筋	吸	筋	魚	鳥
秋	稲	国	稲	七	九
国	圏	桜	圏	西	右
従	徒	鎖	徒	夏	冬
昨	曜	岩	曜	四	六
動	勤	素	勤	後	中

狩	猟	押	猟	男	子
疲	症	畑	症	五	八
胃	背	習	背	母	弟
怖	怪	節	怪	左	前
姻	嫁	看	嫁	十	千
泳	潜	肥	潜	牛	万
桜	梅	姻	梅	友	青
菜	芋	砂	芋	七	犬
押	折	郊	折	男	下
許	討	庫	討	南	女
彩	彰	陸	彰	後	白
岩	岸	閉	岸	上	兄
炎	炭	疲	炭	母	東
習	翌	貧	翌	五	外
素	索	昨	索	四	鳥
宝	宮	雪	宮	魚	九

右 冬 六 中 子 八 弟 前 千

黒 北 左 百 西 赤 十 夏 人

盲 郷 星 剣 炉 堀 福 賃 隆

埋 泳 帯 秋 胃 炎 許 祝 昇

盲 郷 星 剣 炉 堀 福 賃 隆

看 郊 昇 刺 畑 埋 祝 貧 陸

Semantic Categorization Task

radical-category		no-radical-category		fillers	
庫	slanting roof/eaves	旬	hand	男	person
砂	stone	囲	sun/day	北	direction
吹	mouth	均	roof	百	number
肥	flesh	昔	plant/vegetable	赤	colour
帯	cloth	削	animal	十	number
鎖	metal	願	bamboo	四	number
顔	head/neck	腰	metal	上	direction
雪	rain	貧	gate	黒	colour
閉	gate	陽	knife/cut	外	direction
節	bamboo	較	water	白	colour
秋	grain	映	mountain	千	number
国	border	院	rain	子	person
従	steps/stride	城	mouth	下	direction
時	sun/day	席	money/valuables	友	person
動	power	故	border	中	direction

493

狩 animal	陰 eye/look	東 direction
疲 sickness	胆 roof	父 person
怖 heart/feeling	怪 tree	青 colour
胃 flesh	猟 sickness	万 number
姻 woman/marriage	符 woman/marriage	右 direction
酒 water	逮 slanting roof/eaves	円 person
桜 tree	依 design	月 food
菜 plant/vegetable	杯 flesh	今 direction
押 hand	息 wings/fly off	車 colour
許 say/words	級 stone	出 food
彩 design	射 fire	食 colour
岩 mountain	妻 rain	生 direction
炎 fire	房 hill	川 food
習 wings/fly off	般 steps/stride	大 food
素 thread	祭 thread	長 colour
宝 roof	貢 knife/cut	年 person

看	eye/look	肩	woman/marriage	半	food
郷	community	昭	earth	分	number
昇	sun/day	帝	person	本	food
剣	knife/cut	庭	cloth	六	person
畑	fire	脱	head/neck	牛	colour
堀	earth	勉	plant/vegetable	魚	direction
祝	holy announcement	留	stone	兄	number
貧	money/valuables	密	water	正	colour
隆	hill	宿	grain	天	number

Appendix C   Semantic Relatedness Task

			Semantically related?
1	吸	吹	0-----1-----2-----3-----4-----5
2	肥	脂	0-----1-----2-----3-----4-----5
3	砂	砕	0-----1-----2-----3-----4-----5
4	帯	布	0-----1-----2-----3-----4-----5
5	庫	店	0-----1-----2-----3-----4-----5
6	鎖	鉄	0-----1-----2-----3-----4-----5
7	顔	頭	0-----1-----2-----3-----4-----5
8	雪	霜	0-----1-----2-----3-----4-----5
9	閉	開	0-----1-----2-----3-----4-----5
10	節	筋	0-----1-----2-----3-----4-----5
11	秋	稲	0-----1-----2-----3-----4-----5
12	国	圏	0-----1-----2-----3-----4-----5
13	従	徒	0-----1-----2-----3-----4-----5
14	昨	曜	0-----1-----2-----3-----4-----5

15	勤	勤	0-----1----2----3----4----5
16	狩	猟	0-----1----2----3----4----5
17	疲	症	0-----1----2----3----4----5
18	胃	背	0-----1----2----3----4----5
19	怖	怪	0-----1----2----3----4----5
20	姻	嫁	0-----1----2----3----4----5
21	泳	潜	0-----1----2----3----4----5
22	桜	梅	0-----1----2----3----4----5
23	菜	芋	0-----1----2----3----4----5
24	押	折	0-----1----2----3----4----5
25	許	討	0-----1----2----3----4----5
26	彩	彰	0-----1----2----3----4----5
27	岩	岸	0-----1----2----3----4----5
28	炎	炭	0-----1----2----3----4----5
29	習	翌	0-----1----2----3----4----5
30	素	索	0-----1----2----3----4----5

31	宝	宮	0----1----2----3----4----5
32	看	盲	0----1----2----3----4----5
33	郊	郷	0----1----2----3----4----5
34	昇	星	0----1----2----3----4----5
35	刺	剣	0----1----2----3----4----5
36	畑	炉	0----1----2----3----4----5
37	埋	堀	0----1----2----3----4----5
38	祝	福	0----1----2----3----4----5
39	貧	賃	0----1----2----3----4----5
40	陸	隆	0----1----2----3----4----5

1	庫	slanting roof/eaves	0-----1-----2-----3-----4-----5
2	砂	stone	0-----1-----2-----3-----4-----5
3	吹	mouth	0-----1-----2-----3-----4-----5
4	肥	flesh	0-----1-----2-----3-----4-----5
5	帯	cloth	0-----1-----2-----3-----4-----5
6	鎖	metal	0-----1-----2-----3-----4-----5
7	顔	head/neck	0-----1-----2-----3-----4-----5
8	雪	rain	0-----1-----2-----3-----4-----5
9	閉	gate	0-----1-----2-----3-----4-----5
10	節	bamboo	0-----1-----2-----3-----4-----5
11	秋	grain	0-----1-----2-----3-----4-----5
12	国	border	0-----1-----2-----3-----4-----5
13	従	steps/stride	0-----1-----2-----3-----4-----5
14	時	sun/day	0-----1-----2-----3-----4-----5
15	動	power	0-----1-----2-----3-----4-----5
16	狩	animal	0-----1-----2-----3-----4-----5

17	疲	sickness	0-----1-----2-----3-----4-----5
18	怖	heart/feeling	0-----1-----2-----3-----4-----5
19	胃	flesh	0-----1-----2-----3-----4-----5
20	姻	woman/marriage	0-----1-----2-----3-----4-----5
21	酒	water	0-----1-----2-----3-----4-----5
22	桜	tree	0-----1-----2-----3-----4-----5
23	菜	plant/vegetable	0-----1-----2-----3-----4-----5
24	押	hand	0-----1-----2-----3-----4-----5
25	許	say/words	0-----1-----2-----3-----4-----5
26	彩	design	0-----1-----2-----3-----4-----5
27	岩	mountain	0-----1-----2-----3-----4-----5
28	炎	fire	0-----1-----2-----3-----4-----5
29	習	wings/fly off	0-----1-----2-----3-----4-----5
30	素	thread	0-----1-----2-----3-----4-----5
31	宝	roof	0-----1-----2-----3-----4-----5
32	看	eye/look	0-----1-----2-----3-----4-----5

33	郷	community	0-----1-----2-----3-----4-----5
34	昇	sun/day	0-----1-----2-----3-----4-----5
35	剣	knife/cut	0-----1-----2-----3-----4-----5
36	畑	fire	0-----1-----2-----3-----4-----5
37	堀	earth	0-----1-----2-----3-----4-----5
38	祝	holy announcement	0-----1-----2-----3-----4-----5
39	貧	money/valuables	0-----1-----2-----3-----4-----5
40	隆	hill	0-----1-----2-----3-----4-----5

Appendix D   The numbers of participants

The numbers of participants from beginner, intermediate and advanced groups in the kanji recognition tasks.

	T1	T2	T3	T4	T5	T6
Beg	32	30	21 (10)	18 (8)	20 (17)	18 (14)
Int	20	20	19 (16)	21 (19)	40 (35)	40 (39)
Adv	17	17	27	26	17 (16)	16

Note: T1 = character-ness judgement task, T2 = radical identification task, T3 = phonological judgement task, T4 = phonological matching task, T5 = semantic judgement task, and T6 = semantic categorisation task; The figures in the parentheses show the numbers of participants whose results were analysable (e.g. no missing data).

www.ingramcontent.com/pod-product-compliance
Lightning Source LLC
LaVergne TN
LVHW042330060326
832902LV00006B/92